VA

CAMPBELL CHRONICLES

and

FAMILY SKETCHES

Embracing the History of

CAMPBELL COUNTY, VIRGINIA

1782-1926

By

RUTH HAIRSTON EARLY

Baltimore
REGIONAL PUBLISHING COMPANY
1978

Originally Published
Lynchburg, Virginia
1927

Reprinted with "Guide to Family Sketches"
Regional Publishing Company,
Affiliate of Genelogical Publishing Co., Inc.
Baltimore, 1978

Library of Congress Catalogue Card Number 77-93960
International Standard Book Number 0-8063-0798-6

Reprinted from a volume in
the George Peabody Branch,
Enoch Pratt Free Library,
Baltimore, Maryland
1978

Made in the United States of America

Preface

O Virginia county has more of interest to offer the historical student than Campbell, from its formation till the present time—in beauty of situation, staging of events and number of notable citizens. It was the first county formed after the Yorktown surrender, at the period when history making was proceeding with rapid strides; in selection of county officials, survey of boundary lines, choice of meeting places, erection of public buildings, payment of war claims, locating military land warrants; opening roadways, and establishing settlements, with selection of names, and here popular sentiment zealously used those of heroes who had achieved renown in the Revolution, christening the Washingtons, Jeffersons, Lafayettes, Henrys, etc., which mark discontinuance of English designations. Patriotic fervor luxuriated in the opportunity for displaying its breadth of nationalism, even thus with generous impulse Virginia donated her northwest territory to the general government. So with diminished boundary, state and county were meeting the requirements of a new era, each in its adjustment to the situation which had developed.

Receiving at baptism the distinguished name of Campbell, the county has condoned nothing that could tend to dishonor it, and during the course of its one hundred and forty-odd years, can give proof of much that adds to its luster. That its annals have lain dormant must not be construed as signifying lack of abundant records, but rather to the long continued custom of storing them in the guarded shelves of the county clerk's office. Virginia, indeed, has not been backward in creating history, but, though proud of her achievement, tardy in circulating information concerning it. From experience we know that history, in process of making, provides as many thrills of risk and rescue as the pen of fancy can picture, which

PREFACE

if seized in passing would afford sufficiency of eventful material. As residents of Bedford, Campbell citizenry were busy contributing their quota to county annals long before the Assembly decided that Bedford was too large and must be divided; many of the inhabitants had been among the most active citizens of the old county, the slicing of which did not change the location of their residences, though disconnecting them from former associations, and from their records of service in the development of Bedford, which remain incorporated in the minutes of that county, civil as well as military. Thus Campbell started with a blank register in the year 1782, and only what transpired from that date onwards is there inscribed, with names of those who contributed towards the promotion of county interests; including some who descended from worthy forefathers and made good the promise of heritage; others, without known heredity, or apparent encouragement, who sprang into the limelight of public approval and accompanying renown, by meritorious action, and thus furnish example of what determination and energy, guided by due ability, may accomplish. In the opening of new country, many of the later settlers, overflow from more populous communities, were homeseekers attracted by the lure of its opportunities, who also contributed to its industrial advancement.

The effort is made in the following pages to set forth the cause of what happened as well as the matter of fact details of occurrence and while completeness has been the aim of collection, there cannot be surety of that element where information is dependent upon the preservation and accuracy of accessible material. Towards furtherance of full record, family sketches, as far as obtainable, have been included, since much county history is embraced in the activities of private citizens. To the information which has come under my observation and of which free use has been made, county people have contributed, yet the instigation to continued research is due to the suggestion of the librarian of William and Mary College, E. G. Swem, whose familiarity with and interest in Virginia records encouraged me to follow his advice in completing this history of Campbell county as far as possible.

Many of the illustrations have been secured through the assistance of Herman Wells of the J. P. Bell company, and these accurately reproduce originals, as now standing. Should the circulation of this volume lead to the discovery of any omission of actor or deed in the making of the county, one aim of its publication will then become effected through the acquirement of unknown fact. If it were possible to peer through the hedge of silence and secrecy which screens much of Campbell's past, more of it might be recovered from the obscurity into which it has fallen.

Lynchburg, 1926. R. H. Early.

Introduction

Y backward glance into the colonial period we discover what had been transpiring in the section before Campbell was launched into countyship, when the red man used it as a camping ground; for there is proof that the white invader came in contact with him at an early date and needed to dispute occupancy with the savage owner. The finding of arrowpoints and other Indian native stone relics, still brought to earth surface by the farmer's plow, has induced the belief that Indians camped in the locality and this presumption has become confirmed by investigations of the Bureau of Ethnology, which gives the names of the especial tribes that have inhabited the county at earliest times of which there is knowledge, and John Lederer, discoverer, is quoted as authority. Lederer made an expedition May 20, 1670, from the James river falls with a party of "20 Christian horse and 5 Indian," and was received by the Monakins with volleys of shot. Near their village was a pyramid of stones piled together that the tribal priests told Lederer was the number of an Indian colony drawn out by lot from a neighbor country over-peopled, and that they had been led hither by one Monack, from whom they took the name of Monakin. The Monahassans of the Monacan Confederacy, occupied the northern part of the county in the 17th century, on the upper waters of James river. The name, variously spelt, was derived from an Algonquin word signifying a spade; they were allies of Manahaoc and enemies of Powhatan, but spoke a different language from either. Their encampment was on the south side of the river near the Bedford and Buckingham mountains. In person they were tall and war-like, and their totem was three arrows. They were next in importance to Monocan in the Confederacy. In 1671 they were settled 25 miles from the Saponi on Staunton river and a small number of the tribe were living a few miles from Lynch's ferry at the time of Campbell's establishment. These Monocans were better known by the name of Tuscaroras.

The Saponies (Jefferson says were families of Wanamies who had moved down from New Jersey)—an Eastern Siouan tribe—had a village on Otter creek which flows into Staunton river. Continuing his travels in 1670, Lederer tells that he reached Sapon, a village of the Nahyssans, about 100 miles from Manock and situated upon a branch of the Shawan, alias Rorenocke river. The tribal name of Saponi was originally applied to the whole group of Fort Christianna tribes and occasionally included under Tutelo. Their language appears to have been the same as Tutelo to the extent that the two tribes could readily understand each other. Lederer states that as early as 1654-56 the Saponi were at war with the Virginia settlers, at the time of the attack by the Cherokees, probably in alliance with them; that Sapon was a Tutelo town and Pintahoe was another nearby village, giving evidence that the Saponi and Tutelo were living in close and apparently confederated relation. In 1671 they were visited by Thomas Batts with guides. After traveling nearly due west from the mouth of Appomattox river—about 140 miles—they came to Sapong or Sapony's town. Having been harassed by the Iroquois in this locality, the Saponi and Tutelo at a later date moved to the junction of Staunton and Dan rivers, where they settled near the Occaneechi, each tribe occupying an island in Roanoke river in what is Mecklenburg county. The Saponi tribe is now extinct.

In later times other Indian tribes were temporarily in Campbell but not there long enough to leave any remains of consequence.

Between Alta Vista and Leesville there are indications of an Indian camp at a place where are piles of periwinkle shells scattered around, which might have been left there by the Saponi; there are two wigwams noticeable near the Ridge road towards Evington. An Indian trail led through the Blue

Ridge into Goose Creek valley, and from an excavation near Goose creek a half dozen skeletons, stone tomahawk and arrow points were exhumed, in proof of their burying with the Braves their implements of war. Tradition reports that an Indian fort stood near the point of excavation.

Jefferson wrote that he knew of no Indian monument, only of the barrows, some of earth, others of loose stones, which they used as repositories for their dead. A tradition handed down from aboriginals that when they had settled at a place, the first of their number who died was stood erect and covered with earth for support and others following him similarly buried against the first one, determined Jefferson to open one of the barrows in the low grounds of the Rivanna—on the opposite hills of which had been an Indian town—in order to satisfy himself as to their manner of burial. His examination convinced him that burials were made in strata; the first collection of bones had been deposited on the surface of the earth, with a few stones put over it, and then a covering of earth, a second collection had been laid on this, again covered with earth, and so continued. The apparent process convinced him that bodies had not been placed upright and the fact that children's bones mingled with older ones proved that they were not merely bones of those who had fallen in battle. A party of Indians passing through that part of the country where the barrow was found, went into the woods directly to it, without enquiry and having staid about it for some time, with expressions construed to be those of sorrow, they returned to the high road, which they had left about half a dozen miles to pay their visit, and pursued their journey. There are many of these barrows in various parts of the country.

Numerous pipes, as well as other Indian relics, have been found in Buckingham county; among these native stone objects unearthed is a "pipe of peace," having a central bowl with a number of extending stems, proving the purpose for which it was intended, and the fact of its being recovered in perfect condition, indicates that its careful secretion in that locality had some special significance. It is said that one collector alone has obtained seventy-five pipes in the same locality; and many more arrow points, tomahawks and axes. Bedford county also has yielded arrow points.

Through discovery of such relics, traces of Indian abodes are located, traditions concerning which could not otherwise become confirmed, and these remains point to the one-time occupancy of Campbell and adjoining lands by nomadic Indian tribes.

.   .   .   .

It is noteworthy that of the members of the House of Burgesses sent from Bedford, the majority of them were domiciled in that part of the county which became Campbell. These sessions embraced the period 1754 to 1775:

William Callaway, Sr.: sessions Aug. 22, 1754; Oct. 17, 1754; May 1, 1755; Aug. 5, 1755; Mar. 25, 1756; Sept. 20, 1756; April 30, 1757; Mar. 30, 1758; Nov. 3, 1761; Jany. 14, 1762; Mar. 30, 1762; Nov. 2, 1762; May 19, 1763;; Jany. 12, 1764; Oct. 30, 1764; May 1, 1765.

Samuel Hairston, Sr.: sessions Sept. 14, 1758; Nov. 9, 1758; Feb. 22, 1759; Nov. 1, 1759; sessions of 1760 and 1761.

John Talbot: sessions Nov. 3, 1761; Jany. 14, 1762; Mar. 30, 1762; Nov. 2, 1762; May 19, 1763; Jany. 12, 1764; Oct. 30, 1764; May 1, 1765; Oct., 1765; Nov. 12, 1766; Mar. 12, 1767; Mar. 31, 1768; May 8-17, 1869; Nov. 7, 1769; May 21, 1770; July 11, 1771; Feb. 10, 1772; Mar. 4, 1773; May 5, 1774; June 1, 1775.

James Callaway: sessions Oct., 1765; Nov. 5, 1766; Dec. 18, 1766; Mar. 12, 1767; Mar. 31, 1768; May 8, 1769; May 17,

1769; Nov. 7, 1769; May 21, 1770; July 11, 1771, which was prorogued to the fourth Thursday in October, and dissolved Oct. 12, 1771.

Charles Lynch, Jr.: sessions Nov. 7, 1769; May 21, 1770; July 11, 1770; Feb. 10, 1772; Mar. 4, 1773; May 5, 1774; June 1, 1775.

The sessions of 1758-61 prorogued seven times, the last session continuing until October 20, 1760, when the Assembly prorogued, met again for one day and was then prorogued till March 5, 1761; remained in session till April 10, when it was dissolved. The Assembly of 1761-65 first convened Nov. 3, 1761; met by seven successive adjournments, on June 1, 1765, not long after the adoption of the famous resolutions of Patrick Henry, it was dissolved. There was but one session of the Assembly of May, 1769, which met on May 8, and was dissolved on May 17, 1769. On the preceding day the House of Burgesses adopted vigorous resolutions asserting Colonial rights, and on the 17th the governor, Lord Botetourt, called the members before him and said: "Mr. Speaker, and Gentleman of the House of Burgesses: I have heard of your resolves and argue ill of their effects. You have made it my duty to dissolve you, and you are dissolved accordingly."

The delegates sent to the Convention of 1775-6 from Bedford were:

> March 20, 1775, John Talbot and Charles Lynch.
> July 17, 1775, John Talbot and Charles Lynch.
> Dec. 1, 1775, John Talbot.
> May 6, 1776, John Talbot and Charles Lynch.

John Talbot became a captain of militia and Charles Lynch colonel in the Revolutionary army. Upon the formation of Campbell, they were among the first justices to receive commissions, as were also Samuel Hairston and James Callaway (the son of Colonel William Callaway, Sr.).

INTRODUCTION

A general idea of the state of affairs in the locality, preceding the division of Bedford and the formation of Campbell, may be gathered from the following extracts:

James Callaway in May, 1779, gave information that one Robert Cowan, Scotchman and a Tory, who had been refused admission into the state, had in defiance come and settled upon his land.

John Mead, county jailer, in 1780 petitioned for reimbursement of expense incurred while keeping certain persons in jail the past summer, who were arrested on suspicion of conspiracy against the United States.

At the same time, Harry Terrell claimed that the allowance of the auditor had been insufficient when he, and others employed, had been ordered to serve as guards in conveying a number of prisoners, suspected of treason, to jail.

This year the various states had been called upon to furnish in lieu of money, determinate quantities of beef, pork, flour, etc., for the use of the army, called "a tax in kind." Commissioners had accordingly made collections in order to furnish the Continental troops on their march northward from Greene's army; militia under Baron Steuben; Colonel Among's Legion; Bedford Militia; Henry Drovers, etc., all were provided with supplies from this tax, as they passed through the country.

On August 10, 1781, Colonel James Callaway wrote to Colonel William Davies from New London that he had discharged the militia which had been ordered to the south, inasmuch as those from the adjoining counties had been discharged, but ordered them to hold themselves in readiness to march at a moment's warning. He thanked Colonel Davies for the compliment paid to the militia of Bedford, assuring him that if the enemy ever made it necessary they would entitle themselves to credit.

A letter from Captain Angus Rucker, of Madison county, written in September of the same year, reported to Colonel Davies that his instructions in regard to collecting supplies and establishing a magazine at Lynch's ferry had been received, but he recommended Stovall's ferry, fifteen miles below, as a more fitting place on account of less danger from high water. He found abundance of flour and grain, but unless the people were assured of payment those articles could not be procured; Bacon was scarce for want of salt.

An act was passed in May, 1782, for ascertaining the losses and injuries sustained from depredations of the enemy within the commonwealth during the period embraced by the Revolution. Many county people availed themselves of this legislation and presented their claims for reimbursement.

Anthony Bledsoe reported that he had wagons in the service of the state in 1776 and entered bill for them at the same rate as was allowed in the Cherokee expedition, but the auditor refused to pay his charge and reduced the rates.

Caleb Tate asked for payment for whiskey and writing paper furnished Virginia troops in South Carolina at the last battle of Camden; 550 gallons of whiskey and 5 reams of paper; also two teams, which were lost.

William Dudley presented a certificate for 114 lbs. of bacon given to Henry Ward, commissioner of supplies; Robert Baber claimed that he supplied Captain Gammell, Continental officer, with 40 lbs. of bacon; John Connefax furnished Henry Ward with 50 lbs. of beef for the Bedford militia; Charles Lynch, Junior, furnished 3 lbs. of powder; Peter Hennessy supplied Christopher Irvine, commissioner, with 60 flour casks.

John Richardson provided 4 bundles of fodder for the Augusta militia. Vincent Glass furnished a wagon and team five days, during which they were employed in removing military stores from Prince Edward to Bedford; also a wagon and team belonging to him was impressed for Continental service and was not returned. He was allowed £83.16. Oliver Caldwell supplied Maj. John Ward with 350 lbs. of grass beef. Charles Roark was employed 32 days in New London as a butcher and taking care of tallow and hides. Aquilla Gilbert furnished Christopher Irvine a black and a bay horse, and wagon cloth for Bedford militia on the march to Petersburg, which were not returned. Thomas Lewis furnished Christ. Irvine with ½ bu. salt, and Bedford militia, on the march to Cobham, 3 pecks of salt and a cask; shod eleven horses with his own iron; his wagon and team were twelve days in service removing stores from Prince Edward, the same was employed 126 days on the march to Cobham; he lost a wagon cloth, tar-bucket, keg and pot. Thomas McReynolds supplied the militia under Muhlenburg, a wagon and team 97 days, and militia with three gallons of brandy. Thomas Helms' estate also furnished Muhlenburg a wagon and team 97 days. Jacobus Early supplied the deputy commissary of prisoners with 2½ bushels of meal and the "commissary law" with 600 lbs. of beef for the army; Col. Jerry Early's estate furnished sundry Continental troops at New London with 1425 lbs. of beef; Mrs. Mary Stith-Early supplied beef, diets and pasturage and had the care of a sick horse left on her hands by the passing army for six weeks. Robert Alexander, executor of Samuel Hairston, found among the papers of decedent's estate claims against Peter Stubblefield for 3½ gals. of corn, and 8 bundles of fodder; against Andrew Henry for 2 barrels of corn and 203 bundles of fodder, and a quantity valued at £30.10; against John Porter for pasturage of 62 head of cattle and 82 diets, the pasturage for 8 horses and 11 diets; against John Hills for 10 bundles of fodder, 4 quarts of corn, stableage for 1 horse, 2 diets and lodging; against Joseph Poindexter for 1 diet, 2 quarts of corn, and 18 diets; and 18 diets to Bedford Militia en route to Richmond.

These apparently small claims, presented at the time when Virginia was impoverished through expenses incurred during the Revolution—when the state treasurer, Jacqueline Ambler, reported that there was not enough money in the treasury to supply him with the necessary fuel and stationery, and the government had to be maintained with borrowed money—would seem to indicate a lack of public spirit; but the question of making provision for their families justified the claims for reimbursement made by the poor farmers who were then stranded with no means of transportation even if successful in raising crops, and with no avenue for borrowing; even securing bounty land entailed discouragement, delay and often more expense than they were able to incur. Not for half a dozen years were they in circumstances to pay taxes into the treasury. Doubtless no colony sustained a greater blight to industry, because that source of revenue was limited to agriculture.

An instance of the difficulty attending the locating of warrants issued for their services to American soldiers after the wars, is to be found in the petition of one Alexander McCoy (or Mackey) to the Virginia Assembly. The first presentation of this claim was made in May, 1780, when McCoy proved that Captain Alexander McKinzie, a native of North Britain, served as an officer in the French war under Major Grant in 1758 when he was killed; also Roderick McKinzie served as sergeant at the same time and was killed. McCoy's wife, Jean, was second cousin to the two McKinzie's, and was their only relation in this country. On April 30, 1780, John Talbot presented this claim which called for 3,000 acres of land, sending it by Mr. Callaway (Richard Callaway, then in Kentucky county), but the latter could get no one to lay it. It was then laid before the registrar in Richmond, in order to prove that no one had before obtained a warrant for the same bounty land.

By advice of James Steptoe, clerk of Bedford, on Nov. 20, 1782, a note was added to the petition, more fully explaining the circumstances, in stating that Alexander Mackey and Jane, his wife, representatives of Alex McKinzie, who served under Major Grant as a captain and was killed near Pittsburg in 1758 while fighting for his state at a battle called "Grant's Defeat," petitioned for land granted to McKinzie as an officer. A certificate of the register from Bedford court in 1780 had been sent to John Quarles, county lieutenant, but the registrar of the land office refused to grant the petition. In October, 1782, the same certificate was sent by John Talbot, who, upon the insertion of certain necessary words omitted from the original petition, presented it again at the registrar's office; again Talbot placed it in the hands of Christopher Irvine, Jr., of Kentucky to be by him laid, but too late to lay the warrant in good tillable land, so it was returned to the petitioners.

The land was still due when Campbell was formed, and the warrant was sent, with other county petitions, asking that power be granted the claimants to lay their land fit for cultivation on the south side of Green river or any western river where continental or state lines had lands laid off. This warrant presented for settlement many times was finally sent through the hands of James Steptoe, clerk, and Christopher Irvine, Jr., on March 6, 1784; as there is nothing found concerning it after that date we may presume that the land was obtained or the petition positively rejected.

In 1754 Alexander Mackie patented 803 acres of land on the east side of Ward's fork.

1758 Michael Mackey patented 13 acres on Reedy creek.

The McCoy family settled in Campbell at the time of its establishment, but their name, written indifferently McCoy and Mackey, is calculated to cause confusion in research; in the second generation a daughter, Catherine, married (1794) William Arthur, and her name is written Mackey. In 1790 Thomas McCoy married Catherine Strange and 1794 John McCoy married Lavinia Fuqua. In 1783 Martha McCoy sold Jesse Cobbs 100 acres on Little Falling river.

At the beginning of its distribution, land was acquired in various ways. Many of the earliest owners secured large tracts as investments which they afterwards sold in smaller parcels to settlers. Among these land investors were Colonel John Bolling, Nicholas Davies, Colonel Richard Randolph, Governor Benjamin Harrison, Sir William Skipwith, Joseph Ward, John Coles, Patrick Henry, John Alexander, Colonel William Byrd, Thomas Cocke, Drury Stith, Obediah Woodson, Richard Kennon, the Callaway brothers, Peter and Thomas Jefferson, Clement Read and others. Soldiers who served in the French

and Indian wars were given bounty-land; also those who enlisted in Colonel William Byrd's defensive regiment raised in
1760. There was a special proclamation issued in 1763 allot-
ting land bounties to reduced officers and soldiers of the late
wars, which gave to every captain 3,000 acres; to every sub-
altern or staff-officer 2,000 acres; to every non-commissioned
officer 200 acres and every private 50 acres. In August, 1775,
another allotment for pay to soldiers gave tobacco in place of
land; to captain of horse 30 lbs. of tobacco; lieutenant 30 lbs.;
cornet 25 lbs.; to captain of fortsoldiers, 30 lbs.; lieutenant 25
lbs.; ensign 20 lbs. In 1779 officers and soldiers were allowed
twelve months to ascertain their claims to lands.

During the period 1779-81 the Southern states became the
theatre of war and Virginia was invaded. Army enlistment at
this time does not seem to have been compulsory, for in October,
1780, additional bounty of 300 acres was promised soldiers
who would serve till the end of the war. On May 6, 1782, for
recruiting the state's quota of troops in the Continental service,
the call was made for 3,000 men of sound minds and able
bodies at least 5 feet 4 inches high and between the ages of
eighteen and fifty years, one man for every fifteen militiamen;
then in 1784 the national government. gave a bounty to each
non-commissioned officer and soldier, 100 acres of land; to a
captain 300 acres; to a lieutenant 200 acres, to an ensign 150
acres. The state's bounty was also to each non-commissioned
officer and soldier 100 acres, to the officers just the same as the
Continental agreement.

Provision for settlers in 1779 allowed 640 acres of land
whereon villages were situated and to which no other person
had legal claim, in consideration of their settlement; and if such
settlers desired to take up a greater quantity of land, upon payment to the treasurer of the consideration money, they would
be entitled to the pre-emption of any quantity not exceeding
1,000 acres, but no family should be entitled to that allowance
unless they had made a crop of corn in that county or resided
there one year since settlement. The certificates of settlement

were delivered by commissioners stating the number of acres, time of settling, particular location, and adjacent lands, to which the claimant might have right of pre-emption. Commissioners' and clerk's fees were fixed at 10 shillings for each entry and warrant or survey as prescribed.

Contents

Guide to Family Sketches

GUIDE TO FAMILY SKETCHES

Illustrations

County Formation

To Campbell County

Fair Campbell, though thy verdant vales
Resound no shepherd's fabled tales,
For thee no minstrel harp be strung,
And all thy beauties bloom unsung,
Yet thine are charms that might inspire
The pen, the pencil and the lyre.

Land of my birth! to thee belongs
The bard whose humble genius, nursed
On thy kind bosom, loved thee first.
Whose song, though haply low and rude,
Shall yet evince his gratitude.
There is a voice in Fancy's ear,
A voice to Fancy's children dear,
A harp whose soft, enchanting tone
Is heard in solitude alone.

Dear Campbell! Thy romantic plains,
Where wild, in lonely grandeur reigns,
In caves, with spruce and laurel graced,
The awful genius of the waste;
Yet do they hear at close of day
The mystic measures far away,
And listening Solitude profound
Stills every breath to catch the sound.

FREDERICK SPEECE.

Chapter I

Formation

AMPBELL was evolved by a series of slicings from earlier counties, beginning with the original Warrosquoyacki (swamp in a depression of land) which had been named for a tribe of the Powhatan Confederacy of Indians living on the south bank of James river. There was a great stretch of country between the county's eastern border, and its mountain-girdled western boundary, and much of the latter portion was unsettled and unknown: as these conditions became changed division took place, which provided smaller counties.

The first change came in 1637 with the conversion of the county into Isle of Wight, and the creation of Surry in 1652: from these two counties Brunswick was taken in 1720 and from Brunswick, Lunenburg in 1745; then from the latter Bedford was formed in 1753 and what had been court meeting-place in Lunenburg became county seat of Bedford. Bedford embraced a part of what is now Amherst, but was then included in Albemarle and this territory had also received various christenings through county divisions. Goochland formed 1727 from Henrico, was itself divided in 1745 "because of divers inconveniences attending the upper inhabitants by reason of the great distance from the court house and other places appointed for court meetings." The county then formed was named for the Earl of Albemarle, the governor of Virginia. This was the first regularly organized county in James river valley, and it included the whole of Fluvanna, Buckingham, Nelson, Amherst; the larger part of the present Albemarle and Appomattox, with parts of Bedford, Campbell and Cumberland. Among its justices are found names yet held by their descendants: Fry, Cabell, Jefferson, Howard, Lynch, Daniel, Jordan, Lewis, Read, Reid, Anthony, Randolph, Nicholas, Fleming, and others; many of whom were later recorded in Campbell as residents there.

In 1754 the part of Albemarle lying upon the south side of the river, from the mouth of Stonewall creek to the head of Falling river, was added to Bedford: then Albemarle was divided in 1761 to form Amherst; the portion north of the James was marked by a line up the Rockfish river to the mouth of Green creek, thence to the Blue Mountains; east of this line remained Albemarle, west of it was given to form the county then named for General Jeffrey Amherst, hero of Ticonderoga, and it embraced "certain islands in Fluvanna river." This river dividing Bedford from Amherst, now known as James, then called Fluvanna, and in earliest colonial days, Powhatan, —from its confluence with the Rivanna up to the mountains, was the Fluvanna of all early records and in the mountains, Jackson's river. The name of Queen Anne was variously used by the colonists for streams and places; they connected fluv (fluvius, running water) with Anna forming the word Fluvanna, a name later given to a James river county and still retained for it.

When divisions occurred and new counties were established, the old ones usually retained all accumulated court records, so that it often becomes necessary to revert to parent counties for information concerning people, who were formerly resident there, but transferred into a newer county.

Between 1779 and 1782 a dozen or more petitions were forwarded to Virginia Assembly urging the division of Bedford; with as many opposing any change. Some of these appeals were immediately rejected, some promised later consideration; finally one sent in 1781 bearing the signatures of 300 residents, judged to be reasonable and practicable, was favorably acted upon.

The earlier petitions suggested division running south of Staunton river, fertility of its land then attracting attention to the locality; the last petition added the boundary of Blackwater creek. In the call for division, a reason given was that tax assessors could not make their rounds in the required time as Bedford was 70 miles long and 35 miles wide.

The act creating Campbell county did not go into effect for some time after its passage. The Act of Assembly for the division of Bedford and provision for a new county enacted that "From and after the first day of February next, the county shall be divided into two distinct counties by a line to begin at the mouth of Judith's creek on James river, thence to Thompson's mill on Buffalo creek, thence to the mouth of Back creek on Goose creek, then the same course continued to Staunton river, and that part of said county lying east of said line shall be called Campbell and all the residue of said county shall retain the name of Bedford.

"The court for Campbell shall be held by the justices thereof on the first Thursday in every month, after division, in such manner as provided by law for other counties, and directed by their commissions.

"Justices,—to be named—shall meet at the house of Micajah Terrell upon the first court day and having taken the oaths and administered the oath of office to and taken the bond of the sheriff according to law, proceed to appoint and qualify a clerk and fix a place for holding courts as they think fit, provided always the appointment for a place and of a clerk shall not be made unless a majority of justices be present.

"The Governor, with advice of Council, shall appoint a person to be first sheriff of the county, who shall continue during the term upon the same conditions as appointed for other sheriffs. In all elections for a Senator, the county of Campbell shall be of the same district as Bedford.

"It shall be lawful for the sheriff of Bedford to collect and make distress for any public dues or officer's fees, which shall remain unpaid by the inhabitants thereof at the time such division takes place, and shall also be accountable for the same in like manner as if this act had not been made. The court of Bedford shall have jurisdiction of all actions and suits in law and equity which shall be depending before them at the time of the division and shall try and determine the same and issue process and award execution thereon.

"Whereas by division Bedford shall be inconveniently situated, the justices shall have power to fix on a place as near center as the situation and convenience will admit for building a court house and prison, and until such buildings are completed, to hold court at such place as they may think proper." Bedford then abandoned its previous pivotal center and, like the newly created county, turned attention to the selection of a suitable site for its court buildings, which would prove sufficiently central from all directions of its diminished boundaries.

Campbell Court House

Campbell bounds Bedford twenty-one miles on the west.

The act passed in November, 1781, for the formation of Campbell county went into effect February 7, 1782, in the 6th year of the Commonwealth and American Independence. At a meeting held in the house of Micajah Terrell, a commission of the peace directed to Samuel Hairston, Richard Stith, Charles Lynch, John Ward, John Callaway, John Fitzpatrick, Francis Thorp, John Hunter, Robert Adams, Jr., James Callaway, John Talbot, George Stovall, Jr., and William Henderson was read, when John Ward and John Henderson administered the oath of justice of the peace, as by law directed, to Samuel Hairston, who then administered the same oath to Richard Stith and the other justices named. At this meeting Samuel Hairston and John Callaway were appointed commissioners, on behalf of the county, to meet the commissioners who might be appointed by the court of Bedford to superintend running the dividing line between the two counties by survey. Richard Stith, who had served as deputy surveyor to his brother Buckner in Bedford, was appointed surveyor for Campbell and the dividing line was to begin at the mouth of Judith's creek; for running the line Stith was to receive 500 lbs. of tobacco.

No change was then made from the military system, long in use in Virginia, as embodied in the code prescribed by George III at the close of the French and Indian war, which provided that in each county there should be a chief military officer known as the county-lieutenant, below him in rank a colonel, lieutenant-colonel and major. A regiment consisted of 500 men or ten companies of 50 men each; company officers being captain, lieutenant, ensign, and several sergeants. The lieutenant and those above him were known as "field officers" and those of lower rank as "subalterns."

James Callaway, who had been county-lieutenant of Bedford, now become a Campbell resident, received this highest office in the new county by commission from Governor Benjamin Harrison. Charles Lynch was appointed colonel of militia; John Callaway, lieutenant-colonel; and William Henderson, major. Owen Franklin, Thomas McReynolds, William Jordan, John Irvine, Josias Bullock and Thomas Johnson were made captains; with Archelaus Moon, Benjamin Arthur, John Helm, Charles Moile Talbot, lieutenants; and Joseph Stith, Plummer Thurston, Shelldrake Brown, Jr., James Stewart, and Charles Gilliam, ensigns. Francis Thorp received from the governor the appointment of sheriff, with Williston Talbot and Plummer Thurston, under-sheriffs.

Robert Alexander, former deputy clerk to James Steptoe of

Bedford court, was made clerk of Campbell, and he proposed that James Steptoe be appointed clerk of circuit court.

Commissioners to receive the specified tax were: Brown Price; James Campbell to receive the tax at or near Long Mountain; Thomas Lewis to receive it at Ross and Hook's store on Falling river. Christopher Irvine, Josias Bullock and James Adams, commissioners of tax. Harry Innis was admitted to qualify as attorney-at-law.

Charles M. Talbot was appointed to make a complete survey of the county in order to find the center for erecting the court house and other public buildings. John Fitzpatrick, surveyor from Molley's creek church to the ford over Falling river; Thomas Jones, surveyor from the ford on Great Falling river to the county line; Hugh McIlroy, surveyor from Jacob's creek past Hat creek Meeting House to the county line; Moses Fuqua, surveyor from Long Island on Staunton river to Seneca creek road; Charles M. Talbot, surveyor from Molley's creek church to Elisha Rodgers' path.

Terrell's house furnished the meeting place for county court during the following year. In April, 1783, the court nominated and appointed for erecting a court house and other buildings for county use, the place on the Fish Dam road known as "Rust's Meadows" near Long Mountain, 50 acres of which were given for the purpose that day by Jeremiah Rust. This was the initial movement towards establishing the county-seat now known as Rustburg or Campbell Court House and closed the controversy which had been carried on by two factions in the selection of a site.

In 1785 Patrick Gibson was allowed 2356 lbs. of tobacco for building the court house and table bench bar.

In 1787 justices formerly appointed were ordered to sell the lots at the Court House to the highest bidder, embracing the old court house and one-fourth of its lot at six months' credit.

County Given a Hero's Name

General William Campbell, born 1745 in Augusta county, moved to Washington county. At 29 years of age he commanded a company of militia from Fincastle upon an expedition under General Andrew Lewis to Point Pleasant on the Ohio river. After his return on January 20, 1775, he was one of a Committee of Safety appointed by the freeholders of Fincastle to draft resolutions to Continental Congress against the misrule and oppression of the British government; they concluded with the assurance "If no pacific measures be proposed or adopted by Great Britain and our enemies attempt to dragoon us out of those inestimable privileges to which as subjects we are entitled and reduce us to slavery we declare that we are resolutely determined never to surrender them to any power but at the expense of our lives." This address was forwarded to the delegates from Virginia then attending Congress at Philadelphia. Less than nine months afterwards Campbell was called into action; a British ship of war was driven ashore near Hampton during a storm and the captain threatened to burn the town and tried to do so but the Virginia Committee of Safety dispatched three companies of riflemen to the assistance of Hampton, and one of these companies was under the command of Campbell. Later he marched with a regiment of 910 cavalrymen and 50 riflemen in 18 hours to meet British Colonel Ferguson with a force of ·1105 men and won his title of general in the battle which followed at King's Mountain, South Carolina, October 7, 1780, when Ferguson was killed. There, as leader of militia troops, he gained the memorable victory considered as the turning point in the fortunes of the hard pressed colonists, which culminated at Yorktown surrender a year later. For this service Campbell received the thanks of Virginia Legislature and of Congress. But he did not live to see the end of the war, though on March 15th, following King's Mountain battle, he bore a distinguished part at Guilford C. H., North Carolina. In the summer of 1781 he was seized with a fatal illness and died August 22nd at "Rocky Mills," Hanover county, the home of Colonel John Syme, half-brother of his wife who was the sister of Patrick Henry.

His recent death, and the laurels he had won, prompted a memorial to him. It seems fitting that Patrick Henry,— whose name the American cause had cast upon the screen of history,—should have been the one to suggest the name of this Revolutionary soldier, whose bravery in action had covered him with glory, for the new county formed soon afterwards. And thus Henry assisted in measures for launching the county under favorable auspices by furnishing a name which would keep alive patriotism and inspire efforts for the advancement of the community.

Elizabeth, widow of General Campbell m. 2nd General William Russell, also a Revolutionary soldier; her only daughter, Sarah Campbell, married Francis Preston.

Though General Russell won his title in the Revolution, his father, who had held a commission as King's Counsel in Virginia Colony, was an uncompromising Tory and was distressed that his son was a rebel. While Colonel Russell was in service on the Virginia Peninsular, finding himself only a few miles from his father's home, he rode over to see him. Hitching his horse to a post on the lawn, he proceeded to the house and was affectionately welcomed, upon his entrance, by his father. A bell summoned them to the dining room. All the while, the horse with showy military saddle and the colonel's sword hanging from the pommel and pistols in the holsters had been an irritation to the Squire. He could harbor no resentment against his son, but the restless horse pawing holes in his lawn and jingling the trappings in his hearing had aroused intense ire. As they proceeded to the table, Colonel Russell told a servant to take the horse to the stable and feed him; the Squire overhearing the order, halted on the way and taking his son's hand said to him, "William, the ties of blood are strong within me when I look at you, in spite of your treasonable toggery, I can only see my dear son, but Sir," dropping the hand and continuing in great dignity, "I would have you understand, Sir, I will give no corn to a d——d rebel horse."

The office of sheriff combined as it then was with that of county-treasurer was an important one and entailed considerable risk to one holding it; a heavy bond, bearing signatures of several landholders, was required to obtain the office. Many petitions were presented to the Legislature requesting relief from threatened loss. In 1784 John Hunter, then sheriff, complained that he received in discharge of taxes, notes for tobacco at Manchester, which he credited against accounts of persons paying at the rate established by law. When he offered the notes at the public treasury in April, they were refused. The warehouse storing the tobacco was burned and he risked the loss of large sums in consequence.

In 1785-6 John Anthony became security for James Adams, deputy-sheriff, who failed to make good his accounts with the treasurer and he, Anthony, had to pay £193.4 shillings which distressed him very much; he petitioned for redemption of the amount he had paid.

Achilles Moorman was deputy in 1785-6 to Alexander Hunter, sheriff, and made complaint that owing to neglect of the clerk, he was not able to prepare a list of insolvents for the year in the time prescribed by law and he was forced to pay the whole sum into the treasury.

In 1804 James C. Moorman, deputy sheriff for John McAllister, sheriff, was instructed by the county justices to carry Lewis Robinson to Williamsburg lunatic asylum and he took William Arthur to assist him in guarding the prisoner; but Robinson was not admitted into the institution because of lack of room there. The trip was made at Moorman's expense and he therefore asked for reimbursement.

Robert Franklin, administrator in 1811 on the estate of Owen Franklin (deceased) former deputy sheriff claimed that delinquent taxes were charged against him for which he was not responsible; he asked that the commonwealth's claim be relinquished.

Nicholas Harrison, deputy in 1815 to Daniel B. Perrow, sheriff, in danger of heavy penalties, because through circumstances he could not control he was not able to sell as required by law, delinquent lands at the August court, asked leniency as he was sick and not able to attend to his duties and when he made returns they were incorrect and he suffered from the error.

In 1822 Thomas Humphreys, late sheriff, asked that certain laws concerning the management of decedents' estates be amended.

The shrievalty was the most powerful local office in Virginia and the fees and perquisites made it the most lucrative. The church vestry supplemented in dignity and consequence the shrievalty;—the one was civil and evidenced political importance, the other religious and denoted high social status.

Campbell Land Patents

1787. Robert Alexander: 250 acres on Beaver creek; 30 acres
1803.   at southwest end of Long Mountain; 150 acres on Molley's creek.
1789. Christopher Anthony: 9 acres both sides of Trent's ferry road.
1798. Thomas Anderson: 400 acres on branch of Beaver and branch of Archer's creek.
1784. Savage Bailey: 475 acres west side of Falling river.
1817. Matthew Bellamy: 159 acres on Back creek.
1790. Archibald Bolling: 1,200 acres on Wreck Island creek; 70 acres on Elk creek.
1794. Powhatan Bolling: 138 acres on head branch of Joshua creek.
1800. Thomas Boteler: 128 acres on east branches of Stonewall creek.
1808. John Boughton: 100 acres on Falling river.
1799. Henry Brown, Jr.: 784 acres on branch of Staunton river; 1,200 acres near Johnson's Mountain.
1792. Peyton Brown: 225 acres on Long branch and south fork of Falling river including its head.
1815. Polly Brown: 20 acres on Pretty creek; 67 acres on Staunton river.

1806. Stephen Butler: 13 acres adjoining land of William Staunton.

1806. Dr. George Cabell: 688 acres on James river and Blackwater creek.

1810. Frances Callaway: 320 acres on Big Falling river.

1792. James Callaway: 264 acres on Pretty creek, Johnson's and Back creeks, including top of Verdeman's Mountain; 300 acres between Back creek and Plum Tree
1801. branch; 72 acres on Plum Tree branch; 65 acres on
1802. Back and Goose creeks joining Leftwich and Lee; 80 acres north side of Goose creek; 658 acres joining Moorman and Boatwright.

1807. James Callaway and Jas. Steptoe: 940 acres at mouth of Harold branch of Blackwater creek, opposite the mill.

1819. William Campbell: 48 acres adjoining Rose and Thompson.

1819. William Cardwell: 56 acres on Manley's branch, fork of Big Falling river.

1786. James Carson: 300 acres on southeast branches of Wreck Island creek.

1818. Raleigh Chilton: 31 acres on Reedy creek, branch of north fork of Big Falling river.

1818. Robertson Cheatham: 7 acres west side of Big Falling river.

1786. John Clark: 2,177 acres on Flat creek; 400 acres both
1793. sides of Quarry branch.

1803. Micajah Clark: 150 acres on Flat creek, including west end of Waylie's Mountain.

1784. John Cobbs: 300 acres on head branches of Big and Little Falling rivers.

1821. Robert S. Coleman: 100 acres beginning at Conrad Speece's line.

1785. Robert Cowan: 600 acres on Buffalo creek; 950 acres on Otter and Buffalo creeks.

1811. Charlotte Crawford (neé Austin): 634 acres on Buffalo creek.

1806. Henry Landon Davies: 550 acres on Little Falling and Cub creeks; 504 acres on Cub creek.

1796. Richard Davenport: 400 acres on north fork of south fork of Cub creek.

1792. Micajah Davis: 500 acres on branch of Seneca, and branches of Staunton river.

1809. Samuel Day: 565 acres on Luck branch and Big Falling river.

1793. William Dobbs: 3,621 acres on Little Falling, Entray and Turnip creeks.

1818. Joseph Dinwiddie: 26 acres on Manley's branch on the bottoms leading to Falling river.

1804. Edward Douglass: 300 acres on Beaverpond branch.

1810. Daniel Driskell: 285 acres on Great Falling river.

1786. William Dudley: 124 acres on the north branch of Staunton river.

1800. Abner Early: 80 acres on north side of Otter; 2,142 acres on north side of Big Otter.

1831. Peregrine Echols: 110¾ acres on a branch of Flat creek and on Sawyin road.

1791. Thomas Eldridge, devisee of John Bolling: 400 acres on Reedy creek, a branch of Wreck Island.

1789. William Farthing: 390 acres on branch of Rattlesnake, a branch of Falling river.

1787. John Fitzpatrick: 276 acres on Phelps' old road, on branches of Molley's and Buzzard creeks.

1838. Nathaniel W. Floyd: 12½ acres on fork of Turkey Hen branch.

1787. Daniel L. Forbes (legatee of Peter Hairston): 75 acres including head of Fishing creek west branch of south fork of Falling river; 400 acres on north branch, south fork of Seneca creek.

1787. John Forbes: 400 acres on head branch of Beaver creek, upon top and north side of Long Mountain.

1792. John Forbes: 850 acres on Opossum, Rock Castle and Flat creeks; 450 acres on Beaver and Opossum creeks, including a great part of Cooper's Moun-

1795.   tain; also 2,500 acres on a branch of Cub creek and Falling river.

1803.   James Fore: 1,008 acres on Cub and Jenning's creeks.

1804.   John Fore: 446½ acres on Rattlesnake and Beaverpond creeks; 127½ acres on Beaverpond creek.

1793.   Lewis Franklin: 215 acres on Dixon's fork, branch of Falling river.

1808.   William Frazier: 5 acres on Pocket creek.

1809.   Philip Gibbs: 50 acres on Button creek.

1786.   Preston Gilbert: 260 acres on Staunton, including 6 isles, island sluices, rocks and falls.

1787.   Aquilla Gilbert: 104 acres between Seneca creek and a fork of Seneca.

1789.   Vincent Glass: 400 acres on Falling; 670 acres on forks
1797.   of Rattlesnake branch and east branches of Falling river.

1784.   John Hall Glover: 950 acres adjoining land of Dougherty, Moss and Moore.

1809.   Daniel Gray: 35 acres adjoining his own land.

1796.   Nathaniel Gregory: 400 acres on Archer's creek, including the head

1805.   Isaac Grishaw: 40 acres on Falling river adjoining his former entry.

1818.   John Hancock: 98 acres on Matthew's branch, east side of Falling.

1828.   Martin Hancock: 700 acres in Campbell and Charlotte, principally Campbell.

1782.   William Harris: 450 acres on Mound branches, fork
1786.   of Falling river; 378 acres between the forks of
1789.   Falling; 940 acres on Otter, including heads of
1795.   Cheese, Flintstone and Ormsbys creeks; 1,075 acres,
1796.   including branches of Seneca, Minters, Green Spring
and Swan creeks and other branches of Staunton
river; 1,100 acres, east side of Otter, branches of
Troublesome and Flintstone creeks; 350 acres on
head branches of Minters, and valleys of Hills creek.

1786. Thomas Harris: 400 acres on head waters of Falling river.

1796. John Harvey: 177 acres on Panther's branch and other branches of Little Falling river.

1818. Glover Harvey: 10 acres on western branch of Cub creek.

1805. William Harvey: 50 acres on Cub creek.

1810. John Helms: 90 acres adjoining lands of John Caldwell and John Thompson.

1796. Patrick Henry: 200 acres on east side of Falling river in Campbell and Charlotte, the greater part in Campbell; 125 acres on both sides of Falling river.

1819. Alexander Hunter: 5½ acres in a bottom leading to Mulberry creek, fork of Big Falling.

1815. John Hunter: 1,100 acres on Martin's creek and branches of Falling.

1815. Robert Hunter: 85½ acres adjoining Jones, Glass,
1844.   Turner and Martin; 9 acres and 1 rod on Reedy creek and Stonewall road; 28 acres on ridge between Wreck Island and Reedy.

1799. Samuel Hubbard: 130 acres on Molley's creek, both sides of surveyor's road.

1793. Christopher Irvine-Clendenning: 1,140 acres both sides of Flat creek.

1786. David Irvine: 278 acres on Flat creek.

1797. John Irvine: 90 acres on north branch of Hat creek, including head branch of Falling river.

1797. Thomas Jefferson: 800 acres on Dreaming and Buffalo creeks; 100 acres on so. branch Ivy creek.

1799. Jesse Johns: 180 acres on east branches of Little Falling river.

1806. Jonathan Johnson: 9 acres adjoining the land of Norvell.

1791. Thomas Johnson: 330 acres both sides of Windfall
1796—1799. branch and south branch of Molley's creek; 95
1812.   acres on Swan creek; 380 acres on both sides of

south fork of Cub creek; 22 acres on Swan creek.

1791. Thomas B. Jones: 374 acres on north branch of main fork of Falling river; 154 acres on Reedy.

1804. James Jones: 50 acres on south branch of Molley's creek.

1794. Publins Jones: 320 acres on Entray creek, east branch of Little Falling river.

1809. Rowland Jones: 353 acres on Opossum creek.

1813. William Jones: 223½ acres on Reedy creek.

1794. William Jordan: 200 acres on east branches of Little Falling river.

1814. David Lane: 104 acres on Deep branch.

1799. John Lee: 200 acres on south side of Goose creek.

1827. William J. Lewis: 256 acres on Slippery Gut.

1813. Thomas Logwood: 497 acres on Cub creek.

1793. Charles Lynch: 2,300 acres on the west side of Otter river.

1806. Anselm Lynch: 200 acres on Pocket creek; 1810—695 acres on Beaver creek.

1789. John Lynch: 320 acres on so. branch of Lynch's creek
1792. both sides of Lynch's ferry road; 160 acres on Flu-vanna river, including islands and Lynch's ferry
1795. road; 3,453 acres on James river with islands, rocks and bed of rocks; 450 acres on Opossum creek, Fish-
1806. ing creek, Rockcastle creek, including part of Can-
1810. dler's mountain; 44 acres near Lynchburg; 111 acres on James river; 312 acres on Joe's and Fishing
1814. creeks; 3,609 acres on James river and Blackwater and Fishing creeks.

1790. Nathaniel Manson: 550 acres on branches of Little Falling river and Cub creek.

1791. David Martin: 800 acres both sides of Opossum creek; 56 acres on branches of Wreck Island.

1795. Thomas Martin: 230 acres both sides of Opossum creek.

1789. Patrick McCarty: 420 acres on south fork of Catchaway branch, west branch of Seneca creek.

1786. Samuel McCraw: 788 acres on south side of James river.

1818. John Martin: 80 acres on Stanley's creek.

1818. John Merrill: 526 acres on Stovall creek.

1787. Hugh McElroy: 420 acres both sides east branch of Little Falling river.

1801. James McReynolds: 184 acres on east branch of Falling.

1787. James Miller: 200 acres head branches of Beaver creek, northwest side of Long Mountain.

1796. Thomas Mitchell: 380 acres on both sides of Opossum creek.

1787. Thomas Moore: 554 acres head branches Hill's and Cheese creeks, including spring of Seneca.

1786. Achilles Moorman: 200 acres west side of Seneca creek.

1796. Andrew Moorman: 100 acres on Pocket creek; 170 acres on Pocket and Johnson's creeks.

1784. Zepaniah Neal: 204 acres on west branches of Cheese creek.

1810. Thomas Norvell: 810 acres east side Long Mountain; 95 acres on Beaver creek.

1845. Matthew B. Nowlin: 125 acres both sides Hat creek road on branch of Falling river.

1809. Elizabeth and William Pannill (children of David): 1,070 acres on Opossum creek.

1801. Samuel Pannill: 900 acres on Whipping creek and Watkin's road, including head of Little Whipping; 6 islands in Staunton river opposite Big Island, including smaller islands; 141 acres embracing rocks, islands, shoals in Staunton river.

1798. Obediah Patterson: 800 acres, two parcels of land on Reedy and Wreck Island creeks.

1810. James Pemberton and Griffin Lewis: 386 acres on Big Falling river.

1808. Daniel B. Perrow: 26 acres on Beaver creek.

1818. Stephen Perrow: 6 acres on Opossum creek.

1821. Ambrose Plunkitt: 351 acres on James river near Stovall's road.

1808. Zenas Preston: 100 acres on Dreaming creek.

1790. Michael Prewitt: 302 acres on north side of Staunton river.

1787. Thomas Ramsey: 200 acres on west branch of Seneca creek.

1793. John Reid: 392 acres on Little Mill creek, branch of Falling; 420 acres on Big and Little Falling.

1787. John Robertson: 400 acres east branch of Flat creek, including part of Waylie's mountain.

1806. John Robertson, Jarrett Doherty, Catherine and James Russell: 1,314 acres on Flat creek.

1787. David Ross: 400 acres on south side James river, Opossum, Beaver, Archer's, Joshua and Stonewall creeks; 260 acres on west branches of Beaver creek.

1787. Robert Russell: 1,000 acres on Cattail branch, Spring branch and other w. branches of Flat creek.

1821. Philip Rohr: 64 acres along Watkins' road.

1804. Samuel Scott: 114 acres and 54¾ acres on Ivy creek, and south branch of Ivy.

1795. John Shackleford: 350 acres on east side of Otter river.

1784. Robert Shelton: 525 acres both sides of Little Wreck Island creek.

1788. John Steel and Alexander Steel: 54 acres on Reedy creek; 30 acres on main ridge road.

1796. John Steel: 447 acres on Archer's creek, including the head.

1800. John Sled: 53 acres on a great branch of Dog creek.

1785. Richard Stith: 164 acres on east branches of Whipping creek, both sides of Little Whipping; 1,050 acres
1786. north side of Lick creek, including head branches of Molley's creek; 1,050 acres on west branches of Falling river; 1,100 acres on head branches south fork
1787. of Falling River, southeast of Long Mountain.

1801. Bartholomew Stovall: 75 acres on Archer's creek and Wreck Island creek.

1788. Elizabeth (devisee of George Stovall): 788 acres on south side of James river; 85 acres on head branch of Wreck Island creek, north side of the main road.

1798. Nathaniel Strange: 150 acres on south fork of Falling river.

1792. Reuben Simmons: 271 acres both sides of Manley's creek.

1793. Jacob Stemmons: 400 acres on head branches of Flat creek.

1813. John Stratton: 7 acres adjoining his own land and land of Thomas Butler.

1804. Benjamin Tanner: 200 acres on Big Falling river.

1786. John Talbot: 1,265 acres on west side of Otter, on Callaways and Irvine's creeks.

1803. Caleb Tate: 290 acres on Green Spring creek.

1809. Edmund Tate: 16 acres on West side of Blackwater creek.

1794. Nathaniel Tate: 1,000 acres on east branches of Troublesome creek.

1827. Samuel Tennill: 50 acres between the shores of Staunton river.

1787. David Terrell: 178 acres on east side of Seneca creek both sides of Phelps' road.

1809. John Thompson: 81 acres on Little Beaver creek.

1792. Francis Thorp: 140 acres on a branch of Buffalo creek.

1789. Walter Urquhart: 500 acres on west branches of Johnson's creek.

1785. John Ward: 218 acres both sides of Cheese creek of Staunton river.

1799. Robert Watkins: 28 acres at Pilot Mountain, on Campbell's branch, adjoining Bolling's and Campbell's land.

1816. James West: 36 acres lying on Johnson's creek.

1816. Robert White: 268 acres on Beaver creek.

1808. Joseph Wilson: 100 acres on waters of Opossum creek.

1791. John Wimbush: 604 acres both sides of Austin's and other branches of Turnip creek and a branch of Hat creek.

1816. Jonathan Wilson: 360 acres on Big Falling river, east side of Long mountain; 365 acres on Molley's creek.

1805. Benjamin Walraud: 6 acres on main road adjoining Scott and Wilkerson.

1797. Edmund and John Wood: 922 and 505 acres both sides north fork of Falling river on both sides of Lawyers' old road and branches of Molley's creek.

1806. John Wooldridge: 82 acres on waters of Cub creek.

1800. Robert Wright: 34 acres on west branches of Little Wreck Island creek.

It may be noted that among the names listed above, in the order of dates, William Harris, John Hall Glover, John Cobbs, Savage Bailey, Robert Shelton, Zephaniah Neal, Richard Stith, John Talbot, John Ward, Achilles Moorman, Preston Gilbert, Thomas Harris, David Irvine, Samuel McCraw, James Carson, Robert Cowan, John Clark and William Dudley were the earliest patentees of Campbell county land.

Community Settlement

Chapter II

Three Groups of Settlers

NEAR the middle of the eighteenth century there appeared in what was then Lunenburg county, two groups of people who had come to settle, and were later to wield influence in their neighborhoods; one of these groups was a colony of Presbyterians and they located at Hat Creek, the other was Quaker who settled at South river; both came for a similar purpose, that of establishing a community where they could secure freedom in religious observance: there was an interval of ten years between the coming of the first and last group and they were fifteen or twenty miles apart. Here was an anomalous situation of two religious bodies, segregated as it were, with no variant sect or influence to disturb the harmony of their communion, a condition lasting for some years, because of isolation, distance and difficult travel.

Between the two pilgrimages, a third group of home-seekers had established themselves in a different locality, on Buffalo creek; yet their movement was not an outgrowth of religious zeal, but more likely instigated by reports of available land. They were conformists to the Anglican church and enjoyed a certain prestige from that association, for at that time church moved with state; other sects were classed as dissenters and were not accorded equal privileges. A certain degree of sympathetic toleration for this latter class caused the passage of a bill by the Assembly in 1772 entitled "A bill for extending the benefit of the Act of Toleration to his Majesty's subjects dissenting from the Church of England in the Colony of Virginia"; the provisions of the bill did not meet with the satisfaction of those most interested and in consequence the Presbyterians drew up a petition "in behalf of themselves and all Presbyterians in Virginia in particular and all Protestant dissenters in general" for less restricted toleration; to what issue this discontent would have led we can not know, for revolution along other lines soon appeared to divert thought and action.

First Settlement

Hat Creek

Forty years before the establishment of the county—which was to receive the name of Campbell—came into contemplation, the land it inherited was being distributed to various claimants by grant and by transfer. Many names of those so procuring it have already been noted; numbers of these owners never became residents nor contributed towards county development; it remains a question as to whether some of the English people holding title to land in the county ever came to this country. Such, for instance, as "Lady Mary Read," recorded in several deeds of transfer. She may have been the wife of Clement Read (of the adjoining county) who from her prominent social position was known as "Madame Read," or some one who never left her English home; but her land was purchased for the purpose of occupying it by those who became settlers.

The first settlement made in the section which became Campbell, but was then included in Brunswick—was by a colony of Presbyterians from Pennsylvania about the year 1742, following the favorable response to a petition sent in 1739 by John Caldwell, the grandfather of John C. Calhoun, to the governor of Virginia, requesting permission for those of the Presbyterian denomination moving into the state to have the free exercise of their religious liberty. Three colonies of this sect thereupon came respectively into Campbell, Charlotte and Prince Edward, the Campbell contingent of them settling about Hat Creek locality.

John Irvine, pioneer of these settlers, came alone into the virgin forest and blazed the way for others who were to follow him. In a wilderness of thirty-five or forty miles extent, he only found one very old white resident. Patenting there a large tract of land he prepared for the settlement of his family upon it, returning to Pennsylvania for them.

His report of the likelihood of a living being obtainable in this new country induced others to follow, and people then flocked to the neighborhood, for land was cheap and wood for building and for fuel was abundant.

As soon as they had established themselves in their new homes, Irvine persuaded the settlers to unite with him in building a place of worship, and the first church was given the name Hat Creek from that of the nearby stream. Community interests centered around this church and as its membership became extended through the adjoining country, its influence increased and it eventually became the mother of other county churches.

John Irvine continued to be the leading spirit in all progressive innovations. In payment for his part of the building expenses Irvine gave the land upon which the church was erected; and this first rude structure was completed for worship about three years after he came. According to an agreement previously made with Gilbert Tennant of Philadelphia that he would send for him if a preacher was needed, the latter was summoned and took charge of the services, preaching at Hat Creek on Sundays for twelve months following. By the time the year had expired a good sized congregation had been drawn together, cemented in good fellowship by mutual interest in church growth. It became easier to secure preachers less distant, and calls were made for those near at hand.

Succeeding Tennant in the pulpit came Waddill, David Rice, William Mahon, Cary Allen, William Irvine (son of John) and James Allen.

About this time it was found necessary to replace the old church building with a new one, which was more pretentiously constructed of plank; again John Irvine gave of his adjoining land, reserving a few acres for the benefit of the church which still belong to it.

The elders of the church were John Irvine and his son, Major John Irvine, Captain John Marshall, Captain Charles Cobbs, Captain Publius Jones, Joshua and Samuel Morris. No other denominations had erected churches in the community then, so other sects were allowed to preach in their church, provided they did not interfere with the arrangements made for the Presbyterian service: the spirit of toleration also caused those of different belief to meet together as one congregation, whether Presbyterian, Methodist or Baptist.

Among those who availed themselves of this pulpit privilege was William Dodson, a Baptist minister, who made the boast

Hat Creek Church

of a successful revival he had held over the mountains, but enquiries concerning this claim revealed the fact that no revival had taken place. Dodson then was dismissed from the use of Hat Creek church. In leaving, however, he drew some of the Presbyterians into his Baptist fold. Among these were Charles Cobbs, his sons John and Jesse and his daughter Mary. Elder Cobbs ultimately became a Baptist minister. His wife remained a while longer with the Hat Creek congregation and when she finally left she was regarded by the Baptists as a very distinguished convert. Dodson contrived to baptize her at night by the light of torches on the banks of Little Falling river to create an effect of the supreme importance of immersion—that if one of Mrs. Cobb's standing could not wait until daylight, others could not follow too quickly.

John Irvine died in 1788, not long after the completion of the second church, and Elder Morris a few years later. Lacking a Presbyterian preacher those of other denominations were called to Hat Creek and in the interval a Methodist, Bishop Moore, served there, giving much satisfaction. About 1799 Rev. Archibald McRoberts was procured for Hat Creek, but he did not preach during the winter months and the pulpit was then filled by others; at one time by James Tompkins of Old Concord and John Weatherford of the Baptist church. McRoberts died in 1806 and Hat Creek was again without a preacher. In the summer of 1807 John H. Rice came from Charlotte and advised petitioning the next Presbytery to provide supplies. In 1808 Mr. Lumpkin and Clement Read of Charlotte came to Hat Creek, followed by Nash Legrand, with John H. Rice and Clement Read as assistants on sacramental occasions.

At this time a third church, a frame structure as the previous one had been, was built; the elders then were Paulett Clark, Captain William Smith, Benjamin Chapman and William Armistead; but the last named died in the following year. Major John Irvine and Rev. Legrand both died in 1814 and John S. McLain succeeded, being ordained pastor by a Presbytery composed of Drury Lacy, Matthew Lyle, William S. and Clement Read. When McLain became afterwards a student of medicine his connection was then severed. Captain Smith and Elder Chapman having moved away and Elder Marshall deceased, the eldership was renewed with Richard Hammersley, John W. Marshall of Little Concord, Andrew Mann and Paulett Clark as associates; Samuel Armistead succeeded McLain in the pulpit. So far everything had gone on harmoniously at Hat Creek; but a change now occurred. A call was made out for Armistead and sent to the Presbytery. In 1826 Stephen Taylor, by appointment, preached his installation sermon at Hat Creek. After Armistead became pastor, the opposing party would not be quiet, and complaints were sent to Presbytery, which appointed committees to examine into the state of things and make a settlement. The committee after hearing both sides cut off the opposing party and gave them to Little Concord; both parties declared themselves satisfied, until the Presbyterian controversy burst out through the states and the cry of "Old School" and "New School" was heard, when contentions again arose at Hat Creek between those siding with one or the other of the schools, as Armistead sided with the "New," those favoring the "Old" opposed his remaining as pastor, several members withdrawing to worship at Rudd's Old Store, who contemplated building another meeting house, and Mr. Cunningham preached to them. Finally Armistead decided to withdraw. After some delay the parties at Rudd's and Hat Creek agreed to worship together at Hat Creek with Hammersley as pastor. Those also at Little Concord returned and quiet became restored. The elders then chosen were William, James and Christopher Clark, Dr. Robert Smith, Matthew T. Irvine, Brice A. Martin, Sampson Woodall and Captain Robert Armistead, and in addition, Paulett Clark and Andrew Mann. Sunday school was started about 1850. The buryground which had been used since Hat Creek church was first built, was enlarged in 1825 because it had become so filled up and several times its enclosure became renewed. In 1882 a fourth church was built. Elders at the time were Paulett Clark and his son, O. C. Clark, James Clark, Dr. Robert Smith, and Captain Robert Armistead. The church which has been often rebuilt and restored still occupies the old site given it by John Irvine.

Irvine had come into Brunswick county. At its division in 1745 to form Lunenburg he became a citizen of the latter county and when Lunenburg was divided in 1753 to form Bedford he then became a resident of Bedford. At a court held at New London in 1766 "Sundry Presbyterian Protestant Dissenters' new meeting house erected near Six Mile Tree was set apart for the worship of God," showing that Presbyterians were establishing churches in new communities. Again in 1774 "members of Peaks of Otter Presbyterian church asked that elders might be entitled to take and hold lands for the use of ministers under proper regulations." In 1785, three years after the formation of Campbell, seventy signers petitioned against the passage of a bill for the support of preachers of the gospel, "which was an imposition upon the rights of free men for legislation favorable to any one group."

SECOND SETTLEMENT—1753
New London

Around the year 1750 a second group of people came to settle in Lunenburg near its county seat, and they conformed to the established English church. Among these was the family of William Callaway, who had obtained a grant of 15,000 acres of land in different sections of the county: 1,600 acres upon the upper side of Buffalo creek, 4,500 acres lying both sides of Elk creek.

Richard and Francis Callaway, brothers of William, patented land in Lunenburg in 1747; these three settlers are said to have been the first men who cleared land and raised corn on Otter river.

William Callaway was living in the county when on March 12th, 1750, Dr. Thomas Walker passed through it during his second expedition as agent of the Loyal Company. Walker travelled from his home in Albemarle through Nelson and Amherst to James river, which he crossed near where Lynchburg was afterwards established; probably over the ferry Nicolas Davies operated, which furnished communication and transportation from one side of his land to the opposite, as that appears to have been the only ferry in the locality at that period. From there Dr. Walker went on to Callaway's merchant store, supplied himself with rum (an article considered of the first importance) thread and other necessaries; and thence pursued his journey over the main wagon road leading to New river. The home of Callaway was not far from where the town of New London, as Bedford county seat, was located a little later, on Buffalo creek near the main road.

At the formation of Bedford in 1753 there were no public buildings which could serve as court house for the new county and the newly commissioned justices met on May 27th, 1754, in the house of Matthew Talbot. Callaway had applied for the patent on 445 acres of land on both sides of Little Otter—2,350 acres on the upper side of Big Otter adjoining the land of Sherwood Walton and 288 acres on the north side of Staunton river joining Echols' land. When court met at Talbot's on July 22nd, 1754, it was ordered that application be made by the sheriff to the governor, for a writ of adjournment from Talbot's to Callaway's on Buffalo creek; awaiting official authority for change of meeting place, court was held again at Talbot's on August 26th, at which time Callaway agreed to build a prison immediately near the main road; and in case the court house should be established upon his land he was to be paid for the building, if part of Arbemarle on the south side of James river should be added to Bedford and the court house be located on his land—in such event he agreed to give 100 acres at the forks of the road upon which court building and prison could be erected—50 acres in fee simple when required and the balance when he had obtained the patent for it; in the meantime he offered to provide a rough house for court meetings.

At a court held November 25th following, a writ of adjournment from Talbot's to the lately erected court house was produced, and two days later the justices adjourned to the Callaway building. The deed for the fifty acres from himself and wife to the trustees, Richard Callaway, Zachary Isbell, and Benjamin Howard (who had been appointed by order of court in 1755) was recorded March 27th, 1757, at which time it was ordered that the town be given the name of New London.

Callaway received patents for 350 acres on both sides of the south fork of Otter in 1756 and for 390 acres on a branch of Little Otter in 1759. He gave the county in 1761 the other 50 acres promised, with a deed to newly appointed trustees—

Richard and James Callaway, Benjamin Howard, Jeremiah Early, William Meade, John Payne, Jr., and William Stamps.

Proceeding with county affairs it was ordered that town land be laid out in half acre lots and sold, with the previso that they be built upon within a year's time or the land revert back to the county. The court house erected at this time was replaced by order of court, July 23, 1766, for a new one, to be built 24x36 with 12-ft. pitch, wainscoting 4-ft. high, plastered above and six glass windows with underpinning of brick, 1½-ft. from the ground. At a court held there on January 23rd, 1776, of the ten justices in attendance, seven of them came from the Campbell section of what was still Bedford county.

In 1784 Robert Ewing, William Leftwich and Robert Clark, trustees empowered by the Assembly, sold "the late court house, prison and lots" to Christopher Irvine for £125. The building was standing in 1856 but was either burned or pulled down later.

At the time of the Revolution New London contained about 80 private residences, and a number of merchant stores. It acquired importance as a base of supplies, for it contained an arsenal and a long wooden structure used as a magazine, which was kept under guard of soldiers. Its possession of these military stores drew to it the attention of the British forces, and Tarleton was dispatched there to destroy them. His forward march was by Petersburg, Amelia Court House and Prince Edward Court House, reaching New London July 16, 1781; leaving there on the morning of the 18th via Lunenburg and Dinwiddie to join Cornwallis at Suffolk on July 24th. Hunter of the Federal army raided the town en route to Lynchburg, June 16th, 1864, but failed of his object as had Tarleton; thus New London participated in two wars.

On December 13th, 1813, a petition bearing many signatures of Bedford and Campbell people was presented to the Assembly requesting the formation of a new county with New London as the center; and that it be bounded by four lines making a square of it, and the middle of each line be six miles from town; but the petition was rejected as undesirable.

Voice of the Revolution

Patrick Henry delivered his celebrated speech on the John Hook case at New London court house, appearing there as counsel for John Venable, the defendant. He excited the indignation of his audience against Hook, in painting the distress of the American army, exposed, almost naked, to the rigors of a winter's sky and marking the frozen ground over which they marched with the blood of their bare feet. "Where was the man," said he, "who had an American heart in his bosom, who would not have thrown open his barns, his cellars, the doors of his house, the portals of his breast, to have received with open arms, the meanest soldier in that little band of famished heroes? Where is the man? There he stands! Whether the heart of an American beats in his bosom, you, gentlemen, are to judge."

Henry concluded with a description of Yorktown surrender, the British dejection and the patriot's triumphal cry of "Washington and Liberty," then the discordant note, disturbing the general joy, of Hook hoarsely howling through the American camp, "beef, beef, beef."

The legal record of this case is preserved in the circuit court of Franklin county, Virginia.

John Venable was fortunate in the selection of counsel for his defense, and no doubt Henry was no unwilling advocate for the cause in which Hook became a victim of popular political feeling. With such an opponent Hook could have no showing, yet his attorney, William Cowan, proved his ability later by his marked success in his profession. Henry brought to a climax—at which patriotic judgment could give but one verdict —this suit of long standing (once settled in court against Venable) by his appeal to patriotic sentiment, while that feeling in the community was still inflamed; it was as an echo of the oratory, at St. John's church, in Richmond, which had furnished a spark that kindled Virginia's smoldering revolt against England's exactions.

John Hook was a Scotchman by birth. After he had established himself near New London, he became a prosperous farmer and merchant, operating in the latter industry under the firm name of Hook and Ross. Christopher and Mary Irvine sold John Hook and David Ross, merchants in partnership, in 1783, a hundred acres of land lying on both sides of Watery branch, both sides of Irvine's road at Anthony's corner, along John Callaway's line. In 1728 Hook patented 285 acres on Beaverpond creek.

Hook married Elizabeth, the daughter of Colonel John Smith of Goochland county. His descendants are amongst the most respected citizens of the country. His two sons are reported to have died unmarried, but all four daughters married. His daughter Elizabeth married Christopher Clark (3rd of his name, son of Robert and Susan Henderson-Clark, grandson of Micajah and Judith Adams-Clark, great grandson of Christopher Clark, Sr., of Louisa county). Clark was a prominent attorney in Bedford which district he represented in Congress from 1804 to 1806.

The names of Robert and Stephen Hook are found among county records. Stephen was listed in John Hook's store accounts. Robert's will was recorded in 1781. A suit of Robert Hook's estate against Hector Harris, administrator, was conducted by William Leigh, attorney-at-law.

In 1785 John and Elizabeth Hook sold Thomas Jones 200 acres lying on both sides of Little Mill creek, which was part of a patent to Hook and Ross of 565 acres obtained in 1780. Then in 1786 John Hook sold 350 acres of land adjoining Crockett Thompson. At this time he appears to have disposed of all his Campbell county property and removed to Franklin county, where he conducted a store at Hale's Ford, about a mile from the river.

One of the Hook name married Quintilla Adams. This Hook operated a ferry across Staunton river in early times.

Court Penman

Less than a mile from New London, on an eminence over-looking the old town, there still stands the home, *Federal Hill,* of Bedford's first clerk, James Steptoe, familiarly known as "Jimmie." Also remaining within his home grounds is the clerk's office, noticeable for its enormous brick chimney built on the outside, a style prevalent when it was constructed. Here all county business belonging to his office was transacted and the records of his long term in his fine writing are preserved at

Federal Hill, Home of James Steptoe, Half a Mile from New London

Bedford City, the name of Bedford's seat changed in 1890 from Liberty of Steptoe's day.

The *Federal Hill,* seen to-day, replaced an earlier residence, which was destroyed by fire, but is itself over a hundred years old and is a more. substantial building than the one it super-seded. The entrance porch and cornice have dental ornamenta-tion; and chairboarding and stairway are well preserved in the hall and reception rooms.

James Steptoe married a daughter of Col. James Callaway (county lieutenant), and his first wife. Beginning with 1772 he remained clerk of county court during his life; was also clerk of circuit and district court, composed of Bedford, Franklin, Campbell, Pittsylvania and Henry, from 1772 to 1797. At the time he moved to Bedford that section of country was still unsettled and subject to disorders. The tradition is extant of passing Indians coming upon his mother-in-law as she was returning from a spring at the foot of the hill, and pointing a drawn bow at her as long as she was in sight. This incident caused the spring to receive the name of Indian Spring.

The former home of clerk Steptoe was sold about 1850 to a family of Carters from Fredericksburg, a daughter of which married Augustus Labby, son of Captain Pleasant Labby of Lynchburg; she still owns and resides at Federal Hill, and charms visitors by her courteous greeting of them.

Between New London town and the Academy of that name, is the old rock-walled graveyard which contains the graves of Steptoe and many of his neighbors, but the stones have fallen out of position and the inscriptions are barely traceable, though a few have withstood neglect and the wear of time. There can be deciphered Frances Langhorne, 1832; Anne Bowker Callaway, 1834, wife of Col. Wm. Callaway; William Callaway, 1827; Ann Bowker Mennis, wife of Callohill Mennis; Callohill Mennis; Samuel Read; Elizabeth Read; Frances A. C. Mennis and a few others. Wild vines and dense undergrowth with a tangle of briars render a visit to the enclosure one of risk to clothing if not to the person of the intruder. Speece writes of this old landmark, which contains his beloved son's remains as well as his own:

> On Campbell county's western verge
> Where wasting down with slow decay
> New London mourns her better day,
> And here, a little further west,
> The founders have been long at rest.
> Yet now the casual tread alone
> Discovers graves no longer known,
> Whose mouldering tenants cannot claim

The honors even of a name. . . .
Tradition, when affection slept,
In legendary record kept
Their birth, their actions and their age,
Oblivion stole the tattered page,
And shrouded in impervious gloom,
Hid the frail record in the tomb.
Ye noiseless slumberers who repose
From all your wanderings, cares and woes
Low as yourselves, your annals keep,
Involved in night and silence deep.
Your secrets none can now reveal,
Death and the grave have fix'd the seal,
That renders all inquiry vain.

Conrad Speece bought a tract of land lying on Flat creek from Christopher Irvine, which had been granted to Wayley, was surveyed in 1770 for John H. Weaver and conveyed to Irvine by Weaver in 1790.

Conrad Speece, an early Campbell settler, married in 1796 Rachel Claywell. In 1790 he purchased the tract of land on Flat Creek from Christopher Irvine. His daughter, Mary, married Thaddeus Kabler in 1821. A son, Joseph M., married Louise M.. . . . and had children, John, Morton, and daughter, Josaphine N.: sons George W. and Frederick were the executors of Conrad Speece's will. In 1827 Thaddeus and Mary L. Kabler made a deed to Geo. W. Speece, an heir of Conrad Speece, of an equal part of the land and mansion house at the *Water Lick* (Jefferson and Mitchell's pointers were called the Water Lick) 402 acres on Cottontown road (Richard Callaway's former road). Just outside of New London, where two roads meet at a sharp angle, stands the old brick residence of Frederick Speece. None of his descendants remain in the country and his property has passed from the family to a succession of owners. Speece wrote of himself that he was a wayward boy of a melancholy turn, a stranger even in his own home; so he bade adieu to the land of his birth and went wandering afar; yet in the course of a few years he returned well satisfied to revisit his old haunts. It seems to have been at that period of his career that he wrote his "Sketches," which were collected together in one volume, and were issued from New London Academy in 1823. The loss of his young son was a great grief to him, and left him with an only daughter.

In the latter years of his life the impulse seized him to play the King Lear act. He accordingly made a proposal to his

Ivanhoe Lodge, Frederick Speece's Old Home

daughter and her husband to take charge of his property and divide the proceeds with him. He soon discovered this was a most unsatisfactory arrangement, and in his will written in 1868 he covered several pages of it with minute details of the neglect and privations to which he was subjected by his daughter as well as her husband. Yet to that daughter he bequeathed 90 acres of land bounded by the turnpike and Richmond road and to his four grandchildren the property upon which his home stood.

His poetic gift seems to have fallen to a relative, Douglass Kabler-Nelson, who has published two volumes of verse for children, and one number inspired by a visit to Speece's neglected grave in the old New London cemetery. One of Speece's few intimates was Augustine Leftwich, through whose assistance the poems were printed. At the death of Leftwich's beautiful first wife, Speece wrote a touching poem to her memory. His home is called "Ivanhoe Lodge." His daughter, Ann Booker, married Dr. William A. Rice: children, Nannie M. and Sarah F. Rice.

Peter Hunter of Campbell was executer of Frederick Speece's will, witnessed by Dr. J. M. Speece, C. T. and Jerry Hunter, John F. Teas, Joseph Graham, T. L. Kabler and John M. Echols.

In 1751 William Echols patented 317 acres, along both sides of Buffalo creek, a branch of Staunton river, of land adjoining the property of Nathaniel Dennis. The same year Joseph and Isaac Echols patented each several hundred acres on both sides of Straitstone creek and its branches.

In 1831 Peregrine Echols bought 110¾ acres on a branch of Flat creek and on Sawyer's road.

In 1836 Galt, Bullock and Company, trustees, sold a tract of land in New London to Peregrine Echols, which property had been conveyed to Dabney by William C. Bowyer and his wife in 1830. Upon this land Echols erected a building which he used as a tavern. His land extended within the limits of Bedford and about ten years after he purchased it, a deposit of alum was found which led to the discovery of a spring there but no use was made of the mineral water until John R. Maben bought the property, improved the ground and built a hotel and cottages upon it for a resort, and for many years the place attracted health seeking visitors. New London was then embraced in the new community, which was christened Bedford Springs, and it is generally called by that name at the present time.

But tradition, in connection with the spring, goes back to the time of the Revolution and attaches to it the romance of a soldier, who, returning home from Yorktown surrender, found his affianced sweetheart wedded to a civilian. In despair he turned away and worn and weary at nightfall, dismounted and laid down to die. A little girl from a neighboring farmhouse saw his wretched condition and in pity brought him a cup of water from the spring which revived and restored him, and prompted the resolve to live. He never married, and superstition says that periodically, at midnight, this soldier is seen dismounting from his white war horse and mingling, as in toast, his blessing to the water with a curse to the unfaithful one, then he disappears like a shadow, upon the wings of the wind.

When Bedford Alum Springs became discontinued as a health resort a company was organized for the manufacture of salts from the water and located their works on James river near Lynchburg. John Minor Botts Echols, son of the original owner, was associated with the enterprise; but it did not long remain in operation.

Maben, proprietor of the springs, had been one of the party of men who crossed the country as gold seekers in 1849. He married first Sarah Douglass of Campbell and lived not far from New London, where he owned and operated a mill. He was the subject of a suit which resulted in a judgment against him. This disappointment caused him to make complaints in writing his will, of how he had been plundered, harassed and robbed through bribery and perjury by unscrupulous men of what his industry and economy had accumulated. He was an eccentric character:—had travelled to California overland by horseback and brought back upon his return mementoes of his sojourn, one a "pure gold breastpin, and nugget of gold shaped into an American eagle," upon which he set much value. He died around 1900 and in making disposition of his property to his second wife and the children of his first marriage, he provided that the latter should receive their share of their grandfather Douglass' estate; the springs property was directed to be sold for the benefit of his heirs. Special instructions were given in regard to the disposition of an old Bible which he claimed was the first one printed in the United States.

At the time of Bedford's division, the country was sparsely settled and farms covered large areas. New London was the only town and, being county seat, was the general meeting-place in all matters of public interest, regardless of distance. A radical change came with the county division, for Campbell as well as Bedford, took prompt measures to secure more central sites for their court houses; in the interim of construction of these buildings, official meetings were held at conveniently situated homes which were loaned for that purpose.

New roadways, having for their objective, the nearest route to centers and to market, were laid off. New London then lost its prestige, although supreme court continued to be held there under the old district system. In October, 1791 an effort was made to remove this court nearer the center of the district, New London being at the extreme northeastern corner. Those favoring this movement were prompt with their reason for the change. "Houses there, ready for reception, had made an excuse at first but that could no longer be urged; a rich and fertile neighborhood was to be found near Staunton river, and the necessary buildings would not cost more than £100, a trifling sum in *competition* to the equal justice it would cause." This petition repeated next year met with violent opposition from the towns people of New London, who retorted that "District court was established to suit the general convenience. Assembly chose the court house already built and capable of affording entertainment, being most convenient and *centrical* in this district. That the bill was presented by only a few of those most interested, the center of the district, not being the center of inhabitants but a barren, poor country, very hilly, required travel as far out of the way as to New London"; hence an appeal was made that courts of justice reject the previous petition.

For thirty years the center around which a large county's activities revolved, there being no rival town with which to divide honors, then suddenly deposed from prominence, arrested in development and left on borderland—lacking water and rail facilities and shadowed by the pall of blighted hopes and discouraged efforts—it is no wonder that New London started on a downward course which has continued. It has still its memories of past use to secure for it a place in history—perhaps during the somnolent state into which it had fallen, it had its dreams of an awakening and re-establishment—for surely the glamor of glory which came to it through its eminent men clings to it in the association with their achievements and in the preservation of its ambitious name during more than a century of inactivity.

Just at this time a development in the neighborhood has been started by a company of realtors, which embraces the construction of a large lake to be called "Timber Lake," with a surrounding driveway and the adjoining land divided into lake front lots. Towards the carrying out of this plan 325 acres of land at the intersection of three streams, which form Buffalo creek, have been purchased from the owners, T. F. Johnson "Closeburn Manor" tract; L. C. Leftwich, George J. Isaacs and Morton Leftwich. It is planned to stock the lake with fish and to provide boating facilities. A dam 600 feet long, is to be erected to form the lake which will cover 75 acres of ground, the dam to be topped by a driveway, and the property to have two entrances—one from Salem turnpike on the east, and the other from Forest along Bedford Springs road. Interest in this enterprise is already awakened and motorists from near towns are attracted to the scene of the company's operations.

Third Settlement
South River Meeting

The Lynch family was the third group of people to enter the county and establish a settlement there. Charles Lynch, Sr., had patented 200 acres, in one tract, and 123 in another tract on the north side of Staunton river and 87 acres on the south side of Reedy creek in 1741; then in 1747 he bought two tracts of 425 acres and 125 acres from Colonel John Bolling, surveyed by Colonel William Cabell, and located at the mouth of Blackwater creek on James river, including the site of Lynchburg, "being one-half barren and the other plantable." Lynch then moved to *Chestnut Hill* on James river, but lived only a few years, dying there in 1753. He was not a Quaker; his wife joined the Society of Friends in 1750 about the time they moved from Lynch's ferry on the Rivanna, north fork, and settled on lands near the ferry, on Fluvanna, the south fork of James river. Mrs. Lynch qualified as executrix on Lynch's estate, with John and Joseph Anthony and William Cabell as securities. She added to the estate in 1758, 57 acres on the north branch of Fishing creek, and three tracts of 100, 400, and 322 acres in 1759, land on Lynch's and Stovall's creeks, also 3,480 acres on the south side of Staunton, north side of Otter, including Briery creek.

It was through efforts of Mrs. Lynch that a Quaker Meeting was established in the county, and this she started by sitting alone with her children for divine worship; a large quarterly meeting grew out of this small beginning. She provided the site upon which the first building was erected in 1757. The meeting becoming established, drew members and their families from other sections, and by the beginning of Revolutionary times, the community was well populated.

Governmental requirements caused early settlers in Virginia to conform to the established English church. Laws of 1659, 1662 and 1693 prohibited unlawful assembling of Quakers— made it penal for any master of a vessel to bring a Quaker into the colony—ordered those already here, and such as should come afterwards, to be imprisoned till they should leave the country—provided a milder punishment for their first and second return, but death for their third. Prohibited all persons from suffering their meetings in or near their houses, entertaining them individually or disposing of books which supported their tenets. Quakers were escaping from persecution in England and turning to this country as a refuge affording civil and religious freedom. They found that legislation in Virginia only favored the English church, a condition lasting a century. Then other opinions began to be held and at the commencement of the Revolution two-thirds of the people had become dissenters. Laws were still oppressive, but moderation had replaced intolerance, and the determination of the Quakers had won for them respect and recognition. They were already settled in Bedford at the beginning of war, and some of their young men were incited to enter the patriot army, even with the penalty of disownment from the Society. During the war period that restriction caused disagreement among themselves. In 1749 a meeting was established near the Sugar Loaf Mountains with Christopher and Bowling Clark as overseers; this was in the present county of Albemarle near Stony Point. The road between the Camp Creek Quakers of Louisa and the Sugar Loaf meeting was called "Clark's Tract," that family having been among the first settlers in the locality. In August, 1754, the Friends of South River petitioned that they might have a meeting, which being granted them in October of that year, Bowling and Edward Clark were appointed overseers for the meeting which was to be located south of the river three or four miles southward of where Lynchburg was afterwards started, at Lynch's creek of Blackwater, on land given by Sarah Lynch, sister of the Clark overseers.

In 1756 a second meeting was located on Goose creek, a tributary of Staunton river but was abandoned after two years on account of annoyances from Indians.

When the division of Bedford was made Friends aided in the settlement of Campbell and deserve a place in the history of its early days. Many names of South River Quakers are held by descendants of those who remained—Adams, Clark, Davis, Lynch, Pleasants, Terrell, Moorman, Anthony, though we must look in other states for many other names. Inquiry into the history of these Quakers discloses two significant facts: that they were foremost in demonstrating their attitude towards slavery by freeing their slaves; and that whereas women of other sects were merely followers in religious exercises, Quakeresses were accorded equality in church government and furnish first suggestion of female suffrage. Mrs. Sarah

Clark-Lynch was example of the latter, she having taken the initial steps to secure the meeting and provided a place; her daughter, Sarah Lynch-Terrell, was leader in anti-slavery movement, having, before her death in 1773, expressed her sentiments in that connection so forcibly, they were read at meetings as "The last sayings of Sarah Terrell," and were promptly acted upon by Christopher Anthony, Christopher Johnson, Micajah Terrell, Charles Moorman, John Venable and others. Many gave up the Society and held their slaves; others held to the Society and freed their slaves. Some of the latter then moved to Ohio, and other non-slave holding states. Many outside of the Quaker fold were influenced to give up slaves at the time. The discipline of disownments caused breaks in society ties and Mrs. Lynch at her second marriage to Major John Ward, lost place for "marrying out"—Ward not being a Quaker. Her son, Charles, was disowned for taking "solemn oaths" upon his installation into office, instead of the "solemn affirmation" of the sect; besides Charles engaged in war, when patriotic fervor was uppermost in thought and action, and he appears to have remained cast out from Quaker Meetings. John was also disowned, but in 1787 he decided to make confession and humble himself before the society in order to rejoin them. Accordingly he sent to the monthly meeting of governors the following letter: "I have to acknowledge that being off the true watch I have given way to the spirit of resentment so far as to gratify that revengeful spirit by putting forth mine own hand to the dishonor of truth which has been a matter of sorrow to me and do sincerely condemn the same; and notwithstanding such conduct may justly deserve the censure of my friends, yet have I a hope and earnest desire remaining that I may be enabled, through a watchful care and diligent attention to that principle of Light and Grace, to surmount every difficulty that in future may be permitted to attend me. I therefore submit my case to the solid consideration of the Meeting."

To the first Meeting house, erected four miles south of Lynch's ferry in 1757, an addition was made in 1763 and a

graveyard provided nearby.   In 1791 John Lynch deeded to
Achilles Douglass and Ashley Johnson 10 acres where the
Meeting house stood "in trust for the use of the congregation
of people called Quakers; for encouragement and establishment of a public school for the pious education of youth; to
build, uphold and repair the premises for purpose of divine
worship; for regulation of church discipline, and for a burying
ground, with entry in and out of the premises."   Upon the
land, then donated, a Meeting house was erected, walls of which

Quaker Memorial Church

form the base of the reconstructed church now used by the
Presbyterians on Salem road.   Between 1775 and 1800 thirty
Quaker members, some with large families, had brought certificates of removal and good standnig from Fairfax and the
northern Goose creek Meeting to South River; and towards
the end of the 18th century Quakers had become scattered over
the county and had started places of worship at Hill's creek
and other points, but they remained principally congregated
at South River, which was headquarters for the Society until
Meetings were completely laid down in 1858.

Quaker Meeting House on Salem Turnpike

The building of the third Quaker Meeting House was begun in 1790 but not completed for several years afterwards. It was built of rugged natural stone collected and laid by the devout hands of those who later were worshippers within its walls. All councils and meetings of the Friends were held there until death or their removal to far-away sections depleted their ranks, and, finally, caused the disappearance of the sect from this community. Descendants of the Quakers, who remained, connected themselves with the religious bodies replacing this early sect, and in time all trace vanished of the latter as a body—which wore a distinctive dress, laid down and conformed to strict rules punishable with disownment if not observed, simplicity of living, and humility in worship—never to reappear, leaving behind the tradition of a peculiarly conscientious people who for years had exerted an influence for good, in living up to the tenets of their religion, and who had been amongst the earliest settlers in the county.

The rock-walled graveyard in which numbers of the Friends were given a last resting-place, is near the church, and among those whose remains were interred there was John Lynch, founder of Lynchburg. No stone marks his grave, but from existing records it is known that he was buried in the northwest corner. Quakers did not approve of grave stones, and interments were only marked by rough head and foot stones, without inscription; it has long been an enclosed reservation where interments are not now permitted.

Age and the elements combined to dismantle the old Meeting house of its roof and for years the neglected walls alone stood as a reminder of former service. Religious exercises conducted near the old ruin finally created the demand for a church there. The preservation of the ruin was becoming exceedingly difficult and expensive, and while there was every reason for preserving it, the trustees although living in the vicinity found it almost impossible to prevent depredations. It seemed a happy inspiration of the Floyd Street Presbyterian church to acquire the property, and, in restoring it, to prolong its existence as an historic relic, and as a worthy memorial of its founders, by reopening it for religious services.

Dr. John J. Terrell, then living, was one of the last surviving trustees and for 30 years its careful guardian. In his young days he attended services there with his Quaker kindred. His sympathy in the movement for its proposed restoration is expressed in a letter written July 2, 1900, and was as follows: "In association of memories, as connected with Friends' Meeting House and graveyard, I stand nearly alone, and desire to see Christian work revived within its walls again. As expressed, within the past year, to Rev. J. A. McMurray, chairman of the building committee, I am in full sympathy with him and others in erecting a church on the walls as now standing. Unless so preserved, the stone walls, now partially remaining, will be despoiled to their foundation within the next decade or two. This I have prevented during the past thirty years by stress of the infliction of legal penalties." The ruin was reconstructed in 1910 and christened "Quaker Memorial Presbyterian Church." Rev. Arthur Rowbotham, of Alta Vista, former pastor there, has been succeeded by C. E. House, now resident in Lynchburg.

Causes of Disownment in Quaker Government

Enlisting in military service: John Schoolfield and James Martin, 1795. Joining the Free Masons and conforming to sundry practices used amongst them that are burthensome to Friends, such as marching in procession with music and weapons, and also in the uniform of an apron, etc.: Samuel Jordan Harrison disowned 1794.

Following the vain fashions of the world, making "bets" and using profane lauguage: William Harrison 1798.

Attending and answering to his name at a military muster: Benjamin Bradford 1799.

Gaming, using profane language and attending places of diversion: Moorman Johnson 1799.

Dancing and attending places of diversion: Betty, daughter of Charles J. Johnson, 1799.

Taking strong drink to excess, offering to fight, and hiring a slave: Thomas, son of John Johnson 1802.

For marrying (being first cousins) contrary to rules of Friends: Micajah Moorman, Jr., and Susanne Johnson 1803.

Following vain customs of the world and hiring slaves: Christopher Lynch 1805.

Moving out of the state without endeavoring to settle with his creditors, William Johnson, Jr., 1806.

Playing cards, taking oaths, attending places of diversion and joining the Masonic society: Asa Wood 1821.

Disposing of a colored boy, named James, who was entitled to his freedom and who has since fallen into the hands of those who hold him as a slave and said Samuel would not endeavor to restore him to his freedom although Friends urged him to do so: Samuel Fisher 1820.

Rhoda Terrell, daughter of Charles Terrell (who had an education amongst us), contrary to the good order used amongst Friends, joined in marriage to a man not of our Society, and having been repeatedly cautioned against it: disowned from our religious society until she makes satisfaction. 1804.

Neglect in attending religious meetings: Robert Terrell.

Hiring slaves and purchasing several: Jesse Terrell.

Overseer of slaves; active in military service: Caleb Terrell.

Catherine Pleasant Terrell: marrying James Bell (a man not professing with Friends). These were the parents of James Pinkney Pleasant Bell, author of "Quaker Friends," who was born in 1829 and who established the J. P. Bell book stores in Lynchburg and Richmond.

Most of the disownments came through marriages contracted against Quaker rule; in the Terrell family alone there were twenty-two for this cause.

In course of time many confessions followed their disownments, presented by those who were solicitous of returning into the Quaker fold.

Enoch Roberts acknowledged that he had so far deviated from the peaceable principles professed by Friends as to suffer the spirit of anger and resentment so to prevail as to procure firearms for his safety, all of which conduct he did condemn, hoping at the same time that his future conduct would evince the sincerity of his acknowledgement: 1789.

Milly Johnson acknowledged having married contrary to Discipline, for which she was justly disowned, and being

Old Clerk's Office, Standing at Federal Hill and Used by Clerk James Steptoe When New London was County Seat of Bedford. (See page 36)

lately measurably sensible of the disadvantage of such a separation, therefore condemned her misconduct in that respect and desired to be reinstated to Friends again, hoped that her future conduct, etc.: 1791.

Judith Brown confessed that she knew not the worth of the right amongst Friends she once had in taking undue liberty, and suffering herself to be married by an Hireling Minister, which caused her to lose her right, which she had found to be a great loss, when it pleased the Lord to open her eyes and shew her whereabouts she was; therefore like a returning prodigal, she made her request to come under Friends' care again: 1792.

Timothy and David Johnson acknowledged that they had deviated from Quaker principles in kissing the Book, etc., which they were inadvertently drawn into, not knowing the difference between an oath and an affirmation, which they were heartily sorry for, and if Friends could pass by that offense, they hoped in future to be more cautious how they committed errors: 1794.

William Betts condemned his conduct in procuring a substitute to serve in the militia, although by indirect means; also removed and left some accounts unsettled, which had given trouble and uneasiness to Friends, of which he was sensible.

Micajah Johnson condemned his conduct in being married by a hire-preacher.

Achilles D. Johnson regretted the act of fighting, of which he had been guilty on account of its repugnance to the principles of the Society in which he had been raised and in which it was his desire to remain, and trusted that Friends would judge of his case in the spirit of forbearance: 1829.

Some of the Quakers Who Moved From South River Meeting, Campbell

1792—John Stanley and wife Sarah and children, to Westfield Meeting, Surry county.

1795—William Davis and wife, Zalinda, and daughter, Sarah, to Goose Creek, Bedford county.

1795—James Johnson and wife, Penelope, and ten children, to Goose Creek, Bedford county.

1794—John Johnson, son of James, to Cedar Creek, Hanover county.

1794—Abraham Runker to New Garden, North Carolina.

1796—Richard Tullis, Jr., to Goose Creek, Bedford county.

1796—Robert Wright and wife, Rachel, to Fairfax.

1796—Joseph Anthony and wife, Rhoda, and son, Samuel Parsons, to Henrico.

1797—Thomas Burgess to Deer Creek, Harford county, Maryland.

1798—Naomi Davis to White Oak Swamp.

1799—Jesse Williams and wife, Sarah, and children, to New Garden, North Carolina.

1799—Micajah Terrell and wife, Anna, and son, Achilles, to New Garden, North Carolina.

1800—Agatha Dicks and her four minor children to New Garden, North Carolina.

1799—Micajah Davis and wife, Mary, and nine children, to White Oak, Henrico county.

1800—Samuel Carey and wife, Rachel, and seven children, to Westfield, North Carolina.

1800—Cynthia Bradfield and infant, John, to Westfield, North Carolina.

1799—Robert and Annis Pleasants to White Oak, Henrico county.

1801—James and Mary Stanton, and two children, to Centre, North Carolina.

1801—John and Martha James and children, to Westland, Penna.

1801—Robert and Catherine Hanna, and four children, to Westland, Penna.

1801—Jonas Harris to Westland, Penna.

1801—Asa and Mary Holloway, and seven children, to Westland, Penna.

1801—Benjamin and Amy Stratton, and three children, to Westland, Penna.

1801—James Ferrell, minor, and his father, to Westland, Penna.

1801—Daniel and Shady Stratton and five children, to Westland, Penna.

1802—Mary Via, Westland, Penna.

1802—Jacob and Rebecca Stratton, to Westland, Penna.

1801—John and Sarah Tellus and four children, to West-land, Penna.

1801—Joseph and Naomi Stratton and two children, to Westland, Penna.

1803—Nicolas and Drucilla Crew and two sons, to Hanover.

1803—James and Agnes Stanton, to Dinwiddie.

The general exodus of Quakers occurred between 1835-7.

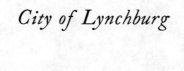

City of Lynchburg

Chapter III

Lynchburg

YNCHBURG, often designated "Tobacco Town" and "City of Hills," received its name from its founder, John Lynch, who displayed wonderful forethought in his selection of the site. New London had been in existence since the middle of the century and Rustburg established several years previously, yet they were soon left behind in progressive movement and now Lynch's town need fear no county rival. Doubtless the city father had an eye for scenery and when he staked his plan upon the power and possibilities of James river, he cast a glance upon the surrounding hills and gained inspiration from their appealing beauty. The town as to its natural features is best described by Anne Royal, first woman journalist, who when travelling through the South, made a visit to the city. She writes she was "astonished to find this garden spot of Virginia which remained in obscurity, unnoticed and unsung" and enthusiastically notes her impressions.

"Daylight disclosed to me one of the richest pictures of scenery to be found. Of all the travels and other notices of this part of the State, I never heard a word on the beauty of the scenery, the most rich and varied within the same bounds of which any town in the Union can boast. Situated on James river, the land on which Lynchburg stands ascends from the water's edge at first gradual then more abrupt and finally terminates in an elevated plain. From this summit you have a view unequalled either for grandeur or beauty. A smooth broad river rolls at your feet and again the opposite shore presents an abrupt high bluff, with huge rocks of terrific wildness, and terminates in smooth conic hills, beyond which are seen farms and houses. The wildest hills and ledges of rocks run up the river's edge and beyond all the Blue Ridge mountains. What distinguishes the scenery of Lynchburg from any I have met with is that such a number of images are drawn within so narrow a compass: the rough, the smooth, the sublime and the beautiful are thickly mingled, combining every catalogue of the picturesque and the fanciful. Whether we regard the boldness of the figures or the variety they assume from different points it is the most finished picture of spontaneous or studied beauty and the town is most happily blessed by nature. The Peaks of Otter, 25 miles distant in Bedford county are seen to rise in sharp blue points almost perpendicularly 4,000 feet. On the north side of the town there is a beautiful view of Tobacco Row mountains in Amherst county and cross-wise Candler's waving range slants in a southeasterly direction."

Mrs. Royal, born 1769 at Newport, Md., fled with her mother from the Indians and settled at Sweet Springs, Va. There she met Capt. Wm. Royal, elderly veteran of the French and Revolutionary Wars whom she married in Botetourt county. After sixteen years of sheltered life she found herself a widow and in poverty. This pioneer of American newspaper women started then her journalistic career at the age of 60 years as editress and chief reporter of *"Paul Pry"* and the *"Huntress."* Her resourcefulness and energy were at their height when she was in search of news.

The notes from her Southern travels were gathered into her first volume of a series, ten in number, which recount her experiences and observations and which won for her national reputation as a clever, observant, entertaining and caustic writer. She revolutionized the press of her day. On July 2nd, 1854 she issued her last number of the *Huntress* and died a few days afterwards.

There are three books extant which furnish history of Lynchburg and which include information concerning the surrounding districts. The first of these volumes, *"Sketches and Recollections of Lynchburg"* is rarely obtainable because it was printed in limited edition. It was written about 75 years ago by Margaret Anthony-Cabell (daughter of Christopher Anthony, Jr., a distinguished attorney of Lynchburg) who was then living in Buckingham county on James river. The *Sketches* originated in her desire to entertain her young children during the long winter evenings, when she was restricted in literary facilities by her residence in an isolated country neighborhood. The recollections of her youth spent in Lynchburg, supplied subjects for these fireside tales, told to interested yet juvenile listeners, in lieu of more imaginative narratives;

Mrs. Margaret Anthony Cabell of Fernley

though, in effect, a lure as of romance seems to hover in the personal description and delineation of character—in the worth and gallantry of her men, the virtue and beauty of her women —which might capture the attention of any age.

Mrs. Cabell, wife of Dr. Clifford Cabell, a practicing physician of Buckingham, was of Quaker ancestry, through both parents, and she lived at a period when Quakerism—so potent a factor in manners and customs of its day—was disappearing from the community and being superseded by influence of other sects. Besides its use as a record of families, her book is valuable because it furnishes annals of the village stage which Lynchburg had not then outgrown, and quaintly expressed seems to reproduce something of the social atmosphere prevailing at the time.

"Sketches and Recollections" was not originally intended for publication; it was not then customary for women to print what they might write. Many confided their thoughts to journals or diaries, but these were kept in their desks and only shown to their most intimate friends. When at length the writer was induced to put her "utterances of happy memories" into print, the small edition was largely distributed as gifts to her circle of friends. The lack of an index, which interfered with its use as family record, has been supplied by a pamphlet index compiled in recent years and now obtainable from the State library at Richmond.

About the end of the nineteenth century and fifty years after the issuance of Mrs. Cabell's book, Rev. Asbury Christian, also a native Lynchburger, using the *Sketches* as background for his *"Lynchburg and Its People,"* brought the growth and outlook of the city to the date of his publication in a volume of full details concerning citizens, many of whom were then active but have since passed away. He rendered timely service in collecting chronicles when Lynchburg was making ready for extended growth and enterprise and it must be a matter for civic gratulation that he seized the opportunity of his residence there to procure these annals while attainable, for the time when the city library would call for them. Taking up the thread of events as they passed, he recalled the agitations of the 50s—the preparation for war and entrance into it—the city's toll in sons who made the supreme sacrifice; the impoverished condition following; military rule and espionage; onwards till around the 70's when control and enterprise became re-established in the hands of citizens and there was renewal of hope and effort; then the land boom which came in 1890, and wild speculation, followed by money crisis and depression in industry; a revival from this stage and activity in suburban development, chief interest in which centered in Rivermont, for a proposition had been made and accepted for the establishment of Randolph-Macon Woman's College and its site was selected in that locality; and in April, 1891, Rivermont bridge, at end of Main Street, was formally opened to the public. This was a time of much rejoicing and the occasion was celebrated by the booming of cannon, the shriek of steam whistles and loud cheers from the crowd assembled. First the officers of Rivermont company went over the structure, the large gathering of people following them.

The bridge had been suggested by Colonel Thomas Whitehead, and his plan was seized by Major Edward S. Hutter, who was largely instrumental in organizing the company. Closing his recital at the end of the century, Mr. Christian stated that Lynchburg was entering upon an era of prosperity unknown in its history.

A third town history contributed by James P. Bell, of Quaker origin himself, gives a statistical account of Quakerism, its followers in the community, its gathering and active operation, and its passing. *"Our Quaker Friends,"* compiled in calendar form, prompts the wish that Mr. Bell, with his early associations and resources, had depicted more of the home life and happenings of this picturesque band of people, whose earnest desire for free exercise of their religion had occasioned their drifting in search of a favorable locality and their removal therefrom when they met with opposition or intolerance. Religious belief and observance made them distinctly peculiar and this was heightened by their dress and mannerism in speech.

These three volumes occupy each their own niche in town history, and serve as a basis of information concerning the times embraced, pointing to the need of a later account of the town of larger interests, grown as it has into a manufacturing center with extended limits and greater population, for at this very time the long contemplated plan of embracing within its bounds contiguous territory is being carried into execution and there may be reasonably visualized further expansion from the operation of its numerous industries. The recent extension adds eight miles of real estate and eight thousand increase in population.

In 1786 John Lynch applied to the General Assembly for the charter of a town to be laid off on 45 acres of land contiguous to Lynch's ferry, the same to be vested in John Clark, Adam Clement, Charles Lynch, John Callaway, Achilles Douglass, William Martin, Jesse Burton, Joseph Stratton, Micajah Moorman and Charles Brooks, trustees. In October of that year the town of Lynchburg was authorized to be established. The first official meeting was held May 8th, 1787, at which assemblage John Clark, Jesse Burton, Joseph Stratton, William Martin, Micajah Moorman and Achilles Douglass were present. Richard Stith was appointed to survey and lay off the town and his plan was recorded at the Court House February 11th, 1805. The town was to be on a single hill called Lynchburg, but was first known as Lynch's Warehouse, for tobacco was engrossing industrial attention. Trustees had no control in the town except over titles of lots. Following the year 1791 owners began to petition for more time in which to improve their lots, so that they might erect better buildings. Several persons had lost their buildings because they were not finished in the allotted time, others wished to improve theirs but feared to do so because of the short time allowed. A petition to the Assembly on November 5th, 1793, asked the privilege of establishing a market house in the town, the structure to serve the double purpose of market and Mason's hall, as the lodge of Free Masons were planning to form a society and were in great need of a hall. Concretely the request was for permission to raise £450 necessary for construction of a hall, and the petitioners were principally Free Masons. Without other legislation, in 1802 Lynch laid off additional lots, several of which were improved. He had a rough map made of the town and demanded that owners should not be compelled to improve them in a specified time, as there was great scarcity of material. On December 8th, 1804, citizens asked for an act of complete incorporation as the town had grown so large the officers could not control riots, vice and law violations. On the 10th of January, 1805, Legislature passed an act for incorporating the town, and for enlarging it; then the half-acre lots adjoining Lynchburg which Lynch had laid off were made a part of the town and a map made and put on record at the Court House. A charter was provided at this date which authorized freeholders and housekeepers to select annually by ballot twelve freeholders, who should meet and elect by ballot one mayor, one recorder and four aldermen, the balance to serve as common councilmen. But no power was given them to contract debts. On May 6th, 1805, the first court of Hustings for Lynchburg corporation assembled at the Mason's Hall: present William Warwick, mayor; Thomas Wyatt, recorder; Geo. D. Winston, Samuel J. Harrison, Roderick Taliaferro and Meredith Lambert, aldermen. This court ordered that William Norvell be appointed clerk of court, and, he being qualified according to law, entered into bond with William Warwick and John Wyatt as his securities. John Davis was appointed sergeant for one year and entered into bond with William Davis and John Lynch, Jr., as his securities. William Davis and John Lynch, Jr., were recommended to the Governor as fit persons to exercise the duties of coroner. On motion of Thomas S. McClelland in behalf of Wilson Davenport and Josiah Leake, it was ordered that they be admitted to practice as counsel and attorneys for the corporation court. It appearing to the satisfaction of the Court that the society of Masons had given use of their hall for the purpose of holding court of hustings, it was ordered that the hall be considered as the court house for the corporation.

1805.—William Davis, Samuel Irvine and John Lynch, Jr., were appointed commissioners to receive proposals for ground upon which to build a jail and to procure a temporary jail with a draft for a new one.

May 7th, the same year, Charles and William Johnson were appointed as constables and Thomas W. Cocke, master-commissioner.

May 8th, William Davis, John Lynch, Jr., and Samuel J. Harrison were appointed commissioners to contract for a jail 12 ft. square, two stories high, seven ft. pitch on Water street, below the market house. This structure, which attracted attention by its quaintness, was eventually pulled down for the purpose of broadening Ninth street at its intersection with Main.

July 1st, Josiah Leake was appointed commonwealth's attorney, thus completing the organization of the court, which was still held in Mason's Hall.

John Lynch donated a lot to the community on June 18, 1805, "lying on the hill adjoining the town," "for the purpose of erecting public buildings and using it as a public square"; but in event the ground should become relinquished from the purpose for which it was given and intended "it should then return to the heirs of John Lynch forever"; thus as long as a court house remains on that site it may be said to own it. The first court house was built upon this ground in 1812; it was taken down and the present one, replacing it, was erected in 1852, and was designed by John Wills, architect, the grandfather of city clerk Thomas D. Davis.

An act of February 19th, 1812, authorized freeholders and housekeepers to elect fourteen freeholders, who should select one mayor, one recorder, six aldermen and the balance to serve as common councilmen.

An effort made in 1813 by freeholders to enlarge the boundaries of the town was opposed by John Lynch, yet the Legislature added to the corporate limits on February 9th "that lot of ground conveyed by John Lynch to the town for a public square" upon which the court house and jail had been erected.

A third extension of the town occurred on February 9th, 1814, when its limits extended to Harrison street "as soon as it was laid off in lots with convenient streets." A plat of this new district was recorded on September 8th, 1814, in the Hustings Court clerk's office. A fourth extension was made on March 10th, 1819, and the Act of that date provided for the town's division into two wards, freeholders of each ward to elect nine men who were to select one mayor, one recorder, and seven aldermen, the remainder to be councilmen. The request sent December 20th, 1825, for further extension of limits was granted January 30th, 1826 and was the first extension to reach the river, giving a narrow frontage from the mouth of Blackwater at the toll bridge to the mouth of Horseford branch at Hurt's mill. A plat of this addition was recorded on September 27th, 1827.

An Act of January 29th, 1830, authorized the common council to raise $40,000 by lottery, and one passed on February 19th of the same year, gave authority to qualified voters of each ward to elect six aldermen and six councilmen, who were to elect by ballot from amongst themselves one mayor, one recorder, and one senior alderman. Petitions were sent for enlarging the town's corporate limits on February 1st, 1843; again on January 31, 1846.

Petitions asked permission to locate a poor-house outside of town limits and to purchase necessary lands. The Act granting this petition was passed March 17, 1849. Act of January 19th, 1848, authorized the common council to guarantee 6% on $500,000 stock in Richmond and Alleghany railroad company, chartered in 1846 to run from Richmond on southwest side of James river to or below the mouth of Kanawha river. At the same time by charter of the Lynchburg and Tennessee railroad, the common council was authorized to guarantee 6% on $500,000 of stock in that road, in both cases without any vote.

By Act of January 16th, 1851, qualified voters were authorized to elect the mayor. A sixth extension of city limits occurred on May 20th, 1852, but this added but little amount to the city's limits of 1826. At this time Lynchburg was made a city and the various acts affecting the charter were reduced into one. By this charter the common council was authorized (upon petition of one-fourth of the freeholders) to direct a vote of the freeholders to be taken as to whether the city should subscribe to the stock of an internal improvement to be constructed near the city and to make the subscription if the proposition was sustained by a majority of the freeholders voting.

The extension which took place December 9th, 1870, was the most comprehensive one which had then taken place, and required a plat of the boundaries included, of Percival's Island, along the James river banks to the ravine at the base of White Rock hill, to the corner of the Presbyterian cemetery, thence to Spring Valley branch, crossing both arms of the Lynchburg and Salem turnpike, to the Meeting house branch on the Forest road, along Blackwater to the abutment of what was then the Orange, Alexandria and Manassas railroad bridge spanning James river. Large districts outside of corporate limits were laid off into squares and streets by the owners, thus a portion of Diamond and Franklin hills were laid off by the Henry Davis estate and on Daniel's hill by Judge William Daniel and others. On February 9th, 1856, in an address to Virginia Assembly a number of petitioners opposed the incorporation of Spring Hill cemetery, an objection which was repeated on December 8th, 1857.

On January 25th, 1860, suburbans petitioned that the town be authorized to levy taxes from the suburbs as soon as the waterworks were enlarged and extended into the suburbs.

Among John Lynch's gifts to Lynchburg was a lot on the town side for Amherst bridge, and land for the public burying ground, known as the "Old Methodist Graveyard," where many of the earlier citizens were interred, but it later became a soldier's cemetery, and for many years past has been the setting for memorial services.

Acts of Assembly in connection with Lynchburg:

January 28, 1811, authorizing John Lynch to build a toll bridge across James river at Lynchburg.

February 28, 1818, authorizing erection of a free bridge across James river.

February 7, 1818, incorporating the Lynchburg and Salem Turnpike company.

March 16, 1836, incorporating the Lynchburg and Campbell Court House Turnpike company.

February 16, 1846, incorporating the Ann Norvell Orphan Asylum.

March 16, 1849, incorporating the Lynchburg Female Orphan Asylum.

March 21, 1851, authorizing three justices to hold Corporation court.

In 1890 the city encroached upon more county area in Rivermont (and later its extension, Peakland), West and South Lynchburg.

In 1926 it incorporated eight additional acres, including Brookville, Burton's Creek, West Lynchburg, Fairview Heights and Fort Hill.

John Lynch (son of Charles, Sr., and Sarah Clark-Lynch), the founder of Lynchburg, born 1740, moved, when twelve years old, to the wooden building on Chestnut Hill, then his father's residence, but acquired later by Judge Edmund Winston, and sometimes called Winston's Hill. Later still it was the home of Henry Langhorne (who married Frances, daughter of James Steptoe), and was burnt during Langhorne's residence, but rebuilt; many years afterwards it became a part of the Elliott estate.

Lynch married Mary Bowles and lived on his farm near the Quaker meeting house, until the establishment of the ferry bearing his name over the James River, when he moved to the house, built at the ferry, remaining there till 1800, then returned to his farm. Still later he built a house (burned in 1820) in Lynchburg, on Court street, where the Presbyterian manse now stands, and lived there till his death in 1820. Lynch was a Quaker, wore their garb, and used their speech. His obituary notice describes him as a zealous and pious member of the society, prompt in the discharge of the duties of husband, father and friend, though laboring for 50 years under a pulmonary complaint which rendered him weak in body; his mind of the first order, with a fortitude and firmness of character seldom equalled. He witnessed the first laying of the corner stone of the town of Lynchburg, its rise and progress from the time when the site was a wilderness.

Such was the veneration the citizens entertained for him that he was regarded in the light of one of the patriarchs of old. Few measures of a general nature were set on foot without consulting him and he was found to be a promoter of whatever tended to advance the general good. A large concourse of people followed his remains to his resting place in the northeast corner of the Quaker burying ground.

A singular fatality amongst his sons left no male descendant in the community to bear his name. His son, Dr. John C. Lynch was poisoned by Bob, a slave, in 1810. The negro was tried for the crime but acquitted because the court was not unanimous, though the majority thought the prisoner guilty. An accomplice in the murder was Lucy, a free woman. William Radford and Samuel Wyatt were assigned as counsel for the prisoner. Courts at the time had not begun using juries and law was administered by justices. Those at this trial were Meredith Lambert, James Stewart, John Schoolfield, and James Mallory. Five days later Lucy was brought to trial before the same court with the addition of John Lynch, when she was adjudged guilty, but was sent on for further trial to the Supreme Court of Campbell in the following April. At the end of the trial, John Lynch, father, and Edward, who was brother and administrator of John C. Lynch, decided to emancipate Bob, of which act there is the following record:

"Nov. 9, 1810.—Having a negro slave named Bob, aged 30 years, fallen under my care by descent from my son, who died intestate, and being fully persuaded that freedom and liberty is the natural law of mankind and that no law, moral or divine, hath given me a right to property in the person of any of my fellow creatures and notwithstanding the injury done to me and mine, by Bob, from his confession and evident circumstances for which he was tried and acquitted by the laws of his country—believing as I do that no circumstances whatever can change the principle, and leaving the event unto Him Who hath said 'Vengeance is mine and I will repay,' I therefore for myself and heirs do hereby emancipate Bob."

(Signed) JOHN LYNCH, EDWARD LYNCH.

John Lynch in 1780 patented 3,000 acres of land on both sides of Blackwater and Fishing creeks; in 1789 patented 320 acres on the south branch of Lynch's creek, both sides of Lynch's Ferry road; in 1792 patented 160 acres on the banks of Fluvanna, bed of the river from the common water mark, including islands and rocks; patented in 1793 450 acres on Opossum, Fishing and Rock Castle creeks, including part of Candler's mountain; also 3453 acres on James river, including islands and rocks; in 1806 patented 44 acres near Lynchburg; in 1810 patented 111 acres on James river, Joe's branch and Fishing creek; in 1814 patented 3609 acres on James river, Blackwater and Fishing creeks.

Children:—

—John Lynch, Jr., was mayor of Lynchburg in 1809; killed 1810.

—Edward B. Lynch, eldest son of John Lynch, Sr., married Mary Terrell, who was said to have been the most beautiful woman ever seen in Lynchburg. They had 8 children; Zalinda, eldest, married Nathaniel Winston; another daughter married Charles Withers; another married Dr. Pretlow; Dr. Micajah T. Lynch moved to Richmond, and Charles E. Lynch to Waynesville, Ohio; three daughters also moved to Ohio.

—Hannah died in early womanhood.

—Micajah married Ann, daughter of James C. Moorman; he was a soldier in the war of 1812, and was stationed at Norfolk; died early in life; s. p.

—Anselm died young.

—William married Jane, daughter of Dr. Humphreys; they and their young son died of consumption. William was a colonel in the war of 1812, stationed at Camp Holly; his regiment was remarkable for its perfect drill.

—Mrs. Alexander Liggat of Lynchburg, was the only member of the family who survived to mature age; she and her son, Alexander (who never married), resided in the old John Lynch home, where the Presbyterian manse on

Court street now stands.   Her daughter married Whit-
well Tunstall, had two sons, John and Alexander, both of
whom have descendants; and a daughter, Nannie, who
died unmarried.

WILL OF JOHN LYNCH

I, John Lynch of Lynchburg, Campbell county, do hereby
dispose of my worldly estate in the following manner:

1st, I lend to my wife, Mary Lynch, the houses and lots
where I now live, known in the plan of the town by numbers
129, 131 and 119, including all improvements, on the same,
all household and kitchen furniture, riding carriage, horses,
cattle and hogs, and the benefit of all the profits arising from
the Lynchburg mills, Liberty and Lynch's Warehouses and
all the profits from the tolls of the Lynchburg Toll Bridge
Company, and rent that becomes due from Peter Detto for
the remainder of his lease of the tenement he now occupies
as a grocery; also the use or profits of the place on Fishing
creek, where Isham Roberts lives, also the use and profits of
the place where the widow Fears now lives, lying between the
turnpike road and the new road to Tate's Lane, bordering on
the town lands; and the rents of the brick house built by my
son Christopher on part of lot number 22 and also rents of
lot No. 33, lying between Liberty Warehouse and Lynch
street on 3rd alley.

2ndly. I give to my daughter, Matilda Roberts, the lot and
improvements thereon where she now lives, bought of Samuel
K. Jennings, being the greater part of lot No. 60, also two unimproved half acre lots on the opposite side of the street numbered 164 and 166, also one other half acre lot lying between
Lynch street and Blackwater, next below and opposite, where
Michael Niger lives on which Enoch Roberts built a stable,
and a tract lying on Fishing creek, supposed to contain 200
acres, beginning on Tate's line where there is a dividing line
between her sister Zalinda Davis and herself, to a large chestnut tree on an old road called the Chestnut Oak Stand to

Richard Perkin's line at his northeast corner to Jonathan and Newby Johnson's line with the same to William Daniel's line onwards to Enoch Roberts' line, being the land he purchased of Achilles Moorman crossing the turnpike road with his line to Tate's line to the beginning with all improvements thereon; also one half acre lot No. 11 and its improvements for which a deed has been executed to her husband, Enoch Roberts, and a square of half acre lots lying between 8th and 9th streets and between 5th and 7th alleys numbered 383, 384, 394 and 395 for which a deed has been executed to her husband—all of which I give unto my daughter Matilda, and her children forever.

3rdly. I give to my daughter Zalinda Davis that tract of land lying on Fishing creek below and adjoining the above tract of her sister, supposed to contain 200 acres, and beginning on Tate's line where the dividing line begins thence with Tate's line to the turnpike along the same till it comes to where the road leading from Lynchburg to the former dwelling house of William Davis, Jr., leaves the turnpike to the land on Fishing creek just above where a considerable quantity of sand has been taken for building purposes, in a straight line till it forms a right angle with the chestnut oak where the line corners, or at the distance of 75 poles with the dividing line to the beginning; also the half acre lot No. 94 on which she now lives, with all improvements, and an unimproved half acre lot No. 98 on the other side of the street opposite No. 94, and No. 9, whereon William Davis, Jr., built a stone house, for which lot a deed has been executed to him, also part of lot No. 3 on 2nd street upon which Wm. Davis, Jr., built a brick house, also the lot which Peter Detto now occupies as a grocery, to extend back the full width of the lot, being part of the old lot No. 3, and to take possession at the expiration of Peter Detto's present lease, also the half acre on which Charles Hoyle's old stable stands between Lynch street and Blackwater now occupied by David R. Edley as a lumber yard and fronting lot 17; also a square of 4 half acre lots lying between 6th and 7th streets and between 7th and 9th alleys, numbered 221,

223, 238 and 239 which lots and appurtenances I give to my daughter, Zalinda Davis, and her children forever.

4thly. I give to my son, Edward Lynch, the tract of land whereon he now lives with all the improvements and the boundary agreeable to a deed executed by me to him, including the grist mill, paper mill, carding machine, etc., on Fishing creek, also the half acre lot No. 35 and improvements thereon, on which lot Thomas Higginbotham and others now live, for which lot a deed has been executed to him, also one other half acre lot on which the widow of Henry Landon Davies lived for several years lying between Lynch street and Blackwater and opposite lot No. 33, all of which lots and lands I give to my son, Edward, and his children forever.

5thly. I give to my daughter, Polly Liggat, the tract of land whereon Nancy Jackson now lives near Candler's Mountain, supposed to contain 200 acres and boundary as follows: by the land of Rowland Jones' estate, Robert Johnson, Samuel Irvine's estate and others, reserving to her mother the privilege of getting firewood and occasionally timber for repairs, also the half acre lot No. 1 on which William B. Perrow lives and opposite Lynch's warehouse, also 40 feet of ground and improvements, being part of lot 3, for which a deed has been executed to her husband, Alexander Liggat, also the half acre lot on which she lives, being lot 117 and improvements, except a small part of the lot which has been taken off for the court house, offices, etc., also 126 feet and 3 inches of ground being a part of lots 43 and 47 lying in front of the lots my daughter Polly and myself now live on, and after the death of my wife, I also give to my daughter Polly the three lots where I now live 129, 131, and 119 with all improvements thereon, to her and her children forever.

6thly. I give to my son, William B. Lynch one tract on the west side of the Meeting House branch adjoining the lands of Richard Chilton, Edmund Tate and others, the other tract on the east side of the Meeting House branch adjoining the former tract and including the houses and lot whereon he now lives, also a square of four half acre lots lying between 7th and 8th streets and 7th and 9th alleys numbered 402, 411 and 412 also one one half acre lot on 2nd street No. 96 with improvements, now occupied by Lawyer Smith for which a deed has been executed, also one other unimproved half acre lot 97. below and adjoining No. 96, also my half of the Blackwater mills and lands attached with improvements thereon and to have possession, at death of his mother, all of which I give to William and his children forever.

7thly. I give to my son, Micajah, the tract of land lying on both sides of Rock Castle creek, whereon I formerly lived supposed to be 600 acres for which a deed has been executed by me to him, also a square of lots on the hill lying between 5th and 6th streets and 7th and 9th alleys numbered 217, 219, 236 and 237 with their improvements, also ground on 2nd and Water streets the full width of the lot being part of No. 3, also a square of half acre lots where Christopher Lynch has brick yards lying between 8th and 9th streets and 1st and 3rd alleys numbered 305, 307, 325 and 327 all of which I give to Micajah Lynch and children forever.

8thly. I give to my grandson, John Davis, the half acre lot No. 95 lying on 2nd street except the part owned by Widow Tompkins whereon she lives, to John Davis and children.

9thly. I give to my three great grandsons, William Powell Roberts, George Edward Roberts, and Christopher Roberts, children of Samuel Roberts, the tract of land whereon —————— Dowdy now lives, supposed to contain 70 or 80 acres with the following boundary, beginning on Ward's road where William Johnson's old meeting house path crosses the road, along Ward's road to the old iron works on a ridge along which William Johnson in his latter time used to go to the Meeting House, then with the said line to William Norvell's line along to William Johnson's old Meeting House path to the beginning on Ward's road—to be equally divided between my three great grandsons or the survivors of them, and I appoint my son Micajah to be their guardian as respects the tract of land that he shall have the care and management for their benefit.

10thly. I direct my executors to sell and convey as much of the residue of my real estate as shall be deemed sufficient to pay my debts beginning with my lands on Seneca creek and then my Amherst lands, reserving that which borders on the river until it goes below the mouth of the branch below the horseford and then lot No. 65 with improvements being the lot formerly owned by David Moore. Whatever remains after my debts are paid to be equally divided between all of my before named children and after the death of my wife, all estates loaned her or of which she is to have benefit, except the three lots where I live which are given to my daughter Polly Liggat, the ground and improvements where Peter Detto occupies which is given to my daughter Zalinda Davis, to be equally divided between my children as before named except the Lynchburg Mills of which my son William B. Lynch is to have no part in consequence of his having my half of the Blackwater mills.

It is my desire that if any of my children should die without leaving a child or children that the portion of such shall be equally divided between the rest of my children. If any misunderstanding or dispute arises between my children respecting my will, I desire and direct that they shall not go to law but submit the same to William Davis, Sr., William Daniel, Thomas Wyatt and Chiswell Dabney, whose decision shall be final. Lastly I appoint my wife, Mary Lynch, to be executrix and my sons, Edward, William B., Micajah and Anselm Lynch executors to execute this my last will and testament, as witness my hand and seal this 10th day of the 8th month 1820.

JOHN LYNCH.

In presence of
WILLIAM DANIEL
CHRISTOPHER ANTHONY
JAMES C. MOORMAN
JAMES STEWART

At a court of Hustings for the corporation of Lynchburg at the court house, Tuesday the 5th day of December, 1820, the last will of John Lynch, Sr., was exhibited in court by Edward Lynch, one of the executors named, and proved by the oaths of William Daniel and Christopher Anthony, two of the subscribing witnesses, and ordered to be recorded. Teste: William W. Norvell, Clerk.

From a start on Lynchburg Hill, of Lynch's provision, with tobacco as the single industry of its early life, the town became, like Rome, a city of seven hills, Court House, Garland, College, Federal, Diamond, Daniel, White Rock. It grew slowly; had its first store in 1790. In 1805 Lynch added more lots to the town, in 1806 added land on Blackwater creek. The same year Dr. George Cabell started a town on his land at the forks of the creek and James river, adjoining his *Point of Honor* home. Tobacco warehouses were built by John Lynch, Dr. Cabell, Wm. Martin, Wm. Davis, and the town earned fame for its tobacco market. It became the largest town in the southwest.

In 1801 Lynch turned his ferry over to Thomas Johnson. In 1811 an Act was passed by Assembly authorizing him to build a toll bridge across the James and the ferry was abolished. Directors in the town's bank were Charles Johnston, Christopher Anthony, Jr., James C. Moorman, John Lynch, Thomas Wyatt and Henry Davis. Thomas Wyatt was the first town recorder.

In 1830 the town contained eleven hardware stores, forty-one groceries, three auction houses, three confectionary shops, one brass foundry, three hat stores, two Bible societies, three rope walks, six tailor shops, three chair factories, three cabinet warehouses, two printing offices (for semi-weeklies), eighteen dry goods stores, three apothecary shops, two book stores, five millinery stores, three tin and coppersmiths, three shoe stores, one tract society, five saddle shops, seven shoe maker shops, three coachmaker shops, one gunsmith shop, two banks; one Presbyterian church, two Baptist, two Methodist (one reformed), one Episcopal (a fine building with church organ), one Masonic hall, court house with a large bell, stone jail

Scene No. 1. Scenes Around Paris. Frescoed Walls in the Home of Dr. J. J. Cabell, Lynchburg

(claimed to be best in Virginia, equal to any in the United States), fifteen lawyers, eighteen physicians, seven tobacco warehouses (inspecting annually from 15,000 to 18,000 hogsheads, each weighing 1,500 pounds, largest inspection in the States). There was exported from 25,000 to 30,000 barrels of flour. About 1,500 batteaux, which were operated between Lynchburg and Richmond, kept about 1,500 hands employed. There were two large manufacturing mills, Scott's and George Callaway's; and the Langhorne brothers were erecting one on a larger scale than any in the upper country, purchasing their water power from the canal corporation. Fifteen manufactories employed from 400 to 500 workers. The town possessed a carding machine, and a powder magazine. In 1852 Lynchburg was chartered as a city.

The Lynchburg Manufactoring Company had been organized in 1828 by Dr. John J. Cabell, John Schoolfield, John Caskie, Ed Duffel, Wm. Morgan, E. Fletcher, Henry Davis, Samuel Garland, Sr., John Hollins and David G. Murrell as trustees, and in January following the Assembly granted them a charter. It was proposed to manufacture cotton, wool, hemp and flax, for which purpose a mill on Blackwater creek was soon completed and the machinery put in place. Michael Connell was employed as manager, and the mill was started with the manufacture of cotton goods. By degrees the town reached into contiguous farm land for territory, and became the home of varied industries, for in trade, as in real estate, it spread itself, as purveyor to demand beyond its borders. Among varied industries, manufacture of shoes took the lead, boasting, in this industry, precedence over other Southern cities, the successful operation being proven by the returns from the capital invested.

A few collapses of corporations, not well established, point to the careful management of the Craddock and Terry Shoe Company, the followers of Witt and Watkins, an earlier corporation supplying the same product, which became absorbed by the later one.

Frescoed Walls. Scene No. 2. (See page 76)

In 1920 Lynchburg, with the employment of a city manager, E. C. Beck, entered upon new methods of administering its municipal affairs.

The policy of larger expenditure of funds was instituted in the promotion of city interests, beginning with street improvement, a measure relieving a tendency to congestion in the direct avenues of ingress and egress, to and from the city, which in earlier times was limited to Fifth and Twelvth streets but later eased by routes through Rivermont and Fairview.

The most important work, so far accomplished, has been the reinforcement with cement of old Rivermont bridge, planned by Manager Beck when it had been considered necessary to build a new viaduct. The contract for work on the bridge was ready to be signed when the city manager died. The plan was designed by Allan J. Saville, Philip Aylett and A. C. Janni, and the construction was done by the Whiting Turner Company of Baltimore, supervised by the Allan J. Saville Company, Inc., of Richmond, actual work by J. M. Hough, resident engineer of the Company.

"Amherst" or Ninth Street bridge connecting Lynchburg with Amherst county was built in August, 1878 by the Western Bridge Company of Fort Wayne, Indiana, and it replaced a toll bridge that had been washed away in the flood of November 24, 1877 when James river rose 33 feet; a former bridge had been carried away by a flood in 1870. A contract between the Lynchburg Toll Bridge Company, the City of Lynchburg and Amherst county was signed in November 1882 providing for the purchase of the bridge from the Company for $25,000, one half of the price to be paid by the city and the other half by the county, and the expense of maintenance was to be borne equally by city and county. The contract was signed by Camillus Christian on the part of the Company and John W. Carroll, Jesse E. Adams, Peter J. Otey, Thomas L. Walker and Thomas Fauntleroy for the city. It had been authorized by the General Assembly January 14, 1882 and approved by the voters of Amherst county on November 7, 1882. The bridge, purchased from the joint stock company owning it, was thrown open to the public as a free thoroughfare.

In August, 1886 the Richmond and Alleghany .Railroad Company instituted proceeding in court to condemn a boundary of land on the northwest side of Ninth street and southwest side of James river known as the "toll-house lot." These proceedings were resisted by the city of Lynchburg and by Amherst county as owners of the lot by purchase from the Toll Bridge Company. It was finally agreed that the railroad should pay $5000 for the right of way for one track across the approach and wing of abutment and that it should remove the toll house.

It is near this spot that the Lynchburg Chapter D. A. R. placed a boulder with bronze tablet inscription to mark the site of the old ferry house which was built by the founder John Lynch when he operated a ferry from this point across the river.

Due to the proposal and efforts of Ernest Williams, a citizen, Lynchburg acquired in 1919 the fine concrete viaduct which replaced the Ninth street bridge spanning James river to the Amherst side, and which was constructed at the expense of the railroad companies (which held contiguous property), the city and the county of Amherst. The picturesque iron bridge, relic of the past, was not at once removed but remained for some years as memorial of its former service, no longer of use, for the viaduct meets all requirements by its breadth, elevation and various entrances; not far apart the two crossways stood as symbols of the past and present; yet at the present writing negotiations are pending for purchase of the skeleton bridge, by Nelson county authorities, for the purpose of removing it to the last named county and re-erecting it across the James river in that section of the country.

Small Towns and Villages

Chapter IV

Ha* Creek.

AT Creek village situated between the creek of that name and Little Falling river, was started about 1742 and grew with the building of the church there; this old church has been rebuilt and renewed several times and the old burying ground is said to contain graves which date back before the middle of the 18th century. A small stream called Entray creek runs between the village and Morris Church which is almost due north of it. Good soil roads lead to Hat Creek, but it is not near a railroad; the Presbyterian church stands about a mile outside of the village, and while the building is new, it stands upon the same site, first selected for it. The church of 1847 was perhaps the building preceding the present one; Parson Hammersley preached there 30 years, dying during the War between the States. A little further is Morris Church, the settlement named for the English settlers there; it was designated "New School"to distinguish it from Hat Creek "Old School"; parishioners at the latter place were Irvine, Clark, Armistead, Hamlet, Asher, Morris, Smith, Williams, and others—descendants of whom are yet to be found in the neighborhood. John Irvine settled at a place afterwards owned by his grandson, O. C. Clark, and Dr. J. Paulett Clark, his son (now resident in Lynchburg). In 1820 William Cobbs, president, and other citizens in the neighborhood of Hat Creek, requested to be incorporated under the name of the Hat Creek Literary Society, with privileges granted in such cases; three years later the same petition was presented by Thomas J. Marshall a new president of the society. In 1829 twenty citizens petitioned for a change of election from the junction of Little and Big Falling river to Hat Creek Meeting House. In 1835 the voters at Hat Creek Meeting House asked to have election moved to Brookneal because of the inaccessibility of Hat Creek house. Little Concord church (Charlotte county) is almost on the county line near Cub creek and but a few miles from Red House (on the Richmond road), a place built by the Hancocks. At the time it had become the custom to paint houses red, and that one took name from its color. Chas. Hunter kept a tavern at Red House about the middle of the 19th century when as an important stopping place for travellers it became well known, and still is used as a guiding point for directing travel along the high-

Bob White Lodge, Hat Creek

way. An old sampler worked in cross-stitch* picturing the house and grounds, is preserved. The fancy for its red color still continues, all surrounding buildings having the same color. A log cabin club house has been built in Hat Creek village within enclosed grounds and given the name *Bob White;* it is owned by a company formed largely of Lynchburg citizens and used as a recreative and hunting lodge.

John Irvine's Hat Creek settlement, lacking but fifteen years of two centuries in age, has seen the rise, the ventures,

---

*Worked in 1824 by Mrs. Ann Harvey.

the growth of all other county towns,—it has grown little but it has retrograded little; now it waits for its wheels to arrive, when it may go forward avoiding the mistakes and losses it has witnessed, in the progress of its neighbors.

Rustburg

Rustburg, the county seat of Campbell, is situated on Route 18, about twelve miles from Lynchburg, and also furnishes a station on the Lynchburg and Durham Division of the Norfolk and Western Railroad.

The public buildings grouped there are the court house, old and new clerk's office, (of brick construction) all within one enclosure, and, at the distance of a square there stands the county jail; beyond the latter is the High School Building also of brick.

The village has a population of around 400 inhabitants, four churches,—Presbyterian, Baptist, Methodist and Episcopalian—the county bank, six merchandise stores, one drug store, two hotels, two roller mills, a tomato canning factory, two garages, and three filling stations. There is a Rosenwald school for negroes, who have also a church in the town. Daily mail is carried to outlying sections, along five rural free delivery routes, from the post office.

The home of former clerk Alexander adjoined the court house grounds but was burned some years ago. One of the Withers' family residences was purchased by Judge Nelson at the time of his removal to Rustburg; it stands at a bend of the road leading from the main street and faces Long Mountain. Among the residents of Rustburg are County Clerks, Goggin and Woodson with their families, and nearby are Merriman, Anderson, Thornhill, Perrow and other homesteads. Sheriff R. L. Perrow lives on Route 18 midway between Rustburg and Lynchburg, where his ancestors settled.

Because of its long period of establishment the Fountain Hotel (1786-1926) has become quite historic.

Henry Finch, received 200 acres of land through military service and agreeable to the king's proclamation of 1763. Bernard Finch, (probably a son of William Finch whose will was recorded in 1811) married in 1804 Sallie Webber. He patented 350 acres along Lawyer's Road upon the head branches of Molley's and Bear's creeks. In April 1786 he was granted leave to keep an *ordinary* (inn) at his house at the Court House; descendants bearing the name have con-

Fountain Hotel, Built 1795

tinued the popular tavern known as the Fountain Hotel, where the fame of its well prepared and generously served viands attracts many guests to this day.

Early marriages in the Finch family were;—Sallie Finch m. Miles Lester in 1788, John Finch m. Nancy Webber in 1796, Blagdon Finch m. Jane Dawn in 1798, Betty Finch m. John Gardner in 1794, Sallie Finch m. Ambrose Rosser in 1800, Elizabeth Finch m. Jesse Rosser in 1818, Polly Finch m. George Bird in 1803; Barnett Finch is recorded in the county from 1825 to 1870.

The Rust family is said to have come from England; one branch of it settled in Westmoreland county. Dr. William Cabell surveyed land for George Rust on Castle creek, upper Tye river, in 1750. Captain George Rust lived in Fauquier county and had a son, William, whose son Albert was an officer in the Confederate army and was commissioned a general; he had previously served in the United States army. Albert Rust married Anne Bouldin a daughter of John Breckenridge Cabell (son of Dr. George) formerly of Campbell county but at that time living in West Virginia.

It is not known to me at what time Jeremiah Rust came to Bedford; he was settled there before its division to form Campbell, and upon the establishment of the latter county promptly made an offer of 50 acres of his meadow land for the new county seat; but other land was offered for the same purpose at that time and a clash of petitions ensued, creating a controversy which lasted a year or more before the final decision was made in favor of Rust's land, and the village then started was given his name. In 1784 John Callaway, Charles Cobbs, William Henderson and Charles Moile Talbot were appointed trustees to receive a deed for the land given the county by Jeremiah Rust for erecting public buildings thereon. In January, 1785 a prison had been finished and was approved as sufficient for the purpose, and in February the court of justices ordered that the new prison then received be considered as the jail of the county to keep debtors and criminals.

Jeremiah Rust lived but five years after the county was formed yet in 1783 a temporary court house had been built upon his land even while the struggle was going on between the two factions, each advocating choice of their sites, the point in dispute being as to which was most central and accessible.

Long Mountain, rising above the meadow upon which the town of Rustburg is situated, at one time bore the name of Rust's Mountain; it stretches the length of six or more miles, and a cave on one side is said to have harbored tories and outlaws during the Revolution. It is one of two detached mountain ranges in the county, the other being Candler's Mountain.

In 1780 Jeremiah Rust patented 458 acres of land on the head branches of Molleys and Beaver creeks. His will recorded in 1787 bequeathed money to his four oldest sons George, Peter, David and Enos; he had already given David land lying between Green and Molley's creeks by the old ford; his wife was given all of his "goods and chattels" for her use in raising the younger children: the tract on Meadow creek and one on the north side of Molley's creek adjoining the town land and the tract below David Rust's was to be sold and the proceeds divided between Rebecca (Mrs. Wm. Lucas) Enos, Isaac, Sarah, Elizabeth (Mrs. Morris Roberts), Anne E. (Mrs. Mack Roberts) and his youngest son Jeremiah. His wife, Mary, and sons, George and Peter, were appointed executors of his estate.

The first school fair in Virginia was held, at Rustburg in October 1908, when prizes were awarded the county public school pupils.

This school fair was started by the Virginia Federation of Women's Clubs with the aid of J. S. Thomas, then school examiner in the district, and with the agreement of the Van Dyke League to help in Campbell. At that time no work of the kind was being done in the state, though the Boys' Corn Club had become organized by the United States Department of Agriculture. The school fair work reached and encouraged the best efforts of a large number of workers, while the Boys' Demonstration work emphasized the value of expert knowledge and training, for which the school fair prepared the ground. In the long list which embraced prizes in agriculture, horticulture, domestic science and art, manual training and literary work, every child of school age had the chance of exhibiting the work he or she could do best.

The Fair Committee consisted of W. L. Garbee, county superintendent of schools, chairman; John Gills and Miss Jennie Mosby from Brookville district;—W. S. Frazier and Miss Mae Brandt from Otter river district;—G. A. Bradley and Miss Bettie Burton from Seneca district;—and J. A. Connelly and Mrs. V. H. Lawson from Falling river district.

The school fair hall was burned, then the fair was discontinued. On November 5 and 6, 1926 Campbell held its first agricultural and school fair at Alta Vista, the fair being strictly educational, athletic events alone furnished entertainment. This fair was sponsored by county school officials and farmers of the county for the purpose of developing keener interest in agricultural affiairs and to stimulate interest by competition and improved school activities and ultimately to induce the diversification of crops,—upon which prosperity of the county depends rather than upon the bulk of any one crop. Men, women and children prepared and entered exhibits, which conduced to the success of the fair.

Mrs. C. S. Ferguson, home demonstration agent for Campbell has been very active in organizing and directing agricultural and home economics clubs of county girls and women, and in securing for the girls home demonstration short courses annually at Lynchburg College. Mrs. Ferguson is also engaging county attention in demonstrations for the development of better poultry and standardization methods.

While housekeepers are thus being aided by the home demonstrator, the farmers are receiving benefit of expert knowledge on crop manipulation from Bruce Anderson, farm agent for Campbell. Tobacco marketing has been a problem of the past year, and farmers have passed through a trial of co-operative sales. The organizations co-operating with the county agents to further boys club work are the Lynchburg National Bank, the Campbell County Bank at Rustburg and the G. B. Lewis Company of Lynchburg.

Marysville

In 1782 Micajah Davis brought to the South River Meeting a certificate of removal from Cedar Creek Meeting. He bought land on Seneca creek where he located and built his dwelling house, merchant mill and store house. In October 1790 a petition was addressed to Virginia Assembly for the establishment of a ferry from the land of John Connefax in Campbell over Staunton river to that of Colonel John Ward on the Pittsylvania opposite bank; as there was then no ferry for a number of miles yet there were roads leading to Micajah Davis' store and mill, Lynch's Warehouse, Oxford Iron Works, Campbell Court House and New London.

In 1792 Davis patented 500 acres on the west branches of Seneca creek, and, the branches of Staunton river, and next year he located a town on his land at Seneca Mills, which being remote from any other place of business, through the encouragement given to farming operations and mechanics, and to tradesmen to settle there, had attracted public attention, and he was thereby encouraged to lay it out in half acre lots in the form of a town, to which he gave the name of his wife, calling it Marysville. Some lots in it were sold and in October 1793 Davis applied to Legislature to enact a law establishing it as a town, which was agreeably done. But it met with no considerable encouragement from investors though acts were passed in 1815-16 allowing further time for improvement. In 1817 the trustees, John Harvey, John Organ, and Benjamin Davis sold Thomas Fox lot No. 16. beginning at Mary's alley to Philip Payne's land and Chestnut Street; again Thomas Fox, Jesse Harvey and Benjamin Davis, trustees, sold Edmund Wade lot No. 7 at Spring street. Sales were slow and infrequent, Micajah Davis became discouraged and decided to leave the community. He and his wife with their nine minor children moved from Campbell to White Oak, Henrico county. Then the town of Marysville which he had sponsored, following the fate of other boom enterprises became little more than a location on a roadway and designation on the map; yet it later revived and acquired stores and dwellings, but they have disappeared: the old mill still remains. Much of the land in the neighborhood became embraced in the large estate of the Payne family. Not far away lies Patrick Henry's grove place which was never dwelt upon.

Micajah Davis, Jr., (son of Micajah, Sr.) b. 1779 married Mary C. Gwatkin, and remained in the county: ch.—William m. Mary Alexander;—John m. Ann Jennings; children, William Minor m. Nannie Hunter Eubank; Christopher, m. . . .; —Mary Jane m. John Henry. Thomas Newman, son of Wm. Minor and Nannie H. Davis married Blanche Thompson and resided in Lynchburg, where he was city collector, an office now held by his son, H. Minor Davis. Thos. N. Davis was a Confederate veteran and prominent Mason.

Samuel Davis married Anne Lipscombe, in 1769; located near Green Springs, Louisa county, later moved to Bedford: children—George Dixon, b. 1805 m. 1840 Mary Ann, dau. of John J. Wills (clerk of Lynchburg court, member of Legislature and architect of Lynchburg C. H.) : Geo. D. Davis died in 1879; his son, Thomas D. was for many years clerk of Lynchburg court.—John Thomas m. Margaret Preston; his dau. Mary m. Camillus Christian, a banker in Lynchburg.

Brookneal

Brookneal, situated between Staunton and Falling rivers, is not far from Halifax and Charlotte county lines. It belongs in a section, the fertility of which, largely contributed to the favorable decision as to Bedford county division and the neighboring farm land continues to produce a rich crop yield: the succession of these broad fields, in full cultivation, furnishes an attractive setting for the town, which is said to have received its name from the intermarriage of the families of Brooks and Neal.

In 1756 William Brooks patented 200 acres on the lower side of Reedy creek.

In 1782 John Brooks purchased 100 acres of land lying on both sides of Little Falling river from Susan Lawson, and her son William, of Henry county, a tract which had been willed to Bartlett Lawson by William Rodgers who in 1753 patented 300 acres on both sides of Little Falling river.

In 1743 Roger Neale patented 200 acres on the north side of Staunton river and both sides of Cub creek, also patented 100 acres on both sides of Whipping creek. Daniel O'Neal patented 300 acres on Sycamore, and 300 acres on Austin and Sycamore creeks. In 1784 Zepaniah Neal patented 200 acres on west branches of Cheese creek.

A petition was sent in 1799 by 500 county residents for the establishment of a warehouse for tobacco inspection upon John Brooks' land along Staunton river, to be known as Brooks' Warehouse: receiving authority then, those interested, erected a warehouse which for two years was operated as designed; at the end of that time 600 petitioners urged the location of a town, there, to be called Brookneal, at the same time presenting a request for establishment of a ferry across the Staunton from Brooks' land in Campbell to that of the late Patrick Henry in Halifax, the ferry to be located at the end of Seven Islands. Activities seem to have lulled in the community, for in the following years several petitions were sent asking for the re-establishment of tobacco inspection and allowance of a longer period for improving lots in Brookneal.

In 1831 a false alarm of a negro uprising in the town caused great alarm in the surrounding district and many persons, in consequence, left their homes and collected together for protection at more distant points: but the rumor proved to be without foundation of fact, excitement subsided, no one sustained injury, and all returned to their abandoned homes.

An appeal was made in 1832 by Campbell, Charlotte and Halifax residents for the reappointment of commissioners to resurvey and lay off Brookneal with the same powers as first appointed. A post office was established in the town in 1835, and during this year it was petitioned that voters in election at Hat Creek Meeting House be allowed to move elections to Francis Callaway's tavern at Brookneal.

Because of the inaccessibility of Hat Creek, again in 1843 the petition was made that cavalry be allowed to muster at

Brookneal, the three adjoining counties joining in the request that such companies as enrolled themselves in the voluntary artillery there be exempt from military duties in those counties.

A volunteer troop of cavalry was formed at Brookneal in 1845 of members from Campbell, Halifax and Charlotte with Dr. Robert E. Withers as lieutenant and drill master. The training of the officers occurred every Spring at the Court House. Two other cavalry companies were formed in the county, one at Rustburg and the other at Leesville near Bedford county line: there were also two regiments of militia in the county, and two companies in Lynchburg: all of the officers were required to drill together.

In 1856 Company "C" of the 11th Regiment (commanded by Colonel Samuel Garland of Lynchburg) was under Captain Adam Clement, with Henry Howard Withers as lieutenant. This company drilled at St. John's Church, not far from Pigeon Run (the present Gladys). Captain John D. Alexander was captain of a cavalry company of Campbell men. Volunteer companies mustered into service one year, then the government issued orders for reorganization.

The ferry across Staunton river at Brookneal was replaced by a steel bridge—constructed by the Canton Ohio Bridge Manufacturing Company, through contract with the Brookneal Bridge Company—for wagons and pedestrians: its length being 90 feet by 16 feet width. Erection of the bridge was placed in the hands of E. S. Moorman of Rustburg, as superintendent of construction. Falling river is crossed by a bridge at Rush's mill near Brookneal.

Substantial brick houses replace the old wooden structures, in the business section of the town, which were destroyed a few years ago by fire. Brookneal has two banks, two hotels, two garages and service stations, three tobacco warehouses, a hydro-electric plant, an ice factory, a flour, lumber and planing mill; it has four churches—Methodist, Baptist, Presbyterian, and a negro church—and a fine school building: one weekly newspaper, the "Union Star," B. F. Ginther, editor and manager.

Two railroads pass through Brookneal—the Lynchburg and Durham, a branch of the Norfolk and Western, on the north, and the Virginian on the south side with freight and passenger stations. The town is also entered by good soil roads, and the State Highway passes through it, thus giving transportation facilities. At this time it is undergoing street improvements and extension of its limits.

Liberty Farm with its notable vineyards is between Brookneal and Naruna and has the largest commercial orchard in the county. The bulk of its grape crop is packed in baskets and shipped to the coal field section of West Virginia: careful attention is given to the cultivation of the vineyard, which is probably the largest in the state.

As an economical measure, Brookneal's two banks have become consolidated into one, the Peoples National Bank of Brookneal. R. C. Blackford, a prominent and well-known Lynchburg attorney, was recently elected to the presidency to succeed C. C. Scott. It has served the community well from the time it was founded several years ago by J. E. Webb and has an unbroken record of growth and progress.

Leesville

Leesville at the junction of Goose creek and Staunton river in the southwestern part of Campbell is now a station on the Virginian railway just west of the thriving town of Alta Vista: grouped in the vicinity are many old homes, as the town was started over a hundred years ago. The first known settler there was Captain Jacobus Early, eldest son of Colonel Jeremiah Early who was a captain of Bedford militia in 1781; a captain of Campbell militia in 1782; he married Sarah, daughter of Colonel Charles F. Wall. His plantation lay on both sides of Goose creek to the mouth of William's branch the north side of Staunton river, by Callaway's corner and adjoining Leftwich property; it embraced lands inherited from his father and 115 acres purchased of Mark and Elizabeth Snow (Henry Snow's patent) along Watery branch. In 1793 Early sold this land to John Lee and in 1794 sold

Edward Bybee 500 acres in Pittsylvania county and then moved to southwest Virginia, his descendants settling in Kentucky and West Virginia.

There was a boom in 1818 for town building along water courses supposed to be navigable for batteaux and John Lee conceived the idea of locating a town on his land, giving it his name. He laid off 100 acres in half acre lots and of these sold sufficient to yield him $20,000, reserving the home and its grounds; then closed the sale. At his death, four years later, his son, Richard, came into possession of the old home and occupied it several years. None of the lots purchased were ever improved and there was no attempt made to transact business there until 1826. At that time Stephen Terry rented the old Early mansion and converted it into a store house, and afterwards, opened a tobacco manufactory, continuing to operate as a merchant and manufacturer till 1830. He became dissipated, neglecting his business, and the buildings were closed in 1831. Afterwards business revived and at one time there were 4 stores of general merchandise, 2 tanneries, 3 black-smiths, 3 physicians, 2 tailors, 2 cabinet makers, 2 carpenters, a wheelwright, a male academy, 2 churches, post office, and near the village, a saw and grist mill, hemp and carding machinery and cotton gin: in 1902 there remained 2 stores, a shoe maker, blacksmith, public school house, 2 churches, post office, grist and flour mill.

When John M. Speed was the Campbell delegate to the Legislature three efforts were made to form a new county of parts of Campbell, Pittsylvania and Bedford in 1845, '48 and '57: it was to be called Staunton with Leesville as the Court House; but the petition was not favored and was finally withdrawn. Near to Leesville there is a stone quarry, with layers of a thickness to be serviceable for building purposes, which has long been used for paving slabs and from which many of the neighboring houses have been provided with steps and platforms. Lumber trade is carried on around Leesville to some extent.

The grave of an Indian girl (containing pottery, beads, etc.)

was found in 1919 by John L. Douglass on the Gordon farm, near Leesville, by the Staunton river: and there have been found many flint arrows and tomahawks in the vicinity.

An early settler around the Leesville community was John Brown, of whose purchase in 1784 from James and Ann Martin and Jos. Eads of 196 acres, the first county deed book makes record; this land lay along Catamount branch of Staunton river beginning at Eads' corner: it is also recorded that he then freed a slave. In 1785 Brown purchased from Wm. and Martha Alford 200 acres, known as Alford's Mountain near the river, witnesses to the transaction being Micajah Davis, Jos. Childress and John Vest.

In 1798 Brown petitioned for a ferry on his land to cross the Staunton. He lived in a brick dwelling at the top of a hill leading to Leesville. One of this name was conspicuous for his habit of wearing a spike-tail coat ornamented with brass buttons and his long hair tied in a cue; thus he would appear riding to mill, or around among his neighbors, with a negro servant behind him: he was a successful farmer and a man of means.

James Brown m. Catherine Leftwich: children,—Fannie m. John Jefferson,—Jane m. Col. Abner Anthony, one time agent at Lynch's;—Ann m. Col. D. Reid Arnold,—Maria m. Albon Arthur,—America m. Jas. L. Arthur, state senator and treasurer of Bedford county,—Virginia m. 1st Fletcher Arnold, m. 2nd Fletcher Lukin,—Bettie m. 1st Col. Frank Board of Bedford, who was killed in Confederate service; Dr. J. J. Board of Lynch's was a son; m. 2nd Alex. A. Arnold,—Thomas married a Miss Brown: Jas L. Arthur m. (2d) Clara Anderson.

Littleberry Moon lived at the top of Moon's Mtn., which took its name from this family. The ancestor of the Moon family went with the Conqueror to England at which time the name was Du Mohon, Mhoon, then Moon. Littleberry moved in 1838 from his father's home in Buckingham county; his mother was Jean Breckenridge, dau. of Wm. Hopkins, who was the son of Dr. Arthur Hopkins of Revolutionary fame. He bought 600 acres from Wm. Anderson upon which he built *Viewmont,* his home, facing the distant Peaks of Otter, and standing not far from Leesville: m. Martha Perkins, dau. of Littleberry Moon, Sr., a wealthy merchant of Scottsville, who had died young, and his wife also, leaving 4 orphan daughters who were then raised by their uncle Benjamin Perkins of Scottsville. *Viewmont* replaced a smaller, quaint old house which was moved to the negro quarters: the land upon which it stood had been the part of Col. Early's large estate devised to his daughter, Mrs. Sarah Anderson. Littleberry's brothers, Overton of Albemarle, and Arthur of Buckingham, were amongst the wealthiest citizens of those counties: the family seem to have confined themselves to the marts of trade, rather than official or military activities. Children of Littleberry Moon, were— Maria m. . . . Gilbert, d. soon afterwards,—Sallie P. m. Col. Goodman,—Jennie B. m. Leverette S. Early, son of Col. Edmund Early,—Elizabeth m. Sam'l C. Goggin clerk of Campbell county,—Littlebery, Jr. d. at Lexington 1858,— Edward was killed in the Confederate army,—John B. moved to a western state.

Robert F. Gaines moved to Campbell from Charlotte; m. Elizabeth Noel; d. 1865; had 6 sons, 1 dau. (m. W. S. Smith)—Charles E. and Richard T. died in Confederate service; William, also a Confederate soldier died in July, 1865; Robert H. (C. S. veteran) m. Margaret Scott; James C. enlisted in C. S. army in the autumn of 1864, was captured April 1, 1865, at Five Forks battle near Dinwiddie C. H., and sent to Pt. Lookout where he was imprisoned until June 13, 1865; m. Rosa. dau. of Robert P. Mattox of Leesville, moved to Rock Wall, Texas, where he now resides.

Other Leesville residents, Col. Abner Anthony; John Anthony m. dau. of Col. Reid Arnold, lived in the old brick dwelling on the hill above Anthony's creek: Dr. Haden, whose home was at top of Haden's hill; Morton Pannill, merchant at Leesville m. 1st Kitty Leftwich; m. 2d Mrs. Brown, neé Moorman; Green Terry, later moved to a farm *Solitude* two miles

away; Wm. A. Lee; Burwell Lee; Dr. Austin; Dr. Withers;
Thos. A. Richardson; John Jefferson; Robt. P. Mattox; James
Camper; Dr. David Ward.

Mt. Hermon community, Wyatt A. Lee, son of John Lee,
had 7 ch.—Lucinda m. Christ. West,—Ann m. Wm. Merritt,—
J. Dibrel m. Bettie Sweeney,—Ed. S. m. Anna Bruce; these
two brothers moved to Missouri;—Robert C. m. Hassie Pear-
man.

King George's Hill is between Staunton and Pig rivers:
an old tombstone nearby is inscribed to the memory of one
"Charles Carter who departed this life on the 9th of May,
1827. He was loved by those who knew him, best loved by
those who knew him best:" Carter was doubtless a resident in a
neighboring county.

Lynch's Old Tavern on Ward's Road

Two Lynch purchasers appeared in Campbell section at an
early period of its land distribution, but whether of the same
family cannot be asserted as their names are spelt differently;
this may have been through choice of the owners or just an
accident in clerical writing.

In 1726 one John Lynch patented a tract of land in Brunswick county on Meherrin river and Fontaine creek; and about
the same period Thomas Linch patented land on the north
side of the Roanoke (Staunton) river: the comparatively
small acreage of their patents seems to indicate that land was
procured for the purpose of settling upon it, and the date
shows that they were among the earliest settlers.

These Lynchs preceded Charles Lynch, of James river
locality, by more than twenty years: they may have been the
ancestors of John Lynch of Ward Road Inn, who must not be
confused with Lynchburg's founder, for if they were connected
with the Quaker family, as similarity of name might suggest,
it is unknown to me. The old inn or liquor tavern, erected on
the main road—which was swathed across the county by Major
John Ward—stands in fair state of preservation and is yet
occupied by members of that Lynch connection though not

now used for public entertainment. The weather-worn building, without trace of paint, suggests long use and haunting memories of peace revelries and war incidents. It is quaintly but conveniently constructed, with low pitched rooms having broad, grooved timber ceilings, and entered through a long covered porch which extends across the front and is blocked at one end by a small detached room: liquors were stored in the latter, and tumblers of the beverage were served customers

Old Lynch Inn, Ward's Road

through a square opening with sliding shutter, cut in the dividing wall for the purpose. The house is finished with gabled roof having three dormer windows, and in plan and location is admirably situated for a wayside inn, standing as it does midway between Lynchburg and Alta Vista on a much travelled route, unsupplied with accommodations for travellers, about a mile or so from Castle Craig settlement.

This Lynch family is allied with the Blankenship, Trent and Johnson families: one John Lynch drew a pension for service in the War of 1812, and Robert Johnson, who married a Blankenship, also served in that war at the battle of Ellicott

City, Maryland.　When he returned to his home he talked so much about the engagement there he was given the name "Ellicott Johnson" which clung to him through the remainder of his life.　His son, Daniel Johnson, born 1804, died 1897 attached himself to the Dearing household at Avoca, where he spent a good part of his life and at death was buried in the Lynch family burying ground.　His wonderful memory was stored with county narrative, with much of which he had been personally familiar and he was ever ready with reminiscences of what had transpired during his long life of 93 years, and of people with whom he had come in contact.

In 1769 Isham Blankenship patented 576 acres on the ridge between Ivy and Tomahawk creeks.

Castle Craig

The settlement at Castle Craig is situated about eight miles from Evington, seven miles from Alta Vista, a mile or more from Lynch's old tavern and two miles from Kingston, on Ward's Road: it is said to have been given its name by an English woman after a place in England.　It possesses a store, a church, post office, several homes and the now (ever present) gasoline station.

John Ward (probably second of the name) sold land to an Englishman, Rev. Mr. Loder, a Congregationalist minister, who preached in the Presbyterian church at Castle Craig.　An old Protestant Methodist church there called Paneuil was replaced by Otterburne, a Missionary Baptist; Boswell Traylor of *Quiet Retreat* preached at the latter church.　Rev. Pinckney Scott preached at *Pleasant Grove,* a free church, for the Methodists.

Edward Estes of Big Lick (Roanoke) about the middle of the 19th century bought *Ridge Valley,* a house built by one Goodman and embracing the family dwelling, tavern and merchandise store, which Estes used for the same purposes. His daughter, Celia, married Henry Williamson, and the daughter of the latter couple, Ann Eliza, m. Anderson Dudley,—

and now widowed, Mrs. Dudley occupies the Ridge Valley home. Henry Hazelwood was the first post master at Castle Craig. There was a second tavern in the settlement called, from the proprietor's name, Simmons-Chapman.

Kingston

John King patented 369 acres of land in 1750 on Cargill's creek the north side of Staunton river: the same year William King patented 400 acres on Smith's creek adjoining John Davis. The first mention of the King name in connection with Campbell is that of William King of Montgomery county, born 1753, who enlisted in the Bedford militia for two months as guard at the lead mines in Wythe county under Captain Robert Adams, and Lieutenant McReynolds of Colonel Charles Lynch's command. King received a pension for his Revolutionary service. After the war he became a resident of Campbell and his will has Sackville King's name attached as witness: the instrument bestows his property on his wife, Mary King, to be by her devised to their children at her death; designating his heirs by name,—Patsy Candler, Jesse W., John W., and Charles W. King and grandson William M. Goodman the son of Achilles Goodman.

The name, Sackville King, is found signed to many petitions from Lynchburg and the county to Virginia Assembly.

Sackville King married Anne, the daughter of George and Judith Burton-Payne. His father-in-law willed him 300 acres of land on Cany Creek, Fluvanna river, where King was living in 1781. He sold Samuel Scott in 1800 a lot in Lynchburg, on Water and Second Streets, upon a part of which Mason's Hall stood—one half acre—reserving so much of the lot as the hall and its eve occupied for its use; the price paid him for the part sold was £100: the lot is now in the city's business center.

In 1824 King petitioned for establishment of a town upon his land lying on Ward's Road and receiving favorable response, started the village of Kingston (situated not far from Castle Craig), named for himself—a place like other paper towns of the time, which acquired no extensive bounds, yet the name given to it clung to the locality, and might more appropriately have been called King's Folly.

King was an eccentric character, often the buffet of fortune. He was twice High Sheriff of the county, an officer so appointed because he had served on the bench of magistrates longer than any other justice: the office carried with it that of treasurer also, and was the most powerful local office in Virginia, the fees and perquisites making it the most lucrative. King was upon the county's charge once when called to fill the shreivalty, being then an inmate of the alms house.

He lived to be very old and was apparently estranged from his family, as during the latter years of his life he staid alone in a cabin with only servants near; had his coffin made several years before his death, kept it under his bed and stored apples in it, said the little negroes would be afraid to steal the fruit from such a container: at that time he appears to have moved to the country.

King's will written in 1838 devised his property of every description, to his grand-daughter, Mary Ann R. Layne, the dau. of James and Nancy King-Layne of Montgomery county and appointed his friend John Teas, of New London, her guardian.

The town he ambitiously started now shows only decay and wreckage: two stores which remain indicate the amount of its former merchandising industry—but windows and doors are barred against entrance. In striking contrast a new residence is being constructed nearby; and its situation on the national highway may attract other homeseekers and bring new interests and settlers to the community.

"Blue Door" church, an Episcopal Mission church is about a mile from Kingston, situated upon a side road.

Beyond Kingston a few miles, Yellow Branch (earlier known as Early's Cross-Roads) is reached: it formerly supplied camping ground for religious gatherings and obtained the name of Tabernacle Ground; it also supplied a site for picnic-grouping. Here neighbor pledged himself to meet neighbor in yearly convivialties, for which bountiful provision was made by the housekeepers and eager anticipation awaited the appointed tryst, when happy abandon characterized the program of amusements, and age engaged with youth in aim of pleasure. These picnics continue as harvest-home gatherings which serve to keep alive the neighbor spirit of mutual interest. Yellow Branch has its school house and not far away stands Early's Chapel.

Twin Oaks lost the home to which it gave name, but the splendid trees yet stand. *Beechwood,* purchased from E. E. Ross, about seventeen years ago by an English family, Mr. and Mrs. Thomas Rogers, is yet occupied by the widow Rogers and her sister, Mrs. Rowles. Next is approached the former home of Lewis E. Williams, now occupied by his descendants: it bears the name *Spring Bower,* from a bold spring nearby, which is shaded by a branching tree covered with the parasitic mistletoe: two brick structures of an earlier period, which furnished home and office building, yet remain.

Approaching Lynchburg we come to the large grant of 1000 acres on Flat creek obtained by Robert Russell and now distributed among his descendants. A portion of this property was obtained some years ago by Lynchburg for its City Farm, upon which necessary buildings were constructed. Within sight of Lynchburg, Senator Glass' country home is reached and nearby the former property of John W. Carroll.

Concord

Concord, known better as Concord Depot, a station on the Norfolk and Western railroad, near Pilot mountain, and situated on the border line between Campbell and Appomattox, contains between three and four hundred inhabitants. It has a Methodist and a Baptist church and a four year accredited high school with attendance of 180 pupils.

The name was taken from New Concord church, (an offshoot of early Hat Creek Presbyterian church) but came near being called instead *Tight Squeeze* from the report of Captain Jack Alexander, county wit, that at the gathering there in celebration of the completion of the station it was a tight squeeze to get anything to eat: Concord church is not situated in the village, but stands 9 miles away.

The first house in Concord was built by Robin Wilson, an Irishman, who owned it but a short time, and sold to James Cardwell one of the first settlers to have a steam saw mill in the county, which he operated from 1800 till 1850-'60: he also owned a foundry, a blacksmith shop, and a threshing machine called a "ground hog" machine, worked by 8 horse power; the teeth of the cylinder knocked out the grain.   Cardwell also made pots, skillets, plows and castings.   His son Charles moved to Missouri.

Rev. Richard Brown, a Methodist preacher, conducted a merchandise store in the village; he was followed by Burks and Fitch: Mr. Scruggs now has their stand.   Nat. Guggenheimer, a Lynchburg merchant, opened a branch store in Concord with Maurice Furber as manager; and Robert A. Doss, (son of Overstreet Doss, owner of a good deal of land around the village) an early county sheriff and treasurer, also had a store, but following the fate of many sheriffs, his office caused his failure. Raleigh Chilton kept a tavern, used also as post office, later owned by Hubbels.

There was no provision for mail distribution from the tavern, and Dr. D. S. Evans and William Dinwiddie would collect and carry it around every few days to the neighbors in the surrounding country.   Major Thomas L. Arrington was the first postmaster and depot agent.   Owners of land nearest the village were Samuel Staples, (father of George, Jeffrey, James and Powhatan) James Cardwell and Sampson Evans.   George Staples and George Abbott drove stages.   Burton Landrum conducted a liquor shop.   James Cardwell sawed ties for the railroad, the first train over which, passed Concord in 1854, creating much interest and excitement.   Concord is reached by a sand clay road from Rustburg and by a tar macadam road which leaves the river near Six Mile bridge, from Lynchburg and is the shortest route from that city.

Concord railroad station was burned down during Hunter's raid on Lynchburg in 1864 by one of his soldiers named Rucker, from Ohio, who was probably the descendant of a former Campbell county resident: the Federal troops were driven away by Early's corps before they could do further damage in that section. Three Presbyterian churches of simi-

New Concord Church, Campbell County

lar names, Old Concord, New Concord and Little Concord, are in the neighborhood of Concord Depot, one in Charlotte, one in Appomattox and the other in Campbell; the latter designated as New Concord was first located on Landrum's land moved to Shaw's and moved a third time; it is a frame structure and stands near the roadside; its minutes have been continuously kept and bound.

Tradition reports that Robert Cardwell (father of James Dixon Cardwell, inventor of the threshing machine) was of notable English ancestry: born in 1762 at Thornhill parish

England, he went first to North Ireland and from there emigrated to America, landing in Virginia, where he arrived shortly after the Revolution. He married and located in Campbell near the locality which became Concord: there he raised a large family of boys and one daughter.

His second son, James Dixon, Jr. b. 1790, married three times, an Elliott, a Cheatham, and a Walker, and owned a large quantity of land towards Pilot Mountain. Jas. D.'s son, Charles Wesley, born 1825, married Dorothy M. 'Franklin; Charles Wesley's son, Robert, went to Missouri, where he graduated from Washington University of St. Louis in 1893. This grandson of James Dixon Cardwell, the inventor, was also an inventor: he patented a number of articles which are in general use, including the Friction Draft Gear (called the Cardwell Gear): Robert Cardwell now lives in Chicago.

John Thomas Cardwell a son of the emigrant remained at Concord, and also had a large family of sons and one daughter. His son Josephus, married Mary, the daughter of Captain Rees and Martha Evans; their daughter Ora, married Daniel Benjamin, the son of Dr. Daniel S. Evans. Members of this family yet live at the Pilot Mountain farm, situated not far from Concord.

Little Concord church is within Appomattox lines.

The two land slices taken from Campbell to add territory to Appomattox county in 1845 and 1848, threw the families then living within that boundary into the latter county and records of these residents were burned with all of the county records when Appomattox court house was destroyed by fire in 1892; unless the families possess duplicate copies, there is no way of recovering those court papers.

Two or three old covered bridges remain in the county; one of these relics of past usage crosses Falling river about ten miles from Concord Station.

Otter River

Otter River was established in the early days of the Southern railroad as an inn, where the trains waited until the passengers were fed. It was run by Captain Stewart from Washington, whose son Frank married Ella the daughter of Benjamin Anthony. *Walnut Hill,* home of the Anthonys, *Arnolton,* home of Colonel Reid Arnold, and *Otter River,* home of Samuel C. Tardy are near; the latter place is now owned by a family of Tweedy, formerly living at Rustburg. Reid Arnold was a lieutenant in the Confederate Army and later made colonel of militia.

Families in the neighborhood, Anthony, Andrews, Douglass, Tardy, Wyatt.

Evington.

Evington, a station established by the Southern Railroad company and,—built upon land owned by Miss Evie Smith— was given her name; it was in former years a community of considerable wealth. Without information to the contrary I am led to believe that the first house erected near Evington was that of Colonel Jeremiah Early, who moved there in 1755 from Culpeper, though in a deed of land purchased from John Gibson of 200 acres in Russell parish, Bedford county, he is recorded as "Jeremiah Early of Augusta county" being then a lieutenant in the Augusta District Militia.

Early purchased 200 additional acres in 1758, from Wm. Bryan of Albemarle county, lying on Elk creek, Bedford, and a parcel of land on the north side of the road to Warwick, from the trustees of Bedford county, upon which he agreed to build within one year; as he is not known to have occupied any other home, the one now owned by the family of Thomas N. Langhorne, a mile or more from Evington, must be the one erected during 1758-9 to which the deed refers. Like many later buildings in the county it was constructed of broad boards overlaid with weather boarding and sealed closely inside with plaster, leaving no space between outer and inner linings, and stands upon a basement of brick foundation, paved with broad slabs of stone.

Early also built a mill and a tavern in the neighborhood. He acquired much landed property and owned the Washington Iron Works in partnership with James Callaway, his son-in-law: at the end of the century of his eleven children only the two youngest Rev. Abner Early and Mrs. William Anderson were left in the county, the former occupying the old family mansion; Jeremiah Early, colonel of the Bedford Militia, died in 1779 aged 49 years.

Irvines, Watts, Saunders, Anthonys, Callaways, Hicks and Hadens were among the earliest settlers in Flat creek section near Evington. Three Hicks brothers came to America from Lancaster, England in 1771: William and Henry went to Defiance, Ohio, Thomas took up homestead in Pennsylvania. After a few years sojourn in Ohio, William Hicks moved to Bedford county, Va. where he bought a farm near Evington upon which he settled. His two eldest sons having gone west, during the latter years of his life be placed his son, James Westmoreland in charge of his farm; one of the other sons later returned home.

Hon. E. A. Hicks, the present delegate from Campbell to the Legislature, lives on a farm owned by his grandfather: he served on the board of supervisors for 20 years, was chairman for 8 years; elected to the House of Delegates in 1920 and re-elected in 1922: he was educated at New London Academy. A large Hicks family connection lives around Evington. R. L. Hicks and Miss M. M. Hicks are employed in the Bureau of Standards in Washington city.

John Callaway b. 1738, son of Colonel William and Elizabeth Tilly-Callaway m. 1st Tabitha, dau. of Henry and Sarah Tate; m. 2nd Agatha, dau. of Major John Ward: resided near Evington. In 1785 his brother, Col. Jas. Callaway was security on his bond to Patrick Henry, governor, for his commission as high sheriff and treasurer. John Callaway in

1786 was one of the trustees of the town of Lynchburg then established. His will recorded in 1821 devised to his three grand-daughters, Matilda, Docia and Sally (daus. of his son William) 160 acres of land on the north side of Otter; to his grandson, George W. Callaway, he devised the land patented to James and John Callaway 67,000 and some hundred acres in Franklin, Botetourt, Henry and Patrick counties. To his beloved friend, Henry Ward, he bequeathed the debt due him from Capt. John Ward.

The John Callaway who moved to Georgia in the last quarter of the 18th century may have been a son of this John Callaway of Campbell. John Hewitt married Sarah A. dau. of John Callaway, Sr. in 1827 and lived on Otter river about a half mile from *Wyndholm*. He built a temporary home expecting to build a better one later in an oak grove on the hill above, but did not live to carry out his plans; both husband and wife died early leaving one son, Richard Newton, and a dau. Kate. Dr. Richard N. Hewitt added to the house built by his father and lived there; he married Frances Dorothea, dau. of Jonathan and Pamela Michie of Louisa county and their dau. Anna K. married Thomas Nelson Langhorne (dec.) and lives at *Wyndholm*.

First William Watts, and then his son-in-law, Judge Fleming Saunders lived at *Flat Creek,* a house built by the former, and later occupied by Captain Fleming, a son of Judge Saunders, who married Mary Gwaphmey of Norfolk; the property is still owned by the family of the latter couple. Major Robert Saunders married Carrietta Davis, and resided at a place named for her, called Caryswood, which also remains in his family.

John Anthony, who was a justice of Albemarle in 1845-6, moved to Campbell and acquired a large estate in land: in 1754 patented 1012 acres on both sides of Otter river adjoining William Stone and in 1780 patented 1300 acres on the south branch of Otter creek, in 1759 patented 674 acres at the head of Ivy creek a branch of Blackwater creek: in 1785-6 he was deputy sheriff to John Callaway: in 1801 Mrs. Elizabeth An-

thony's will (then recorded) mentioned children;—John, Jr.
. . . . . —Elizabeth Cowan,—Abner. . . —Mary
Menges,—Elizabeth Robertson,—Lucy Jones,—grandson Col.
Charles m. . . —Sarah Bradford,—and grandson John A.
Callaway: there is still a large connection of this family in
the locality.

Rev. Abner Early lived in his father's old mansion;
his son Jacob moved with his family to Indiana; son William moved to Mississippi; family of his son, John W.
moved to California; sons, Abner and Edmund remained in
Campbell, and the latter heired his grand-father's home: but
later moved to a place built by himself.

William Irvine, a Scotch settler, purchased land on Otter
river where he built a home called *Otter* and married Mary
Anthony: he died when William, his only son, was
small. He was one of the first justices of Bedford, and an
active citizen there. William, Jr. married Martha, the dau.
of Jesse Burton, who assisted in laying out Lynchburg and lived
near Burton's creek, named for him and changed from Rock
Castle creek: a gr. grandson, Dr. James Sinkler Irvine, (who
m. Evie Saunders) owns the old Irvine home place.

Haden is another name still found among residents in the
neighborhood: in 1793 John Haden m. Rachel Reynolds, 1795
Rachel Haden m. John Moorman; 1810 Jas. C. Haden m.
Nancy Johns. In 1812 James M. Haden was captain of a
company of Grenadiers in the 3rd Va. Reg. which served in
the war with England. In 1821 Margaret D. Haden, married
Henry T. son of Rev. Abner Early. In 1814 Jane Haden m.
Samuel C. Tardy, who lived near Otter River, a station on the
Southern R. R. Cornelia F. dau. of Dr. Madison Haden m.
Judge John G. Haythe of Gladys: his son Dr. J. W. Haythe
was severely wounded in a battle near Petersburg. Capt. Chas.
Anthony m. Martha Haden.

Colonel Alexander Austin's old home was on the road to
Evington; his dau. Sarah married Peter Rawlings and her
family now occupies the old home; his son Thomas moved to
Missouri.

Type of the Old South.

Rev. Charles Carter Randolph, born in 1846 at *The Grove* near Warrenton, Fauquier County, Va. was 3rd son of Captain Charles C. Randolph (son of Robert and Elizabeth Hill Randolph of Charles City County) and his wife, Mary A. Fauntleroy-Mortimer. When a lad of 14 years Federal soldiers sacked his home and the family were forced to seek refuge in the home of a kinsman. In 1862 he entered Co. "F" 6th Virginia Cavalry in which a brother-in-law was lieutenant. That year he saw service in the Valley of Virginia and at the battle of Port Republic first met Stonewall Jackson. In crossing a stile Jackson dropped his glove and the little soldier picked it up for him, an act that attracted Jackson's attention to the youthful and diminutive figure. After enquiring his name, the general ordered him to put down his gun and return to the rear, but so persistent was the young soldier's refusal to obey this order, that Jackson became impressed with his earnestness and took him on as courier for oral dispatches and ordered him to overtake the army, which Randolph reached at Malvern Hill engagement, the climax of the Seven Days Fight. The boy carried dispatches for Jackson at 2nd Manassas and went with him to Frederick and Antietam where he rode hard all day carrying dispatches through heavy fighting around the Dunkard Church. Jackson thought him too young for continued military service and recommended him for a scholarship at Virginia Military Institute which Randolph entered in February 1863.

May 15, 1864, as a member of Co. "C" of the Cadet Corps, he took part in the battle of New Market. As the boys charged up the hill to take the battery, he was wounded and left for dead on the field, where later a comrade found him and brought a surgeon to him: after several weeks he recovered but lost his hearing in one ear. Only three days before New Market battle his oldest brother, Captain Robert Randolph, of the Black Horse Company of Fauquier, was killed at Meadow Bridge near Richmond.

In 1866 Charles Randolph re-entered Va. Mil Inst. and graduated in 1870.

In 1872 he entered the Theological Seminary at Alexandria, graduated in 1876 and next year was ordained by Bishop Whittle. After serving the parishes of Christ Church, Matthews Co., Va., St. Thomas', Baltimore Co., Maryland; and Woodville, Botetourt Co., Va., with two years at Americus, Georgia—in 1899 he became rector of Moore Parish, Campbell Co. with charge of the churches—Good Shepherd, Evington; Trinity, Rustburg; St. Peters, Lynch Station (afterwards moved to Alta Vista); Christ, (built by him) near Winfall; *and* St. John's near Gladys for a short while; also Union Church at Castle Craig and Blue Door Mission near Kingston.

After a devoted ministry in Moore Parish of 17 years, he retired in 1916. However, he continued to supply various town churches till the autumn of 1924. He married 1st Sallie T. Anthony of Botetourt, who died a year after her marriage; m. 2nd Sarah Blair dau. of Rev. Wm. McGuire of Essex Co.: children; Bessie Carter, Mary Mortimer, Charles C., Wm. McGuire and Robert: Rev. Chas C. Randolph died in 1925 at Richmond. Builder of mission churches and preacher for 48 years he was an unfailing friend and minister to all classes, colors and religious beliefs: those who came near him recognized the earnestness of his Christian spirit and he was dearly loved. Among his friends he showed himself the chivalrous gentleman, tolerant and magnanimous: all who knew him felt the influence of a personality of exceptional sweetness and charm.

Good Shepherd Episcopal Church was built through the efforts of Captain Fleming Saunders of *Flat Creek:* vestrymen of the church were John Thompson Brown, Captain Saunders, Thomas Langhorne, and Captain James G. Begg. The rectory formerly occupied by Rev. Charles C. Randolph, has been sold, and the minister officiating there now lives at Alta Vista. In 1872 Begg (born 1829 at Kinross, Scotland, a great nephew of Robert Burns) purchased *The Grove* near New London, and lived there 35 years: he died in 1909 and was interred at the churchyard of Good Shepherd church. He was educated at Edinburg, and had been connected with the iron works at Lochgelly and Coatbridge, and was captain of the 29th Lanarkshire Volunteers, which had been organized as a Home Guard. He sold his interests in the iron works and emigrated to Virginia. Since his death *The Grove* has passed through several ownerships and been renamed *Closeburn Manor*.

Confederate Soldiers from Evington

Arthur, John A.
Anthony, John W.
Early, Leverett S.
Farmer, Bogus
Farmer, William
Haden, Benjamin
Haden, Clarence V.
Haden, Dr. Joel W. of Capt. Jordan's company, Wise brigade; severely wounded in battle near Petersburg.
Haden, Mark A.
Haden, M. H.
Irvine, Captain Edward
Irvine, Captain Jesse
Irvine, John B.

Irvine, Dr. William H.
Hicks, James H.
Hicks, James W.
Hicks, R. W.
Hicks, W. H.
Hunter, J. A.
Hunter, Robert
Fields, Daniel
Mason, John L.
Murrell, D. B.
Phillips, William
Pribble, C. J.
Saunders, Captain Fleming
Saunders, Major Robert C.
West, William H.

Lynch (R. R. Station, Clarion)

The land which Lynch Station covers was originally owned by the family of Lee who were large landholders in that section; the Lee home, built partly of stone, was said to be over one hundred years old when it was recently burned. In 1825 Mt. Hermon (Methodist) church, one mile west of the present town, was built on land donated by John Lee, and, excepting one at Leesville, was the only church within a radius of many miles: pastors there were Milton Andrews, Nathaniel Thomas, J. A. Proctor, John Hannon, Joshua Hunter, etc. The old church was torn down and a larger one erected in 1875; the discarded timbers were used in the construction of a school house which was taught by Mrs. Charles Douglass, dau. of Ralph Smith: prior to this a private school was conducted on Ralph Smith's land by Miss Elizabeth Lambert.

Upon the completion of the Lynchburg and Danville Railway in 1873 a station was settled upon land belonging to William Frazier, which he had purchased from the estate of John Laughon, who married into the Lee family. It was given the name Lynch Station because Charles Henry Lynch, a landowner several miles east, had been instrumental in securing subscriptions for financing the railroad. The Fraziers had long been landholders in the vicinity, their home being a mile northwest of Lynch's. Other near residents were John W. and Benjamin H. Anthony; Rev. Milton E. Andrews; Wyatt, Alexander and D. R. Arnold, Henry W. Adams; Benjamin and Alexander Brooks, Rev. Milton L. Bishop; Charles A. Douglass, Sr.; Edward Lynch; Dr. Thomas L. Dillard; the Dearing family, Anselm and Wm. O. Frazier; Gaines family; William Goodman; Wm. and Charles Hall; Charles Hughes; John Laughon: Wyatt, Richard and Moses Lee, the sons of John Lee; Moorman family; Wm. Merritt; William Pannill; Benj. W. Porter; Ralph Smith, Benjamin Tardy; Hardaway Turner; John and Kenneth Urquhart; James Wood; Whitfield and Charles West; Judge Robert H. Ward; Christopher West.

The railroad which has been given several names, but now called Southern Railway System, was three years under construction and furnished work for country people, who had returned from the war in great need. The name of the station being similar to Lynchburg, another station on the road, was changed to Clarion but the post office retained the first designation. The first building erected was the home of John B. Omohundro, section foreman for the company. William Ould's store conducted by his son Eugene, (who later represented Campbell in the Legislature) followed. Wyatt A. Andrews with Haden and Bragg in sawmill business, procured several acres in connection with a sawmill and that was the first industry. James A. Traylor erected several homes, and two stores, one of brick, which were laid by Samuel Crawford, veteran of the Mexican war.

The first station agent and post master was Abner Anthony from Leesville, who while in his office was struck over the head by burglars and lay in critical condition for weeks afterwards: Oscar M. Turner succeeded in the office and he also practiced law: Eugene Taylor, pioneer citizen, was also a postmaster. Wyatt A. Andrews and John L. Douglass were merchants in partnership till the former opened a drug store: Andrews was a confederate veteran, married Annie R. Bishop. John L., son of Chas. A. Douglass, m. Lucy Hardwicke of Tennessee, and was identified with railway mail service for 40 years. John L. Webb of Orange county was associated with the J. T. Marshall Lumber Co. in the operation of a mill not far from the village; married Valeria M. Snow. Dr. John J. Board (son of Col. Frank H. Board, killed at Winchester battle) practiced medicine, and his brother-in-law, Dr. T. C. Dennis, dentistry, when Lynch's was in its infancy; the latter married Lily Board and Dr. Board m. Lily B. dau of D. R. Arnold, lieutenant in the Confederate army. John C. Thompson, a pioneer, married Clara Victor Snow; Joseph Tyree m. Mary E. Douglass, and conducted a merchandise store.

Jesse, son of Wm. Frazier received a bullet during service in Confederate service which was never extracted: he travelled through the west but returned to his home ultimately.

In 1880 James Hardwick and James Traylor published a weekly called the *Campbell County Record,* which was later taken to Rustburg. After a few years the press was brought back to Lynch Station and the *Campbell County Clarion* published for some years by B. J. Wilkinson, an attorney and Confederate soldier: Wilkinson m. 1st Mollie Turner, m. 2nd Virginia Traylor. Two of the most successful merchants were John

J. Anthony and Paul T. Anthony, brothers and partners in business.

Wm. C. Arthur 40 years in Southern Railway service m. Theresa Laughon; he was wounded in Confederate service. Charles A. Douglass, Jr. m. Kate Boisseau of Petersburg; he died in 1926.

Lynch Station was incorporated as a town in 1884, with Oliver Peak as first mayor. One of the ordinances provided that no vehicle should be driven through the main street at a speed over six miles per hour. Before 1900 the charter was allowed to become inactive.

Prior to the settlement of Alta Vista, three miles to the south, more business was transacted at Lynch Station than at any other point in the county, excepting Lynchburg. It was the nearest point for residents of Ward's Road section and for the people fifteen or twenty miles to the west in Bedford county. Their farm products were carried to the local merchants there for purchase or for shipment: many train loads of lumber and wood were shipped and there was a large output of ore from the manganese mines, at one period of the town's history.

James Traylor, Thomas Fauntleroy and H. M. Oliver were instrumental in securing the erection of a Baptist church 'at the station in 1879: the first preacher was Rev. James Eubanks, who taught a boys' school at *Sunnyside* in Bedford. Other ministers who officiated there were Dr. Frank Fisher, Rev. C. A. Woodson, Rev. W. D. Barr, and Rev. Charles Anthony. John Adams, a Confederate veteran, was superintendent of the Sunday school for many years.

About 1890 Rev. Dr. Jaeger visited the county as a missionary for the Episcopal church and was active in raising funds for the erection of St. Peters church which was consecrated in 1892. Rev. James F. Plummer was the first regular minister with H. W. Adams, Sr., John C. Thompson and Thomas Payne as vestryman. Rev. Frederick Le Mosey followed in the pulpit, but he was killed by a runaway horse; after him Rev. Charles Carter Randolph took charge. In 1910 the membership of St. Peter's was moved to Alta Vista.

Benjamin Porter was among the first settlers in the locality; he moved from Orange county in 1790 and acquired land upon which he built his dwelling and a merchandise store near the present Arnolton, which received its name from the Arnold family, who later came into possession of it. The store was used as a post office before the construction of the railroad. Captain Porter died during the heavy snow storm of 1857 which drifted ten feet deep in places, and there was difficulty in attending his funeral. His sons William, John and Benjamin moved to Missouri; dau. Elizabeth m. . . Rogers of Orange county: dau. Anne F. m. Kenneth son of Walter Urquhart who came to Virginia from Scotland and settled in Campbell at the foot of Johnson's Mountain. In 1789 Walter Urquhart patented 500 acres lying upon the west branches of Johnson's creek. Shiloh church stood near the homes of the Porters and Urquharts near Johnson's Mountain, some miles above Lynch's.

Alta Vista

The name of the town, Alta Vista, was suggested by its situation: lying on the Staunton river, at the junction of the Southern and Virginian railroads, it was founded by Henry Lane, (one of its present active citizens) at the time of the building of the last named road, upon land formerly belonging to a member of the Adams' family.

The Staunton's water power has furnished an important factor in the town's development and foremost among its enterprises are the Lane Brothers' Cedar Chest and Alta Vista Cotton Mill Companies which have become well established and much advertised; the former is claimed to be one of the largest manufactories of cedar chests in the world. The town possesses also a mallet factory, stove factory and ice plant, which, with the above named industries, make it the second important manufacturing center in the county: it provides a market for tobacco in its two warehouses, one each for bright and dark tobacco, also boasts ownership of the largest High School in the county, excepting Lynchburg.

Here there is seen a fine post office building, public library, two banks and six churches,—Episcopal, Baptist, Methodist, Western Methodist, Presbyterian, Pentacostal Mission and Church of the Living God; two hotels, two newspapers,— one, the *Alta Vista Journal* (weekly) and the *Tri-County Democrat,* a semi-weekly issue; two drug stores, three garages and service stations, and two automobile agencies.

Near the locality is Otter-River or Ward's Bridge which crosses the Otter, a tributary of the Staunton. In 1810 Major Ward replaced his ferry with a toll bridge, now a free bridge furnishes passage across the river for travel along Route 14.

Members of the Ward, Adams, Lynch, Dearing and Fauntle-roy families lived in the immediate neighborhood, where some of the old homes still stand, and some representatives still live. Unusual beauty, in name selection, for their estates, was manifested, such as *Otterburne, Monteflora, Avoca,* and the like, prompted doubtless by the natural beauty of the scenery.

Romantic interest centers around Otter bridge from its connection with the Otter River picnics started about the middle of the last century on the banks of the Otter near its junction with the Staunton and not far from Alta Vista. They were inaugurated with the purpose of drawing county people together, and formal invitations were issued by appointed committees for a two-day festival. The picnickers assembled in a romantically situated glen just beyond the bridge, where a dance pavillion was erected and long tables provided to receive the spread of daintily prepared food from bountifully laden baskets; and benches supplied to seat the company: nature lent a hand in furnishing vine and root, trunks and abundance of shade, with the lulling sound of flowing water on river banks below. An invitation of August 26 and 27, 1870, gives committee names, Dr. Wm. V. Adams, Chiswell Dabney, Dr. Maurice Early, Mosby H. Payne, C. R. Payne, T. L. Anthony, G. E. Coleman, with those of managers, Maj. Chas. H. Lynch, Maj. J. C. Ward, Dr. F. A. Perrow, Bowling Clark, Colonel H. W.

Adams, Captain Wm. E. Johns, and J. A. Payne: without distinction of age, here extremes met and two of the promoters of the festivities were bachelors of 70 years.

As time wore on one day sufficed for this neighborhood gathering but the same spot lures the pleasure seekers to its attractive shelter.

Alta Vista has an enthusiastic chapter of Daughters of the American Revolution named for Colonel Charles Lynch, whose residence was near there.

Winfall

Before the construction of the Lynchburg and Durham Railroad, through the locality, the present station of Winfall was simply a trading point possessing one general merchandise store. In earlier times the family of Elliott, who held the English king's grant of land, had settled in the neighborhood, descendants of whom remain there. The building of the railroad gave the community its post office and station which was named after a small stream flowing at the foot of the hill: the present post master is S. W. Elliott, who also operates a store there.

In 1797 Thomas Elliott bought a tract of land, upon which stood a mill, on Falling river from James McReynolds; again in 1803 bought 400 acres lying on both sides of Mountain Run from McReynolds. In 1811 William Elliott purchased land on Troublesome creek from John Pribble. An allottment was made in 1810 of Thomas Elliott's estate—land adjoining that of Robert Elliott, Jr.—to Prudence, Tabitha, Thomas P. and Archibald Elliott, beneficiaries. In 1814 a deed transferring property from Thomas Elliott to Robert Elliott was recorded.

Besides its station and post-office Winfall has a school building, a gasoline station, 2 stores, a Baptist church, with a Methodist church nearby on the main road and five miles beyond the station, on east ferry road, Grace Episcopal church, the land upon which it is erected, having been given by W. C. Mitchell.

Families around the community are Elliott, Mitchell, Brown, Daniel, Page and others.

General Wyatt Elliott, C. S. Veteran, and clerk of U. S. Court in 1896 and one time resident in Lynchburg, was a member of the Elliott family at Winfall.

Gladys

The village which now bears the name of Gladys, and is a station on the Lynchburg and Durham railroad, started as Connelly's Tavern, and that was used as a relay post for the mail which was brought on horseback from Rustburg by Mt. Zion, Marysville and Brookneal; the first post master having been Mr. Stoner. Later the place received the name *Pigeon Run* from the pigeon roost which near the middle of the 19th century was observable in a densely wooded section known as *The Barrens* where changing locality at night flocks of pigeons more than a mile in length continued to roost till early spring time. Almost every autumn wild pigeons would sweep over the forests searching for nuts and acorns; they would settle down on a piece of forest land marching in solid mass, and closely examine the ground, roosting in the undergrowth but when they were disturbed by hunters, they changed their roosts to the tall pines of the unbroken forest. Hundreds of huntsmen from the contiguous county would throng to their shelter every night in wagons, buggies and vehicles of all kinds, and form a regular encampment, spending the night in search of the birds, which did not remain in the same place but often changed their quarters. Their range extended from four to six miles in width and from ten to fifteen in length, and they would commence moving off in the morning as soon as it was light.

Churches then were the meeting places for neighbors, and the first heard of in this locality was situated about 100 yards from the Alexander home in a grove of fine oaks and called Molley's Creek church, but the old structure was blown down during a storm in 1830. It was used by Methodist and Baptist alike, but located on Alexander's land he exercised a proprietary right over it. The next church, St. John's Episcopal, still used, was erected through the efforts of Mr. Osgood, a ministerial student, who was employed as a teacher in the neighborhood: Wesleyburg of the Methodists followed, then the Baptist erected Mt. Calvary, but the latter was replaced by Kedron, land for which was donated by Richard Morgan.

School started in a one-room log cabin, and was taught by Dr. Moorman; in 1820 the school acquired 2 rooms, to which was added a third in 1913, fourth in 1917, and in 1919 it possessed 8 rooms; it was converted into Seneca High School in 1917 and since 1920 it has been an accredited high school with seven teachers in charge. Large tracts of land around Pigeon Run were owned by the Withers' family; Gladys Inn was built by Dr. Robert Withers. The Moyer house was also used as a post office and the Haythe house as a store. After disposing of his Shady Grove property Richard Morgan moved to the Haythe house and his son, Dr. Morgan built a drug store which he used as a dental office also, during his residence in Gladys.

The Lynchburg, Halifax and North Carolina railroad completed in 1890, placed Robinson's Crossing at Kedron church; a station was established at Pigeon Run and called Woodlawn, but changed later to Gladys, its present name, at the suggestion of Major Otey. president of the railroad company, after the name of a stockholders' daughter. This road was afterward sold to the Norfolk and Western railroad company as a branch line, with the name Lynchburg and Durham, and is yet operated as such. With the choice of Gladys for the station, the village numbered its third change of name, and from then parted with the one which had been suggested by the roosting of pigeons in the neighborhood.

Situated in a tobacco and grain growing section of rolling country, Gladys possess two churches, three stores, hotel and school house, two garages, a blacksmith shop, mail and rail service, a grist mill, a physician and two pastors: rural free delivery was started in 1902. The first improved wagon road was built in 1917 extending from Gladys to Long Island.

Grouped in the neighborhood are a number of old houses, which were the homes of families who were once active in the county affairs and who dispensed hospitality to such extent that it made those homes notable, but those owners have all gone and other tenants now occupy them. These country places are not near enough to be seen from the station, though in easy access, over good soil roads which now prevail. Not far away stands St. John's Episcopal church, and its nearby burial ground furnishes a resting-place for many of its former parishioners. Among the places, become historic by association with the past, are Robert Alexander's *Rock Castle* (which later was the Robert W. Withers' home); Adam Clement's *Oakwood;* Spotswood Henry's *Shady Grove* (later home of Richard Morgan, still later of Captain William Perrow); a house built solidly of rock, the residence of the Page family; Paynes, Lemmons', Haythes' properties not far distant.

Naruna

Naruna (a name which is said to be of Indian origin) is situated in open country on the Lynchburg and Durham division of the Norfolk and Western railroad: fine pine forests are seen near. Perhaps its chief interest centers in its High School which in 1923, through contribution of its patrons and an appropriation from the state was erected for the instruction in vocational agriculture and home economics, and thus became a Smith-Hughes Agricultural School. The principal of this institution is Miss Rose Gilliam, who resides in the old Gilliam home a few miles distant and who, in conjunction with two other teachers, Miss Rachel Whitlow of Rustburg High School and Mrs. Elizabeth Clarke of Fairview Heights graded school, prepared the Campbell County Geography Supplement in 1925 under the supervision of Dr. Wilson Gee of the school of Rural Economics and Rural Sociology at the University of

Virginia—a booklet published by the Campbell county school board.

Near Naruna is the large apiary of Tanner C. Asher, who has besides colonies of bees in Halifax and Charlotte counties. Bee-raising is a growing industry which is now fostered by conventions of bee-raisers. In 1920 there were 2555 hives in Campbell and the yield of honey and wax amounted to $15,770: the sources from which the bees obtain honey are the sour wood, tulip, poplar, clover and fruit blossoms, asters and sumac; that these furnish sufficiency is proven by the fact that bees do not materially depredate upon the neighboring vineyards.

A property situated between Naruna and Brookneal and known as *Liberty Farm,* now established on a commercial basis, is conducted by Samuel A. Ford and sons, and is largely devoted to apple orchards and vineyards, about eight acres, (with around a dozen varieties of grapes) constituting the space covered by the latter. The crop of grapes is packed in baskets and shipped to West Virginia markets principally, though much of it finds a local market. This Ford family is of Huguenot origin, the spelling of the name having been abbreviated into its present form. An early ancestor was the first sheriff of Buckingham county; the present head of the family married the daughter of Dr. Samuel Taylor of Richmond, who is said to have been a brother of Chancellor Creed Taylor. Samuel A. Ford was a member of Company "G" 3rd Va. Cav. Wickham's brigade, and was with the command under General Early in the Valley campaign; having entered service in 1863 at the age of 17 years. Of the captains of his company, George Matthews was killed at Mitchell's Ford, Edward Garrett killed at Amelia C. H., and Robert Page was last in command. Samuel Ford purchased Liberty Farm about twenty-five years ago; a property which had passed through various hands. Report says it was first owned by Hancocks, and the present residence was the site of slave quarters. More authentic seems the information that it was owned by John J. Callaway. Ford obtained the land from Foster, a liquor mer-

chant of Lynchburg. Perhaps his apple crops afford the largest market return, as culls and dropped fruit are run through
press, the cider from which finds ready sale locally.

Near 'Liberty Farm' is a negro settlement which bears the
name 'Cake Walk'.

County Almshouse

Campbell appears to have made as good provision as falls to
the lot of other county almshouses, yet it is not possible to dis-
sociate the pathetic, the tragic, from the lives of inmates of an
institution, which (from long usage of the term) we commonly
call the *poor house*—that is the refuge for those who have come
to the end of their resources, who must wrench themselves
from old ties and face a situation of dependence upon the community and its provision. The most touching feature is that
this fate comes principally to the old, the infirm, the helpless,
and that under the most favorable circumstances their lives
pass out in shadow, even in many instances in invalidism.
In order to reach the institution it is necessary to take the
highway which connects Lynchburg and Rustburg then leaving
that road midway between these two places, turn to the right,
cross Beaver creek and the railway track and follow a road leading up hill: the stables for county mules and horses are first
reached in nearing the institution. Then there comes into view
the white washed brick buildings around a quadrangle; frame
houses in the valley below and on the hillside, beyond the main
buildings, and a chapel for religious services. The superintendent of the almshouse, C. E. Blankenship, has a screened
white-washed brick house, with porches also screened, and low
ceilings. Fronting the quadrangle, and across from it, there
is a double-dining-room, one side for the white inmates, and the
other for negroes; for both there is provided bench-seats at
the oil-covered tables. A negro, hired for the purpose, is cook;
and a white woman is employed as nurse and assistant in the
care of the sick and aged.

The white residents are housed in four brick buildings, one and a half stories high, having two downstairs rooms in each building and two in the upper half story.

Negroes are allotted rooms in the frame house in the valley. The cook prepares three meals a day—of vegetables, meat, bread, coffee and milk. Beds, quilts and blankets, pine dressers, kerosine lamps and wash-basins comprise the furnishings, without attempt at ornament.

Screens furnished are not acceptable to the inmates, and the screen doors are found propped open and even taken down and carried away in protest against their usage. Perhaps these unfortunates reach a stage of contentment, that fate is so far benignant, and realize that for them the elements of gladness, of happiness do not exist, unless in retrospect or else in reflection from the lives of those more happily situated.

Rivers and Creeks, Ferries and Bridges

Chapter V

Water Courses

AMPBELL is peculiarly favored in water courses. Along its northern and northeastern border flows James river; along its southern and southeastern border the river which locally passes by the name of Staunton, and emptying into the latter, a short distance from Alta Vista in the western section, Otter river flows in from Bedford: near Leesville, Goose creek, also from Bedford sources, joins Staunton river. In the east Falling river, with its tributary, Little Falling, has numerous branches feeding it, which form a network of streams. There are many creeks large enough to be designated by names and these are fed by numberless brooks, from valleys between the hills and mountains.

Tussocky and Little Beaver add their overflow to Beaver creek which empties into the James near Mt. Athos.

Little Opossum and Opossum having source in Candler's Mountain, flows (near an island of the same name) into the James, and not far off Fishing creek empties into the James at Lynchburg.

Whipping, Hills, Seneca (aided by Little Seneca), Cheese, Bishops and Back creeks add to Staunton's volume, while Buffalo, Johnson, Tardy, Flat and Troublesome creeks contribute to Otter's waters.

Marrowbone creek, Steel branch, Jennican branch, (from Appomattox); Beaver pond branch, Cane branch, Entray creek into Little Falling; Burger branch, Pulliam branch, Rattlesnake branch, Molley's creek, Suck creek, Hat creek into Falling, which with the additional waters of Little Falling, then empties into Staunton river at Brookneal. Burton (formerly Rock Castle) and Tomahawk creeks join to form Dreaming, which, with Ivy, forms Blackwater creek and that in turn empties into James river at Lynchburg.

Lynchburg procures its water supply from Pedlar basin in Amherst county fifteen miles distant: but in earlier times it made use of James river water, until that river received the waste from dye mills along its course. There were also a number of bold springs in the town, which furnished fine drinking water before a water system was established; these springs were filled over as the town grew and building space became congested: one, on the premises of Captain Early in a

Old Covered Bridge Over Falling River

depression near Main and 6th streets, of which he gave the city the use, supplied all the neighborhood with water. The Acadmey of Music now covers the site of the spring, water from which was piped across the street to a pump placed there for the convenience of those who used it.

The river locally designated Staunton, is called Roanoke from its source in Montgomery county to the point at which it passes through the Blue Ridge Mountains, and resumes the latter name when it unites with the Dan in Mecklenburg county. The Jefferson and Fry maps use *Staunton* for the western end of the river from its confluence with the Dan to its source: but in his "Notes on Virginia" Thomas Jefferson makes no mention of the name Staunton, but calls the whole stream by the Indian shell word *Roanoke*. The dual name is said to have arisen from the fact that when white settlements were first established in Staunton river vicinity in order to protect them from the incursions of Indians a company was organized to patrol the territory of Roanoke river from the mountains to the mouth of the Dan and placed under the command of a Captain Henry Staunton. From this circumstance that part of the stream came to be called first Staunton's river and later Staunton by which name it appears on the map and is known to the people of the surrounding country. Captain Staunton served in the Revolutionary War, but probably received his title during this patrol work.

During the time he was patrolling the country, Mary Crawford, a girl about twelve years of age who lived at the White settlement (a place in Pittsylvania county about a mile and a half from the present Hurt Station and back from the river) was stolen by the Indians and taken to their camping ground above Smith's Mountain, where she was kept a prisoner for four days. In the search made for her recovery, Captain Staunton succeeded in discovering where she was held, and watching a chance he stole into the camp, rescued her and brought her down the river, through which he waded and swam a good part of the way in order not to leave foot tracks by which the Indians could pursue and retake her. This story of Mary Crawford's rescue was related by Colonel Abner Anthony, a nonagenarian and he had been told of it by older people who knew of the occurrence. Colonel Anthony was familiar with the county's early history and contributed articles concerning it to local newspapers, and through these contributions information has been preserved which otherwise would have passed into oblivion. The family he represented was originally of the Quaker sect and he was of the branch which remained in the county, descendants of whom still bear the name of Anthony.

Staunton river has ever provided sport for fisherman, one of whom reports that fish were always abundant in that stream, the spawning period being in early Spring time when they frequent the falls of the river, and wherever they can find a swift current over a bed of gravel, they collect in shoals and deposit their spawn. The fish can be captured in large numbers with a seine from eighty to one hundred feet in length, not drawn to shore when filled, but after the seine is enclosed, the fish taken out then in the middle of the stream.

The first fish to run in the spring are found to be the salmon trout, which must be caught in March; next to these come the winter or black sucker, followed by the sorrel-horse, or red fin sucker, the largest of that family; then in turn come the blue fin, later the May sucker and after these the black bass. Fine game fish have been found in the stream known as *King William perch* and the mill ponds in spring and autumn furnish a good stock of pike or jack fish, red eyes and silver perch, mill pond and flat back suckers.

The Norfolk and Western Railway Magazine provides hints as to where anglers should throw their lines in Campbell waters, thus locating fish haunts in the Otter, Seneca and Falling rivers, (tributaries of the Staunton) in Buffalo, Flat, Opossum, Beaver, Bear, Goose, Molley's and Bishop creeks. This territory is not mountainous and is consequently deficient in the large cold springs necessary to the welfare of trout and small mouth bass. A few big mouth bass are found in James river but mostly New River cats, suckers and eels and abundance of carp. The Otter contains mud cats, red horse, perch, a few big mouth bass and eels. Falling river and its tributaries have red horse, suckers, mud cats and eels. Red horse fish from the Staunton run up into Otter river, its tributary, while mud cats suckers, perch, and carp remain in the larger stream.

Ferries and Toll Bridges

In 1778 John Ward, who had kept a boat for the free use of those crossing Staunton river from his land in Bedford to that in Pittsylvania, asked to be allowed to have a ferry there: in 1780 David Ross petitioned for a ferry from his land at the mouth of Archy's creek, on James river in Bedford, to the land of Robert Bolling in Amherst. John Lynch, who had operated a ferry, which was not used in 1782, asked for repeal of the act discontinuing it, across Fluvanna river from his Bedford to his Amherst land.

In 1790 Campbell and Pittyslvania residents petitioned for a ferry across the Staunton from John Connefax' land in Campbell to John Ward's in Pittsylvania.

There had been a ferry from Moses Fuqua's land in Campbell to Joseph Echols in Halifax, but it became abandoned, and Campbell, Halifax and Pittsylvania people requested in 1793 a new one started from Echol's land to John Hix' in Halifax: their petition not meeting with response they repeated it in 1797, explaining that Samuel Pannill then owned Fuqua's land, and they asked that Pannill be allowed to run the ferry at the same rates. A year later a petition was made for a ferry across the Staunton from Thomas East's in Pittsylvania to John Brown's in Campbell. In 1801 a petition was made for a ferry across the Staunton from John Brooks' in Campbell to the late Patrick Henry's land in Halifax at lower end of Seven Islands.

On December 22nd 1807 Edmund Tate petitioned for permission to erect a toll bridge across Blackwater creek on the road leading from the county line by Samuel Scott's place to Lynchburg.

Three years later John Lynch, Sr., petitioned to build a toll bridge across the river (James) to his land, he had been informed that another petition would be presented to Assembly with request to construct a bridge about 100 yards above his ferry and he asked that he receive justice in the case: no action being taken, a few days later fifty Lynchburgers sent in a petition stating that in their opinion John Lynch should be allowed a toll bridge. A second petition followed that of John Lynch from 600 Campbell citizens for a toll bridge across James river at Lynchburg and asked that commissioners be appointed to open books of subscription for that purpose.

In 1810 John Ward petitioned for permission to establish a toll bridge across Staunton river from his land in Campbell to that in Pittsylvania.

In 1817 a remonstrance was sent by the president and directors of the Lynchburg Toll Bridge Company against a petition of Amherst people and town of Lynchburg for a free bridge: this was followed by a petition from Amherst and Lynchburg for erection of a new bridge across James river from the land of Benjamin Schoolfield in Amherst to the land of George Cabell near Lynchburg.

In 1821 a remonstrance was sent by stockholders of Lynchburg Toll Bridge Company, against a petition of James C. Steptoe that he might take over the Lynchburg Toll Bridge.

In 1823 Lynchburg citizens petitioned for another toll bridge across the James river and completion of the road leading to it.

Two petitions were sent in 1831 for permission to build a toll bridge from Schoolfield's land in Amherst over James river to William Daniel's land on the opposite bank: this was followed by a remonstrance from the Lynchburg Toll Bridge Co. against that petition. Schoolfield made a second petition for a bridge near his ferry across James river.

In 1841 Samuel Pannill asked that the tax on his bridge across Staunton river for that year be refunded and the bridge be exempt from future tax: in 1844 he sent a similar petition.

In 1842 William J. Isbell asked to establish a ferry across the James from his Amherst land to opposite bank in Campbell.

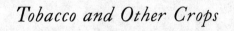

Tobacco and Other Crops

Chapter VI

King of field and trade

TOBACCO growing in the wilds of America, was first discovered by the Indians who taught white men the use of it, exchanging their tobacco for English brandy. One of the first objects to which the industry of the colonists was directed was the cultivation of tobacco. In 1619 Virginia imported into England 20,000 lbs. of the weed that being the entire crop of the previous year. The labor of the colony became almost exclusively devoted to the cultivation of tobacco. So popular an article was easily converted into a circulating medium; private debts, salaries and fees were paid in it. When money was introduced—the keeping of accounts in tobacco being inconvenient to foreign merchants—an act was passed "whereas it hath been the usual custom of merchants and others to make all contracts and to keep all accounts in tobacco, it shall be enacted that in future they shall be kept in money." Twice a year at a general meeting of merchants and factors at Williamsburg, they settled the price of tobacco.

Governor Spotwood was author of an act for improving the staple of tobacco and making tobacco notes the medium of ordinary circulation. These notes were made current within the county or adjacent county and were in use at the beginning of the 19th century. Salaries of county officials were paid in tobacco or notes representing it; thus a day's attendance at court called for payment of 25 lbs. of tobacco: the first payment made by Campbell court was 500 lbs. of tobacco to Richard Stith for running the dividing line between Bedford and Campbell. The towns of Lynchburg and Brookneal were started as warehouses: John Lynch had two houses; one near the ferry and the other across the river at Madison in Amherst; then he established a third called Spring warehouse in the new town.

The first inspectors at Lynch's ferry in 1786 were William Martin, Jonathan Rosser, Griffin Lewis and John Venable, and the amount of their salaries was regulated by law which occasioned many petitions being sent to Assembly for increase, as what they received was not sufficient for the support of their families: inspectors also were taxed, and they petitioned to have their tax of 6 shillings per hogshead lowered to 4 sh. 6 d. as they had to pay 1 sh. 6 d. for warehouse rent and those who shipped tobacco from below avoided rent expense. In 1793 inspectors and coopers at Lynch's Amherst and Spring warehouses, asked that as more nails and more care in coopering was required because of its longer journey, more money be allowed for nails and coopering. In 1796 William Martin and Achilles Douglass, inspectors at Spring Warehouse claimed that they handled more tobacco than any other warehouse in the state. 1797 John Lynch, proprietor of 3 public warehouses reported that the upkeep of the houses amounted to more than the rent he was allowed, as much damage was done to the warehouse by carelessness of persons there. Charles Johnson and Benjaman Arthur inspectors at Lynch's in 1798 asked more pay because of the increase in amount of tobacco passing through their hands and because prices of commodities had almost doubled. John Hubbard and William Snead were pickers at Spring warehouse in 1799; pickers, as well as inspectors, were appointed by the county court. The loss of 7 hogsheads of tobacco at Lynch's caused an appeal from inspectors there, urging that if they were forced to pay for the tobacco with the damage to other hogsheads, it would cause their complete ruin; that the warehouse had been without fence, gate, lock or key for a considerable time.

There was much rivalry in the building and use of warehouses: John Lynch made complaint that he went to the expense of building another warehouse because of the great crop that had been grown and that his houses suffered damage from carelessness of inspectors and boatmen in handling the tobacco, and he urged that they be made to keep the houses in repair. In 1801 a thousand petitioners requested additional in-

spection of tobacco; James Martin offered to build a warehouse on his land and reported in 1802 that by order of the
Assembly he built one of stone near Lynchburg and contracted
with Charles Curle to make tile for the roof, but Curle failed
of his contract and the house would remain uncovered unless
covered with shingles. This structure was the one in Lynchburg so long known and used as Martin's warehouse. In 1799
five hundred signers, in that neighborhood petitioned
for establishment of tobacco inspection on John Brooks' land
along Staunton river to be known as Brooks' Warehouse,
which was the beginning of the town that later developed into
Brookneal.

In 1805 George Cabell, owner of land on Blackwater creek
and James river conveniently situated for a warehouse,—
backed by the signatures of 250 of his neighbors—petitioned that
as there was great need for a warehouse near the town of
Lynchburg, one be built on his land. At this time George Mc-
Daniel and James Martin, inspectors at Martin's gave notice
that the new house was being built and when finished, would
greatly increase their labor. Samuel and Lodowick McDaniel
became inspectors at Blackwater Warehouse. In 1806 there
were seven places for tobacco inspections with petitions for
three others in the town. William Davis asked for erection of
a warehouse on his land. Jonathan Johnson, first inspector at
Spring warehouse, asking for increase in salary, suggested that
the increase be made by increasing duty on the tobacco that was
shipped. In 1817 Charles Williams of Lynchburg made application for a warehouse on his land and the appointment of
inspectors. Inspectors asked increase of salary sufficient to
pay for the trouble of the position and insure getting good
men for the positions. In 1820 William Johnson and Zack
Wade were inspectors at Friend's warehouse.

The first record found of the manufacture of tobacco in
Campbell was in 1804 when leave was given Charles Johnson
to stem and manufacture tobacco. In 1827 the stemmers and
manufacturers in Lynchburg asked for a change in bond and
oath required of them so as to enable them to ship refuse to-

bacco. That year Brookneal citizens petitioned for an act reviving inspection of tobacco in that town.

On February 18, 1832 a petition was addressed to the President and Common Council by the citizens of Lynchburg for the appointment of a weighmaster of tobacco: in 1835 the inspectors petitioned for a law making their salaries uniform and permanent, and payable out of the public treasury: two years later owners and proprietors of warehouses petitioned to have rates of storage restored to what they had been before May 1, 1823. A change in the laws for tobacco inspection was requested in 1837.

In 1839 Campbell, Bedford and Amherst citizens requested passage of a law forbidding the sale of loose and unprized tobacco which had not been carried to a warehouse inspected and weighed, with the quantity and owner's name entered on the books. In 1849 there was a repeal of the act requiring loose tobacco to be taken to warehouses and weighed: county residents remonstrated against any change in laws respecting inspection of loose tobacco, urging that if change be made, it might be to put the law into immediate effect.

The cultivation of tobacco, which had long engaged earlier communities, was continued as the principal dependence of Campbell landowners, and so it is found that more attention was given to that than any other crop. From clearing and seeding of plant bed, hilling of fields, drawing and resetting plants, fighting the tobacco worm, succoring, cutting and final stringing for storage in the curing houses this crop furnishes "daily dozen" labor for the grower.

Need of transportation introduced the custom of packing tobacco in hogsheads which were supplied with wooden pins in each head and to these adjusted a pair of rude shafts in the way of a garden roller, and thus drawn to market by horses: the process was called "tobacco rolling" and roads were made for their conveyance over them. Warehouses when first established were designated rolling houses because tobacco was rolled to them. The manner of opening hogsheads for inspection of their contents, gave rise to the term "tobacco breaks," which now is used to signify sales also.

In 1827 planters received warning that a petition would be presented to the Legislature asking that public inspectors be required to break the hogsheads in four different parts in order to detect the many impositions practiced in prizing, and that certain warehouses where such frauds were connived at and where inspectors refused to break tobacco in such places as they were desired to do by the purchasers, might be suppressed.

Tobacco sales or "breaks" took place in the sheds of the warehouses; each lot as it was removed from wagon to the building, being weighed and given floor space and bore a ticket giving its weight and the name of the owner. When the auctioneer, who "cried" the sales, appeared and buyers came, then a signal blast, from a long horn, notified the public that breaks were ready to start and the crier rapidly proceeded to "knock down" invoices of leaf tobacco which was openly exposed to inspection.

The manufacture of tobacco was for many years the chief industry of Lynchburg hence it became known as "tobacco town." Fortunes were made through investment in it and trough speculation, also lost in it. Samuel Miller was the most successful investor. But the outstanding figure in local tobacco industry was John W. Carroll, whose first appearance in the community was as a cabinet maker in 1849 with the firm of Folkes and Winston. Later he engaged in the manufacture of tobacco and in 1859 started his "Brown Dick" and "Lone Jack" brands of smoking tobacco, by which he amassed a fortune and which have become world known and used.

Carroll was president of the Lynchburg Council for a long time and was connected with leading commercial enterprises. He owned a country place along the lowlands of Candler's Mountain named *Lone Jack Farm* where fine cattle were raised: recently this property was divided into parcels and sold.

Two towns, one in Ohio and another in Texas, received the name of Lynchburg through the extension of tobacco business into those communities; but manufacture of tobacco in Lynchburg has greatly decreased and become superseded by various other industries. During the war of '61-65 warehouses were turned into hospitals for the reception of wounded and sick soldiers; these were Christian's, Knight's, Ferguson's, Ford's, Saunders', Candler's, Langhorne's, Wade's, Claytor's, Miller's, Crumpton's, Booker's (formerly Jesse Hare's), Burton's, Taliaferro's, Planter's Warehouse, and Massie's factories; Lynchburg became the base hospital center.

On the premises of the Bowling Clark home there is an unusual brick building, so far not discovered on any other private property, which was erected for the purpose of storing wood ashes and in size is smaller than the necessary smoke house (for curing meat) which has always formed part of a country gentleman's establishment. The custom of using ashes in the preparation of land for crops was not unusual but Jefferson was the first in the section to suggest a method by which best results could be secured. The manufacture of potash was one of the earliest chemical industries, the London Company having sent eight Poles and Germans to the Virginia colony in 1608 to make soap ashes, pitch and tar; and the shipment of wood ashes to England was begun immediately in a small way. Wood was cut down and burnt upon the ground, then the ash was boiled with water to yield lye, which evaporated, left salt and that calcined became potash; this last was packed in barrels and exported. Potash being a commodity universally used, it was not easy to overstock the market but excessive duty and lack of transportation facilities prevented too great manufacture. In 1751 Parliament remitted duties on potash, then five years later Thomas Stephens came to America and started an abandoned factory on the Rappahannock. Increased consumption of potash for bleaching, calico printing and soap making—as well as award of medals for success in production—made the manufacture one of the most flourishing industries preceding the Revolution. But the process was crude and wasteful and many who engaged on too lavish a scale, suffered losses. The trees giving best results were hickory, oak, beech, birch, elm, walnut, chestnut and maple: crude potash was treated to get pearl ash. Agricultural development through the enormous waste in the manufacture, suffered in loss of soil fertility and the forced abandonment of many farms. There are no traces of this manufacture in Campbell for other than private use on farm land. Though export suffered a check during the Revolution, it was afterward resumed with vigor owing to the encouragement of bounties. The profits to be derived from the enterprise aroused Jefferson's interest, and he addressed a letter to Judge Archibald Stuart in which he urged the manufacture and use of potash, as he was persuaded the contemplation of the subject would end in Stuart's adopting the business and be the means of introducing it among the Virginia people.

He formulated the notes on pot and pearl-ash for guidance in their manufacture as follows:—

"A Man will cut and burn $2\frac{1}{2}$ cords of wood a day.

A cord of wood yields 2 bushels of ashes (neither pine nor chestnut will do).

A bushel of ashes sells for 9 cents.

It will make 6 lbs. of brown salts, which makes 3 to 5 pounds pearl-ash in a common way and 5 lbs. of pearl-ash in Hopkin's way.

For a small work, 2 kettles suffice to boil the lie into brown salts and 1 to melt up the brown salts.

$\frac{1}{4}$ cord of wood a day maintains one fire, which will do for 5 kettles.

To keep 3 kettles agoing will require the attendance of a man and a boy.

There should be 15 or 16 tubs of 100 bushels each.

3 kettles will turn out 1000 lbs. of pearl-ash a week.

Consequently will require 100 cords of wood a week and 7 cutters to keep them constantly at work.

Each kettle costs 24 doll.

Potash is worth in England ———— the ton, and in America $114\frac{2}{3}$ D.

Pearl-ash is worth in England £40 sterling and in America £40. lawful.

An estimate of the profit and expense of such a work at 3 lbs. pearl-ash to the bushel of ashes, which is 100 lbs. pearl-ash a day, and counting 5 days to the week, which would give only 500 lbs. of pearl-ash a week, instead of 1000 lbs. the common calculations, results;—

500 lbs. pearl-ash a week is 13 tons a year @£40.
    Virginia currency £520.00
To this added;

	£ s d
7 cutter's hire @£12. a year, add maintenance and clothing	128.16-0
A manager for his hire and provision	50.00-0
A boy	10.00-0
Implements annually	10.00-0
A wagon, team and driver, all expenses included	111.15-0
	310.11-0
Clear profit in cash	209.09-0
	520.00-0

At 4 lbs. pearl-ash to the bushel (a very moderate calculation) it would add 5 tons a year, worth £200; at 5lbs. to the bushel £400.

Add to this the clearing 150 acres of land a year, whatever it is worth."

"Note. I was told that ashes burnt in the open field cannot be made into pearl-ash in the common way. This, if certain, is a very important circumstance in Virginia."

Campbell county has an active Agricultural Advisory Council of its farmers, among whom are E. C. Dunkard, J. C. Gilliam, C. L. Hutcherson, W. B. Moyer, C. B. Feagans, J. E. Protheroe, W. L. Wineberger, T. C. Asher, H. C. Winston, J. L. Brooks, S. C. Goggin, W. E. Mason, E. A. Hicks,

Henry Lane, J. J. Fray, A. M. Harmon, N. Wooding, E. G. Peerman, and Harry Farmer. The officers elected at a meeting held December 8, 1926 were G. W. Griffin, president; C. B. Feagans, vice-president; Bruce Anderson, (county farm agent) secretary.

The council urged the production of pure certified seed; that each farmer have a good home garden; enough food for home use, and feed for all live stock. It recommended reduction of acreage for dark tobacco, and a better grade on smaller acreage, and that each dark tobacco grower produce one ton of soy beans or cow peas for each horse or cow on his farm. That in addition to bright tobacco as a money crop, each farmer have a second money crop such as Laredo soy beans for seed; that bright tobacco acreage be curtailed and some other paying crop be substituted.

After a survey made to locate better sires for breeding, the report given was 93 pure bred and grade dairy sires, 41 pure bred and grade beef sires, 53 pure bred and grade hog sires, 19 pure bred and grade sheep sires, 62 scrub sires, including cattle, hogs and sheep.

The recommendation was made that grades and scrubs be replaced with pure breds during the year; and that each farmer fence in land to pasture live stock on the cheaper soils. The council urged a renewal of pure bred sire campaign and organizing of a cow-testing association.

As the pig market production shows a 25 per cent increase farmers were advised that it is unwise to increase the number of brood sows and recommended only pork production for home use, with a small amount for sale, and that pure bred sires be used.

A curb market has become established in Lynchburg for farm-garden, poultry and dairy produce, which serves well the farmer and housekeeper, especially in the open season of growing crops. This market is a spectacular sight in its display of fruits and vegetables spread upon impromptu stands and is of the nature of foreign (open) produce markets, though in the instance of this curb market it is housed in a large tobacco warehouse with accessory market wagons and machine trucks: often there is observed a side market of second hand clothing, which also is a reflection of foreign street sales, and adds to the picturesqueness of a constantly changing scene: but this is a species of town enterprise reversing salesman and purchaser; town providing articles for sale and catering to a very limited purse of the smaller country producers, generally of the colored race.

Situated in the south-central part of Virginia, Campbell county has an area of 557 square miles lying entirely within the Piedmont Region. Its natural features are those of a high and rolling plateau, deeply cut by many large and small streams, forming a network of rivers and rivulets which irrigate while draining all sections of the county. From a rolling plateau it rises in its northern and western portions to high hills and ridges, notably, near its center, in two disconnected ranges—Candler's and Long Mountains—each about six miles in length with elevation of 1400 feet, the highest in the county, the average height being from 850 to 900 feet: Candler's Mountain is broken at its top by nine, nearly uniform, and picturesque knobs.

Campbell's climatic conditions,—moderately cold in winter and, from mountain proximity, usually pleasant in summer,—are favorable for cattle and other stock, providing a season of about nine months for grazing and this prerequisite has induced many farmers in the county to engage in cattle and hog raising of finest breeds.

An average uniformity prevails in its soil conditions—gray to reddish surface soils, underlaid by stiff red clay subsoils: twelve types being found which vary from heavy clay to light sandy loam. The most extensive of its predominant soil types, sandy loam, clay loam and clay occur in its northern, western and southwestern portions, and are known as *red land,* one of the best soils for general purposes: deep fall plowing is very important, and failure to observe this requirement as well as inadequate fertilization, occasions shortage in crop yield.

The principal crop of the past has been tobacco varied by lesser sowings of wheat, corn, oats and clover, but effort is being made to discourage a monoply in tobacco and increase in grain crops. Cultivation of fruits is also encouraged, with decided success in the matter of apples and grapes and, for summer season, melons: in potato cultivation the county has never aimed at an outside market.

The original fine forests have been greatly depleted of timber in the preparation of land for farming purposes; in 1910 report was made that 36 per cent of land area was cleared and farmed: the forests consist of hard wood and soft wood or evergreen trees, the latter being abundant in short leaf and spruce pines: commonest hardwoods are oaks, yellow poplar, red maple, hickory and locust: in the mountainous section there is yet much cedar growth, but its doom seems to be ultimate extermination in the interest of fruit cultivation.

The principal minerals found in Campbell are manganese, barite, granite, gneiss, iron, soapstone, limestone, diabase and sandstone. Near Mt. Athos, Evington, Lynch's, and east and south of Lynchburg, are large deposits of managnese which were worked for many years; the principal mines are the Piedmont Manganese mine formerly known as the Lerner mine, Leet's mine near Mt. Athos, the Saunders mine near Evington and the Bishop mine near Lynch.

Barite appears in a belt of deposits starting near Evington and running south into Pittsylvania for a distance of about 30 miles. A barite mine a few miles from Evington, is one of a few mines at present worked in the county.

The Southern Railroad, near the barite belt for its entire length, gives facilities for its transportation.

The soapstone belt extends through the Piedmont section of Virginia; crosses James river above Lynchburg and runs west of the city.

Gneiss deposit near Diamond Hill Presbyterian church several miles from Rustburg, caused that church to be given its name, the glistening mineral suggesting diamond brilliance. A few miles west of Concord remains the site of the "Old Gold Mine."

On Moon's mountain, near Leesville, there is a quarry of white stone in slab formation, which was popularly used about dwellings for outer steps and paving.

Iron mines were worked before the Revolution. The Oxford Iron Mine was owned and operated by Colonel James Callaway and during the Revolution, his son-in-law, Harry Innes, was superintendent there during its operation for supplying the patriot armies with materials of war: these were the first iron works above Lynchburg.

In October 1793 a petition was made to the Virginia Assembly for a ferry across Staunton river to and from Ross' iron works. Presumably these were the same as the Oxford Iron Mines which David Ross acquired in 1787 when he secured two tracts of land, 260 acres on the west branches of Beaver Creek, and 400 acres on the south side of James river, both sides of Opossum, Archer's, Joshua, and Stonewall creeks; this property embraced the old Oxford Iron Mines, which then became known as Ross' Mines. Formerly Ross had been a partner with John Hook in merchandise business and they together patented 565 acres on both sides of Little Mill creek of Falling river, both sides of the main road between Falling and Little Falling river. When Hook's suit against Venable was terminated, the former moved from the county and the partnership with Ross was dissolved. Ross seems then to have entered into more extensive business operations, and in 1785 is found one of the directors of the James River company of which Washington was elected president.

Ross' Iron Mine was on top of an elevation two miles south of Six Mile Bridge, the furnace, a few hundred yards from the mine was built during Callaway's ownership. In 1781 Jefferson reported it was making 1600 tons of pig iron annually.

Iron ore was shipped from Lawyers about fifty years ago.

In the construction of wall and walkways around his premises Samuel Pannill freely used red sand stone which was found in his vicinity, and across the river in Pittsylvania county, in large quantity.

It is said that when a site for the town of Lynchburg was

under consideration the proposal to locate it at the point which became in 1793 Ross' ferry, was opposed by him as interfering with the operation of the iron mines; these he secured by purchase, a year afterwards, about the time that Colonel Callaway changed his citizenship back to Bedford county.

Igloe Dairy

Dairies

Ferdinand Hutter, son of Maj. Geo. Hutter, owned an estate which joined the Sandusky property, home of his brother Risque. He gave this place the name *Igloe,* which was suggested by a friend who had travelled to Alaska and brought back this word signifying *Little Hut,* used by the Indians there to indicate their abodes, and implies that the original house was small; the building replacing it is a handsome brick structure. This property was acquired by A. P. Craddock, Sr., who after some years' ownership sold it to Charles B. Segar now of New York (formerly of Louisiana) its present owner.

Here in 1922 Segar established the Igloe Dairy, operated by Edward Vosberg, manager, and stocked with a herd of a hundred Guernsey cattle. The dairy is situated about a half mile from Salem turnpike, opposite the Quaker Memorial church. In addition to the dairy department there has been more recently introduced poultry raising, with at present a flock of two thousand white Leghorn fowls. The enterprise is completely equipped for its manipulation, and from the near highway furnishes an attractive picture in its freshly white coated dairy and poultry houses with beautiful brown and white cows pasturing in front or chewing their cud, while resting on the green sod. Adjoining this dairy farm is Chestnut Hill farm belonging to A. P. Craddock of Lynchburg which is stocked with finest breed of Duroc Jersey hogs.

Beyond the old Quaker church and its rock-walled burying ground—where the N. & W. (branch line) R. R. cuts a passage through the fields, causing construction of two bridges to span the gaps it has made,—there lies property once embraced in the large estate of Charles Henry Lynch, son of Charles Lynch (2nd of the name). This farm Lynch sold to Alexander Spotswood Grigsby, a prominent politician and orator of his day. Grigsby married Caroline Garrard of Kentucky and had a family of six sons, all of whom served in the Confederate army, and several daughters: his son Clay Grigsby was a teacher in the Lynchburg public schools, but later moved to Texas. Afterwards the Grigsby property was sold and passed through the hands of several owners; a dairy, known as Edgewood Dairy was conducted there, first by R. D. Martin, of Lynchburg; since whose death it has passed into the hands of a company at the head of which is B. E. Hughes of Lynchburg.

Other dairies supplying Lynchburg market with their products are:

J. P. Adkins	W. D. Holland	Norfolk Ave. Dairy
D. O. Apperson	Ferd. Hutter	Oak Grove Dairy
E. H. Brockenbrough	Ivey Creek Dairy	C. A. Padgett
T. C. Coleman	J. R. Jackson	J. W. Phelps
C. W. Falwell	Wm. King, Jr.	Rivermont Dairy
Fort Hill Dairy	Leaward Dairy	Sanitary Dairy
Hill Crest Dairy	Lone Jack Dairy	Service Dairy

Transportation and Education

Chapter VII

Stage and Boat

URING the period of Campbell's establishment, transportation was a serious problem either by land or water on account of the conditions of the road and streams, these being full or rocks and holes. Alexander Patterson was the first person to venture running stages between Lynchburg and Richmond. At the time he started his line of *leathern conveniences,* the road between the two towns was almost impassable, and he only undertook to ply forth in once-a-week trips. The coaches were little better than wagons, and the passengers clambered into them by the way of the driver's seat at the front. When they acquired side-doors they became more convenient and were considered very luxurious. They began then to make two trips weekly, finally tri-weekly trips, and when these started they were regarded as the greatest progress at which public convenience could arrive. Notable stopping places along the route were Upper Patterson's, Lower Patterson's, French's, Raines' Tavern, etc.

There was another stage line called the "Piedmont Stage Route," which during the first half of the nineteenth century ran between Washington and Danville, also to Salem, intersecting at the latter point with the valley line. Its course, Tuesdays, Thursdays and Saturdays, was through Fairfax, Prince William, Fauquier, Culpeper, Madison, Orange, Albemarle, Neison, Amherst to Lynchburg,—thence through Campbell and Pittsylvania to Danville: time to the latter town, distant 268 miles—three and a half days—fare $18.00. From Washington to Salem distance 253 miles, the same length of time, fare $17.25. From Lynchburg a line also ran to the Virginia Watering places (as Springs were then called) travel to which was made altogether in the day time, distance of 103 miles, fare $8.50 and from 6 to 9 hours was allowed for sleep each night.   William Flint was the agent for these stage lines.

When the canal and later railroad came into operation, stage travel gradually lessened and wayside stopping places lost their prestige.   For a while packet boat and stage lines issued combined passes from Lynchburg to Staunton; these tickets notified the bearer that they must be handed to the captain.   To-day tradition alone recalls this leisurely and sociable mode of travel, which gave ample opportunity for enjoyment of the picturesque scenery along the route; its lack of speed in transportation never entered into consideration.

Roads were under the government of the county court which ordered new roads to be opened wherever they thought them necessary.   The county was laid off into precincts to each of which was allotted a portion of public road to be kept in repair and bridges to be built, else the court employed workmen to build at the expense of the county, or, if that was too expensive for the county, then application was made to the General Assembly which in turn authorized individuals to do the construction and take a fixed toll from all passengers: hence arose toll-gate system.

Ferries were permitted only at such places as were pointed out by law and rates of ferriage were fixed by same method. Certain ferries had long been established in Bedford and as demand became peremtory others were permitted in Campbell.

In December 1811, Campbell, Bedford, Botetourt, Greenbrier and others petitioned for the establishment of the Great Western Turnpike road from Hunter's on main Richmond road through Lynchburg to Lewisburg.

December 1825 sundry Lynchburgers asked for a turnpike road from the lower gate of Lynchburg and Salem road, running in at the upper end of the town.   The same month William Davis, president, and Directors of the Lynchburg and Salem Turnpike Company, asked for improvement of Ward's ferry road which intersected with Salem pike.   A year later John Early and the Commissioners (under an act authorizing an extension of Lynchburg and Salem pike to Cocke or West street) asked to have their body perpetuated and that the land, on which the road was laid off, be vested in them authorizing additional subscriptions to repair and preserve the road. Next year the Commissioners of this branch of the road asked that Hustings Court be allowed to allot hands on the road in order to keep it in repair.

December 1828 Campbell, Buckingham, Charlotte and Prince Edward asked the incorporation of a company to construct several new roads.

February 1830 Stockholders of Lynchburg and Concord Turnpike Company applied for amendments to their charter.

January 1831 Lynchburg and Salem turnpike asked to be released from constructing the road further than already made: February 1833 this company requested the incorporation of an incorporating company to construct an extension road to Salem.

February 1834 Lynchburg and Blue Ridge Pike Company asked for increase in their capital stock. December of that year Lynchburg and Salem Pike Co. asked permission to appropriate entire tolls of the company to complete the pike and reduce width of road.

January 1836 Campbell citizens requested the incorporation of a company known as Lynchburg and Campbell C. H. Pike, for the purpose of building a pike between the two places.

February 1836 Lynchburg and Pittsylvania Co. asked that the Commonwealth subscribe to their stock.

December 1841 Lynchburg asked for the construction by the state of a macadamized road from the Tennessee line to the most eligible point on James river.

December 1845 citizens of Lynchburg and Campbell C. H. asked for increase in capital stock and permission to make changes in the road.

February 1847 the President and Directors of Lynchburg and Buffalo Springs Turnpike Company requested payment for loss incurred in the sale of state scrip.

December 1850 petition for a macadamized road from Lynchburg in the direction of Amherst C. H.

January 1852 petition from Lynchburg and Pittsylvania Company, concerning joint road.

December 1855 damages demanded by Lynchburg and Salem Turnpike Company.

Travel through the country in early times was commonly by horseback, gig or chair (a term used to signify a carriage of that period) for people and batteaux for produce and merchandise. Country merchants were supplied with their wares by means of a chain of wagon-trains, and there was the unique mode of rolling tobacco, to the various ware-houses, in hogsheads.

The eminent need for travel facilities gave the impulse which produced a system of canals, James River and Kanawha Canal in Virginia being the second one projected. Governor Spotswood conceived this undertaking, having in view a connection of the coast with the west by a canal from the James to the Kanawha river. Following Spotswood's suggestion, General Washington introduced a bill, which successfully went through Virginia Legislature, authorizing the construction of the canal, and he was made president of the company in 1785. Directors were John Harris, David Ross, William Cabell and Edmund Randolph.

The Legislature passed an act extending the navigation of James river from the land of Nicolas Davies in Bedford county to the mouth of Cow Pasture, a measure it was considered would be of general utility. The shares of the James River Company were $2.00 each.

Subscriptions were started for financing the enterprise and were made in milled (Spanish) dollars or other silver or gold coin of like value. One hundred shares of the stock were vested in George Washington; this was the stock which he later donated to Liberty Hall Academy.

The Act of 1783 seems to indicate that James river was open for use eastward from Lynchburg, yet in October 1787 Campbell residents appealed to Legislature in the interest of better transportation there, reciting that as the Appomattox headed up adjoining the county, this would afford within a few miles, navigation for transporting produce to market if cleared of obstructions which then hindered the use of it and by the removal of rocks, would be sufficient for passage of batteaux or canoes for a course of eighty or ninety miles above Petersburg, which was prevented by mill dams constructed without locks or slopes. The exhausted state of the soil, taxes, and the impoverished condition of the country, showed the necessity for advantages, particularly inland navigation, in order to increase resources and encourage industry. The petition drew attention to the fact that here was a fine navigable river shut up for the emolument of a few, thus sacrificing a good part of the commonwealth. Dams and obstructions should not be allowed to remain under any promise made to correct locks or other evasions.

The time was ripe and the community ready to take hold of the canal project, then zealously advocated by the *Press,* a Lynchburg paper, which urged the incorporation of the new company and active participation in measures for its promotion.

Towards the close of the 18th century the canal was finished sufficiently around the lower rapids of the James for boats to load and unload at Richmond. By 1816 a sluice navigation was opened for batteaux, which, however, were soon found to be insufficient for the growing commerce of Lynchburg and other settlements along the river. Opposition to further construction of the canal developed from sectional politics, and was the beginning of continued wrangling which made the fortune of the project uncertain; yet did not altogether halt progress in construction, and boatmen were making use of the waterway, for we find David Staples on February 3rd, 1830, petitioning for permission to run a packet boat between Lynchburg and Richmond.

In 1832 a new James River and Kanawha Company, a private stock corporation, was chartered, but work on the canal was not started till 1836, and after the expiration of two years it was seen that the original capital of five million dollars was insufficient for carrying on the proposed undertaking, because a large part of this fund consisted of stock of the old James River Company.

Officers and agents of the new company were: President, Joseph C. Cabell; J. H. Cocke, Randolph Harrison, Richard Simpson, Sidney S. Baxter, Chapman Johnson, Hugh Caperton, (Bishop) John Early, Bernard Peyton, Samuel Marx, Corbin Warwick, John R. Triplett, Charles Ellis, John Brockenbrough, Thomas M. Bondurant, John A. Lancaster, Smithson H. Lewis, Samuel McCorkle, Allen T. Caperton, John H. Harvey, William H. Chittenden, Edward H. Gill, Ezra Walker, Richard Reins, James P. Tyler.

President Cabell urged the General Assembly to subscribe for three-fifths of the six additional million dollars needed, in stock, but instead of acceding to this proposition, the company was forced to borrow funds from the state on which interest had to be paid, thus diminishing the company's income. Through legislative enactments, other restrictions came to handicap progress on the canal. Increased difficulties arose when some of the Lynchburgers proposed that the canal be completed only as far as Lynchburg. This suggestion precipitated a fight, but in the end the proposition was turned down, and a resolution was passed for the construction of a thorough water route.

In 1840 the canal was completed from Richmond to Lynchburg and its swarm of packet and freight boats began to ply between the two points. Construction proceeding slowly, the canal reached Buchanan in 1851. There was a splendid scheme of making a long tunnel through the mountains to connect the rivers, but lack of money caused postponement of this undertaking. The State continued its policy of forcing the company to extend its improvements upon bonds instead of new capital stock, and interest charges grew larger every year. Hence there was furnished good cause for opposition to an enterprise which threatened loss to investors and failure of its completion.

Among the aggressive opponents to the canal's construction was one Milton J. Jones, editor of the *Salem Register,* who,

(after the boats began to run up James river) wrote a prophetic
poem, emphasizing the opinion he had expressed in his editorial columns, a prophecy he lived to see verified in 1880:

> As, vain man, thy sight is short
> Thy wit is often dearly bought.
> For millions have been spent for naught
> Beside that same old river.
> Soon will your ditches fill with mud,
> Your dams give way before the flood,
> And all your dreams of coming good
> Lie prostrate by that river.
>
> The boat horn's soft and mellow note
> That through the neighboring valleys float
> Will at a time not far remote
> Be hushed beside that river.
> And in its stead, the engine's scream
> Will startle babes along that stream
> And break the spell of folly's dream,
> Forever and forever.

The borrowing policy inaugurated by the state, proved dis-
astrous to the enterprise. Then charges of malfeasance were
brought against the officers, in answer to which President
Cabell wrote "The Defense of the James River and Kanawha
Canal," defending in detail the objections which had been
brought forward.

By 1850, from the extension of the canal fifty miles beyond Lynchburg, increased receipts from tolls and freight
charges began to encourage the promoters, but interest charges
also increased, and the company was still dependent upon bonds
for improvements. Realizing at last that unless the company
was aided in a better manner than before, all the money which
had been spent would be lost, the Assembly agreed to exchange all of the bonds owned for new capital stock. In 1861
a proposal was received from a French firm of contractors to

take over the enterprise and pay the state a perpetual annuity of $135,000. A new company was organized as "The Virginia Canal Company" with a capital of $35,000,000 to complete the water route to the Mississippi, but the scheme was delayed by the war of 1861-65, and afterwards Virginia was unable to consider a second offer from the French contractors. The Underwood constitution of 1868 prohibited the state from taking any part in internal improvements.

Two floods in James river during the '70s damaged the canal to such an extent that the corporation was induced to sell it in 1886 to the Richmond and Alleghany Railroad Company, a transaction which did not meet with the general approval of those who were not financially interested. A few long-period mill leases left stretches of the canal undisturbed in its narrow channel and bordering tow-path, but not again was heard the packet horn in announcement of approaching boat. As no disposition could be made of old packets and barges they fell slowly into decay along the abandoned bed; yet for a long time much sentiment centered on the old packet *Marshall,* which had conveyed General Thomas Jackson's remains to Lynchburg, and which in its later years afforded shelter to an aged couple. The canal was in operation for thirty years, but the cost of repairs was so heavy it was never able to pay dividends, yet it had well served the purpose of transportation before railways were introduced.

Railroads

The first effort made to obtain a railroad in the county was through a petition sent December 15th, 1830, by citizens of Lynchburg and its vicinity asking the passage of an act to incorporate a company for construction of a road from Lynchburg to New River. Permission being received, the company started upon the work and on February 3rd, 1832, Henry Davis, president, and the directors, sent a second petition asking that the state subscribe to the company's stock.

On December 9th, 1835, Campbell and Bedford citizens petitioned for the formation of a company for construction of a railroad from Lynchburg to the Tennessee line, to connect with the road from New Orleans, and to run from Lynchburg to Richmond or allow the James River and Kanawha Company to do this. On January 10, 1839, the request was made that the state take over the road's construction to Tennessee line as all private enterprises had failed and there was great need of the road.

December 25th, 1849, Lynchburg contributed $500,000 to the capital stock of the Virginia and Tennessee R. R. Co., partly by direct subscription and partly by a guarantee of 6% dividends on the stock to be taken by others. January 2nd, 1850, the president and directors of the company asked for confirmation of the Council's action granting right of the use of a street and alleys in Lynchburg and permission to hold four acres purchased by the town as site for a depot. On February 18, 1852, the first locomotive, the *Virginia,* of this road, made its appearance, and created a sensation, for few of the citizens had ever seen one. The cars were made at the Piedmont Works by Frank B. Deane, Jr. An excursion was run as far as Forest depot and on April 1st the road was opened as far as the town of Liberty (now Bedford City.) The main road of this line runs through Campbell from Clay's Crossing to Concord on the county's border.

About the middle of the year 1854 Lynchburg became interested in the proposition for securing a second railroad and 53 citizens were appointed to canvass for subscriptions. The aim was to extend what was then known as the Orange and Alexandria railroad to Lynchburg. The effort to obtain $100,000 was not successful but private citizens took stock, and Blackwater Warehouse was secured for a depot.

January 14th, 1860, the new road was completed to the Amherst side.

At this time the Lynchburg Locomotive and Machine company and the Lynchburg and Richmond Railroad Company were incorporated.

The first train on the Southside road reached the island depot on November 2nd but was not allowed to connect with the Virginia and Tennessee road. Passengers were conveyed from the depot of the latter road to the Orange and Alexandria terminus in omnibuses.

In 1866 a plan was started to consolidate the Virginia and Tennessee and the Southside railroads, which after much opposition was carried into effect in June, 1870.

Lynchburg having subscribed $60,000 to the Lynchburg and Danville road, was asked in 1871 to raise the amount to $200,000 and this was done through an election. In 1873 the Orange and Alexandria, and Lynchburg and Danville roads were consolidated into the Washington City, Virginia Midland and Great Southern Railroad, but since then the name has been abbreviated into the Southern Railroad; with Campbell stations at Lynchburg, Durmid, Montview, Lawyers, Evington, Otter River, Clarion (former Lynch), and Alta Vista.

Several petitions for new railroads never materialized. February 25, 1853, construction of a road in the direction of Leesville towards Leaksville, North Carolina, and for one from Lynchburg to the North Carolina line in direction of Smith's river, the latter petition was repeated January 9th, 1856, by Campbell and Pittsylvania citizens.

The eastern section of James river and Kanawha canal had been operated profitably and with Federal aid for its improvement it was thought that the original design of slack water navigation for James river could have been readily carried out as far towards its head waters as Lynchburg, with much assistance to the valley of the James. But despite many protests the property and franchises of the James River and Kanawha Canal Company were sold to a company, composed largely of non-residents, bearing the name "Richmond and Alleghany Railroad Company," in 1879, and on April 1st that road was begun at Richmond, and was completed and formally opened for public service on October 15th, 1881, Campbell stations being Lynchburg and Tyreeanna. The road now goes by the name of James River Division of the Chesapeake and Ohio Railroad.

In 1886 a new railroad company was organized as the Lynchburg, Halifax and North Carolina Railroad Company, with Major Peter Otey of Lynchburg as president. Two months later a special election was held to determine by vote of the people, the question of subscribing $200,000 to its capital stock, a test which resulted in a victory for the road by a large majority. The building of the new road caused a quickening of trade and many advantages accrued from the opening of an avenue which had been closed for lack of transportation. But it was not long operated by the original company. In 1893 Lynchburg and Durham Railroad was leased to the Norfolk and Western R. R. Company and merged into the latter, it became a branch line with county stations at Lynchburg, Bocock, Lone Jack, Rustburg, Winfall, Gladys, Naruna and Brookneal.

The next railroad constructed through Campbell was the Virginian, connecting tidewater section more directly with the western part of the state. Following the course of Staunton river, it passes through the two larger towns of Alta Vista and Brookneal, intervening stations being Melrose, Long Island, Seneca, Tabor, Perrows, Mansion and Leesville.

Now that the automobile has come into general use, the question by that mode of travel is determined by the condition of the roads, and the latter receive the attention necessary to bring neighbors into closer intercourse, and to attract those living at greater distance. Thus progress follows good roads and the farmer reaps benefit in accessibility of market for his produce. Captain J. D. Fauntleroy, federal representative, has supervision of construction work on highways in Virginia where federal aid is involved, and he has made a check of the distance of all state highways, where such enter or leave Lynchburg. He has also made a survey for a new approach to the city from Amherst county across Williams Viaduct spanning James river, a contemplated improvement upon the present steep grading.

The highway commission has announced the allocation for the Lynchburg area, a district which embraces:

Route 10.   Appomattox—east.

Route 10.   Farmville—east.

Route 12.   Jones store, Halifax county.

Route 12.   End concrete, Henry county line.

Route 14.   Alta Vista—north.

Route 14.   Overhead crossing Southern R. R., 3 miles out of Lynchburg.

Route 14.   Sycamore—Hurt.

Route 18.   Volens—Halifax.

Route 18-28.   Albemarle county line.

Route 20.   Bethel church—Phoenix.

The surfacing of macadam bitumen on the north side of Locke's Mountain is discontinued for the present on account of cold weather. Putting up guard rails, painting them, widening dirt shoulders, and other tidying-up processes are being done on state highway routes which reach or leave Lynchburg.

.   .   .   .   .   .

A College Proposal

When it became known that Washington intended to donate his stock in the James River Canal Company to the cause of education at such place as the Legislature should recommend, then, on January 29, 1796, the people of Lynchburg convened at Mason's Hall in that town, to formulate a petition to Washington recommending the selection of a site for the proposed seminary in Lynchburg. Inducements offered were— that it was the most suitable place in the upper part of Virginia, from its situation on the south side of James river and nearly central in the state, having more constant intercourse with the western country than any other place. That because of its commercial importance, being near the head of James river navigation, it thus prevented the possibility of competition, and this made it the emporium of merchandise suited to the demand of the western part of the state—produce which passed through that channel for exportation; also because Lynchburg was the chief center of information and of intelligence in the upper part of the state.

Further pleas of advantages were that Congress had established a mail route from Richmond westward, and also a cross post from Fredericksburg by Charlottesville on through that section; that a weekly newspaper had been in circulation through the back country for four years; and that the only educational institutions above Richmond were those at Staunton and Winchester.

In event of favorable response to Lynchburg's appeal, John Lynch, "proprietor of an extensive estate in the town," proposed to convey to the trustees of the seminary 420 acres of land in the neighborhood, about a mile from the river and convenient to excellent springs. There had been prospectively raised 2256⅔ dollars, and considerably more had been promised conditionally upon favorable response to the town's proposal. A material consideration advanced was the fact that from the trade of the town arose a large part of the funds of James River Canal Company, through the assessment for the school tax, from traffic carried on by the inhabitants. Incorporation of the town would speedily follow acceptance; but whatever decision Washington made would be cheerfully acquiesced in as impartial and indicative of the purity of his intention.

The petition bore the signatures of John Lynch, chairman, and William Norvell, secretary. The interest and anticipation in the outcome of this proposal—which had been dictated by its desirability—throughout the small scattered community, may easily be imagined, as well as the subsequent disappointment, for the appeal was charged with apparently incontrovertible arguments in its favor.

Provision for Education

The aim to diffuse knowledge generally through the mass of the people caused a revision of the early laws affecting education.

Jefferson formulated a plan to lay off every county into small districts of five or six miles square, called hundreds, and in each of them to establish a school for teaching reading, writing and arithmetic. The teacher was to be supported by the hundred and every person in it was entitled to send their children three years gratis, or, by paying for it, as much longer as they pleased. The school of the hundreds was to be the first stage of education where the masses would secure educational opportunities; those whom the wealth of parents destined to higher degrees of learning might go on to a second stage—the grammar school—the University constituting the last stage. At that period the College of William and Mary was the only public seminary of learning in the state. For advancement of education the state provided a literary fund from which the counties received financial aid to a limited extent.

The first effort made in the locality to establish a school was when in November, 1794, townspeople of New London and its vicinity petitioned that they might be allowed to raise $10,000 by lottery for a proposed academy in their neighborhood. From its incipiency, an ambitious plan for its extension was entertained. Virginia Assembly encouraged the movement by appointing in 1795 a self-perpetuating board of trustees, to whom was granted a charter for the founding of an academy near New London. The next year these thirteen trustees were granted authority to raise by lottery the requested amount to defray the expenses of erecting a building and to enable them to establish a permanent fund for support of the school. Whether they were not entirely successful in raising the money, or the estimate of cost fell short of requirement, insufficiency of funds caused James Callaway, clerk of the institution—representing the trustees in 1798—to apply to the

Assembly for assistance in erecting the necessary buildings. The small buildings then constructed were put into immediate service.

In July, 1831, Harrison Chilton was elected a trustee to fill the vacancy caused by the death of Samuel Read. This led to the bequest from Chilton of the money which should be raised from the sale of his lands, negroes and personal property, with all of the debts which might be owing to him, the annual interest of which was to be used for the benefit of the Academy. This fund amounting to $6,000 in state bonds was turned over to Bedford and Campbell superintendents to whom the school was leased in 1887. Bishop Nicolas H. Cobbs was once president of the Academy, as was also Samuel Miller, (later president of a Pittsylvania College).

Colonel Girard Alexander, president of the Academy in 1839, petitioned in the name of the trustees, for an appropriation from the literary fund for repairs found to be needed. It is said that the early records were lost or destroyed, some of them at Poplar Forest, the home of Edward S. Hutter, secretary, where they were burned by Federal troops during Hunter's raid in 1864. Captain Winston was at the head of the institution about that time. In 1900 an additional building and two dormitories were erected at the Academy.

In the interest of its advancement a bill for conveying New London Academy to the school trustees of Campbell and Bedford, introduced by Captain West of Bedford, resulted in its conveyance to the joint boards by act of legislature in 1910. The measure provided that each county should appropriate one-twentieth of its school fund to the Academy.

As now established in addition to the regular High School course, there is here offered four years of Agriculture and Home Economics. The course allows a total of six units for the work in agriculture and is divided into "Plant Production," "Animal Industry," "Farm Engineering and Horticulture," "Farm Shop Work," and "Home Project Work." Two other units are required in the Academic Department for graduation. The Academy is well equipped with a boarding department and dormitories for accommodation of boys and girls and it embraces a group of well constructed buildings situated two miles from the old town of New London (better known as Bedford Alum Springs) and is reached by highway from Forest Depot on the Norfolk and Western Railroad and also by the old Salem turnpike.

As the plan of financing the institution has not proven altogether satisfactory, a committee from the Board of Managers have formulated another plan which is to be presented for legislation with the purpose of changing the present law, by which method the funds are derived from five per cent of the county levy each of Campbell and Bedford, with all expenses over and above the amount from these funds paid by the two counties upon the per capita basis.

It is said that Jefferson, who owned several tracts of land and had a residence (Poplar Forest) in the vicinity, took under consideration the suitability of the Academy site for his University. He became sufficiently interested in the institution to enter his grandson, Francis Epes, though it is reported that as he did not find there a bed to his liking for the young student, he supplied lumber from his forests and had the piece of furniture made according to a design of his own, his intent being apparently that the dimensions should not be large enough to accommodate a bed fellow.

Campbell's nature poet, Frederick Speece, was at one time associated with New London Academy and from there in 1823 issued his volume of poetic sketches. In its long enrollment of pupils there may be found many names of those who have gone forth into distinguished service and renown.

Before the introduction of public schools, county pater familias employed special tutors in their homes and among these the "Yankee School Master" was often installed. An entertaining account is furnished of those who officiated around Pigeon Run neighborhood, beginning with one Mr. Osgood, "an excellent teacher," who took great pains in instructing his male and female pupils, ranging in age from six to twenty years. Mr. Osgood was more than a trainer of youthful ideas, for it was through his efforts that St. John's Episcopal church was built. After him followed, into the schoolroom, a professor of mathematics, who was but a poor scholar himself; then a fine French teacher, not interested in other subjects; succeeded by an Irish teacher of Latin, so unpopular with the pupils that the patrons took their children away from school. Next came a Virginia native who made too free use of a handy rod. Then a very well liked Vermonter contrasting agreeably with the crippled, crabbed Presbyterian minister who replaced him. None of the incumbents seemed to tarry long and country children scholastically were not faring well in the schoolroom. But there were other educational ventures. In 1837 county school commissioners asked that the literary fund quota for 1833, which had become forfeited, be replaced. Reedy Spring Academy requested incorporation in 1840. School District No. 4 petitioned permission to erect an academy. Commissioners appealed for the appropriation of 1845 to liquidate the expenses of 1842; various teachers of private schools in 1833-'42-'44 and '58 demanded compensation from public funds for teaching indigent children who had been placed under them for instruction by the county commissioners, for which service they had received no payment; all of which goes to prove that though inadequate, Campbell was paying certain attention to the education of the youthful aspirants within its borders, and that they were ready for the opportune training which the public school system at length placed within their reach.

Virginia Constitution, as adopted by a majority vote on July 6th, 1869, provided that a uniform system of public free schools should be established in all the counties of the state by the year 1876 or as much earlier as practicable. At its next ensuing session, 1869-70, General Assembly passed the necessary laws to put into effect the constitutional provision in regard to free education and on April 5, 1871, five years in advance of the date fixed by the constitution, the public schools began their first session. Together with the other counties, Campbell then was divided into school districts which since have been under supervision of a resident superintendent. At first the schools of the county and Lynchburg were under the supervision of Colonel Abraham F. Biggers, but in 1878 the town and county were made separate divisions for school administration. R. A. Hamlet was appointed superintendent of county schools, and E. C. Glass of Lynchburg. High Schools rapidly came into service, at Alta Vista, Brookneal, Concord, Naruna, Rustburg, and Seneca. W. L. Garbee, for. sixteen years Division Superintendent of Schools, laid the foundation

R. E. Lee Junior High School

for these schools. There has been a County Teachers' Association in Campbell for 20 years which conducts a Teacher's Institute. At present J. J. Fray of Gladys is County Superintendent of Schools.

Veteran Superintendent

The first superintendent of Lynchburg Public Schools was Abraham F. Biggers, who was admirably equipped for the position which he held up to the time of his death in 1879. He was succeeded by Edward C. Glass, son of Major Robert

H. Glass, (former owner and editor of the *Lynchburg Republican,* later editor of the *News* and at one time Lynchburg postmaster). Senator Carter Glass is a brother and Miss Meta Glass, president of Sweet Briar College, a sister of the school superintendent.

Dr. Edward C. Glass, in point of service, is the oldest superintendent of schools in the United States, having held the office 48 years and numbering 55 years of teaching, all in connection with the schools of Lynchburg, and under every superintendent of public instruction in Virginia.

During a visit to England Dr. Glass made the first arrangement for an international exchange of teachers and has been connected with all Virginia progressive movements in education. He was a member of the first educational state board when foundations for state public school system were laid, and he was instrumental in bringing many leading men and women of this country—who represented the most advanced educational thought and practice—to Virginia as members of the faculty of the Summer School of Methods from 1889 to 1904, conducted by him and his associate, W. A. Jenkins of Portsmouth. A valuable contribution to educational progress in the state was this School of Methods conducted first at Lynchburg in 1889-'90; at Bedford City in 1891-'92-'95; at Salem in 1893; at Charlottesville in 1896-'98; at Roanoke in 1899-1900; at Staunton in 1901; at Virginia University in 1902-4, at which time the University authorities took it over and developed the summer quarter, now a regular part of the University's academic work. This School of Methods acquired a national reputation, and it was during the session of the school under the direction of Dr. Glass, and his coadjutor, that a Virginia State Teacher's Association was inaugurated and thus began the work of an organized teaching body which has developed into a powerful educational force in the state. In 1895 Superintendent Glass provided for the systematic instruction in music, dancing and physical training, and, a few years later, manual training and domestic science, organizing all of this instruction under expert supervision. He has served on various educational boards of the state; as a member of the Board of Trustees of William and Mary College he was honored with a degree of L.L. D. by that institution, the same degree was conferred upon him by Washington and Lee University.

Recently to the large number of Lynchburg schools there has been added the Robert E. Lee Junior High School, Professor W. T. McCullough, principal, which greatly assists in providing for the increased school attendance, incident upon the annexation of outlying suburbs.

Lynchburg is fortunate in its possession of three colleges: Randolph-Macon Woman's College, a handsome group of brick structures facing Rivermont Avenue; Lynchburg College, a co-educational institution situated in West Lynchburg; and Virginia Episcopal School for boys, just beyond Peakland, yet overlooking it. Of importance and interest also are the three orphanages, "Lynchburg Female," "Presbyterian," and "Odd Fellows," all located in suburban sections and propitiously situated for the training of community boys and girls, who are bereft of home's shelter and supervision.

County Public Schools in 1926

Brookneal District
  Brookneal School

Brookville District
  Fairview Heights School
  West End School
  Fort Hill School
  Rivermont School
  Central Point School
  Tyreeanna School
  Cox School
  Bocock School
  White Hall School

Falling River District
  Naruna School
  Hat Creek School
  Morris Church School
  Crosby School
  Union Hill School
  Fork of Falling School
  Rock House School
  Poindexter School
  Mountain View School
  Flat Rock School
  Border School
  Red Hill School

Carwile School
Edge School
Spring Mills School

Otter River District
Alta Vista School
Evington School
Leesville School
Lawyer's School
Lynch Station School
Wilcox School
Argenda School
Forest School
Robertson School
Blackwater School
Pacoman School
Perrow School

Rustburg District
Rustburg High School
Concord High School
Gravel Ridge School
Diamond Hill School
Red Oak School
Shervill School
Plum Branch School

Three Forks School
New Chapel School
Woodland School
Rode School
Leet School
Faegan School
Providence School
Garbee School
Yellow Branch School
Duiguid School
Callahan School

Seneca District
Gladys High School
Marysville School
Brown School
Peerman School
Hubbard School
Winfall School
Stone School
Perrow School
Greenwood School
Long Island School
Island School
Dry Mountain School
Melrose School

Elementary schools are provided for the education of colored residents in the county and through the aid of the Jeanes and Slater funds and the State Board of Education, a negro training school has been established at Rustburg. This institution provides two-year high school course and instruction in manual training and domestic science: A negro supervisor is employed for these schools.

At Fairview Heights, now incorporated within the bounds of Lynchburg, Virginia Theological Seminary is accomplishing good work for the race. Effort is being made to supply the county with Rosenwald form of building to meet increased demand for school buildings.

A new brick schoolhouse was erected on Salem turnpike during the year 1926 and opened with an enrollment of 150 white pupils. The Cox school and the Central Point school were consolidated in this school and the teachers of the two smaller schools were transferred to the new building. James E. Strickler is principal of the school.

This building was erected for the purpose of offering high school work as well as elementary work to the pupils of Brookville district but no high school curriculum has been planned for the present session, as it was not deemed practicable at this time.

Three trucks are being operated to the school to take care of the transportation of pupils who live farthest away. These trucks run along Salem turnpike, Leesville road and Ward's road.

Campbell County Teachers' Association passed resolutions for the retention of school examiners, believing that the services of division superintendents could be better dispensed with than those of the examiners. The following resolutions upon the subject were entered upon their minutes;—

"Resolved, that we, as teachers of Campbell county, respectfully protest against the abolition of the school examiners.

"We believe they have done more to improve the schools of the rural districts and to arouse the interest in education than all other influences combined and we respectfully ask our representatives to use their influence to retain their services."

Religion, Law, Politics and Finance

Chapter VIII

Religion

BEFORE the period of the Revolution—church moving along with state—as in governmental affairs, so in religious observance, all control of the situation emanated from English authority and surveillance.

The first known minister of the gospel in Bedford county was the Rev. John Brander (unmarried) of the Established Church of Great Britain. A deed was made to him by Benjamin Arnold of Buckingham county, conveying to "Revd. John Brander, Minister of Russell Parish in Bedford and his successors, for the use of the parish, 496 acres" in the county, which was paid for by the Church Wardens. Later this tract was sold by the trustees to Rev. John W. Holt, clerk of Russell Parish, who also belonged to the Established Church. In 1774 Rev. John Brander petitioned to receive the same salary at price and rate as other ministers of the commonwealth.

In 1772-73 Brander acquired two tracts in the county, amounting to fourteen hundred acres, and a large number of slaves and other property. He made his will in 1777, which was probated in 1778, devising his whole estate to his nephew, John Brander, then residing in the county. In the meantime, on January 27, 1777, the following order had been entered in court records:

"Ordered that it be certified to his Excelly. the Governor & Council that John Brander, Jr. & James McMurray, subjects to the King of Great Britain and residing in this county, are Agents for two Companies of Merchants in Great Britain; they have not manifested a friendly Disposition to the American Cause, and are both unconnected with Wives and Children in this State." On the 7th of October, 1779, the whole of Brander's estate was escheated to the commonwealth and the record of it was made in the clerk's office.

On November 16, 1782, William Gill sent a petition to Virginia Assembly stating that he was the only blood relation of the Rev. John Brander in America. That Brander willed his estate to his nephew, John Brander, a British subject, but the estate was escheated to the Commonwealth, and he asked that the estate be given him. The petition was received as reasonable, so it may be presumed that Gill came into possession of Bránder's estate. Gill had become resident in Campbell.

On May, 1779, an act passed by the Assembly for disposing of the Glebe of Russell Parish vested the authority in Rd. Stith, Wm. Leftwich, Jas. Callaway, Jeremiah Early and John Quarles, gentlemen, in trust, the money to be laid out into a more convenient glebe. In 1782 the residents in Russell Parish asked for a division of the parish along the county line of Campbell and Bedford, as the parish was extensive and inconvenient. This occurred at the time of county division, and pretty soon thereafter Moore parish, Campbell county, was formed.

Ministers of the Gospel, who were authorized to celebrate the rites of marriage:

Anthony, Abner, of the United Baptists, May 28, 1827.

Anthony, John, of the Baptist Society, August 28, 1781.

Brander, John, of Russell Parish, Bedford, 1762.

Cobbs, Nicolas Hamner, of Protestant Episcopal Church, July 26, 1824.

Douglass, William, April 27, 1801. Baptist.

Early, Abner, Methodist, of Rehoboth church, Campbell county. Missionary.

Early, William, of the Methodist Church, June 22, 1795. Missionary.

Fuqua, Isham, of the Baptist Church, June 27, 1796.

Fuqua, William, of the Baptist Church, October 23, 1815.

Holt, John White, of Protestant Episcopal Church, July 25, 1785. Took oath of allegiance Aug. 25, 1777.

Hunter, Andrew, of the Methodist Church, January 25, 1790.

Hunter, Samuel, of the Methodist Church, June 23, 1817.

Jennings, Edward, of the Baptist Church, October 24, 1808.

Leftwich, James, of the Baptist Church, February 27, 1826.

Leftwich, William, Jr., of the Baptist Church, October 24, 1808.

Mitchell, James, of the Presbyterian Church, September 26, 1783.

Moon, Joseph, of the Methodist Church, May 27, 1799.

Moorman, James H. L., February, 1805, of the Methodist Church.

Moorman, William, January, 1804.

Morris, James, of the Methodist Church, January 27, 1812.

Rucker, James, of the Baptist Society, August 28, 1781.

Rice, David, of the Presbyterian Church, November 26, 1781.

Rucker, George, of the Baptist Church, February 28, 1803.

Russell, Daniel, of the Presbyterian Church, July 27, 1829.

Scott, James, of the Methodist Church, February 22, 1808.

Turner, James, of the Presbyterian Church, January 28, 1793.

Terry, Enoch, of the Baptist Church, June 25, 1810.

Annulment of Marriage Ties

Request for a sundering of marriage ties soon found place among petitions to the Assembly, for then there was nowhere a ready-made divorce court offering prompt service to patrons.

The first petition was presented in 1809, six years after the applicant had discovered that he had been deceived into marriage by the defendant. His request was received by the Assembly as reasonable, but made no record of its decree.

The second petition in 1816 was from a "free man of color," whose application was rejected.

A third petition sent in 1820 was also rejected.

The fourth petition came in 1822 from the wife for divorce from her husband, and was labeled by Assembly "petition to lie," which indicates a question as to its reasonableness, and probably awaited investigation.

In 1823 John Rosser asked that a law be passed legalizing his marriage to his deceased wife's sister.

In 1826 petition was presented by a husband asking divorce from his wife, in which he was joined by "sundry citizens," asking that his request be granted, but followed by a counter-petition from his wife that it be rejected. The first two petitions were rejected and the latter was retained as reasonable.

A petition for divorce in 1834 was promptly rejected though backed by sundry (100) citizens of Lynchburg.

Two divorce petitions of 1841, sent the same day, one from a wife, the other from a husband, were rejected.

In 1844 the tenth divorce petition was presented.

The eleventh petition of a wife for divorce from her husband, was sent in 1851 and was referred to the Courts of Justice. This closes the record of divorce applications to the date of 1862. It would seem from the record that the Assembly was inclined to deal leniently with the wife, or else that circumstantial evidence showed the husband to be most in fault.

County Court

County court was established in Bedford in 1764 and the first court was held on the fourth Monday of May following. The courts were presided over by magistrates until 1870, when the office of county judge was created.

With the establishment of the circuit court, a clerk for that court became necessary and the first one appointed to the position was Benjamin Howard, a native of the county, who received his appointment from the colonial government. He was succeeded by James Steptoe, a personal friend of Thomas Jefferson and appointed by him. His son, James Callaway Steptoe, followed. When Campbell was formed, while Robert

Alexander was made county clerk, James Steptoe held that office in the circuit court until his death.

County Court Clerks:
Robert Alexander, 35 years, from 1784 to 1819.
John Alexander, 19 years, from 1819 to 1838.
William A. Clement, 7 years, from 1838 to 1845.
George William Dabney, 14 years, from 1845 to 1859.
John D. Alexander, 6 years, from 1859 to 1865.
Wm. A. Clement, 3 years, from 1865 to 1868.
Military Appointee, 3 years, from 1868 to 1871.
Robert Woodson Withers, 22 years, from 1871 to 1893.
Samuel C. Goggin, 32 years, from 1893 to 1925.
C. W. Woodson (present incumbent), from 1925.

Clerks of Circuit Court:
Robert Alexander, 10 years, from 1809 to 1819.
John Alexander, 19 years, from 1819 to 1838.
John D. Alexander, 30 years, from 1838 to 1868.
Robert A. Clement, 15 years, from 1871 to 1886.
W. K. Alexander, appointed pro tem., 1 year, 1887.
R. E. Reid, elected May, 1887, served till 1893.
John E. Withers, 11 years, from 1893 to 1904.

The first County Court Judge was appointed by Governor Underwood in 1870:

1. Judge John G. Haythe, of Gladys, moved to Lynchburg.
2. Judge Robert H. Ward, of Staunton river, Campbell county.
3. Judge Frank Nelson, of Warrenton, moved to Rustburg, appointed to fill Judge Ward's unexpired term, then elected to office.
4. Judge (Captain) Stephen Adams, (C. S. Veteran), of Lynchburg, appointed by Legislature. Served till 1904.

County Court, a system of adjudicating that remained in operation for a century and a half, and occasioned monthly gathering of neighbors, passed out of existence in 1904. Circuit court then embraced Halifax, Campbell, Lunenburg, Mecklenburg and Lynchburg.

Judge William R. Barksdale, of Halifax county, filled the judgeship from 1904 to 1925. Circuit Court became restricted to the City of Lynchburg and Campbell. Succeeding Judge Barksdale, Judge Don Halsey (present incumbent), of Lynchburg.

Insufficient record in the old system of indexing wills caused passage of a law requiring name details wherever included in the original instrument. The new General Index to Wills in Campbell county, now being prepared by Clerk C. W. Woodson, will show not only the name of the decedent or testator, but will give that of each devisee under the will, that is, the name of each person to whom property is bequeathed by the will. When this law becomes generally carried out by the various county clerks, genealogical work will be very much simplified for the genealogist.

Lawyers who qualified in County Court, Bedford-Campbell, from 1754, later in Campbell:

Anthony, Christopher, Jr., February 26, 1810.

Branch, Samuel, May 22, 1909.

Carrington, Paul, June 23, 1755; King's Attorney from May 24, 1756.

Cowan, William, September 23, 1780.

Clark, Christopher Henderson, May 26, 1788.

Clements, Alexander, November 23, 1812.

Cralle, Richard K., of Lynchburg, November 23, 1829.

Daniel, Walker, July 25, 1780. Settled in Danville, Ky. Killed by Indians, 1784.

Dabney, John, May 28, 1792. Judge of Superior Court of Law of Bedford county, 1813.

Dabney, Chiswell, of Lynchburg, July 22, 1811.

Davis, Samuel R., August 27, 1821.

Elliott, John, June 27, 1769.

Edley, David R., of Lynchburg, March 22, 1824.

Fontaine, Edmund, December 22, 1788.

Gilmer, James B., August 28, 1809.

Gilmer, Peachy, January 26, 1818. Appointed States Attorney, June 22, 1818.

Garland, Samuel, of Lynchburg, March 27, 1820.

Garland, Maurice H., of Lynchburg, June 26, 1826.

Goggin, William L., of Bedford, April 28, 1828.

Hancock, George, August 26, 1782.

Holcombe, Thomas A., of Lynchburg, July 22, 1816.

Innis, Harry, October 27, 1778. Deputy States' Attorney and Escheator. Moved to Kentucky.

Irvine, Edmund, March 22, 1824.

Leftwich, John T., of Bedford, March 27, 1826.

Madison, John, May 23, 1797.

Morgan, Haynes, March 26, 1771. Sergeant-Major 80th British Regiment, 1758, seven years.

Miller, Thomas, September 23, 1780.

McAllister, James S., of Bedford, August 23, 1813.

Mosby, Charles L., of Lynchburg, November 23, 1829.

Nash, Thomas, January 27, 1755.

Reade, Clement, May 27, 1754. Sworn King's Attorney May 27, 1754.

Read, Clement, Jr., July 25, 1757.

Read, Isaac, February 26, 1765. King's Attorney from February 26, 1765.

Risque, James, November 25, 1794.

Robinson (Robertson?) July 23, 1798.

Roane, William R., of Lynchburg, May 23, 1814.

Risque, Ferdinand W., of Lynchburg, June 22, 1829.

Rives, Nathaniel, February 23, 1824.

Rives, William, March 28, 1815.

Stuart, Archibald, May 28, 1816.

Tucker, George, of Lynchburg, February 23, 1818; later Professor of Law at University of Virginia.

Urquhart, John D., February 28, 1814.

Watts, William, May 22, 1764, Bedford.

Ward, Henry Chiles, of Lynchburg, June 22, 1829.

Ward, Giles, of Lynchburg, August 27, 1822.
Wyatt, Samuel, January 26, 1807.
Winston, Edmund, June 26, 1764. Judge Superior Court
of Law, 1809.

Judges of the Superior Courts of Law, of the Circuit Superior Courts of Law and Chancery and of the Circuit Courts of Bedford and Campbell:

Dabney, John, 1813.
Daniel, William, Sr., 1816, of Cumberland and Campbell.
Daniel, William, Jr.
Gilmer, George H., 1853.
Shumaker, Lindsay M., military appointee, 1869.
Taylor, Creed, of the Richmond Circuit.
Taliaferro, Norborne, 1846.
Wilson, Daniel A., 1829.
Winston, Edmund, 1809.

James Steptoe, clerk of Bedford, placed on record, August 25, 1783, the following unusual deed from the Presbyterian Congregations of Otter Peaks, Bedford:

"Be it known to all men that whereas these Congregations found it inconvenient to support a Minister of our Denomination by yearly subscription, therefore various well disposed Members of said Congregations and others have contributed considerable sums of Money by which Slaves were bought viz: Kate, Tom, Jerry, Venus and said Slaves' issue: Nance, Ishmael, Sall, Moses, Herod, Cyrus, Pharez, Jinney, Charles, Milly and their Issue forever are vested in the Regular Elders of said Congregations in Bedford county, Virginia, and their Regular Successors in Trust only faithfully to apply the neat profits of said Slaves and Issue forever in said Congregations to supporting a Regular Minister of said Denomination in said Congregations and for purchasing lands for said Slaves to work on and to keep decent Houses of Worship in Repair and for such other Charitable uses as said Elders and Majority of said Congregations may agree upon . . . should at

any time the profits of said Slaves arise to such a surplus
Know all Men therefore that we the Purchasers, Heirs at
Law, and next of kin to said Purchasers of said Slaves, Tom,
Jerry, Venus, Purchased with the above-contributed Money,
Do hereby each on our respective parts Warrant and forever
defend the above named Slaves, and their Issue forever, for
the above Mentioned Purpose from us and each of our
Heirs and assigns forever. Witness Whereof we hereunto
set our hands and affix our seals this 28th day of July One
Thousand Seven Hundred and Eighty-three.

"In presence of:

"James Turner	Robert Ewing (Seal)
"Samuel Beard	W. Ewing (Seal)
"Adam Beard	John Trigg (Seal)
"George Dickson	William Trigg (Seal)
"John Ewing	David Rice (Seal)

"At a Court held for Bedford county 25th August, 1783,
This Certain Writing was acknowledged by Robert Ewing,
Wm. Ewing, William Trigg, and

"At a court held for the said County the 22d day of September following the same was further proved as to David
Rice and ordered to be recorded.

"Teste, JAMES STEPTOE, C. C."

Voice of Law

Chancellor Creed Taylor, son of Samuel and Sophia Covington Taylor, owned property in Cumberland county, two
miles from Farmville. He married Sally, daughter of Miller
and Mary de Graffenreid-Woodson; built a home, "Needham" (named in honor of his wife's grandfather, Sir Thomas
Needham, of Shropshire, England). They had no children,
but adopted several young relatives, whom they reared at
Needham. Chancellor Taylor was judge of Richmond Chancery Court. He travelled to Campbell over old Lawyer's

Road, which received its name from its use by the lawyers in their journeys to and from court; now crossed by the Southern railroad. A station was established there and the name was curtailed to Lawyers.

Taylor resigned his judgeship and opened a select class of law students—sometimes enrolling as many as fifty students —and erected cottages to accommodate them on his premises. He died in 1843.

In her *"Sketches,"* Mrs. Cabell gives a list of the distinguished lawyers who attended Chancellor Taylor's talented and brilliant court, held May and October in the old court building at Lynchburg:

> Judge William Daniel, Sr., of Campbell and Cumberland district.
> Daniel Sheffey and Colonel Townes of Pittsylvania.
> Judge William Leigh of Halifax.
> Peachy Gilmer, Christopher Anthony, Jr.; Callahill Mennis, Chiswell Dabney, Blair Dabney of Campbell.
> Judge Allen Taylor of Botetourt.
> Judge Thomas Bouldin of Charlotte.
> Major James B. Risque and others. John W. Wills, clerk of court.

The following incident is told as having occurred during Judge Taylor's last visit to Lynchburg, when weakness from declining health had changed his marked courtesy of manner to impatience and irritability, requiring great self-restraint to preserve politeness to the members of his court:

Adjourning session for the day he appointed the hour of noon on the following one for reassembling. As time drew near next morning, he became restless before eleven o'clock and caused the court house bell to be rung long and loud. In great haste the lawyers came pouring in to meet his ireful glance. He first accosted Mr. Gilmer, reproaching him in an angry voice for being so dilatory; whereupon his victim ventured to remark that it lacked three-quarters of an hour to the appointed time. The Chancellor then losing all control of himself exclaimed in a passionate voice, "Gentlemen, I will have you in future to know, that when I take my seat, it is twelve o'clock."

Cause of Disagreement

Two political parties long struggled for supremacy in Virginia. Since the time of Jefferson the state had been Democratic, but there arose and flourished a strong party known as Whig (a term borrowed from England and intended to signify progress) which aimed at wresting the control of the state from the Democrats. The county of Campbell was for years a battleground, as the people were pretty equally divided in sentiment, first one party and then the other would elect its candidates for the Legislature, the personal popularity of the candidate being a controlling factor in elections. In 1836 Martin Van Buren had been nominated as president, and the Whigs were anxious to defeat the Democratic candidate. Each party in the county tried to bring out their best man. The Democrats chose Judge William Daniel of Lynchburg and Colonel James Dearing of Campbell for the House of Delegates, and for state Senator, Dr. Joel W. Flood of Buckingham. In opposition the Whigs brought out Mr. John Wills, an attorney-at-law of Lynchburg and Dr. Robert W. Withers of Campbell as Delegates, and Colonel Thomas M. Bondurant of Buckingham for Senator. There were few precincts in the county at the time and a large vote was cast at the Court House, where the party which was victorious usually carried the county. Elections at that time were conducted differently from now; every voter came up to the judge's table, announced his name and that of his candidate in an audible voice—which was repeated by the sheriff who "cried" the votes, and they were then recorded by the clerks, the result giving general satisfaction as an expression of popular sentiment. Each candidate was present at the Court House, seated on the Magistrate's bench. Those receiving the votes made a bow and returned thanks to the voters. With the final poll of votes at this election Wills, Withers and Bondurant becoming successful, the Whigs celebrated their victory with great rejoicing.

A Whig electoral ticket for 1848, with Zachary Taylor of Louisiana, presidential candidate, and Millard Fillmore of New York for vice-president, gives the names of Virginia Electors: 1st District, John J. Jones, of Norfolk City; 2nd District, George W. Bolling, of Petersburg; 3rd District, Henry P. Irving, of Cumberland; 4th District, Joseph K. Irving, of Lynchburg; 5th District, William Martin, of Franklin; 6th District, William C. Rives, of Albemarle; 7th District, Robert E. Scott, of Fauquier; 8th District, Henry T. Garnett of Westmoreland; 9th District, John A. Meredith of Richmond City; 10th District, Robert Saunders, of Williamsburg; 11th District, Andrew Hunter, of Jefferson; 12th District, Alexander H. Stuart, of Augusta; 13th District, Samuel McD. Moore, of Rockbridge; 14th District, Conally F. Trigg, of Washington; 15th District, George W. Summers, of Kanawha; 16th District, Gideon D. Camden, of Harrison; 17th District, Francis H. Pierpont, of Marion.

This ticket bears the autographed signature of William H. Tardy, on the reverse side, which was the name of the Campbell county voter who had used it.

Around the year 1860 public issues calling for state action aroused heated debate and violent partisanship. About that time Andrew Johnson passed, by railway train, through Lynchburg at great personal risk, because of excited political feeling, but he was protected from molestation by the prompt strategy of the Whigs, and safely continued his journey to Washington.

Never was a more earnest body of delegates gathered together in Richmond than in the convention which followed party agitations of the time.

A wag wrote an amusing account of this Assembly, calling it "The Animal Parliament," giving to each member the trait of an animal. One especially obdurate Whig was designated a terrapin because he was so slow to move from his stand-pat position for preservation of the Union. In the midst of pleading oratory, earnest advocates on both sides, an unlooked-for bolt fell spreading doubt and consternation: strong men wept. This was the call made by the government for armed troops of invasion, an action which instantly dissolved Whig and Democratic distinction and merged the Assembly into brotherhood with a message to carry and a purpose to defend, even if their zeal for maintenance of right became pitted against the power to win—so staking their fortunes, hearths, lives, and facing cruel, deadly war—they tried out their purpose in a conflict covering four dark years. War, the synonym for horror, for tragedy, however glorified by display of valor and self-sacrifice, paralyzed industrial enterprise, excepting for necessities of war's prosecution, and that of mercenaries, even far away Campbell had its two-day immediate contact with the destroyer. The county paid its quota in toll of soldiers, in maiming of youth and mature manhood, and in levy of available substance. Like its neighbors it also suffered from the appalling aftermath which deprived it of the freedom of action. Thus at that period it chronicled a decade of arrested progress, records of which lie buried in its archives, but memory sacredly treasures them in the hearts of those to whom they have come in heritage. The symbolic flag had not been tarnished, and reverently handled, it was now laid away and become superseded by the flag of Union. Implements of peace replaced those of war, when with earnest will and determination the followers of Lee bent their efforts towards the restoration of their homes, become dearer through the enforced absence from them. Though much which was valued had been lost, adherence to right principle remained and Virginia claimed their earnest service in placing it once again as example in leadership among the states with which it now renewed partnership. In line with other sections of the state, Campbell then became divided into two political parties, Democrats and Republicans, which still continue.

Progress in Finance

A protest was sent in November, 1780 to Virginia Assembly against making debts and loan certificates payable according to the depreciation of money issued by Congress and by the state; and during 1786 certain inhabitants calling themselves "Sons of Liberty," addressed a petition, complaining that though maintaining themselves by the utmost exertion of industry and frugality, they were oppressed with taxes and grievously harassed with debts, augmented with insupportable scarcity of a circulating medium, by the subtlety of a few who wrested from them what money remained from the craft of the mercantile line. They requested the adoption of some mode of relief, an emission of paper currency, which would abolish apparent confusion hanging over their heads, menacing them with insupportable slavery or irrevocable destruction, and begged a sufficiency for the redemption of military claims and all others that involved the state with interest and consequently accumulated endless taxes thereon.

In 1810 a thousand residents of the counties of Campbell, Buckingham, Prince Edward, Charlotte, Halifax, Pittsylvania, Bedford, Franklin, Patrick, Henry, Amherst, Nelson, Rockbridge, Bath, Botetourt, Greenbriar, Montgomery, Grayson, Wythe, Washington, Russell and Kanawha, requested the establishment of a branch for discount and deposit of the Bank of Virginia at Lynchburg—a petition which was received by the Assembly with favor, but was submitted several times before it was carried into effect, and then "sundry persons dealing with the office of discount and deposit" made complaint that the Board of Directors gave partial and unjust bank administration in granting accommodations to inhabitants of the town in preference to those of the country, and they asked for Assembly's consideration and adjustment of the matter in the interest of the country people.

At the session of December 16, 1835, the Lynchburg citizens requested passage of an act establishing a Bank of Lynchburg in the town. The next year a petition was made for establishment of the Planters' Bank of Virginia in the town with capital stock of $1,200,000 and privilege of increasing it to $2,000,000, with branch banks at any place they might see advisable. Through John Wills, delegate at the time, in 1837 petition was made for an Independent Bank, and in 1838 incorporation of the Citizens Savings Bank of Lynchburg. In 1842 officers and stockholders of the Mechanics Bank asked its incorporation. The same year stockholders of the Farmers' and Mechanics' Saving Institution of Lynchburg petitioned for its incorporation, and citizens of the town and surrounding counties requested the redemption of specie payments by the bank. In 1843 the same petitioners made application for the amendment of laws in relation to breaches of trust by the trustee and commission merchants. In 1848 Campbell residents asked for the passage of an act incorporating the Aberdeen Savings Institute. Lynchburgers again in 1850 called for an Inde   dent Bank there, and petitioned in 1852 to have the Citizens Savings Bank of Lynchburg issue notes and give certificates of deposit for sums of money less than $5. William Organ, Allen L. Wyllie and Thomas Dillard petitioned for additional compensation as commissioners of revenue for Campbell county, repeating it in 1854. In 1862 Lynchburgers asked for release of the Savings Bank from the penalty of the law against issuing notes as currency.

Standing to-day near the summit in industrial development of the South and as an important financial center, Lynchburg possesses four banks which represent a capital of $8,000,000, with their total resources of $30,000,000. There are, besides these banks, many building and loan associations which promote the acquirement of homes. The Lynchburg National Bank stands in the class of Federal Reserve banks.

In the Public Eye

Chapter IX

Lynch Court

URING progress of the Revolution the loyalists in Bedford-Campbell section were menaced by foes both within and without their community, for while they were straining every effort to render assistance in support of armies in the field they suffered from depredations of enemies within their own confines. The whole of the mountainous portion of Virginia was infested with Tories and desperadoes who plundered the unprotected property of the loyalists. Efforts made to control the situation were without avail, because the unsettled condition of the time gave the culprits immunity from punishment, though they were frequently caught in the act. At one time Tories were subjected to double taxation, at another treble taxation, though afterwards they were allowed retribution: the call for prompt and strenuous action arose.

County courts were merely examining courts in such cases. For final trial for felonies there was but one court in the state, which sat at Williamsburg, 200 miles from Campbell, and the war rendered the transmission of prisoners thither and attendance of witnesses necessary to convict them next to impossible. The officers in charge of prisoners would often be attacked by outlaws and forced to release their captives or be captured themselves by British troops. The operation of civil law was thus rendered difficult and often impossible. In addition to this disordered condition, a conspiracy to overthrow the continental government was discovered in process of formation at a critical period, with the aim of aiding the British by all possible means.

Colonel Charles Lynch, together with several neighbors, Captain Wm. Preston, Captain Robt. Adams, Jr., Colonel Jas. Callaway and other loyalists, decided to take active steps to frustrate the conspirators and restore order and quiet in their neighborhood as far as possible. They knew the risks they assumed but made no attempt at secrecy. A company was formed for the purpose of effecting their object and Lynch was chosen as head of the organization. Under his direction, suspected persons were arrested and brought to his house, where they were tried by a court of the leaders as associate justices. The accused was brought face to face with his accusers, heard the testimony against him, was allowed to defend himself by producing mitigating circumstances and witnesses in his behalf. If acquitted, he was allowed to go free, with apologies and reparation; if convicted, he was sentenced to receive thirty-nine lashes on his bare back, and if he did not then shout, "Liberty forever," was hanged up by the thumbs until he gave utterance to that sentiment. The penalty of death was never inflicted. When found guilty the prisoner was tied to a large walnut tree (yet standing) in Lynch's yard and the stripes were inflicted without delay. After the sentence of the court had been executed the culprit was released with *words of admonition.*

One of the Tories was found to have papers of great importance, relating directly to the conspiracy against the government and the documents were discovered concealed in the cavity of a large square bedpost. Owing to the character of this information the conspirator was not allowed to go at large, but was assigned lodgings in an outhouse on Lynch's premises with injunctions not to leave, under penalty of severe punishment. No guard was assigned but the method of reproof was so impressive that the order was scrupulously observed.

Many suits for damage in the infliction of Lynch law were taken to court from the community, and, in order to protect patriot defendants, Virginia Legislature passed a special act of indemnification that "Whereas divers evil disposed persons in 1780 formed a conspiracy against the government—and that William Preston, Robert Adams, Jr., James Callaway, Charles Lynch and other faithful citizens aided by volunteers

did by effectual measures suppress such conspiracy and whereas measures taken by them may not have been warranted by
law though justifiable from the imminence of danger, Be it
enacted therefore that sd. Preston, etc., concerned in suppressing the conspiracy or executing measures for that purpose,
stand exonerated from all penalty on account thereof."

Thomas Jefferson, who appears to have been conversant
with the affairs of his time, gave as a proof of the lenity of
the government, that when the war had raged seven years not
a single execution for treason had taken place. He had occasion to visit in the vicinity of the scene of Lynch's court, and
no doubt knew what was presented at Assembly meetings.
We may believe then that he had reason for his assertion. It
has become the custom to compare pitiless mob law to that
administered by loyal vigilants for the purpose of preserving
order as far as possible. *Lynch Law* is thus distorted from its
original significance, and serves to confirm misinformation
concerning its derivation, giving it meaning, opposite to the
original, in suggestion of lawlessness.

On the lawn of the old Lynch property near Alta Vista
stands the old walnut tree upon the limbs of which Lynch law
was administered. A portion of it has died and it bears the
marks of age but great care has been taken to protect and
preserve the living portion.

Bishop John Early

John Early, son of Joshua, Sr., and Mary Leftwich Early,
of Forest neighborhood, reared on a farm, was up betimes,
hauling tobacco or other field crop to market ten miles away,
arriving back home in time for a farmer's breakfast. He was
a product of the years which followed the Revolution, when
energy characterized endeavor, and being among the
younger members of a large family, energy needed to be
utilized. Thus we find that the zeal he exerted in the duties
of boyhood days, grew apace in the spiritual labor he selected
for his manhood. Eventually he located at Lynchburg which

remained his working center and, until age enfeebled him, took part in every movement started for benefit of the city. It is said that he converted and baptized his own father and soon after entering the ministry participated in a Methodist

Bishop John Early

camp meeting revival at Yellow Branch, Campbell county, during which a thousand aspirants were brought to their confession of faith. As time passed he sharply silhouetted his zealous activities upon the screen of religious progress and John Wesley had no more ardent a follower. His first appearance in public was at a conference held in 1808 at the Methodist Meeting House where he was among the candidates for ministry who were received on trial, though he had joined that church in 1804, was licensed to preach two years later and admitted to Virginia Conference in 1807. He began his religous labors among the slaves of Thomas Jefferson at Poplar Forest and was conspicuous for his interest in that race's religious advancement. In 1812 he had charge of a church at Greenville; writing from there to his brother, Rev. Thomas Early at Bedford at that time, he told of the volunteer enlistment of young men in Brunswick county for the war and that the captain had solicited him to go as their chaplain, a position he declined feeling that he had a more important work in the care of the churches. At the age of 27 years he was made presiding elder in the Meherrin District; was a founder of Randolph-Macon College and its rector for many years. He took active part in measures that resulted in the division of the church in 1844 and in the organization of the Methodist Episcopal Church, South, at its convention at Louisville, Kentucky in 1845; and was the president pro tempore of its first General Conference at Petersburg, Virginia, where he was elected its first book agent. In 1854 he was made one of its bishops at a conference held at Columbus, Georgia.

John Early married first Anne Jones, who died s. p., m. 2nd Elizabeth Browne, dau. of Anthony and Mary B. Green-Rives, a descendant of Colonel Henry Browne, a Councillor under General William Berkeley. Bishop Early died at Lynchburg in 1873 after an illness of two years, the result of a railroad accident; children:

—Mary Virginia, born 1822, married James Leftwich Brown; a grandson of whom, James Rives Childs, graduate of Randolph-Macon College and Harvard University, took part in various departments of service in the World War, afterwards was in the American Relief Administration in Southern Serbia and in the devastated section of Russia, later U. S. Consul at Jerusalem, and now occupying the same office at Bucharest.

—Dr. Orville Rives married, 1st Mattie Blunt; married, 2nd, Gertrude Cornelius; married, 3rd, Mary E., daughter of Judge Thomas A. Chevis. Dr. Early was a graduate of Transylvania College, dean of the Medical College at Memphis, Tenn.; served as surgeon in the Confederate Army with the rank of major; had charge of a hospital in Richmond and later in Lynchburg; afterwards made his home at Columbus, Mississippi.

—Rev. Thomas Howard, educated at Randolph-Macon College and at Transylvania, Ky.; studied law, the practice of which he pursued in partnership with Robert J. Davis; entered the Methodist ministry and held charges at Petersburg, Rappahannock and Charlottesville. As a member of the school board at Lynchburg he assisted in securing the establishment of the High School and in fostering its development.

—John Fletcher, married Eliza J., daughter of Harding P. Bostick; educated at Virginia Military Institute. He became connected with the Methodist Publishing House at Richmond, Mobile and New Orleans. Finally located at Nashville, Tenn., where he died. A grandson, John Early Jackson, now associated with the Appalachian Power Company, is resident in Lynchburg; a daughter of Bishop Early, Frances P., resides at the old homestead in Lynchburg.

Bishop Early was a member of a board for establishment of a school for education of poor children, called Lynchburg Charity School, and incorporated in 1823, the first local organized effort for public education. In 1825 he started a colonization society for raising means to send to Africa, all free people of color who desired to go and all slaves who were freed on that condition. The same year he was a member of a committee for bringing water to the city, a proposition which seemed impracticable, but was successfully carried out in 1829. He was among the applicants appointed to petition Legislature to incorporate the Lynchburg and Tennessee Railroad with the aim of connecting that road with the Nashville and New Or-

leans line.   A bill in 1836 was passed authorizing construction
of the road from Lynchburg to Richmond.   In 1841 a state
educational convention was held in Richmond, to which
Bishop Early went as a delegate, in favor of free education.
He was an advocate at a town meeting for a western road
starting from Lynchburg, to be called the Richmond and Ohio
Railroad.   In 1853 he purchased from John Crouse a tract of
land leading from Salem turnpike to Jones' Mill, and at this

Bishop Early's Home, 700 Court Street, Lynchburg

time he and his wife deeded to the citizens of Lynchburg a
portion of this tract for a suitable cemetery.   An association
was formed, with Rev. John Early as President, and in June,
1856, the reservation christened Spring Hill cemetery, was
formally dedicated.   One of the large circular lots laid off was
set apart for the family of Bishop Early and a shaft to his
memory was later erected upon it by ministerial members of
the conference.   The old Early home, at corner of Court and
Seventh streets, stands unaltered, as designed after a popular
plan of his time, on straight lines with ample room space; the

interior of which has fine hand work on mantel, chair-boarding and stairway.   The ground site was purchased from Breckenridge Cabell, whose father, Dr. George Cabell, was one of the early settlers, and it adjoins the lot given by Mrs. George Cabell as site for St. Paul's Episcopal Church.   Diagonally across the street is Court St. Methodist Church, where for many years Bishop Early swayed his congregations and directly opposite from the church stood the home of Dr. Robert S. Payne, who ministered to the body as Early did to the souls of many in the community.

In this connection it is well to refer to a couple from a Northern state who established a school in Lynchburg, thus ministering to the youthful mind of the town and in so doing grafted themselves upon the affections of their scholars; it is doubtful if there has lived any one then associated with Amos Botsford, who does not recall him with appreciation and gratitude for his patience and kindliness in efforts to direct the young idea; and his wife, Julia, as well, though it may be the shadow of her ruler—sometimes brought to bear upon unruliness and unpreparedness—will leave her a little behind her husband in tender memory.

Temperance Apostle

A temperance society was organized by Rev. W. A. Smith in 1828, which lasted for a long time and was effective in lessening intemperance.   When Father Downey came to take charge of the Catholic congregation, he started a total abstinence society among his parishoners and delivered speeches on temperance.   The Catholics formed the St. Francis Xavier Total Abstinence Beneficial Society in 1873, with Patrick McDivitt, president; Patrick Doherty, vice-president; James O'Brien, secretary; John Casey, treasurer; John Kelly, steward, and the Rev. J. J. McGurk, spiritual director.   The society met every third Sunday and during its continuance accomplished much good.   The credit is given Captain Thomas A. Holcombe for being the most earnest advocate of the temperance cause, in organizing societies, distributing tracts and traveling over the state in the interest of this work. He died in 1843, and the temperance societies erected a monument over his grave in the Presbyterian cemetery. The work he had started did not cease at his death; a long peitition was presented in 1846 to the Common Hall requesting that sale of liquor not be allowed in the town; yet the demand was rejected, leaving work in interest of temperance still to be pursued. In 1860 upon completion of the new Centenary Methodist church, their old building, erected in 1811, was sold to the Sons of Temperance, on condition that it be used only for meetings, lectures, literary and scientific entertainments. It was named in honor of Captain Thomas A. Holcombe "Holcombe Hall."

In 1879 the question arose as to whether this hall, formerly the old Methodist church, could be used for a theater, and if the Sons of Temperance were not exceeding permission granted them by the Methodists in holding theatrical entertainments there. The case was carried into court in 1879 when Judge James Garland rendered the decision that by the terms of the deed it must be confined to its use for moral, religious and scientific purposes. The proposition then undertaken to turn the building into a public library failed. Eventually it was converted into housing tenements and with the alteration of the structure, the name which served to recall one of the town's most active citizens, disappeared in connection with the cause to which he had devoted so much time and energy, but the general campaign for prohibition developed to effectually carry on the work he had taken up. Captain John B. Tilden, a second temperance apostle, died in 1877.

In 1849 Lynchburg members of the Independent Order of Odd Fellows, and the Pendleton and Abner Clopton divisions of the Sons of Temperance petitioned for an act of incorporation allowing them to hold a limited amount of real estate in the town.

In 1855 a division of the Sons of Temperance was formed in Campbell county.

Young Poet

The earliest Lynchburg poet, of whom record is found, was Bransford Vawter, son of a tailor who was among the first settlers in the town. Born in 1816, he early developed talents of a superior order, and his death at the age of twenty-three, was a disappointment to his many friends. Even though so young he was made an officer in a military company called "Invincibles," and president of the Patrick Henry Debating Society. It was thought he would have attained high rank as a poet had he lived. His poems were not collected in book form, but he was a contributor to the *Southern Literary Messenger* and a few of his writings have been preserved, which are considered best specimens from his pen. One of these was copied into other magazines and, set to music, was circulated over the states, though few knew its authorship, which became revealed through the offer of a prize upon announcement of the writer's name. It was said to have been inspired by an unhappy attachment to a Lynchburg lady; but appeared in print without heading as well as without signature. The plaintive lines suggest the chivalrous feeling which prompted them and are as follows:

> "I'd offer thee this hand of mine
>   If I could love thee less,
> But hearts so warm, so fond as thine,
>   Should never know distress.
> My fortune is too hard for thee,
>   'Twould chill thy dearest joy;
> I'd rather weep to see thee free,
>   Than win thee to destroy.
>
> "I love thee in thy happiness,
>   As one too dear to love,
> As one I think of but to bless
>   As wretchedly I rove.
> And oh! when sorrow's cup I drink

All bitter though it be,
How sweet 'twill be for me to think
It holds no drop for thee.

"And now my dreams are sadly o'er,
Fate bids them all depart,
And I must leave my native shore,
In brokenness of heart.
And oh! dear one! when far from thee
I ne'er know joy again
I would not that one thought of me
Should give thy bosom pain."

A later Lynchburg poet, Cornelia J. Matthews-Jordan, has bequeathed "The Grave of Bransford Vawter," thus memorializing his burial place in the old Methodist cemetery. Mrs. Jordan's poems were collected together by her daughter, Mrs. Theresa Ambler; many of them written during the war period of 1861-'65 are characterized by the pathos of ever recurring tragedy which fell to the share of the community that had contributed its quota of victims to shot and shell.

Two young Lynchburg poets, Murrell Edmunds, graduate of law, and Abe Craddock Edmunds, L.A., of the University of Virginia, sons of Mrs. W. Murrell Edmunds, have attracted much attention by the publication of two (recently issued) volumes of their poems, which display unusual poetic talent.

Two County Writers

John Kennedy patented 400 acres of land on a branch of Hurricane creek. His son, John P. Kennedy, moved to Baltimore, Md., was author of "Horseshoe Robinson," "Rob of the Bowl," and other stories. "Horseshoe Robinson," a South Carolina narrative, laid about 1780,—first published in 1835, then again in 1852,—was suggested by a visit Kennedy made to the western section of South Carolina in 1789, from an incident heard there which he used in the plot of his story, and his introduction to his hero, Horseshoe Robinson, then around 70 years of age. After Kennedy published his "Tale of Tory Ascendency in South Carolina," he sent Robinson a copy of it which was read to him and won from him the voucher that "It was all true and in its right place."

Colonel John H. Latrobe is given as authority for the statement that John P. Kennedy furnished Thackeray for the account of George Warrington's escape from Fort Duquesne on his journey through the wilderness to the banks of the Potomac, as Thackeray had never seen the valley through which his hero fled after his daring escape. The story is told as follows: Kennedy was at a dinner in London, with Thackeray, Anthony Trollope, Wilkie Collins and other notables. The dinner was over, and the guests were settling down to the wine and cigars, when Thackeray, who was entertaining the company, suddenly stopped and, looking at his watch, exclaimed:

"Gentlemen, I must leave you. I have promised the printers a chapter of *"The Virginians"* tomorrow morning and I haven't written a line of it yet. The printer is inexorable. So wishing you all another meeting when I can be longer with you, I bid you good evening."

Thackeray had almost reached the door, when Kennedy called him back and said, "Perhaps I can write the chapter for you. What are you going to describe?" The great novelist seemed a little surprised, but said, "Kennedy, you are extremely kind, and gladly would I let you write that chapter for me, for I hate to leave a jolly party." "Then don't," all the company cried. "Stay with us and let Kennedy write the proposed chapter." "I've half a mind to let him do it, just for the fun of the thing," said Thackeray. "It is a chapter chiefly of description giving an account of George Warrington's escape from Fort Duquesne and his journey to the Potomac." Kennedy responded, "If that is what you are writing about, I can do it, for I know every foot of the ground." "All right, then," said Thackeray resuming his seat, "let me have it early tomorrow morning." Going to his hotel

Kennedy wrote the fourth chapter of the second volume of *"The Virginians,"* and thus it happened that the narrative of George Warrington's flight was so accurate as to the topography of the country through which he passed.

A later writer, one time Campbell resident, was Dr. George W. Bagby, whose father was a merchant in Lynchburg, and his mother a member of the Evans family. Dr. Bagby at 18 years of age began the study of medicine in which he graduated at the University of Pennsylvania at Philadelphia, and started the practice of his profession in Lynchburg, (where his father lived), but later became editor of the *Lynchburg Virginian*. His editorial articles were afterwards collected and included in a volume with "The Old Virginia Gentleman," which describes Clerk James Steptoe of Bedford and his home at Federal Hill, about 3 miles from Poplar Forest, Jefferson's Bedford county home. Bagby's book tells that Steptoe was beloved by every one, especially by his slaves, whom he had had taught different trades that they might support themselves after his death, when, by his will, they were set free. Born 1750 at Hominy Hall, Westmoreland county, Va.; died 1826 in Bedford county. Children:
—Major James, married Catherine Mitchell.—Dr. William, married 1st, Nancy Brown, married 2nd, Mary Dillon.—George, married Maria Thomas.—Robert, married Elizabeth Leftwich.—Thomas, married Louise C. Yancey.—Elizabeth, married (2d wife) Hon. Charles Johnston of Sandusky.—Frances, married Henry S. Langhorne, of Lynchburg.—Sallie, married William Massie of Nelson county.—Lucy, married Robert Penn of Bedford county. Rt. Rev. Jas. Steptoe Johnston, Bishop of Western Texas, was a descendant of Chas. and Elizabeth S. Johnston.

Dr. Bagby moved to Richmond; he became a writer for other magazines, succeeding John R. Thompson as editor of *The Southern Literary Messenger*, in 1860-64. Partial loss of his eyesight led him to enter the lecturing field, where he received great applause.

An Active Life

Campbell has had no more distinguished a son than Dr. (Colonel) Robert Enoch Withers who lived a long useful life of constant activity and, in his declining years, penned the reminiscences of his varied experiences.

After early preparation by private tutors, and attendance at Samuel Miller's "Woodburne Classical School" in Pittsylvania, he matriculated in 1840-1 at the University of Virginia in the medical class, from which he graduated as a licensed doctor before his twentieth year. He then returned to join his father in the practice of his profession at Rock Castle, but at the end of a year received appointment as one of the resident physicians at the Alms House Hospital, about two and a half miles west of Baltimore, where he remained another year, then returned to his native county. During his practice following (1845) the community was visited through its high rolling portion by an epidemic of Enteric fever, which lasted for nearly five months—and which he successfully treated— the first and worst appearance of the disease in Virginia.

His marriage to Mary V. Royal of Lynchburg occurred in 1846. After this he made his residence in his father's home for a short while, but soon moved to a place he named *Briery,* because it was located upon worn-out land over-run with blackberry vines. To improve this property he decided to apply Peruvian guano, which had just begun to attract the attention of farmers, though none of his neighbors had previously experimented with it. Thus he introduced its use into Campbell. In 1858 he was induced to sell Briery (a residence afterwards burned), and moved to Danville. There he was commissioned captain of the Danville Grays, and, at the formation of a battalion of three companies, received the commission of major of the regiment, which had been called "Third" upon its organization, but later was numbered as the 18th Virginia Infantry.

Colonel Withers was dangerously wounded at the battle of Gaines' Mill and carried to Richmond, where he was discovered to be seriously injured. The doctor attending him, reported the likelihood of his death, but he became well enough in the following autumn to return to the army, yet a severe rheumatic attack caused him to give up active service and he then took charge of the prison post at Danville, and was resident there when that city became the seat of the Confederate government (following Richmond's evacuation) and later when it was under Federal administration.

At the solicitation of his political friends he canvassed as a candidate for Congress, but, as his was not at that period the popular side of politics, his opponent won over him. About this time he entered upon the lease of a grazing farm in the rich portion of Tazewell county and would then have taken up his abode there, but was offered and accepted the position of editor of the *Lynchburg News,* of which Christian and Waddell were proprietors. In 1867 he was induced to enter the race as candidate for governor of the state, but in the interest of his party, afterwards withdrew from the field. When county government became reorganized he was elected supervisor of Tazewell where he was then living.

In 1870 (the year when public schools were being established in Virginia), Colonel Withers was employed by the University Publishing Company of New York, as their agent, to secure the adoption of their series in the state schools, and after the first year of that service he was made general agent for all of the Southern states. In 1873 he, together with Commodore Maury, was appointed by Governor Kemper to represent Virginia at a meeting of the National Agricultural Association which met in St. Louis, Missouri. In the previous year Withers and General Kemper had been Electors at Large from the Conservative party to the National Democratic convention.

At this time Withers was again in the campaign for governor, and his friends made a good fight for him, but the majority party being opposed to him, again won the race for their candidate. Then, by the overwhelming demand of his party, he was induced to accept the office of lieutenant governor and this secured for him the position of president of the Senate.

In 1875 Withers resigned as lieutenant-governor and entered the United States Senate, to which he had been elected. There he met Senator Thurman of Ohio—the head of the Democratic Senators—whose ancestors had resided in Campbell, from which county his family had moved, and settled in Ohio. While serving as Senator, Colonel Withers was elected one of the Board of Regents of Smithsonian Institution. It was at this time that the decision to erect a mortuary chapel to General Robert E. Lee at Lexington was made, and at the laying of the corner-stone a public ceremony was arranged with Colonel Withers, as a Virginia Senator and Confederate Veteran and General Joseph E. Johnston as the speakers.

1881 saw the close of Colonel Withers' political career. In 1885 he received the appointment of Consul to Hong Kong in place of Colonel John S. Mosby, removed. He held the post four years, then resigned from the consulate and returned to Virginia.

Wholesale Pioneer

Many years ago James Bruce, a resident in a neighboring section to that which became Campbell county, drew public attention to himself by his great financial success in his system of operating wagon-trains for the purpose of supplying country merchants with their wares. This was before water and rail carriers had been brought into service, and when transportation was slow and difficult because of the unimproved condition of roads. While reaping the benefit of his operations, Bruce was also a benefactor to the merchants and their patrons who might have fared badly lacking this systematized service. His enterprise and profit seem not to have prompted his neighbors to follow his example, thus not having to contend with competition in his line of work, he managed to amass a large fortune, and became classed with the few capitalists of equal possessions in his day.

He lived when accumulation of land and slaves for field cultivation and care of crops, especially of tobacco in its varied manipulation and distribution, were objects more appealing to the planter than trade, and when engagement in the latter occupation was not considered the proper one for the gentleman who could otherwise provide support for his family. As time wore on this point of view changed, and there was awakened a perception of trade's use upon ambition's ladder, for it could lead to the expansion of fortune and influence.

Long before advance was made towards the operation of chain stores—as at present generally established—a hint was imparted by the action of Nathaniel Guggenheimer, Sr., a merchant of Lynchburg, in his starting a branch merchandise store at Concord about seventy years ago. This merchant was of the race which has ever evinced a genius for successful mercantile operation. While he may not have reached the pinnacle of financial success at which he aimed, he furnished the initiative which probably influenced Max Guggenheimer, his brother-in-law, in his far-reaching efforts towards the introduction of wholesale merchandising in Lynchburg. The younger Guggenheimer rendered service to his state as a Confederate soldier. At the cessation of war activities he returned to Lynchburg. The older merchant having passed away, he took charge of and conducted the retail business of his predecessor; started a wholesale department, which ultimated in the establishment of Guggenheimer and Company, the first wholesale house in the community. Had the policy of money manipulation by investment in corporated industry been as zealously pursued as now and had public interest in trade expansion been as keen, Max Guggenheimer would be generally recognized as pioneer in wholesale business which gave the city its first impulse towards extended activities, thus paving way for new industries, increase of operators, expert workmen with their families, and consequent growth in population.

Father of Army Dental Bill

Robert Withers Morgan, son of Richard and Sophia W. Jones-Morgan, and named for Dr. Robert Withers, was reared at *Shady Grove,* near Pigeon Run (now Gladys). He enlisted when a youth in his teens in Company "E" of the 11th Virginia Regiment of Pickett's Division, was wounded at the second battle of Manassas and again at Gettysburg and was captured at Milford on May 21st, 1864.

After the close of the war Morgan studied dentistry at Baltimore Dental College, receiving there his degree. His army experience in seeing soldiers suffer from lack of attention to their teeth—though himself at an age when youth is not generally very thoughtful—suggested the idea of having a dental corps in the regular army. Following this thought he formulated a bill, which Major Peter J. Otey presented to Congress and which was passed in 1900, providing for a Dental Corps to be attached to the Medical Unit as a regular part of the army, the dentist to have the rank of major.

In recognition of his having formed and introduced the bill, Dr. Morgan was appointed by the Secretary of War in February, 1901, one of three dental surgeons forming the first supervising and examining Dental Board, stationed at Washington. Later Dr. Morgan was sent to the army post at Havana, Cuba, but the climate there disagreed with his health, and he returned to Lynchburg, where he had previously established his home and dental office. He never regained his health and died in 1904.

Such importance is now attached to the condition of the teeth, as furnishing a seat of disease, it may be realized that no more auspicious movement has been started than that of Dr. Morgan for the benefit of a national branch of service, especially in view of the fact that army posts are often situated in remote sections of country which lack the improved facilities of dental practice.

Daniel Monument

Lame Orator

Campbell has ever exhibited the attitude of paying honor to John W. Daniel. His personality and ability inspired respect, his career as soldier, orator and statesman confirmed it, and caused him often to be chosen as county mouthpiece. At his death popular sentiment, calling for voluntary subscription, erected a monument (which was executed by Sir Moses Ezekiel) to his memory in a small parking reservation upon the highest point of Lynchburg, the place where he was born in 1842. When the war of 1861 started Daniel was a youth of 18 years attending Dr. Gessner Harrison's University School, but immediately enlisted into service, and was soon made a 2nd lieutenant in Company "A," 11th Va. Reg.; then became 1st lieutenant, and adjutant later. He was commissioned in the Spring of 1863, at General Early's instance, assistant adjutant-general upon the latter's staff, with the title of major, in which capacity he served for over a year. He was wounded several times, first at the first battle of Manassas, again at Boonsboro, Md.; then so severely wounded May 6, 1864, at the Wilderness, as to be lamed for life—this happened when he was attempting to lead one of Pegram's regiments to General Gordon's assistance, and while behaving with great gallantry, was shot twice, once in the leg, which permanently disabled him and ended his war service.

After the war terminated he took a course of law at the University of Virginia, then returning to Lynchburg entered upon the practice of his profession. His first call to public life was his election to the State Legislature as a member of the House of Delegates, in which he remained for three years, and in 1875 he was elected to the State Senate, and re-elected four years later. In 1884 he was elected to the House of Representatives, and was chosen to succeed Gen. Wm. Mahone in the U. S. Senate, his term beginning in 1887, holding that position to the time of his death. He was a Democratic elector-at-large in Virginia in 1876, and delegate-at-large from Virginia to the national Democratic conventions of 1880, 1888, 1892, 1896, 1900, 1904 and 1908. Senator Daniel was the author of two law books, "Daniel on Negotiable Instruments" and "Daniel on Attachments," which are accepted as standards by the profession.

About a year after the death of Senator Daniel, his son, Edward M. Daniel, collected into book form many of his father's speeches, and in thus preserving them said he felt that he performed a service that was not without real value to the state which the senator had served so faithfully, a sentiment to which everyone will assent, for there is embodied in these speeches only expression of fine principles.

In 1866, while a student at the University, Senator Daniel made an address before the Jefferson Literary Society in which he asserted that "the great achievements that have dignified and embellished the annals of mankind have been performed by a few earnest men gathered together in the spirit, as well as in the name of right and acting under impulse of a glorious sentiment." Called to South Carolina to deliver the oration at the Centennial Celebration of the battle of Kings' Mountain, in 1880, he told of the great battle fought there by the people clad in coarse, homespun garments, with knives in their belts, and flintlock rifles in their hands, but not a bayonet nor cannon, no ambulance or wagon, no general officer, not even a regular soldier in the army of victory, yet they climbed the strong breastworks of the rugged mountain, through onsets of enemy bayonets and laid low in battle or led captive, every soldier who defended it. "Complete to the wish," Colonel William Campbell, as the commandant, said of their victory.

One-fourth of the army of Cornwallis was annihilated by an inferior force, with a loss of but 28 killed and sixty wounded. Daniel quoted from John P. Kennedy (of Campbell county parentage), in "Horseshoe Robinson," as he depicted the battle "from this turning point the cause advanced to a speedy end, the victory was a fresh fountain of strength and the parent of new triumphs, and resulted ultimately in the consummation of our independence."

A singular test fell to Daniel in a request from Vice-President Hobart, that he would speak at a Lincoln dinner in New Jersey. The answer given was that to speak on such an occasion a speaker should be in whole-hearted sympathy with his subject; that some one better fitted should be selected. Asked to reconsider his decision, the senator, looking over one of the war president's biographies, found a page which so impressed him with its absence of hostile thoughts, that he consented to the request made of him. These were the words he read, and which were said at the first meeting of the Cabinet after the news had been brought of Lee's surrender: "Gentlemen, before you take up public business, I have a remark to make on my own account. I hear cries here and there, 'Hang this man, hang that man.' There has been enough blood-shed in this country, and I can say to you for myself that instead of catching anybody and hanging anybody, I wish all of those who feel that they might leave their country for their country's good, might go away without anybody's catching them." There seems in these words almost a suggestion of regret that he had once evoked the spirit of war.

Concerning the War of the Confederacy, Major Daniel said: "Revolutions imply the impossibility of compromise and never begin until overtures are ended; after that there is no half-way house between victory and death. Had surrender come before its necessity was manifest to all mankind, reproach, derision and contempt—faction, feud and recrimination—would have brought an aftermath of disorder and terror; and had it been based upon such terms as those which critics have suggested, a glorious revolution would have been snuffed out like a farthing candle in a miserable barter over the ransom of slaves. Though the Confederate soldiers did not achieve the independence of the Confederacy, they did preserve the independent and unshamed spirit of their people, and in that spirit the South finds shield against calumny, title to respect, and incentive to noble and unselfish deeds."

It seems very fitting that Senator Daniel should have been called upon in 1888 to second the nomination of Allan G.

Thurman for the office of Vice-President of the United States, in doing which he gave the record of his nominee: "Fifty years ago, and more, there went beyond the Alleghanies, from the town of Lynchburg, a preacher of the Gospel, who carried with him his wife, his boy, his Bible, and household goods. He settled in the splendid young commonwealth of Ohio. The boy became the father of the man. The man by his force of character rose to the high places of the people's confidence. They made him their representative in Congress. They clothed him with the ermine of the Chief Justiceship of their court. They made him governor of their state. They sent him as a senator of the United States, and then he was a statesman of country-wide and world-wide renown; and wherever there were difficult conditions to be confronted and difficult theories to be expounded, he measured the breadth of every occasion until he became the beacon of the people's hope and the center of the state's desire." It was a proud moment for speaker and listener, the old and the young countrymen met together on such an auspicious occasion.

John W. Daniel's was a life of miraculous escape from tragic death, for besides his war encounters, he was a near victim at the falling of the capital building at Richmond, where so many of those then associated with him were killed or injured.

The country home of Senator Daniel, *Westerly,* was the former property of Colonel Peyton Leftwich, and situated on an eminence at the foot of which was Blackwater creek. Here the Senator spent the latter years of his life. At the time of Lynchburg's last annexation all of that land was incorporated within the city limits, and is now owned by Richard Carrington of Lynchburg Shoe Company.

Benovolent Hand

Samuel Miller, a native of Arbemarle county, born June 30, 1792, on Humpback Mountain, was the son of a poor widow and had few advantages. As a young man 18 years of age, he moved to Lynchburg and secured employment in the store of Benjamin Perkins. By application and economy he managed to go into business for himself. He began by buying tobacco and finally, by operating in stocks and securities, succeeded in amassing a fortune. In 1829, at the age of 31 years, his health failed and he retired to his farm near the Quaker Meeting House, a short distance from Lynchburg, where he lived alone with the exception of his few servants. Devoting his attention to his bonds, stocks and newspapers, he spent his days, polite to all callers, but never courting company. He accumulated a fortune of several million dollars, chiefly by two great financial strokes—first in cornering the English market in hemp, and second by cornering tobacco, also in the English market. Several years before his death he donated 40 acres of land for the establishment of the Lynchburg Female Orphan Asylum, which was given his name at first but changed back to the designation he had chosen for it. In his will he bequeathed to the city its finely wooded park which also bore his name, but is now known as City Park. Further bequests to Lynchburg were $20,000 towards construction of a reservoir on College Hill and $300,000 as a fund for support of the orphanage.

Miller died in 1869 and was buried within the Orphanage grounds, where a granite memorial shaft was erected in recognition of his charities. Besides his beneficence to Lynchburg he gave $2,000,000 to found an industrial school for boys in Albemarle, his native county. A suit, lasting many years, was brought to set aside his will, but was finally settled, the bulk of his property going as provided. As time passes, his charities become more far-reaching, and have paved the way to advancement for many a girl and boy, equally poorly circumstanced, as he had been in early life. The city park, obtained through his provision, remained for many years the only one in the city, furnishing a recreative reservation for those seeking the shade of its fine oak grove and repose from city noises. Thus it happens that the money for collecting which Miller devoted the longest period of his life, has brought blessings not only to residents of the county where he was born and reared but also to those in the county of his adoption.

Wailes Perkins, one of Miller's beneficiaries, not inspired by his benefactor's thriftiness, said it did not pay to work; he had tried it, following the plow one whole day, when he had worn out a pair of $10 boots. He claimed that he could have hired a farm hand to do the same work for 50 cents.

An incorporated Company, Lynchburg Female Orphan Asylum, was formed June 10, 1868, the purpose of which was the education and support of destitute white females of Lynchburg and its immediate vicinity. The names of officers for the first year were Ambrose B. Rucker, president; John G. Meem, vice-president; Jas. O. Williams, secretary and treasurer; with Geo. D. Davis, Lorenzo Norvell, Chas. W. Button, David E. Spence, Wm. A. Miller, J. F. Slaughter, Thos. E. Murrell and D. P. Halsey, members of the Board. According to the constitution the entire management was vested in the 13 Board Members, who were to be elected by the stockholders, one each from the Protestant denominations in Lynchburg and the remainder from the stockholders, not communicants of any church. No child over 12 years of age could be admitted. On Feb. 2, 1875, two children were received into the orphanage, since when more than 400 women have passed out to business communities and homes of their own. By various purchases the original tract has been increased to 93 acres, the greater part of which is woodland. About 30 acres under cultivation, provides vegetable, fruit and corn maintenance, while dairy and poultry furnish milk, butter and eggs. Meat is also supplied on the premises. Since 1869 more than a million dollars has passed from the orphanage into city business channels, yet during its existence no demand has been made upon the city for financial assistance.

Jones Memorial Library

George M. Jones, a successful merchant and financier of Lynchburg, having lost his only children, two beautiful daughters, in their girlhood, decided to give a library to Lynchburg as a memorial to them, and made some provision for it in his will.

In 1896 Jones gave the Randolph-Macon Woman's College $15,000 for a Memorial Library.

In 1905 his widow formed the George M. Jones Library Association and incorporated it with a body of seven trustees. The building was erected, equipped and opened for one day in October, 1907, for a reception of the citizens with the assurance from Mrs. Jones that they would soon have the pleasure of using the books; and this occurred in June, 1908. She provided an endowment of $50,000 at that time, together with the ground and building.

At her death she left to the Library her whole estate, which amounted to a little over $500,000, making the total of $550,-000, the interest upon which provides the present income for maintenance of the library, now containing upwards of 21,000 volumes.

The work is carried on at present in the Main Library, with three branches—the Fort Hill branch in the Fort Hill Community Club-house on Memorial Avenue; the College Hill branch in the Robert E. Lee Junior High School building on Floyd and 13th street; and a branch in the Dunbar High School for use of colored citizens.

Three members of the Board of Trustees were on the original board when the library was incorporated by Mrs. Jones—A. R. Long, Walker Pettyjohn and O. B. Barker. To this number was added four others, Dr. E. C. Glass, R. T. Watts, J. D. Owen and J. R. Gilliam.

The members of the staff are Miss J. M. Campbell, Mrs. E. K. Peck, Mrs. Warren Dickerson, Misses Sallie Hamner, Josephine DuPuy, Elizabeth Dirom and Claudine Kizer. Mrs. E. Spencer is in charge of Dunbar School branch.

The library with extended and improved grounds, is situated on Rivermont Avenue at its intersection with Victoria Avenue, upon an elevation sufficient to moderate the noise from street traffic, and protect it from other disturbance, as the locality is as yet detached from the business section of the city. Since education has become largely featured in all progressive movements, this Jones' Memorial well serves the city within which it is located, by its timely establishment and endowment.

Valuable Papers

About twenty years ago, Professor Denny of Lexington, Va., returned some boxes of papers in his possession—which were the property of Richard K. Crallé—to the family of the latter, which papers were found upon examination to be of a public character. These letters were received at the time when Crallé was chief clerk and occasionally acting secretary of state, to John C. Calhoun, at the time the latter was Secretary in President Tyler's administration—and as they were exclusively of a public nature, they were given to Custodian Hunt of the Document branch of the Congressional Library. There the letters were bound together in handsome folio volumes, entitled "The Crallé Papers," as further examination had proved them to be of unique value in settling certain mooted points, especially in regard to the establishment of our northwestern boundary line. Secured in their new home from damage or loss, they are also accessible to historical students and writers. Rd. K. Crallé left a Mss. volume of his poems which were destroyed in a fire at the Cabell House in Lynchburg.

He moved to Lynchburg from Lunenburg county, and married Judith Scott, the second daughter of Dr. John J. Cabell, and resided in the Cabell home on Main street (where the Elks building now stands), and there his wife, after a few years, died, leaving a daughter. He moved to Washington City during the period of his secretarial work. Married the second time Bettie Morris, and built a residence on College Hill which acquired the name *Crallé's Folly*, because it was unusually large and pretentious. This structure was afterwards converted into a college for young men, and it embraced a military department. At the beginning of the war of 1861 a company was formed of the students there. Afterwards the college was used for residences.

Rd. K. Crallé moved to Greenbrier county, W. Va., where he died leaving a large family of children. His daughter, Mary, of the first marriage, married N. H. Campbell, of Bedford county, who was a leading attorney in Lynchburg for some years, but moved to New York City; returned to Lynchburg and died in 1867. Judge J. Lawrence Campbell, one time member of Virginia Legislature and judge of Bedford court.—Rd. K. Campbell of Washington City, who held government position of Commissioner of Immigration at Eastport, Maine, and New Brunswick, then in Immigration Department at the U. S. Treasury, later head of Bureau of Naturalization in the Department of Labor; lastly, on Special Review Board of Bureau; and Henry Terry Campbell, a leading Norfolk banker, were grandsons of Richard K. Crallé, Lynchburg attorney-at-law, and his wife, Judith Cabell-Crallé.

Settlement of State Debt

Randolph Harrison, son of Henry and Jane St. C. Cochran-Harrison, of the legal firm of Harrison, Long and Williams, at Lynchburg, was appointed a member of the commission for the settlement of the debt between Virginia and West Virginia, and was also attorney for the commission in the protracted litigation only ended in 1920, when final settlement was accomplished.

Randolph Harrison had been a delegate from Lynchburg to Virginia Legislature in 1893. A narrative, which reads like fiction, appeared in a Virginia paper in connection with West Virginia's honoring Virginia deferred certificates, issued in 1871, for West Virginia's share of the state debt incurred prior to the separation of the two states.

For years the deferred Virginia certificates could be bought in Virginia as low as 10 cents on the dollar. Many holders, despairing of their ever being paid, threw them away. They were almost in the class of Confederate money. The litigation, resulting in the West Virginia debt settlement, gave them real value.

When the settlement for these certificates was made it was discovered that there was approximately $500,000 which had not been presented for payment, and of this amount, certificates representing a face value of over $70,000 had been issued to Charles and Alfred Morrison of England. Clerk H. B. Churmside, of Charlotte county, becoming acquainted with these facts and recalling that his aunt married Alfred Morrison, who died in 1897, communicated his information to his British relatives. These reported that they did not have the certificates and that they must have been destroyed or lost. Urged to make a more thorough search, they were finally found in a safe box in the office of one of the estate's solicitors.

West Virginia honored the certificates then presented by English heirs of Charles and Alfred Morrison, sending gold bonds in payment, half of which will go to the heirs of Alfred Morrison, among whom are Hugh Morrison, member of Parliament, Major Archibald Morrison, Viscountess St. Cyres and Lady Stephen Gatting.

Charles Morrison lived in London, an unknown millionaire. When he died in 1909 England was astonished to discover that he had left an estate of $75,000,000, of which $55,000,000 was in personal property.

Fitzhugh Lee

Before General Fitzhugh Lee's appointment in 1896 as Consul General to Cuba he held the position of Internal Revenue Collector for the Western district of Virginia, and during his incumbency of that office, he made his residence in Lynchburg. His characteristic manner of speech caused him to be an agreeable companion and served him in securing great popularity, for jest—the spirit of jollying too serious outlook on life,—was instinctive with him. Intercourse between Generals Lee and Early (devoted friends) was, ever in speech or correspondence, in the nature of good humored badinage,

the one twitting the other with some real or accredited pecu-
liarity.   On one occasion when they were discussing Early's
correction of certain written history, Lee banteringly warned
Early that a good many writers were waiting for him to die.
Perhaps, as often happens in similar cases, because of his well-
known trait, many witticisms were attributed to Lee, of which
he was not the author.   After he had donned the United States
uniform it was told of him that upon retiring one evening, he
requested his wife to put his U. S. suit out of sight for he
was afraid (he told her) that he might get up in the night and
shoot at it.

He has been credited with the tribute to United States'
world prominence when at a meeting of the nations, after most
of them had toasted their own countries, and the United States
was taking its turn, alphabetically along with the remaining
small American nations, an Eastern representative arose
and modestly, but impressively, gave the natural bounds of the
country.   Not satisfied that this information had inspired
sufficient respect, a Westerner then followed to tell of its possible bounds.   Following this champion of his country's
cause, not sure that due effect had been produced, Lee
hastened to give the bounds of its promise: "on the north by
the Aurora Borealis, on the east by primeval chaos, on the south
by the procession of the equinoxes, and on the west by the Day
of Judgment."   He thus compassed the dream of America's
most ambitious citizen.

U. S. Senator

Senator Carter Glass came of Scotch-Irish stock, his emigrant ancestor having settled in Virginia before the Revolution.   His grandfather, Thomas Glass, born in Fluvanna county, purchased land in Amherst and settled there,
and was captain of a militia company.   He married Lavinia,
daughter of Richard and Ann Williamson-Cauthorne.   His
oldest child, Robert Henry Glass, married Elizabeth, daugh-

ter of Judge Samuel Christian, and grand-daughter of Captain Henry Christian, an officer in the Revolutionary war. R. H. Glass devoted his business life principally to newspaper work, becoming editor and proprietor of the Lynchburg *Daily Republican,* and papers in Petersburg and Danville. He was postmaster in Lynchburg before and during the war of 1861 and while holding that office issued a special Lynchburg war stamp, now valued because of its rarity. Dur-

"Montview," Senator Glass' Home

ing part of the war he served on the staff of Gen. Floyd with rank of major.

We find Senator Glass starting out to carve his own career, having lost his mother, at fourteen, the age when most youths are still hovering about that parent. His first work was on the *Lynchburg Republican.* Familiar with the newspaper business, he continued in that profession and in 1876 engaged with his father on the *Petersburg Index*, but returned to Lynchburg at the expiration of one year, and held the office of clerk in a railroad auditor's office for three years. In 1880 he was on the local staff of the *Lynchburg News,* which had been founded in 1866 by Robert Waddell.   Two years later he bought out the *News,* then bought *The Virginian,* and merged it with *The News,* and also acquired *The Advance,* an afternoon paper.   In 1886, as clerk of the city council, together with John W. Carroll, president of the council, he signed the agreement giving the Richmond and Alleghany railroad right of way for one track through the city upon payment of $5,000.

Senator Glass was elected to the State Senate in 1899, and served two years.   In 1902 he was elected a member of the State Constitutional Convention and took a prominent part during agitation of the suffrage article in the new constitution. In 1902 he was elected to Congress from the 6th district to fill the vacancy caused by the death of Major Peter J. Otey.   Taking his seat in December of that year, he was placed on the banking and currency committee, having previously served on a similar committee in the State Senate.   For ten years he made a careful study of the banking systems and in 1911 was second ranking Democrat on that committee.   Later, chairman, with the election of Woodrow Wilson to the presidency, he began the framing of what is now the federal banking system.   During the fight for a new banking system for the United States, Senator Glass was closely associated with President Wilson, and took an important part in pushing the reserve system through congress.   His service in connection with the enactment of the Federal Reserve law, combined with his authority on financial matters, led to his appointment to the cabinet, as Secretary of the Treasury, succeeding Wm. G. McAdoo.   Upon the new treasurer fell the task of putting over the Victory Loan of 1919.   When Senator T. S. Martin died in 1919 Treasurer Glass, upon being offered the appointment to the senate vacancy by Governor Davis, resigned the portfolio in the cabinet and took his seat in the Senate in February, 1920.   His last address (heard by the war president in 1923, Armistice Day), was at a pilgrimage to the Wilson home and was an endorsement of the League of Nations.

Senator Glass is engaged upon a history of the Federal Reserve Act and other events in the Wilson Administration. He married Aurelia Caldwell; has two daughters and two sons, Powell and Carter, Jr., the latter of whom has charge of the active management of his two Lynchburg papers; owns a stock farm at *Montview* along the low lands of Candler's Mountain, where he built a home upon native stone foundation on the foot hills, a location which affords a fine view of the neighboring country. His farm is stocked with pure bred Jersey cattle,—for dairy and breeding purposes—which include some of the finest registered cattle to be procured.

Recently Senator Glass has been honored by the philanthropist, George P. Baker, of New York City, in the selection of his name for one of the buildings to be erected at Harvard University, for the use of the economic research division, which are to be named after secretaries of the treasury. It is designed to deposit the original Mss. of Senator Glass' speech— upon the occasion of his presenting the federal reserve act in the House of Representatives on September, 1913—with the archives of the Carter Glass Hall.

Campbell watches for Senator Glass' next movement.

Notable Neighbors and Visitors

Chapter X

Last Homes of Patrick Henry

OHN HENRY, son of Alexander and Jean Robertson-Henry of Aberdeen, Scotland, came to Virginia in 1728. He seems to have been a relative (and became the friend) of Colonel John Syme, a Hanover Burgess, who lived at *Studley,* Hanover, and there Henry visited him. Col. Syme married Sarah, dau. of Isaac and Mary Dabney-Winston, but died in 1731, and several years afterwards his widow married John Henry. They continued to live at *Studley,* a frame house with beautiful grounds, on the Tottipottimoi river and there three sons, John Syme of her first marriage, William and Patrick Henry were born, the last named, in 1736, and a few months afterwards his parents moved to *Mt. Brilliant* in the Rocky Mills neighborhood near the South Anna river. In 1765, though living in Hanover, Patrick Henry filled the vacancy in the representation of Louisa, in the Assembly. In 1779 he purchased a large tract of land in Henry, the county named for him, an estate called *Leatherwood,* which numbered 10,000 acres and there he resided until 1784. Retiring from the governorship in 1786, his next move was to Prince Edward county. At this time he was poor and in debt; then—though he had reached the age of 50 years,—he set himself the task of repairing his fortunes; this was accomplished principally by investments in land. In 1794 he purchased Long Island, Campbell county, upon which he lived before settling at *Red Hill,* and even afterwards he alternated between the two places for some years. As his last and preferred abode, *Red Hill* became a historic place. Standing but a few miles from Brookneal and on the Staunton river, was the old one story and a half house with a lean-to, in which Henry was content to spend his last days, for he liked to hear the rain pattering on the roof; and he appears to have been a man of simple tastes, with no desire to build a *mansion* having many rooms like those of his neighbors.

His home was much enlarged afterwards and several generations of descendants occupied it, but it was burned down a few years ago and not rebuilt. He, and members of his family, are buried in an adjoining enclosure where tombstones mark each burial place. To the patriot's old homestead and last resting place many visitors have made pilgrimages.

Red Hill, Home of Patrick Henry

In the neighborhood of Red Hill, beside an old road leading through the woods, there stands Cub Creek Presbyterian church, a building of unusual style of architecture—erected for the Charlotte Presbyterian colony from Pennsylvania,—which is still in a good state of preservation. In colonial days people drove many miles to attend worship there, and among its congregation were a number of large land owners from adjoining counties: also in the nearby churchyard there are graves of many who had been prominent in their generation. Founded about 185 years ago the church took its name from the adjoining stream.

Staunton Hill—former home of Senator Bruce (of Maryland)—a handsome structure which was built by his father, Charles Bruce, in 1848, is about 2 miles from Red Hill. Situation and construction cause it to be a "show place" in Charlotte county; its fine pillared front of Italian marble making it especially noticeable. The reception rooms are finished in hardwood panelling and colored glass window decoration is unique. A broad double stairway reaches the top story, from which fine views are obtained of the river low lands. Thomas N. Page married a daughter of Charles Bruce, and is said to have written *Red Rock* while on a visit there.

A few years ago this fine estate was acquired by a company of realtors and became incorporated as *Staunton Hill Lodge* with the aim of making it a recreative club house for its shareholders, but failure to realize their expectations in the investment, caused the company to dispose of it at a considerable loss. Recently it has been repurchased by a member of the Bruce family who plans to restore and occupy it.

In his will Patrick Henry directed that all the lands in his Long Island estate be divided into two parts; by Randolph's old road to the new road from the overseer's house to where Davis' mill crosses the road, thence to Potts' spring at the old quarter place and along to the upper part where Philip Payne lived, Long Island and other islands and 100 acres of back land most convenient for timbers, to be included: these estates were left in fee simple to his wife for two of their sons which she was to name and point out. To his wife he gave all of his lands at or adjoining Red Hill (property purchased from Fuqua, Booker, Watkins and others out of a tract called Watkins' order) and at her death they were to be given to two of their sons. Leatherwood (Henry county), Prince Edward, Kentucky and Seven Islands lands and those "lately purchased of Marshall Mason, Nowell, Wimbush, Massy and Prewitt" were directed to be sold and after payment of his debts the residue equally divided between their two other sons. All the rest of his estate, whether lands, slaves, personal estate, debts or rights, he gave to his wife to enable her to educate and bring up their children. If the debt for the lands he had covenanted to sell Judge Wilson, in Virginia and North Carolina, could not be recovered, that property should be given his wife for the benefit of their children, but in case his wife married again he revoked and made void every gift, legacy, authority or power mentioned and directed that she should have no more of his estate than she could recover by law; nor should she become the guardian of his children, nor executrix of his will: his friends, Edmund Winston, Philip Payne and George D. Winston were made joint executors.   Mrs. Dorothea D. Henry, his widow, married Judge Edmund Winston, and litigation followed, when court commissioners divided the various tracts of land.

A codicil to his will had become necessary by his contract to sell his Leatherwood land to George Hairston and transfer of the proceeds in the purchase of two shares of the Saura Town lands (amounting to 6314 acres) and this property devised to two of his sons in lieu of his former bequest to them of the Leatherwood estate, etc.   Red Hill, Long Island and Saura Town estates then furnishing seats for his six sons, whose names he gave as Patrick, Fayette, Alexander Spotswood, Nathaniel, Edward Winston and John; and grandson, Edmund Henry, to whom he bequeathed 1000 acres of land where his father Edward died, joining Perego's and Coles' lines and intended for his son Edward (dec.): names of daughters given are Dorothea S. Winston, Martha Catherine Henry, Sarah Butler Henry, Anne Roane, Elizabeth Aylett and Martha Fontaine. Henry's Red Hill estate contained 2920 acres; Long Island 3522 acres; two of the Campbell tracts embraced 1030 acres and 440 acres, which perhaps were *Shady Grove* (given his son, Spotswood Henry) and *The Grove,* a place upon which no residence was erected.

Jefferson's Bedford Home

In 1750 Peter Jefferson patented 713 acres of land in Lunenburg county on Staunton river adjoining the property of Benjamin Clements.   In 1797 Thomas Jefferson patented 800 acres on the branches of Dreaming and Buffalo creeks, and 100 acres on the south branch of Ivy creek. He sold Samuel Jordan Harrison in 1811 the latter tract and one on Ivy creek containing 474 acres (which had been granted to Richard Tullos in 1771), for £400. and the further sum of £800. guaranteed to be paid. Ivy is a tributary of Blackwater creek, which adds its overflow to James river at Lynchburg. Tomahawk creek has its source on Jefferson's land and owes its name to an Indian battle which took place near the stream in early times: numberless tomahawks and arrow-heads have

Popular Forest, Bedford, Home of Thomas Jefferson

been and may still be found along its banks. Tomahawk unites with Burton and forms Dreaming creek in Campbell's northwest corner. Jefferson's land lay not far from New London town and the Academy. A two-room farm house stood on his 800-acre tract, and Jefferson made many visits there. When disabled by a fall from his horse he recruited at this Bedford place. The plan of building Poplar Forest home was formed when he was caught at his farm house, without resources during a long rainy spell; the home, several years under construction, was completed about 1810. His first letters written there, which are embraced in his published works, are dated August, 1811. In 1821 he made four visits to the Forest, which he describes as an excellent house— inferior only to Monticello—"where he was comfortably fixed and attended with a few good neighbors; and he passed his time there in a tranquility and retirement much adapted to his age and indolence." Enormous poplars suggested the name chosen, for many of these trees cluster in groups so close together as to present the appearance of giant poplars.

A descendant of Jefferson also has given a description of this historic and interesting home "built of brick according to a design of his own, one story in front, and, owing to the fall of ground, two in the rear, the lower story being a basement with a wine cellar underneath; an exact octagon in shape, with a central hall, 20 feet square, lighted from above, a room which served as a dining room and which contained a portable dumbwaiter with shelves; around the dining room were grouped a drawing room, four bedrooms, and a pantry. A terrace extends from one side of the house and a portico in front connected by a vestibule with the central room, and in the rear, a veranda upon which the drawing room opens with windows extending to the floor." Two large mounds of earth on either side of the house serve to screen from view outbuildings behind them.

Jefferson's journeys to and from Bedford, made in his private carriage drawn by his own horses, consumed three days in travelling over 100 miles. Stops were made always at the same inns: at Ford's tavern between Monticello and the Forest, the following incident occurred during one of these journeys:

Upon his arrival Jefferson was shown into the best room where a respectable looking stranger was seated. The latter opened conversation without having an idea as to Jefferson's identity. He introduced the subject of certain mechanical operations which he had recently witnessed, inquiries and remarks made in response, satisfied him that he was conversing with an eminent engineer. Agriculture was next introduced and he then made up his mind that his companion was a farmer on a large scale. Finally, the topic of religion was broached and the clergyman (who was Rev. Charles Clay, known as "Parson Clay"), began to suspect that he was conversing with a member of his own profession, but could not discover to what particular persuasion he leaned. When Jefferson retired, Clay sought the landlord and asked the name of his fellow lodger. "What," said his host, "Don't you know the Squire? That is Mr. Jefferson." "Not President Jefferson?" exclaimed his enquirer. "I tell you that was neither an athiest nor an irreligious man, one of juster sentiments I never met." From this recounter, of these two neighbors in the county, a warm friendship ensued and letters passed between them have been preserved, a half dozen from Jefferson to Clay are included in the former's published writings. One written from Monticello January 27, 1790, states: "I hoped that during my stay here I could have the pleasure of seeing you in Bedford, but I find it will be too short for that. I wished to visit again that greatest of our curiosities, the Natural Bridge, and did not know but you might have the same desire. I understand you are a candidate for representation of your district in Congress. I cannot be with you to give you my vote, but I am sure I shall be contented with such a representative as you will make, because I know you are too honest a patriot not to wish to see our country prosper by any means, though they be not exactly those you would have preferred. Wishing you every prosperity in this and in all your other undertakings (for I am sure from my knowledge of you they will always be just), I am, dear sir, your friend and servant." Another letter written January 29, 1815, tells of his sending, as a gift, a complete set of spectacles, from early use to old age, as a token of his friendship for the Reverend Clay.

Thomas Jefferson is said to have acquired the Poplar Forest estate through his marriage to the widow Wailes, neé Skelton. There was a well known tract in Bedford-Campbell section in earlier times called "The Forest," mentioned in several early deeds. One, dated previous to the formation of Bedford, records purchases of land by Rev. William Stith in conjunc-

tion with Nicolas Davies and, in the division of their investments, *The Forest* fell to Stith, who died in 1755.   Afterwards, Colonel John Payne acquired *The Forest,* a property he divided and in his will bequeathed one part each to
the sons of his second marriage, Philip and John Smith Payne.
Nothing has been found showing that this was the same property as that held by Jefferson, who sometimes called his place
"The Forest."   His manager there was Peter Yancey.

In May, 1926, there was staged upon the lawn of this historic
place the pageant "An Afternoon of Retrospection," under the
direction of Mrs. Roy A. Ralph, author of the play, who por-
trayed the part of the "Spirit of Democracy," and was assisted
in her presentation by patriotic societies.   This pageant, given
under the auspices of the Woman's Club of Lynchburg, was
divided into four parts, as follows:

1. The Beginnings of Religion—a reproduction of the first
religious services at Jamestown, in 1607—the cast, the Boy
Scouts of Lynchburg.

II. The Beginnings of Education—the granting of the charter to William and Mary College, London, 1693; produced by
Blue Ridge, Lynchburg, and Poplar Forest,—the three Lynchburg Chapters of D. A. R.

III. The Beginnings of Independence—Jefferson submit-
ting his draft of the Declaration to the Committee, 1776—
presented by the Little Theatre of Lynchburg.

IV. The Beginnings of Social Culture—Dolly Madison and
her friends, 1809-1817—produced by the Lynchburg Committee of Colonial Dames.

Poplar Forest is now the country residence of C. S. Hutter.
The only change which has taken place in the house since
Jefferson occupied it, has been in the roof, originally with a
dome elevation, which became badly injured in a storm and
being considered unsafe, was not renewed.   A circular driveway leads to the front steps, facing which there is a solid
circle of dwarf boxwood, planted there by Mrs. Sextus Hutter,
mother of the present owner.

Hero of New Orleans

The war cloud which hung over the country from 1812 on through 1814 lifted, and the preliminaries of peace between the United States and England were signed at Ghent on De-

Frescoed Walls.   Scene No. 3.   (See page 76)

cember 25th, 1814—a glad celebration of this Day among days. News of the action reached New York on February 11th, 1815, and was flashed over the country and followed by general rejoicing, and fêting of the military leaders who had borne the brunt of battle. During the following April Lynchburg was honored by a visit from General Andrew Jackson, the hero of New Orleans, who was en route to Washington, and made a stop at *Poplar Forest,* the Bedford home of Thomas Jefferson.

A committee of citizens from Lynchburg was sent out on the Forest road to meet him as he drove along in a four-horse vehicle with Jefferson, his host, and they were escorted to the court house, where speeches were made welcoming Jackson to the Hill City; the party thence proceeding to the Bell Tavern. A public dinner, presided over by Mayor James Stewart, was served at Martin's warehouse, and was followed by a fashionable ball that evening at the same tavern. Next morning the distinguished guests crossed the ferry and pursued their onward course to Washington city; the memorable occasion causing much local satisfaction, for even in anticipation the visit of General Jackson aroused enthusiastic interest among the citizens—especially among those who held the same political opinions—and extensive preparations were made for his reception. Many private homes were newly decorated and furnished in his honor.

It was the time when the fashion of frescoed papering was in vogue and a number of householders invested in that fashionable and costly wall papering. Among others, Dr. John J. Cabell—an ardent admirer of Jackson—selected papering for his home on Main street, depicting scenes around Paris—of Verseilles, Trianon, etc., the fine quality of which was proven by its remaining on the walls in fair state of preservation for nearly a hundred years, and when the property passed into the possession of the Elks' society in 1903 it was taken down and portions of it are yet preserved. Other wall paper decorations represented English hunting and pastoral scenes and one pattern reproduced Don Quixote illustrations, one of the latter used in the home of Captain Labby,—also situated on Main street,—was of Sancho Panzo tossed in a blanket, papering which was still untouched when last enquiries were made concerning it.

Returning in the triumphal march of Jackson through Bedford and Campbell were soldier citizens of the two counties who had served in the southern engagement during the war of 1812, and among these were members of the families of Read and Alexander.

Frescoed Walls. Scene No. 4. (See page 76)

Other Distinguished Visitors

President Andrew Johnson, entertained in 1869.

President Rutherford B. Hayes, entertained in 1877.

President Grover Cleveland, visitor in 1895 for a few hours.

Honorable Henry Clay, of whom Lynchburg had been an enthusiastic supporter when he was a candidate for the presidency.

Senator Allan G. Thurman, in 1874.

At the time that the South was under military control, General N. M. Curtis of New York was sent to take charge of the Lynchburg District. The political atmosphere was unfavorable for his reception. His predecessor had blundered. He realized that the people were still sore from their recent disappointment and were chafing under the coercion to which they were subjected. He brought to bear upon the situation a sense of justice and that spirit, called the milk of human kindness, which enabled him to understand the local point of view and deliberately set himself the task of winning the people's confidence. He asked for their co-operation. When he left he had not only gained their respect but their friendship as well and the assurance of a welcome whenever it was his pleasure to return. He cemented his tie with the community by joining the Lynchburg Society of Masons, and thus strengthened the brotherly feeling he had created by his good will and service.

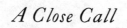

A Close Call

Chapter XI

Hunter's Raid

LESS than 100 years had elapsed, after Tarleton's fruitless effort to capture patriot stores at New London, when a similar incursion was made into Campbell with Lynchburg as objective point. Both had for aim the weakening of resources of the opposing armies. In early June of 1864 it had become known that Lynchburg held stores which belonged to the Confederate government. Hunter was accordingly detailed to make a raid and destroy what he found. This order was carried out very thoroughly both as to public and private property along the route. Sure that success awaited him, this commanding officer moved with deliberation and meeting no invincible stone walls on his forward course, he foresaw easy conquest. Arriving near the Quaker Meeting-house he chose *Sandusky* Major George Hutter's residence for his headquarters, and there held council with his officers as to the plan of attack of what was to be a "walk-over" for them. Circumstances seemed to favor him, for though brave Confederate cavalry under McCausland and Imboden had managed to delay final issue, they were not adequate, even with aid from the hastily collected force of the town, to withstand Hunter's well-equipped and trained army, and the second day's engagement was anticipated with considerable anxiety by the people in the town.

The 2nd Corps, Army of Northern Virginia, was near Gaines' Mill on June 12th, when General Early received instructions from General Lee to move to the Valley by way of Charlottesville, strike Hunter's force in the rear and if possible destroy it, then move down the valley and threaten Washington city; also to communicate with General Breckenridge, who would co-operate in the attack on Hunter. Railroad and telegraph lines had been cut by Hunter's cavalry between Charlottesville and Lynchburg; by Sheridan's cavalry between Richmond and Charlottesville, so there was no way of communicating with Breckenridge. Riding in advance of his troops, Early reached Charlottesville on the 16th and there received a telegram from Breckenridge at Lynchburg, informing him that Hunter was in Bedford county. Early arranged for transportation of his troops to Lynchburg, and some of the latter reached that city on midday of the seventeenth. Breckenridge had been disabled by the fall from his horse, killed under him, and unable to go to the field, was replaced by General D. H. Hill, then in Lynchburg, who rode out with Early to make a reconnaissance of the country, the inspection of which determined Early to meet the enemy with his troops in front. As it was of the utmost consequence to the army at Richmond that Hunter should not get into Lynchburg, Early did not feel justified in attacking him until he could do so with a fair prospect of success, and therefore contented himself with acting on the defensive until the whole of his force had arrived in the afternoon of June 18th.

Arrangements were made for attacking Hunter on the 19th, but an unlooked-for change had taken place, Hunter taking flight in the darkness, thus served notice that he declined further battle, and abandoning his forward march, he more hastily turned backwards, having received impression that a superior force faced him. He could have reported, as did Tarleton, that he had found no military stores at the place to which he had been sent, but had he moved forward more promptly he might have secured a different result.

Of the battle on the outskirts of Lynchburg, June 18th, 1864, in an account given by Colonel J. Floyd King (who took part in it), he states that he was detailed, personally, by President Davis to report to General Breckenridge in the valley, and that commander placed him at the head of all of his artillery. On his march to Lynchburg, holding to the mountains, a cloud of dust could be seen on the horizon for miles in length, marking the advance of Hunter's army. It became a race as to which of the two armies would reach Lynchburg first.

Hunter had been joined by Generals Crook and Averill, and his army was then 26,000 strong, but they were skillfully opposed by Vaughn, with his Tennessee, and McCausland, with his Virginia cavalry brigades. Breckenridge, without resting

General Jubal A. Early

his troops, put them in line with these cavalries five miles beyond the city on June 17th.

That afternoon, General Early, commander of the 2nd Army Corps, A. N. V., arrived and took command by superior rank. He promptly ordered Breckenridge's line (including Vaughn and McCausland) back to enable him to place his right flank against James river and thereby give more secure protection to Lynchburg, at the same time, shorten and straiten his line. This was done at night. Next morning Early at once advanced his entire line to Blackwater creek and ordered redoubts, which were quickly thrown up. The enemy arriving in front, deployed and kept up a fire of artillery and sharpshooters until nightfall.

As chief of artillery, Col. King tells that he had under him 32 guns. Among these were Chapman's, Bryan's and Lowry's batteries, carrying 20 guns, all of them Virginia troops. About mid-day the enemy threw forward a full line of sharpshooters, followed by a line of battle to the right and north of the turnpike. He developed firing to the left, then advanced but a short distance when he met the galling fire of the Confederate infantry and steady aim of artillery, which caused him to fall back under such natural cover as he could find. For four or more hours he kept up a roar of artillery and rattle of musketry, as though it was a pitched battle. Towards sunset firing lulled and died down to a hum of hostile camps. That evening, all of the 2nd Corps having arrived, Early called a council of war and made dispositions for attack to begin at daylight next morning. His plan comprehended turning the enemy's right and flanking him by that means with Gordon's division, while the rest attacked in front. Early's available force at this juncture, including Breckenridge's, did not reach 13,000 men.

Taking alarm, the armies in front, double his numerical strength, stole away in the night and when day dawned there was nothing in front save their empty camping ground, covered by a scattered line of mounted riflemen, who for a short time kept up a desultory fire, then disappeared.

Early's entire command marched in pursuit, but did not reach the enemy near enough for attack of any consequence until near Salem, when Hunter's rear was crushed. The flight, however, continued without stop to Ohio, 200 miles away.

Diary of Captain W. W. Old, A. D. C.

(Kept from June 13th, 1864 to August 12th, 1864)

The operations of Lieutenant General Jubal A. Early, June, 1864:

June 13—Monday: Left the trenches around Richmond, with corps composed of Gordon's Division, Major General John B. Gordon, commanding; Rode's Division, Major General Robt. E. Rodes, commanding; Early's Division, Major General S. D. Ramseur, commanding; Wilson's and Braxton's Battalions of Artillery, Brigadier General A. R. Long, commanding. Marched to Goodall's Tavern.

June 14: Marched to Gardner's Cross Roads, Louisa county.

June 15: Marched to Valentine's and West's Mills, Louisa county.

June 16: Marched to Keswick Depot, Albemarle county.

June 17: Took cars for Lynchburg at daylight and arrived there about noon with Lewis' (Hoke's) and Johnston's brigades of Ramseur's division; Pegram's brigade (Brigadier General Lilly, commanding) of Ramseur's division; and Gordon's brigade; and a small part of Terry's brigade of Gordon's division. Arrived late in afternoon. Formed line in battle. Some artillery of King's battalion on the line. Imboden's men stampeded. Jackson's cavalry also ran but were reformed and remained in line all night. Some artillery firing and skirmishing.

June 18: Lay around Lynchburg in line all night. Some skirmishing and artillery firing. The troops arriving slowly; all in by 3 p. m. Troops moving into position.

June 19: Marched at daylight in pursuit of enemy (who began to retreat by sending off their trains at 2 p. m. yesterday). Ramseur in front. Reached Liberty (Bedford) and drove the enemy through the town.

8:00 p. m.: All quiet; marched 25 miles.

June 20: Marched at daylight. Enemy moving nearly all night.

Hunter's Raid Described by One of His Soldiers

On June 8, 1864, General Hunter was reinforced by a division of infantry commanded by General Crook and a brigade of cavalry under General Averill. One of this command furnished the following account of their march to Lynchburg:

"All the commands, under Hunter as head general, left Staunton on June 10 and marched to Lexington, where there was a lively skirmish with the Confederates. The Federals encamped in Lexington. It was noticed that hundreds of soldiers were running to some point, and then discovered that it was General Jackson's grave, and the soldiers were carrying away by piece-meal, the head and foot boards of the grave, and were cutting small pieces of wood from the flag-pole with their knives. Virginia Military Institute was burned by Hunter's orders. The army remained about Lexington the 12th, which was Sunday. Monday, June 13th, orders were given to form into line and march. Colonel Jas. M. Schoonmaker, a Pittsburg millionaire, commanding the 14th Penn. Reg., but then in command of the brigade, ordered Capt. Miles to take the 3rd Battalion of the Regiment as advance guard. Near Natural Bridge these troops came upon McCausland's Confederate cavalry brigade. Miles charged on them for a short distance, and then commanded a halt. The Confederates charged and the Federals got back a short distance, where they met the regiment, and again charged, when Capt. Miles was wounded. The rest of the brigade came up, and the Confederates fell back a short distance. General McCausland formed a line on the top of the hill. The Federals dismounted and were driving the Confederates back, when one of their rear batteries mistook them for Confederates and began to throw shell among them. The Confederates fell back and the Federals mounted and went on a charge to Buchanan, where they found that the bridge across James river had been set afire, and the cavalry and artillery had to ford the river, infantry crossing on pontoon bridges. When Hunter's infantry came up the soldiers were covered with thousands of snowballs roses and lilacs which they had pinned to their coats. Hunter encamped around Buchanan, and sent out several detachments of cavalry on scouting expeditions. One went to Fincastle, where they broke open the jail and liberated the prisoners, a Union soldier, two Confederates and four negroes. One of the latter was asked why he was put in jail, he said "for stealing ducks, but when I'se stealing, I steals chickens, not ducks." On June 15th, Hunter crossed Blue Ridge Mountains and encamped near the foot of Peaks of Otter. Next day moved only ten miles, passing through Liberty. Had a skirmish with the Confederates. June 17th, moved towards Lynchburg. All that forenoon saw no enemy; halted for an hour within six miles of the city; at 2 p. m. were within four miles, and found the Confederates in line. Ordered to dismount and form a skirmish line to the right of the pike. All companies of the regiment were soon up and joined this skirmish line. This regiment was armed with Spencer rifles and fired a terrific volley at their opponents. All the brigade was soon in line. When the infantry and artillery came up the latter moved farther over to the left and the infantry took their place. They found they were opposed by Breckenridge's division of infantry. From 5 to 7 o'clock that evening the cannonading was very heavy. The battle lasted till dark.

General Lee had heard of Hunter's movement so he detached Ewell's corps of his army commanded by General Early to move at once to Lynchburg and drive Hunter back. On the morning of June 18th Hunter's army was in line of battle early. The forward brigade was sent over to the left of the army and put into line. They could hear the whistle of the engines which were hauling cars filled with Confederate troops into Lynchburg, and could see the movements of both armies; saw some of Hunter's staff officers galloping after stragglers, and some of Crook's division fall on the field of battle. This brigade appeared to be doing it all. That was a long day, and many would go off into a doze but shell from the enemy now and then would waken them up. The battle lasted until dark, then Hunter withdrew his army. When the last brigade was ordered in they were surprised to find that all of the troops had left the field and their brigade was the rear guard.

Had Hunter listened to Generals Crook and Averill he would have routed Breckenridge's division, commanded by General Wharton, the day before. Lynchburg could then have been taken; but the afternoon was too late, for General Early's army was on the field and it must be recalled that three months later it took Sheridan with an army three times larger than Hunter's to defeat General Early. Besides Hunter was out of ammunition and provisions and 300 miles away from all supplies. The army retreated all that night and next day. A small fight occurred near Liberty on the afternoon of the 19th, when a Confederate brigade of cavalry charged upon the regiment which was the rear guard. But that turned upon them and with the assistance of the brigade drove them back. From Liberty Hunter retreated through Buford Gap in the Blue Ridge mountains. Averill's cavalry pushed ahead towards Salem and took up the railroad track of the Virginia and Tennessee railroad, June 20th. During that night Hunter's whole army reached Salem. The next morning when the army was passing through a gap, a body of dismounted Confederate cavalry charged upon the artillery, dismounted one gun and blew up some caissons.

The Lynchburg raid is known as "the hungry raid," for there were many soldiers who travelled for days on the retreat over the mountains who had nothing to eat but birch bark and sassafras leaves. Many gave out and were captured or died along the route. In Charleston some died from eating too much.

. . . .

Rumors of wanton destruction and lawlessness preceded the invading army and spread alarm and terror among the old and young throughout the community. Little children understood that it was an army of wild creatures.

General Early made his city headquarters at the home of Captain Samuel Early and many commissary wagons were

left there. While the battle was going on some of the prisoners, then taken, were sent in, and to relieve the guard that he
might get his dinner, Captain Early took his place. His small
niece seeing him so engaged approached and asked, "Uncle
Tham, what's them?" He answered, "These are Yankee soldiers." She was so accustomed to being teased, she suspected
him of doing it then, and quickly retorted, "You can't fool me,
they's folks."

SECOND ARMY CORPS, 1864

LIEUTENANT-GENERAL JUBAL A. EARLY, *Commanding*

Gordon's Division—MAJOR-GENERAL JOHN B. GORDON—
Brigadier-General Harry T. Hay's brigade.

Regiments—
5th Louisiana, Col. Henry Forno.
6th Louisiana, Col. William Monaghan.
7th Louisiana, Col. D. B. Penn.
8th Louisiana, Col. A. DeBlanc.
9th Louisiana, Col. Wm. R. Peck.

Gordon's brigade (Evans' brigade)—Col. E. N. Atkinson
commanding, and containing 12th Georgia battalion.

Regiments—
13th Georgia, Lieut.-Col. J. H. Baker.
26th Georgia, Col. E. N. Atkinson.
31st Georgia, Col. C. A. Evans.
38th Georgia, Col. J. D. Matthews.
60th Georgia, Col. W. H. Stiles.
61st Georgia, Col. J. H. Lamar.

Brigadier-General John Pegram's brigade.

Regiments—
13th Virginia, Col. J. B. Terrell.
31st Virginia, Col. J. S. Hoffman.
49th Virginia, Col. J. C. Gibson.

52nd Virginia, Col. Jas. M. Skinner.
58th Virginia, Col. H. F. Board.

Hoke's Brigade.—Brigadier General Robert F. Hoke:
Regiments—
6th North Carolina, Col. R. F. Webb.
21st North Carolina, Lieut.-Col. W. S. Rankin.
54th North Carolina, Col. K. M. Murchison.
57th North Carolina, Col. A. C. Godwin.
1st North Carolina Battalion, Major R. W. Wharton.

Johnston's Division—MAJOR-GENERAL R. D. JOHNSTON—
Stonewall brigade—(William Terry's brigade).
Regiments—
2nd Virginia, Col. J. Q. A. Nadenbousch.
4th Virginia, Col. William Terry.
5th Virginia, Col. J. H. S. Fund.
27th Virginia, Lieut.-Col. Chas. L. Haynes.
33rd Virginia, Col. F. W. M. Holliday.

Steuart's brigade—Brigadier-General George H. Steuart.
Regiments—
10th Virginia, Col. E. T. H. Warren.
23rd Virginia, Col. A. G. Taliaferro.
37th Virginia, Col. T. V. Williams.
1st North Carolina, Col. H. A. Brown.
3rd North Carolina, Col. S. D. Thruston.

Jones' Brigade:
Regiments—
21st Virginia, Col. W. A. Witcher.
25th Virginia, Col. J. C. Higginbotham.
42nd Virginia, Col. R. W. Withers.
44th Virginia, Col. Norvell Cobb.
48th Virginia, Col. R. H. Dungan.
50th Virginia, Col. A. S. Vanderventer.

Stafford's brigade—Brigadier-General Leroy A. Stafford:

Regiments—

1st Louisiana, Col. W. R. Shivers.
2nd Louisiana, Col. J. M. Williams.
10th Louisiana, Col. E. Waggaman.
14th Louisiana, Col. Z. York.
15th Louisiana, Col. E. Pendleton.

Rodes' Division—MAJOR-GENERAL ROBERT E. RODES—
Daniel's brigade—(Grimes').

Regiments—

32nd North Carolina, Col. E. C. Brabble.
43rd North Carolina, Col. Thos. S. Kenan.
45th North Carolina, Col. Samuel H. Boyd.
53rd North Carolina, Col. Wm. A. Owens.
2nd North Carolina Battalion, Major John M. Hancock.

Ramseur's brigade—Brigadier-General Stephen D. Ramseur.

Regiments—

2nd North Carolina, Col. W. R. Cox.
4th North Carolina, Col. Bryan Grimes.
14th North Carolina, Col. R. T. Bennett.
30th North Carolina, Col. F. M. Parker.

Johnston's brigade:

Regiments—

5th North Carolina, Col. T. M. Garrett.
12th North Carolina, Col. H. E. Coleman.
20th North Carolina, Col. T. F. Toon.
23rd North Carolina, Major C. C. Blacknall.

Doles' Brigade—Brigadier-General George Dole:

Regiments—

4th Georgia, Col. Philip Cook.
12th Georgia, Col. Edward Willis.
21st Georgia, Col. John T. Mercer.
44th Georgia, Col. W. H. Peebles.

Battle's brigade—Brigadier-General Cullen A. Battle.

Regiments—

3rd Alabama, Col. Charles Forsyth.
5th Alabama, Col. J. M. Hall.
6th Alabama, Col. J. N. Lightfoot.
12th Alabama, Col. S. B. Pickens.
61st Alabama, Major (Lt.-Col.) L. H. Hill.

The Virginia Military Institute Cadets, under Colonel Scott Ship, who came to Lynchburg to assist in its defense, were encamped in the old Methodist cemetery. In this band of youthful heroes were several Lynchburg boys, among whom were Frank T. Lee, R. Spotswood Payne, J. Cabell Early, together with Charles C. Randolph (later rector of Campbell's Episcopal churches, and resident at Evington) and a young Richmond boy, Moses Ezekiel, who afterwards won fame as a sculptor and who contributed a memorial of his workmanship, in honor of his fellow cadets, which was erected at Lexington.

No incident of the war proved Lee's strategic ability more forciby than the expedition of 1864. Commander of a pitifully dwindling army and faced by an immensely superior force in numbers and equipment, with bold strategy he sent Breckenridge with his cavalry (eyes and ears of the army) to patrol the valley and interrupt the progress of the advancing enemy. When it was found that Hunter, commander of that army, was gaining ground in his forward march, Lee then ordered Early to the assistance of Breckenridge. The command, under Early, reached Lynchburg in time to prevent its capture and the destruction of army stores there, a result of great import as the town was the store base of his supplies. Further orders had been given Early to march to Washington and threaten that city, which he knew was inadequately protected. Lee accomplished both of his objects—his stores at Lynchburg were saved, and a portion of the Federal force in front of him was diverted for the defense of Washington city. It can scarcely be presumed that either Lee or his fearless follower hoped to hold Washington even if the Confederate contingent was successful in entering it. The flag pole in front of Walter Reed Hospital at Washington marks the point of

Fort Early Arch

nearest approach to the city reached by Early, and thus this institution, for the treatment of disabled soldiers, serves to preserve the site of a war adventure in a manner satisfactory to veterans of the armies of both North and South.

Hunter's attack was made at a point on Salem turnpike near land then owned by Frank T. Lee, Moorman's and neighboring farms. Here earthworks were thrown up by Early's orders and left undisturbed afterwards. At the close of the war Mr. Lee gave the site of the fortifications for a county school-house, one of which was erected within the enclosure and used for some years, but about the end of the century, this school was moved near the Quaker Meeting House, leaving the fort site unused. It seemed peculiarly appropriate that an old soldier, Robert B. Dameron, who had served behind the works when they afforded shelter from the enemy guns, should have called attention to their abandonment and through David Walker (who as a small boy witnessed that June day fight and was son of a Confederate soldier killed in battle) sent a recommendation that the Old Dominion Chapter, Daughters of the Confederacy, make an effort to secure it. Prompted by these two citizens, and with their aid, the reservation was acquired through the chapter president, by deed of gift from the Campbell school trustees in 1905, and in 1924, sixty years after the battle there, the chapter erected a commemorative arch of Bedford, Indiana stone, at the opening in the fortifications which had been made for the scholar's' entrance, the old sally-port, opening upon private property, not being available for the purpose.

A 30-foot shaft of Barre granite had previously been reared by private subscription to Early and his soldiers at a point of land nearby where two streets merge into Salem pike, the site for which was donated by Howell C. Featherston for the purpose, and is now incorporated within city limits. Several other war works which circled the town at the time of Hunter's raid have been levelled for utilitarian purposes; one, situated near Tyreeanna, several miles distant, remains unchanged except by a thicket of 60 years' tree growth. Fort Early also possesses a 63-year-old oak. This war relic, which received its name from the command that erected it, was in 1920 placed by the O. D. chapter in the charge of residents, near, composing the Fort Hill Woman's Club, who are conveniently situated to look after it, and who built a club house within its enclosure.

That Hunter's army felt sure of success in his expedition, may be known from the fact—as afterwards reported by officers under him, that several of them carried letters of introduction to citizens within the town and a few of the prospective guests returned in later years and were entertained by those to whom the letters had been addressed; they were interested in revisiting the scene of their repulse. Colonel L. W. Kennon (afterwards on Crook's staff) detailed at War Department in Washington, was also a visitor to the fort, having been informed of the engagement there by his superior officer, who with Averill had joined Hunter in his raid. Many persons come who request further information concerning the battle-ground of which they have heard through participants there in 1864.

Negro Types

Chapter XII

Man of Color

THE humorist, Polk Miller, told the story of his joining the Confederate army at Manassas, carrying with him a negro servant. A few days before the battle took place, he received the following letter:

"Dear Polk—I hear you are likely to have a big battle soon, and I write to tell you not to let Sam go into the fight with you. Keep him in the rear, for that negro is worth a thousand dollars. Your loving father."

Other masters held the desire of safeguarding their slaves against war risks. Silas Green, a veteran now of eighty-odd years, lived in Franklin county. He was a very zealous volunteer into Confederate army service, enrolling himself along with other county men; but when the time came for them to join the army in the field, his master refused to let him go. Not daunted by this failure of his hopes, he then raised a company of his own which he drilled and prepared for camp, but again he met with disappointment, and witnessed the company's going off without him, for his master considered him too valuable a piece of property to chance the shot of marksmen with fell intent. Green came to Lynchburg, where he pursues the calling of drayman.

Edward Graham, luckier than Green in becoming an active participant in war, made the proud boast that he "dun fout wid sogers roun' Richmun'." Graham was a very self-respecting colored man. He was a gardener by trade, and otherwise an exhorter to his people to do right and thus gain their reward. He was mowing Captain Early's front lawn when an itinerant photographer came along, who was so pleased with Graham's appearance he asked for his picture to illustrate the old song, "There was an old nigger, and his name was Uncle Ned," in a magazine article. The picture given is the one then taken.

"His Name was Uncle Ned"

Gabriel Hunt, the present janitor at Campbell court-house, was formerly one of Samuel Pannill's slaves at *Green Hill,* though, like many old timers of his race, he does not appear to be as old as that proves him to be. He fills the duties of his position satisfactorily and is an interesting raconteur of the happenings on Pannill's plantation, which he describes with the pride of one who participated there. Gabe (as he is called), is a Confederate veteran pensioner.

John Milton, of New London, has even prouder distinction in his association with the town's past history. He was trained by his master, a New London blacksmith named Thomas Stephens, to the same trade, a calling he pursued for nearly sixty years in the old town magazine of Revolutionary times. He married a slave, from the Alexander estate, who claims prestige over him, because of that circumstance. Milton retired from blacksmithing and has since become a financier.

Perhaps the negro of tenderest association was Blind Billy, long remembered for the soft, clear notes of his flute; for like all blind persons he possessed a talent for music, and, because of his talent, was a very important personage at balls and military parades. Billy was owned by Dr. Howell Davies, but known to all, no one passed him without at least a kindly word. He died while still a slave.

Armistead Pride was liberated by his master as a reward for his faithful service.

Isaac Harrison purchased his freedom and established a bathing establishment in Lynchburg. The wealthiest colored county man was Adolphus Humbles (recently deceased), of Fairview Heights, who accumulated a considerable fortune, and rendered assistance to the educational institutions of his race in that community.

There are two types of the race, passed away now, but which memory can vividly recall; one, the leader of choral voices the volume of whose sweet melodies more than filled the factory spaces, during the period when their hands were shaping tobacco into marketable form; the other, soother of child troubles,—the black mammy of the nursery,—who, having similar childlike disposition, met her charges on a sympathetic plane of understanding, while she won them back to good humor or crooned them to slumber with such songs as "Blueberry john sing all the winter long."

These are figures of yesterday, no longer to be found, for their molds were broken sixty-five years ago.

War's Roster

Chapter XIII

Succession of Wars

1760

HILE still under the dominance of the mother country, soldiers of the community enlisted with the regiment raised by Colonel William Byrd for the immediate defense of the state in a war called the Cherokee Expedition.

1776

Many county names are included in lists of officers and soldiers who served in the war with Great Britain, called the War of the Revolution, and as late as 1835 veterans of this war were receiving pensions.

1812

The first call to United States colors was for national defense against English attacking forces and called the War of 1812; several county regiments engaged in this war and there were a number of fatalities among officers and men.

1848

The Governor of Virginia called out the 24th Virginia Regiment of Volunteers to serve in the war of 1848, known as the War with Mexico, and though not engaged in any important battle, they served otherwise as guards, etc., and remained till the end of the war.

1861

In the war of 1861-1865, known as the War between the States, the county contributed in zeal, soldiers and supplies according to its capacity; it suffered heavily in battle victims and in property losses; it also furnished the battle field for one engagement; neither extreme youth nor age were used as a shield against enlistment, which was usually voluntary.

1899

In the war of 1898-9, (one of sympathy in the cause of a sister nation) known as the Spanish-American War, Campbell sent a volunteer regiment to Cuba. Its soldier victims were more from accident and disease than actual conflict.

1918

When the United States entered actively into the European war, known as the World War, the county promptly put itself in line with other national contributors and reaped heavy toll in the maiming and killing of its youth through disease, accident, and battle.

Cherokee Expedition

In 1760 the 2nd Virginia Regiment was formed for immediate defense of the state, with Colonel William Byrd as commander, in an expedition against the Cherokees. Many of the soldiers in the regiment lived in the Campbell section of Bedford, or moved there later and sent in their claims for bounty land, because of that service. John Adams was a sergeant in Captain John Smith's company; John Anderson was sergeant; Henry Austin was sergeant, and Benjamin Austin corporal; Roger Cock Bailey was a corporal in Captain James Gunn's company; James Arnold was a private; also James Board; Richard Baldock was sergeant, Levi Baldock, a private; John Brown was corporal; William Barlow, George Coleman, James Davis, Thomas Davis and Henry Dawson, privates; John Fitzgerald, sergeant; Henry Finch, a private; James Floyd, sergeant; Stephen Hancock, William Heath, William Gibson, Griffin Johnson, privates; Richard Johnston, lieutenant; Charles Jordan, Thomas Lewis, John King, privates; Thomas

Matthews was a member of Captain Gunn's company; William Murrell was sergeant; John Payne, a lieutenant in a frontier battalion; James Russell, a private; Stephen Smith, Thomas Smith and Charles Turner, privates; James Walden, a private; William Watts in Captain John Smith's company; James Wells, a private.

Other claimants for bounty land were John Anthony, captain of a company of rangers by particular order of the governor; James Buford, guardian of John Buford and executor of Thomas Buford (dec.), lieutenant in 1754-'59; John Clarke, sergeant in 1st Virginia Regiment, entitled to 200 acres of land by proclamation of 1763; Benjamin Clements, in Captain William Temple's company till end of the war; Peter Clarkson, soldier of 1755 campaign, Captain Samuel Overton's company of Rangers; Samuel Daniel, in regiment raised for immediate defense; Henry Davis, under Colonel William Byrd; Willian Davis, of Captain Dickerson's company; John Harvey, in Regiment for defense; James Johnson, a sergeant in Captain Rootes' company of Regulars; William King, a volunteer under Captain Christopher Hudson; Samuel Miller, under Col. Byrd; Abraham Moon, in Captain Bullett's company of Regulars, legally discharged; Haynes Morgan, of the 80th British Regiment (James Grant, commandant), sergeant-major for seven years; John Thorp, regular soldier (Wm. Thorp, heir); Wm. Thorp, sergeant, 1755-62; Charles Wall, in Col. Wm. Bryd's regiment, David Wall, heir; Justinian Wills, sergeant-major under Col. Byrd; Thomas Elliot, paymaster and lieutenant in Virginia Battalion of Regulars, commanded by Col. William Peachy.

Campbell County Officers During the American Revolution

Adams, James; Captain		1781
Adams, Robert; Captain		1778
Alexander, Robert; Captain		1779
Anderson, Jacob; 2nd-Lieutenant		1779
Anthony, Joseph; 2nd-Lieutenant		1778

Arthur, Benjamin; Captain 1781
Brown, Daniel .... ——
Brown, Shelldrake; Ensign 1781
Bullock, James; Captain 1780
Bullock, Josias; Captain 1781
Butterworth, Benjamin; Captain 1781
Callaway, Charles; Captain 1781
Callaway, C. D.; 1st-Lieutenant 1778
Callaway, James, Sr.; County-Lieutenant 1778
Callaway, James, Jr.; Captain 1781
Callaway, John; Major 1781
Callaway, Richard; Colonel .... ——
Callaway, William; Lieutenant-Colonel 1778
Chiles, John; Captain 1778
Clark, Micajah; Ensign 1781
Cobbs, Edward; 2nd-Lieutenant 1779
Cobbs, Robert, 1st-Lieutenant 1779
Daniel, William 1781
Davis, Samuel; 1st-Lieutenant .... ——
Davis, Henry; 1st-Lieutenant .... ——
Dearing, James; Captain .... ——
Early, Jacobus; 1st-Lieutenant 1781
Early, Jacob; Captain 1780
Early, Jeremiah; Colonel 1778
Franklin, Edmund; Ensign 1778
Franklin, Owen; Ensign 1778
Fuqua, Moses; 2nd-Lieutenant 1780
Haythe, Thomas; 1st-Lieutenant 1781
Hunter, John Jr.; Ensign 1779
Innis, Harry; Ensign 1781
Irvine, John; 2nd-Lieutenant 1780
Johnson, Thomas; Ensign 1778
Jones, Thomas; Ensign 1781
Jones, William; 1st-Lieutenant 1780
Jordan, William; Captain 1781
Leftwich, Augustine, Jr.; 1st-Lieutenant 1781
Leftwich, William; Lieutenant-Colonel 1780

Leftwich, Uriah; Ensign 1779
Lynch, Anselm; 1st-Lieutenant 1780
Lynch, Charles; Colonel 1778
McElroy, Hugh; 1st-Lieutenant 1780
McReynolds, Thos.; Captain 1779
Miller, Simon; Ensign 1779
Moon, Jacob, Jr.; Ensign 1779
Patrick, John Fitz; Ensign 1780
Rice, Benjamin; Captain 1781
Russell, James; 2nd-Lieutenant 1780
Slaughter, John; Ensign 1779
Snow, Thomas 1779
Stith, Joseph; Ensign 1780
Talbot, Haile; Captain 1780
Tate, Jesse; Ensign 1778
Terrell, Henry; Major 1781
Walden, Richard, Jr.; Ensign 1780
Walden, Richard, Sr.; Captain 1778
Wall, Charles F. .... ——
Ward, John, Sr.; Major 1778

Others serving (titles and dates unknown):

Cocke, Anderson	Smith, Joseph
Christian, Henry	Ward, Henry; Major
Goggin, John; Lieutenant	Ward, John, Jr.
Hairston, Peter	Ward, William
King, William	Withers, Enoch
Ready, Isaac	Yancey, Joel

Revolutionary Pensioners in 1835

	AGE		AGE
Adams, Henry	73	Browne, Henry	74
Anderson, Jacob	72	Brooks, James	74
Arthur, William	72	Brooks, Nelson	75
Bailey, Philip	80	Campbell, William	85
Blankenship, Abram	74	Candler, William	82

Carson, William	85	Hughes, Benjamin	69
Cabbage, John	76	Hunter, John, Jr.	—
Cobbs, John	75	Mann, Joseph	85
Cobbs', Robt. (widow)	79	Matthews, Samuel	71
Corneile, Jacob	83	Moore, Thomas	85
Diuguid, George	72	Pribble, John	75
Evans, Sampson, (Sgt.)	81	Scott's, Samuel (widow)	76
Franklin, Thomas	75	Snow, Richard	81
Franklin, Thos. P.	71	Story, Edward	77
Graddy, Joseph	77	Truitt, William	74
Hall, Isham	71	Walker, Charles	74
Harvey, Thomas	72	Walthall, Henry	72
Howard, James	71	Wray, Henry	71

Requests for Pensions, Through War Claims

1782. Isaac Ready stated he served under Col. Charles Lynch, was wounded in the hip at Guilford C. H., wound unhealed; had a family to support; he died before his petition was reported; widow was relieved by a later petition.

1827. Richard Daniel petitioned for pension for Revolutionary service.

1827. Edward Gibbs petitioned for pension for Revolutionary service; petition rejected.

1830. John Prebbles petitioned for pension for Revolutionary service; petition rejected.

1831. William Truitt claim for compensation, allowed bounty land.

1833. Isham Perdue claim for service in war of 1812; petition rejected.

1839. Thos. W. Wilcox demand for assistance for war service; petition rejected.

1849. William A. Talbot asked compensation for record book furnished 131st Virginia Military Regiment.

Other Campbell claimants to Revolutionary service:

Adler Arrington	William Leckie
Henry Blankenship	John May
Richard Daniel	Samuel Matthews
George Diuguid	James Pettit
Thomas Franklin	John Pribble
Edward Gibbs	William Rosser
Edward Herndon	Jesse Thornhill
Thomas Howey	Leborix Williamson
Benjamin Hughes	James Whitaker
William King	

Warrants Obtained for Service

William Allegree: Campbell County, 14 October, 1788. Matthew Allegree being sworn on the Holy Evangelists of Almighty God, saith that he had a son named William Allegree, which in the time of the late war enlisted in Colonel Joseph Crockett's Regiment and *dyed* at the Falls of the Ohio in the service, and that "my son Giles is next oldest son of the same mother." This affidavit is signed *Christopher Irvine,* who was doubtless Christopher, Jr., commissioner for Bedford in 1781, and later empowered to locate military land warrants for Campbell county soldiers in Kentucky.

Exec. Dept., 18th December, 1832. *William Truit* (Trewitt), is allowed land bounty for his services as a Soldier in the State line for the war, John Floyd, Governor.

William Truit of Campbell county, Virginia, appointed James G. Denning of the same county as his Attorney, 22 January, 1833, signed before Charles Henry Lynch, Justice of the Peace, Campbell county. Warrant No. 7303 was issued to William Truit, January 29, 1833, for 200 acres of land.

County Militia

In 1778 John Quarles, county-lieutenant of Bedford, received instructions and money from the governor for the purpose of enabling him to appoint recruiting officers in the county. The latter failed in their work and returned the money received. At this time Harry Terrell and assistants were ordered to serve as guards and convey a number of persons, suspected of treason, to jail.

In 1825 David Rodes asked compensation as adjutant of the 85th Reg. Va. Militia. Three years later seventy-five Lynchburgers requested certain amendments to the militia laws. Officers of the First Division, Twelfth Brigade, 53rd, 117th and 131st Virginia Regiments petitioned on February 2d, 1835, that militia laws be so changed as to restore and continue brigade inspectors.

On January 4th, 1838, Lynchburgers petitioned for the passage of a law exempting from the payment of annual levy and poll of capitation tax, each person belonging to a volunteer corps, so long as he continued to be an active and uniformed member of the corps. Then on the 18th of the same month the officers of the 131st regiment requested an act fixing the training and instruction of those officers.

At the beginning of 1841, Campbell, Bedford and Pittsylvania citizens residing near the boundary lines of those counties asked authority to raise a troop of cavalry for the protection of the neighborhood. Two years later residents of Campbell, Halifax and Charlotte requested permission to form a company of cavalry in that district to muster at Brookneal. This same district petitioned that such citizens as enrolled themselves in a voluntary artillery company at Brookneal in 1849 might be exempt from military duty in Campbell. Officers and members of the Lynchburg Mechanic's Company asked to be furnished with 4 four-pounders, swords and pistols, that they might drill properly and have exchange of arms. The cavalry troop of the 53rd regiment requested proper arms.

In 1844 the officers in the 131st regiment were: James A. Turner, colonel; William B. Brown, lieutenant-colonel; James M. Langhorne, major. In the 53rd regiment, Allen B. Wylie, colonel; Moses Arnold, lieutenant-colonel; Zachariah Moorman, major. In the 117th regiment, William Arrington, colonel; Benjamin W. Nowlin, lieutenant-colonel; Thomas H.

Franklin, major. The officers of the three regiments requested permission to train at any place that the majority of the officers agreed upon.

In 1845 a volunteer troop of cavalry was formed at Brookneal of members from Campbell, Halifax and Charlotte, with Robert E. Withers, lieutenant and drill-master. Training of the officers occurred every spring at the Court House. Two other cavalry companies, one at Rustburg and one at Leesville, near Bedford county line were formed and two companies of volunteers at Lynchburg and two regiments of militia in the county; the officers of all of which were required to drill together.

In 1852 Lynchburg Rifle Guards petitioned that they be furnished sixty bronze percussion rifles.

In 1860 a battalion of "Second Class Militia" at Lynchburg offered their services to the state.

First Call to U. S. Colors

Seventy signers sent a memorial to the Legislature stating that in pursuance of a notice published in the newspapers, *The Star,* and *The Press,* of Lynchburg, they met on December 14, 1809, to take into consideration the alarming situation of the country and that they beheld with the utmost degree of horror and solicitude that the country was at that time menaced with war by both the belligerent powers of Europe. "Feeling that they have suffered insults and deprivations from this condition of things they think it their duty to stand firm and unshaken in defense of their rights and liberties and they request that the militia be armed."

Two companies of soldiers were formed in Lynchburg to serve in the war which followed with Great Britain—one commanded by Captain James Dunnington, under Colonel John H. Cocke—to serve from March 22d to August 22d, 1813, and which was stationed at Camp Holly; the other commanded by Captain Samuel Wyatt under Lieut.-Colonel George Huston, to serve from July 31st to August 22d, 1814.

The county furnished two companies to the 3rd Virginia Regiment—Captain James H. Haden's company of Grenadiers, and Captain Joshua Early, Jr.'s company, which served from August 13th till November 3d, 1814, at which time Cap-

Colonel Samuel Hairston

tain Early was killed in the engagement at Ellicott City, Md.

Among other county soldiers who took part in this war, William Lynch, son of John, of Lynchburg, was colonel of a regiment stationed at Mount Holly, remarkable for its perfect drill. His brother, Micajah Lynch, served as a private.

Capt. Maurice Langhorne commanded a company (d. 1865).

Robert Strange, major of the 117th Regiment, 1st battalion.

Joel Leftwich gained the title of general in this war. His brother Jabez Leftwich was adjutant under him. Gerard Alexander a colonel.

Samuel Hairston, 2nd lieutenant of 20th Regiment, promoted major.

——— Garland and ——— Owen were captains.

Micajah Clark and James Saunders were surgeons.

Alexander Austin (New London), Adam Clement, Jas. C. Anderson, Jacob Early (Washington College student then), Robert Johnson and John Lynch (Ward's Road Inn), Samuel Parsons Anthony, Richard Lee (Leesville), Isham Pardue, John Rosser, Charles West, Thomas Wilcox, Joel Yancey, Vincent Snow.

The state library has lists of Virginia soldiers who served in the war of 1812, but it is difficult to discover from which county they enlisted, and Campbell has no recorded list of the men it furnished.

Lynchburg Companies in War of 1812

Captain James Dunnington's company of Virginia Militia, stationed at Camp Holly, first under Major Armistead, then under Colonel John H. Cocke from March 22nd, to August 22nd, 1813:

Captain, James Dunnington.	Corporal, Isaac Gregory.
1st Lieutenant, Peter Dudley.	Corporal, Christopher Clark.
2d Lieutenant, Wm. B. Lynch.	Corporal, Robert Thurman.
Sergeant, John Robinson.	Corporal, French G. Gray.
Sergeant, Edmund B. Norvell.	Drummer, William Pickett.
Sergeant, Samuel Garland.	Drummer, Benj. Crenshaw.
Sergeant, James Banagh.	Fifer, William Yowell.
Corporal, William Martin.	

Enrollment of Privates—44

Anderson, John N.	Booker, Peter E.	Davis, John, Jr.
Askew, John D.	Campbell, David	Doyle, William
Bradford, Fielding	Cobbs, Charles G.	Ellis, Hezekiah

Gray, Robert
Gregory, Isaac
Horsley, Nicolas C.
Lee, Shelly
Mays, John
Mays, Joseph
Mason, David F.
McAllister, John
Mitchell, Gideon
Mettart, George
Murrell, Hayden D.
Mattox, John

Norman, John H.
Pierce, Cornelius
Puckett, Isham
Parten, Pleasant
Roy, John B.
Rose, Littleton
Rose, Hugh M.
Royal, Joseph E.
Reid, John
Robinson, Harrison
Rives, Wm. M.
Smith, David

Strong, John
Staples, David
Thurman, N. B.
Tait, Netherland
Vawter, John
Wright, James T.
Wyatt, Edwin
Williams, Orrin
Waterfield, James
Waterfield, Micajah
Young, Daniel

The Lynchburg Rifles

In the service of the United States, 4th Regiment, commanded by Lieut.-Colonel George Huston, from July 31st, 1814, till August 29th, 1814:

Captain, Samuel J. Wyatt
Lieutenant, Powhatan Ellis
Ensign, Paulus A. E. Irving
First Sergt., Thomas Cohen
Second Sergt., Wm. Sumpter
Third Sgt., Edmund Anderson

Fourth Sergt., Henry Jacobs
First Corporal, Henry Allison
Second Corp., Griffin L. Lackie
Third Corp., Robert Rives
Fourth Corp., Gideon Shaw

Enrollment of Privates—45; Servants—3

Akin, Alexander
Bernard, Smith
Bridgland, Solomon
Booker, Joseph P.
Cobbs, William
Cobbs, Edmund
Cobbs, Anthony
Crandall, Thomas
Cohen, Joseph
Dinwiddie, Wm.

Daugherty, Peter
Dickens, Rd. H.
Echols, Moses
Fox, George
Gwynn, John
Garthright, Saml.
Henry, Holman
Hancock, Ammon
Jennings, Philip
Joseph, Charles

Jones, Robert W.
Johnson, Caleb
Lester, John
Lambeth, Washington
Lipscomb, Francis
Mitchell, Geo. W.
Mitchell, Thos. W.
Mitchell, Thomas
McGee, Wm.
McKenny, James

Medaris, Benjamin
Neighbours, Thomas
Otey, John B.
Plunkett, Jonathan
Rose, James
Rohr, Philip
Strong, John

Saunders, David
Strong, Thomas
Scott, Wm. W.
Thomas, Nelson
Terry, Thomas
Tait, Bacon
Tyree, Samuel

Servants

Peter Knapper
Daniel Ellis
Henry Hill

In the war with Mexico, following upon the annexation of Texas, the regiment of volunteers from Virginia was called for by the President of the United States. Jubal A. Early, who had served as a lieutenant in the Seminole war of 1837-38, had resigned from the U. S. army and was practicing law in Franklin county, Virginia. He was then mustered into service January 7, 1847, and received from Governor William Smith and Council of State the appointment of Major under Colonel John F. Hamtramck and Lieut.-Colonel Thomas B. Randolph. The regiment was ordered to Fortress Monroe and superintendence of the drilling there and the embarkation to Mexico were entrusted to Major Early. Two extra companies were allowed to the regiment and on account of delay in their organization the last detachment of these companies did not sail until March 1st. They arrived at Brazos, Santiago, on the 17th, proceeded up the Rio Grande, and assembled at Camargo, then moved April 1st to Monterey by way of a town called China, as escort for a provision train, one-half of the regiment being left at China under Col. Randolph, and the other half under Major Early moved to Monterey. Colonel Hamtramck was too ill at the time to remain on duty. Early's battalion encamped at Walnut Spring near General Taylor's headquarters, but after a short stay there, relieved an Ohio regiment which was garrisoning Monterey. Here Major Early was for two months military governor of the city. In June the whole regiment moved to Buena Vista, a few miles from Saltillo, remaining near this locality the rest of the war, for the most part inactive, as all fighting on that line, except an occasional affair with guerillas, ceased after the battle of Buena Vista.

Colonel Hamtramck returned to Virginia on February 1, 1848, on recruiting service, and Major Early commanded the regiment during the remaining time. Returning to Fortress Monroe, the regiment was mustered out of service the first part of April, 1848, Early being the only field officer with it. He reports that the regiment had had no opportunity for reaping laurels during the war, but that it had not sullied the Virginia flag, which constituted the regimental colors, by misconduct or acts of depredation. Among the county men enrolled in this 24th Regiment were Charles Ward, son of John Ward (3rd), who remained in Mexico and died in Texas; Samuel Crawford and Samuel Thacker of New London, James Terrell.

In 1847 Captain Wm. A. Talbot with 20 Lynchburgers, enrolled, completed his company in Richmond: John J. Bunting, 2nd lieutenant; and W. F. Norris, 2nd Corporal, of Lynchburg, were members of Captain Talbot's company. Thomas B. Dornin also served in the Mexican war. Dr. M. R. Bohannon, who died at Lynchburg in 1895, was also a Mexican war veteran.

John Lee Manson, son of Nathaniel Manson, died in the Mexican War in 1848.

Southern Guard (Company B) 11th Va. Reg. C. S. Army Roll
Enrolled at Yellow Branch, Campbell County:
Preserved in State Records

Captain, Robert C. Saunders.

1st Lieutenant, James E. Lazenby.

2nd Lieutenant, Thomas B. Horton; wounded at Drainsville and Gettysburg; twice imprisoned.

3rd Lieutenant, Joseph A. Scott.

1st Sergeant, George W. Lazenby; wounded at Gettysburg, Drury's Bluff, Five Forks; imprisoned 2½ months.

2nd Sergeant, Alfred H. Burroughs.

3rd Sergeant, Samuel N. Carson; died Sept. 28, 1861.

4th Sergeant, John Moore.

1st Corporal, William A. Sandifer; severely wounded at Seven Pines.

2nd Corporal, William J. Bowling; severely wounded at Seven Pines.

3rd Corporal, William M. Phillips; wounded at Gettysburg and Drury's Bluff; prisoner 3 months.

4th Corporal, John E. Phillips; wounded at Gettysburg; prisoner 3 months.

Privates

John P. Arthur, prisoner 3 mos.; Peter S. Arthur; John W. Anthony, wounded at Seven Pines and Manassas; Benjamin H. Anthony; Wm. T. Anthony, severely wounded at Five Forks; Jacob I. Atkerson, killed at Seven Pines; Augustus L. Austin; Jacob W. Bondurant; Wm. B. Bondurant, severely wounded at Seven Pines; Cicero W. Brooks, severely wounded at Seven Pines; Whit. R. Brooks, wounded at Seven Pines; John J. Brooks; E. F. Brown, killed at Frazier Farm; John T. Bruce; E. P. Burroughs; John W. Burress; Thomas G. Burress; John E. Burress; Alex T. Bateman; Daniel Cassidy, severely wounded at Seven Pines; E. W. Callahan, wounded at Plymouth, N. C.; Jas. W. Campbell; Thos. Carson; Wm. T. Clement; M. G. Clark; Chas. H. Crouch, wounded at Seven Pines; Saml. H. Cox; Geo. E. Daniel; John T. Davis, killed at Williamsburg; V. F. Deaton, severely wounded at Frazier Farm; John R. Depriest, wounded at Seven Pines, killed at Drewry's Bluff; Wm. M. Dooly, severely wounded at Seven Pines; Moses C. Dooly; D. P. Dews, wounded at Williamsburg and Sharpsburg; Wm. H. Dews; John W. Dinwiddie, wounded at Manassas; James Dowdy, killed at Drewry's Bluff; John A. Dudley, prisoner 3 months; Wm. H. Dudley, wounded at Gettysburg and Hatcher's Run, permanently disabled; Washington Elliotte, wounded at Gettysburg, prisoner 2½ months; Lafayette R. Elliotte; Taiplett T. Estes, wounded at Seven Pines; John W. Edmonds, wounded at Seven

Pines; Edwin H. Ewart, prisoner 3 months; Thos. L. Franklin; Saml. H. Franklin; Robert Franklin; Wm. F. Farthing, severely wounded at Frazier Farm; John W. Farmer, killed at Seven Pines; Edward Farmer, wounded at Seven Pines; Wm. Farmer, prisoner 2½ years; Arthur Farmer, wounded at Drewry's Bluff; Jno. P. Farmer; Wm. H. Farmer; Jas. M. Farmer; Thos. Farmer; Martin Fariss; Jas. M. Finch, wounded at Frazier Farm, prisoner 3 months; Chas. H. Finch, wounded at Gettysburg; C. B. Finch; Jno. Frazier, permanently wounded at Frazier Farm; Thos. Gereghtery; Jesse H. Gill, wounded at Seven Pines and Five Forks, prisoner 21 months; Wm. E. Goolesby; C. V. Haden, wounded at Gettysburg and Drewry's Bluff; M. A. Haden, severely wounded at Drewry's Bluff; E. R. Horton, wounded at Frazier Farm, prisoner 5 months; Wm. D. Hendrick; Jos. T. Hendrick, prisoner 2½ months; Allen W. Holcombe, wounded at Drewry's Bluff, prisoner, died in 1864; B. W. Hughes, prisoner at Pt. Lookout; Jas. R. Hay; Wm. H. Hillsman, prisoner at Pt. Lookout, died 1865 in camp; Jno. C. Hillsman, severely wounded at Gettysburg; Wm. H. Hazlewood, died 1862; B. Harvey, wounded at Drewry's Bluff, died on the field; W. H. Harvey, died in hospital; Thos. W. Hill, wounded at Manassas, died on the field; Jerry M. Johnson, wounded at Gettysburg; Geo. T. Johnson, wounded at Frazier Farm, prisoner at Pt. Lookout; C. C. Johnson; John Johnson; Thos. H. Jefferson; Geo. Kern; Jas. W. Lindsay; Jas. Lindsay; Richard T. Little; James T. Little, paroled at Williamsburg; Geo. W. Little, wounded at Boonsboro, prisoner 3 mos.; Peter Moore, wounded at Seven Pines; Jas. D. Moore; Wm. T. Moore; Jno. B. McAllister, wounded at Frazier Farm; P. L. McCormick; Geo. E. Mason, wounded at Williamsburg, 1862, died on the field; Saml. E. Moorman, wounded at Gettysburg, died there; Jas. A. Morriss, wounded at Gettysburg, prisoner 6 mos.; Thos. J. Morriss; Patrick Murray; James McNamee, wounded at Seven Pines; Robert McNamee; Thos. W. Mattox; S. G. Matthews; Benjamin Musgrove; Jas. W. Olds; Obediah Phillips; Barnabas A. Phillips; Lewis G. Phillips, wounded at Frazier Farm, died on battlefield;

John N. Phillips, wounded at Gettysburg, died and buried there; Wm. M. Phillips, prisoner 3 mos.; Morriss Phillips; John T. Pribble, wounded at Frazier Farm, prisoner 3 mos.; John M. Pribble, prisoner 3 mos.; John R. Pribble; Henry T. Patrick, wounded at Seven Pines; Wm. J. Patrick, wounded at Frazier Farm; Jas. A. Powers, wounded at Seven Pines, prisoner; Alex. D. Perrow, wounded at Seven Pines; Edmund W. Russell, wounded at Seven Pines; John W. Reid, wounded at Sharpsburg; John D. Richardson, wounded at Williamsburg; John Roberts, prisoner 3 months; John T. Shelton; Wm. W. Scott, wounded at Williamsburg, Seven Pines and Drewry's Bluff; Wm. S. Simmons, wounded at Williamsburg; Thos. J. Sandifer, wounded at Dinwiddie C. H.; Alex F. Sandifer, wounded at Williamsburg and Manassas, prisoner 3 mos.; Geo. P. Sandifer, wounded at Drewry's Bluff, prisoner 3 mos.; Robt. F. Sandifer, wounded at Drewry's Bluff; Sebastian Shaner; N. B. Thurmond; Pleasant L. Thurmond, wounded at Williamsburg and Gettysburg, prisoner 18 months; Walker G. Thurmond, wounded at Drainsville; Jas. A. Taylor, wounded at Seven Pines, died on the field; Jesse E. Tompkins, died 1863; Dr. Geo. W. Thornhill; John H. Trent; Amon Tucker, prisoner 3 mos.; Daniel Updike; Patrick H. Vermillion; Robt. A. Vermillion; Thomas Webber; Marcus D. L. Webber, wounded at Gettysburg; John T. Wells, severely wounded at Drury's Bluff, prisoner 3 mos.; Joseph D. Wells, prisoner 3 mos.; John R. White; Wm. H. Williamson, wounded at Williamsburg; John Williamson; Thos. W. Wills; Whit. A. Ward.

Soldiers of 1861-1865

Eleventh Virginia Regiment, formed at Manassas, Colonel Samuel Garland, commander; composed of four Lynchburg companies:

Rifle Grays, Company A, Captain Maurice S. Langhorne.
Beauregards, Company E, Captain C. V. Winfree.
Home Guard, Company E, Captain Kirkwood Otey.
Jefferson Davis Guards, Company H, Captain Risque Hutter.
Campbell County, Company C, Captain Adam Clement.

Campbell County, Company B, Captain Robert Saunders.
Botetourt County, Companies H and K.
Fauquier County, Company I.

Second Regiment Virginia Cavalry: the first mounted regiment organized in Virginia, at Lynchburg, May 8, 1861; Colonel J. A. Early, mustering officer:
Company A, Captain William R. Terry, Bedford county.
Company B, Captain John S. Langhorne, (known as Wise Troop) Lynchburg.
Company C, Captain Andrew L. Pitzer, Botetourt county.
Company D, Captain G. W. B. Hale, Franklin county.
Company E, Captain Edgar Whitehead, Amherst county.
Company F, Captain James Wilson, Bedford county.
Company G, Captain R. C. W. Radford, Bedford county.
Company H, Captain Joel Flood, Appomattox county.
Company I, Captain J. D. Alexander, Campbell county.
Company K, Captain Eugene Davis, Albemarle county.

This regiment, later under command of Colonel (afterwards General) Thomas T. Munford did not surrender, but cut its way through the line and came back to Lynchburg and disbanded at the spot where it was formed in 1861. Through the efforts of General Munford a stone marker was erected at the exact spot in the City Park.

Brigadier-General Samuel Garland, promoted after the battle of Williamsburg—the son of Maurice and Caroline M. Garland, of Lynchburg; was an attorney-at-law; married Eliza C., daughter of John C. Meem. General Garland was killed at South Mountain, near Boonsboro, Md., September 14, 1862, and his remains were interred in the Presbyterian cemetery at Lynchburg.

Major-General Robert E. Rodes, son of General Robert Rodes of Lynchburg, was killed at Winchester, September 19, 1864. Robert E. Rodes, graduate of Virginia Military Institute in 1848, was an assistant professor there; resigned to follow the profession of civil engineer. In 1859 he returned to the Virginia Military Institute to take the chair of Applied

Mathematics. When the war of 1861 broke out he went to Alabama and raised a company of infantry of which he was elected captain and when the regiment was formed, was made colonel.

A Young General

Born at *Otterburne,* Campbell county in 1840, the son of James G. and Mary A. Lynch-Dearing, James Dearing, Jr., was in 1858 appointed by Hon. Thos. S. Bocock a cadet at West Point Academy, from which institution he resigned and returned home in 1861 in order to enter the Confederate army. He chose the artillery service, becoming a lieutenant of the Washington Artillery of New Orleans: later he was elected captain of the Latham Battery which had been organized in Lynchburg. His record in that command led to his promotion to a battery attached to Pickett's Division. He participated in the principal battles of the Army of Northern Virginia until after Chancellorsville when he received the title of major and was put in command of a battalion of 18 guns in the reserve artillery of Longstreet's Corps which became known as "Dearing's Battalion," and which was with Pickett's Division at Gettysburg and took part in the artillery duel that occurred on the 3rd day. In the winter of 1863-64—Pickett having been assigned to the District of North Carolina and finding himself in need of cavalry, he collected companies of mounted men and asked to have Major Dearing assigned to the command of them, which was accordingly done. A few days later General Lee—in ordering the Newbern expedition—wrote that he proposed Major Dearing for the command of the artillery in that expedition.

On April 5, 1864, Dearing was assigned to the command of the horse artillery of the Army of Northern Virginia. The regiment collected by Gen. Pickett was called "Dearing's Confederate Artillery" and other cavalry commands were placed under his charge during the Newbern expedition. At Plymouth, North Carolina, on April 19, 1864, it is said that he ordered the first charge of artillery known in the annals of warfare. In command of cavalry, Dearing was charging a fort when he recognized his old artillery battalion and ordered it to charge with the cavalry. Plymouth was then captured and Dearing was promoted brigadier-general,—not yet having reached his 24th year.

General James Dearing

General Dearing was called to Petersburg at the opening of Grant's campaign in May, and stationed on the Welden Railroad. His command consisted of his old regiment, a Georgia regiment and two North Carolina regiments of cavalry, a Virginia battalion and Graham's light artillery. He was ordered to the line at Swift's Creek and Drury's Bluff to meet the advance of Butler. His command drove Grant's cavalry at Reservoir Hill from the field and made a gallant stand, by an impetuous charge against the advance of the Federals. Subsequently Dearing commanded a brigade of W. H. F. Lee's cavalry division and still later was assigned, by General R. E. Lee, to the command of the Laurel Brigade.

While covering the retreat of the army in a charge on the enemy who were endeavoring to burn High Bridge (on the Norfolk and Western railroad) Dearing was mortally wounded by an accidental shot from one of his own men. He had at that time in his possession a letter from General Lee stating that papers for his promotion to major-general were in the hands of the Secretary of War "a promotion too long delayed by reason of my inability to fill your present command of the Laurel Brigade." General Dearing was carried to the Ladies Relief Hospital at Lynchburg where he died three weeks later and was buried on his 25th birthday.

Lynchburg was the base hospital-center as well as the base of supplies for the Confederacy during the war of 1861-65. Seventeen tobacco factories and warehouses, together with the buildings at the old Fair Grounds, were converted into hospitals, the Fair Ground buildings being used for wounded and sick Federal prisoners. The total number of soldiers who died during the war was 2,701, of which 187 were Federal soldiers, whose bodies were removed in 1866 to the Federal cemetery near Norfolk. Wounded soldiers were quartered in private homes and lodging houses as well as regular hospitals, such as College Hospital (formerly a youth's College), Ladies' Relief or City Hotel Hospital, the Warwick House, Pratt's, the Wayside, Camp Davis, Camp Nichols, Temperance Hall, Odd Fellows' Hall, all came into service, for Lynchburg's proximity to battlefields caused many of the disabled soldiers to be brought to the town and nursed.

In 1862 smallpox epidemic broke out in the hospitals, and there were 99 deaths from that disease among the wounded Confederate soldiers. The ravages were more serious during the winter months than other seasons. The first soldier who fell a victim to this disease was John Smith, of Company "L",

2nd Mississippi Regiment at Christian's Factory Hospital in October, 1862, and the last was John Pugh of Company "C", Virginia Cavalry, in April, 1864. A special smallpox hospital was established back of the Methodist cemetery and a special lot was provided for victims of the disease. There were 1,251 deaths among the soldiers during the year 1862; the year 1865 having but 51, the smallest of any year during the war; year 1861 having 127 soldier deaths; year 1863, having 677, and year 1864 having 593 deaths. 2,701 soldiers were buried in the old Methodist cemetery, and the Ladies Memorial Association, besides providing each with an individual grave marker, erected a shaft of stones representing all the Southern states. In 1926 they placed a stone arch at the entrance of the soldiers' reservation.

The Federal soldiers who died in Lynchburg were from Ohio, Maine, Pennsylvania, New York, Indiana, Maryland, Vermont, Massachusetts and Michigan. When the Federal authorities removed their bodies in 1866 the records of George Diuguid's Undertaking Establishment were used as a basis of identification and location.

Lynchburg had its local Florence Nightingale, in the person of Mrs. John M. Otey, wife of Captain John M. Otey, who sent seven sons into the Confederate service, Kirkwood, Dexter, Van, Peter, Hays, John, Gaston, and David Walker, a son-in-law, the last two of whom were killed in action, or died from wounds. Mrs. Otey organized a relief corps of nurses and took charge of the old City Hotel, then converted into the Ladies Relief Hospital, during the period of the war. With unflagging zeal and continuous supervision and service, she kept at her self-appointed post, in the care of sick and wounded soldiers.

A note from Mrs. Otey to John R. McDaniel, when she had charge of the Ladies Relief Hospital, tells of the need of fuel and her efforts to procure some, and is as follows:

"Dear Mr. McDaniel: Please instruct us, in some way, to procure a load of coke, our coal having suddenly given out. We will *pay for it* but having no steward to do this promptly for us" (she asks) "please instruct the bearer (a young man) and tell him, or give him, such an order, as will get a load directly, and oblige,   "Mrs. Lucy M. Otey, *for*

Ladies Relief Hospital."

The answer, written on the note, says: "I gave an order for 100 bushels."

A memoir of this Otey family, beginning with John M. Otey and wife, Lucy Mina Otey, tells that he presided over the city council of Lynchburg for a quarter of a century and that he impressed his character with such force upon the community that no steps were taken in the government of the town or in the development of its enterprise without his approval.

Before entering upon her hospital work Mrs. Otey equipped her seven sons for the field and sent them to battle for their country.

A military company called the Home Guard was formed November 8, 1859, with Samuel Garland, Jr., captain, and Kirkwood Otey, first lieutenant. Other lieutenants were Marcellus M. Moorman (afterwards Captain of Stuart's Horse Artillery), John G. Meem, Jr., and Samuel M. Simpson. Before the company saw any service, Garland was made Colonel of the 11th Virginia Infantry, and the Home Guard was incorporated as Company G, composed of several hundred men. On the 6th of May, when Garland was made colonel, Otey received his commission as captain of the Home Guard. He received several serious wounds in battle, one when as colonel of the 11th Regiment, he engaged in the historic charge of Pickett's division at Gettysburg. In January, 1865, he was seriously disabled and during the last three months of war was forced to retire from the field.

The six brothers of Colonel Otey were: Lieutenant *Dexter Otey,* of the 2nd Virginia Cavalry. While drilling his company, his horse fell with him and so injured his spine that he was unfitted for service and died soon afterwards. *Van R. Otey,* First Sergeant of Company B, 2nd Virginia Cavalry, served two years in the field but his health broke down and he retired, surviving only a few months. *Walter Hayes Otey,* adjutant of the 56th Virginia Infantry, afterwards captain in the Ordnance Department. *George Gaston Otey,* captain of Otey's Battery of Richmond, wounded at Lewisburg, May 24th, 1862, died from effects, October 21st, of same year. *John M. Otey, Jr.,* was Assistant Adjutant-General for General Beauregard during the entire war. *Peter Johnson Otey* was Major of the 30th Virginia Battalion of Infantry. Major Otey represented his district in the United States Congress, elected to office, 1894.

Lucy, only sister of the seven Otey brothers, married John Stewart Walker, of Richmond, who was captain of a company in the 15th Virginia Regiment and was killed at Malvern Hill in 1862.

Last Message to Lee

Samuel Hy Early, a staunch Whig until that political party dissolved in 1861, at the age of 48 years enlisted as a private in Captain John S. Langhorne's 2nd Virginia Cavalry company, the Wise Troop of Lynchburg, but shortly after entering the field, transferred to Captain John D. Alexander's Campbell county company. A little later he was detailed to serve on the staff of Colonel Wheat, who commanded the Tiger Battalion of Texas: when Colonel Wheat was mortally wounded at the first battle of Manasses, Early assisted him off of the field. Shortly afterwards Early was made aide-de-camp on the staff of Brigadier-General J. A. Early, his brother, with rank of captain, and served in that capacity at Sharpsburg, 2nd battle of Manassas, Williamsburg and Seven Pines in every fight in which the army of Northern Virginia engaged, until the battle of Malvern Hill, he having been slightly and his horse badly wounded at Antietam. Had a horse killed under him at 2nd Manassas by cannonball shot in his flank, and a second horse shot three times while he was riding him. Capt. Early was badly wounded in his left leg at Gettysburg, necessitating his leaving the army and he and Col. Kirkwood Otey (also wounded in that battle), were driven back to Lynchburg by Cabell, aged 15 years, son of Early, a courier on the field, who borrowed a buggy and horse for the purpose. After the engagement at Malvern Hill Capt. Early had an attack of pleurisy, from which he never entirely recovered, having recurrent spells, and was never well enough to engage in field service, but acted irregularly as scout. He was a fine marksman and amateur sharpshooter. He was detailed on the staff of the conscripting officer at Lynchburg, and so engaged until war was ended. When the news reached Lynchburg of the evacuation of Richmond by the Confederate army, Captain Early was dispatched immediately to Danville for the purpose of giving President Davis information of what had taken place. He travelled by horseback at night, reaching his destination in six hours, and after an interview with the President there returned to Lynchburg with the following letter, written on the day of the surrender:

"Danville, April 9th, 1865.

"Captain Early,

"Dear Sir: Please give to General R. E. Lee information as to movement of the enemy through Patrick and Henry and their reported purpose. Also all the information you have of our condition here. He will be able to advise Generals Echols, Lomax and Colston as to the best course for them to pursue. The purpose of your trip to this place with the message borne by you will show him all which can be needful for him to know in regard to affairs at Lynchburg.

JEFFERSON DAVIS."

Prisoners at Johnson's Island

Charles Norvell, Lieutenant, 14th Virginia Cavalry, captured at Winchester June 12, 1862; J. R. Hutter, Captain of Company "H", 11th Virginia Infantry, captured at Gettysburg; I. Marshall Steptoe, Lieutenant, Company "D", 7th Louisiana Volunteers, captured at Rappahannock Station, November 7, 1863; Richard Tyree Lacy, born 1842, son of Moses and Anne Lynch Tyree; John Cabell Ward, Captain in 11th Virginia Infantry, captured at Gettysburg, died 1867 of consumption contracted in prison from his two years' confine-

Capt. Jno. Cabell Ward, Prisoner at Johnson's Island

ment; Lieutenant Thomas Fauntleroy, imprisoned four months at Johnson's Island.

The Clifton Grays (name suggested by Richard Morgan)

A company under this name was organized at Pigeon Run in 1860 with the following roll, as given by sergeant W. H. Morgan, a member of it:

Captain, Adam Clement; promoted to major, wounded and disabled at Sharpsburg.

Lieutenant, Jos. A. Hobson, retired at the end of the first year of the war.

Lieutenant, H. H. Withers, retired at the end of the first year.

Lieutenant, James A. Connelly, missing at Gettysburg.

Lieutenant, Jake R. Rosser.

Lieutenant, Robert M. Cock, captured at Five Forks.

Orderly Sergeant, W. H. Morgan, promoted to first lieutenant and captain, captured at Milford, May 21, 1864. Author of "Personal Reminiscences of the War of 1861-5."

Sergeant, Thomas M. Cock; promoted to orderly sergeant.

Sergeant, E. M. Hobson, detailed as regimental ordinance sergeant.

Sergeant, E. G. Gilliam, badly wounded at Five Forks.

Sergeant, George Thomas Rosser.

Sergeant, Robert M. Murrell.

Sergeant, George W. Morgan.

Corporal, Ed. A. Tweedy, captured at Milford, May 21, 1864.

Corporal, G. A. Creacy, wounded at Drury's Bluff, May 16, 1864.

Corporal, Charles A. Clement, promoted orderly sergeant, captured at Five Forks, April 5, 1865.

Corporal, W. T. Tynes, killed at Five Forks.

Corporal, W. Hendricks, killed at 2nd Manassas, August 30, 1862.

Privates, Charles Allen, killed at Drury's Bluff, April 16, 1864; Reuben Allen; John J. Brooks; Allen Bailey, killed at Drury's Bluff, April 16, 1864; Miffram Bailey, killed at Williamsburg, May 5, 1862; Harvey Bailey, died near Yorktown, April, 1862; Abner Bateman, wounded at Plymouth, North Carolina, April, 1864; Silas Barber, killed at Seven Pines, May 31, 1862; George A. Brown, captured at Milford; James A. Brown, captured at Milford; W. Lee Brown, wounded at Gettysburg and Milford, and captured May, 1864; George W. Bell, lost an arm near Petersburg, March 30, 1865; Charles E. Blankenship; Leslie C. Blankenship; James B. Cocke;

George W. Clement; Thomas C. Creacy; Daniel R. Caldwell; Samuel Caldwell; Peter Cary; Moses H. Callaham, captured at Milford, April 21, 1864; Charles M. Callaham; Lee Dunnavant; John R. Depriest, killed at Drury's Bluff, May, 1864; John A. Daniel; Hairston Eads; William Eads; Robert A. Elliott; H. O. Elliott, color sergeant, killed at 2nd Manassas; Samuel T. Franklin; Edmund L. Franklin; John B. Frazier, now blind; Benjamin Faris, killed at Williamsburg, May 5, 1862; John Gardner; W. H. Hobson, mortally wounded at Dranesville, January, 1862; Nathaniel Hobson; Andy Hughes; Crockett Hughes, killed at Williamsburg May 5, 1862; Richard C. Harvey; Stephen Hall; Thomas W. Harvey; Joseph Hendricks; Ellis H. Holcombe; Robert H. Jones; George W. Jones; Joshua Jones; James T. Jones, captured at Milford, April 21, 1864; J. Wesley Jones, captured at Milford, April 21, 1864; Charles Jones, killed at Gettysburg, July 3, 1863; Walker Jones, wounded at Gettysburg; James Chap. Jones, lost an arm at Gettysburg; Linneous Jones, killed at Gettysburg; Robert W. Jones, wounded in battle; Jasper Jones; Monroe Jennings; Frederick Kabler, captured at Milford, April 21, 1864; W. S. Kabler, captured at Milford; Jack Kabler; Len Kelley; John Keenan, detailed as drummer; Peter A. LeGrand; David Layne, killed at Williamsburg, May 5, 1862; John Layne, died near Fredericksburg, January, 1863; Miffram Layne; Robert W. Morgan, wounded at 2nd Manassas and Gettysburg, captured at Milford; Thomas E. Moorman; James Martin, detailed as cook; John Monroe, killed at Drury's Bluff, May 16, 1864; William Monroe, killed at Plymouth, April 18, 1864; William T. Monroe, captured at Milford, May, 1864; Henry Martin, killed at 2nd Manassas, August 30, 1862; Richard Moore; Maurice M. Mason, Jr., killed at Gettysburg, Charles Miles, shot accidentally; Charles Murrell, killed at 2nd Manassas; Emory Murrell; William Matthews; John Organ, killed at Williamsburg, May 5, 1862; James Organ; Daniel Pillow, missing at Gettysburg; William Pillow, detailed as cook; John Puckett; Thornton Phillips, died in service; James Pugh; Nat Pugh; Michael Quilly; Walter C. Rosser, wounded at

Williamsburg and Drury's Bluff; Alfred S. Rosser, killed at Drury's Bluff; Granville Rosser, killed at Williamsburg; John W. Rosser, captured at Five Forks; Thomas W. Rosser; Joe Rice, killed at Sharpsburg, September, 1862; Aleck W. Rice, captured at Milford, died in prison, buried at Arlington; James Terrell, killed at Seven Pines, May, 1862; G. Dabney Tweedy, killed at Gettysburg, 1863; Bennett Tweedy, killed at Plymouth, July, 1864; Ferdinand Tweedy; Joseph Tweedy; Robert C. Tweedy; Isaac Walthall, company commissary; George W. Walker, mortally wounded at Drury's Bluff; Wash W. Wood, killed near Petersburg, 1865; Bruce Woody, killed at Drury's Bluff; John Wood, killed at Williamsburg, May, 1862; James L. Watkins; John J. Woodall; W. A. Wilkerson, captured at Milford, May, 1864; Whit. B. Williams, wounded at Williamsburg; William H. Wilson, killed at Williamsburg, May 5, 1862; W. S. Withers, detailed at hospital steward; W. H. Wingfield; James Wood, killed at Seven Pines.

The company was armed and entered service May 1, 1861, at Lynchburg, enlisting for one year. It was mustered into service by Colonel Jubal A. Early as one of the ten companies of the 28th Regiment of Virginia Infantry, Colonel Robert T. Preston, commander; with enrollment of 85 men from around the neighborhood of Pigeon Run.

General Officers of the Confederate Army
Born or Lived in Campbell County

Lieutenant-Generals Authorized by Act of C. S. Congress
Approved May 31, 1864
(Provisional Army with Temporary Rank)

—Jubal A. Early, born in Franklin County, Virginia, November 3, 1816; appointed Brigadier-General from Virginia, August 28, 1861, to rank from July 21, 1861, confirmed Aug. 28, 1861 ; promoted to be Major-General, Provisional Army, April 23, 1863, to rank from Jan. 17, 1863; appointed Lieutenant-

General, Provisional Army, with temporary rank, May 31, 1864, confirmed May 31, 1864; lived in Lynchburg from 1870 to 1894; died there March 2d, 1894.

Major Generals; Act approved February 28, 1864: "That such forces (provisional for the Confederate States of America) may be received . . . ; and the President shall appoint, by and with the advice and consent of Congress, such general officer or officers for said forces as may be necessary for the service."

—Robert E. Rodes, born at Lynchburg, Va., March 29, 1829; appointed from Alabama, Brigadier-General, October 21, 1861, to rank from same date, confirmed December 13, 1861, promoted to be Major-General, Provisional Army, May 7, 1863, to rank from May 2, 1863. Killed at Winchester, Va., September 19, 1864.

—Thomas L. Rosser, born in Campbell County, October 15, 1836; appointed Brigadier-General from Texas, October 10, 1863, to rank from September 28, 1863; confirmed February 17, 1864; appointed Major-General, Provisional Army with temporary rank, November 4, 1864, to rank from November 1, 1864. Died near Charlottesville, Va., March 29, 1910.

—John Echols, born in Lynchburg, Va., March 20, 1823; appointed Brigadier-General from Virginia, April 18, 1862, to rank from April 16, 1862, confirmed April 18, 1862; paroled at Greensboro, N. C., May 1, 1865. Died at Staunton, Va., May 24, 1898.

—Samuel Garland, Jr., born in Lynchburg, Va., December 16, 1830; appointed Brigadier-General from Virginia, May 23, 1862, to rank from same date; confirmed September 30, 1862. Killed in action at South Mountain, Md., September 14, 1862.

—Fitzhugh Lee, born at Clermont, Fairfax County, Va., November 19, 1835; appointed Brigadier-General from Virginia, July 25, 1862, to rank from July 24, 1862, confirmed September 30, 1862; promoted to be Major-General, Provisional Army, September 3, 1863, to rank from August 3, 1863, confirmed January 25, 1864; paroled at Appomattox C. H., Va.,

April 9, 1865; lived at Lynchburg, 1895-6; died at Washington, D. C., April 28, 1905.

—James Dearing, born at Otterburne, Campbell county, in 1840. appointed Brigadier-General, Provisional Army, April 29, 1864, to rank from date of appointment; paroled at Lynchburg, Va., April 14, 1865; mortally wounded at High Bridge.

Brigadier-Generals of Artillery, authorized by Act of C. S. Congress: "That the President be authorized to appoint with consent of Congress in the Provisional Army and in the volunteer corps officers of artillery above the rank of captain, without reference to the number of batteries under the actual command of the officers so appointed, not to exceed in number however one brigadier-general for over 80 guns."

—Armistead L. Long, born in Campbell County, Va., September 13, 1837; appointed Brigadier-General from Virginia, September 21, 1862, to rank from same date, confirmed February 17, 1864; paroled at Appomattox C. H., Va., April 9, 1865; died at Charlottesville, Va., April, 1891.

Special Provisional Army authorized by Act, October 13, 1862: "That the President is authorized to appoint 20 general officers in the Provisional Army and to assign them to such appropriate duties as he may deem expedient."

—James M. Goggin, appointed Brigadier-General from Virginia to rank from December 4, 1864.

Officers assigned to duty as general officers, who were not appointed by the President:

—Thomas T. Munford, Born in Richmond, Va., in 1831, moved to Lynchburg during later years of his life. Colonel of the 2nd Regiment, Virginia Cavalry; assigned to duty as Brigadier-General, by Major-General Fitzhugh Lee, and served as such; died in Alabama, remains interred at Lynchburg.

Confederate Soldiers, Lynch Station

Adams, John R., deceased, interred in family buryingground.

Adams, James, John Adams, sons of Joel Adams; Thomas Adams, son of Thomas, Sr.—all three killed in a skirmish at Campbell courthouse about the time of the surrender.

Andrews, Robert, E., son of Rev. Milton Andrews; buried near Lynch Station.

Anthony, Benjamin; buried in Mt. Hebron cemetery.

Anthony, Thomas; buried in Mt. Hebron cemetery.

Anthony, John W.; buried in family burying ground.

Andrews, Wyatt Arnold; living at Lynch Station.

Arnold, Alexander A.; buried in Mt. Hebron cemetery.

Arnold, Lieut. D. R., buried in Mt. Hebron cemetery.

Arnold, Fletcher H., buried in Mt. Hebron cemetery.

Agnew, William S.; living at Lynch Station.

Brooks, Cicero, son of Benjamin Brooks; buried near Lynch Station.

Crumpton, William; buried near Lynch Station.

Douglass, Charles A., buried in family burying-ground.

Dowdy, Aldridge Greene, buried near Lynch Station.

Frazier, James (Texas); buried in Mt. Hebron cemetery.

Frazier, Anselm; buried in family burying-ground.

Frazier, Jesse W.; buried in family burying-ground.

Frazier, William O.; living at Lynch Station.

Fauntleroy, Thomas; buried in family burying-ground at Avoca.

Foster, Truck; buried near Lynch Station.

Gaines, Robert (one of five brothers in service); buried near Lynch Station.

Gill, Jesse; buried in Mt. Hebron cemetery.

Grubb, Joseph; buried in Mt. Hebron cemetery.

Hughes, Charles; buried near Lynch Station.

Hall, Charles R.; buried at Mt. Hebron.

Hall, William A.; buried at Mt. Hebron.

Hogan, Charles W.; buried at Mt. Hebron.

Hogan, Enos; buried at Mt. Hebron.

Jenks, James A.; living at Lynch Station.

Keesee, Booker T.; living at Lynch Station.

Laughan, Edward, William A. Laughan, sons of John Laughan; buried near Lynch Station.

Lee, James W., Robert C. Lee; buried in family burying-ground.

Mattox, Samuel (married the widow of James Adams); buried near Lynch Station.

Mattox, Wm. H., living at Lynch Station.

Merrett, M. T. C.; living at Lynch Station.

Moorman, Achilles. H.; buried near Lynch Station.

Morris, William; buried in Mt. Hebron cemetery.

Richardson, John; buried near Lynch Station.

Roberts, William; buried near Lynch Station.

Snow, Robert, William Snow, sons of Abner Snow; buried at Lynch Station.

Snow, Vincent, son of Osborne Snow; buried at Lynch Station.

Terry, Sanford W.; buried in Mt. Hebron cemetery.

Tucker, Amon; buried in family burying-ground.

Tardy, B. F.; buried in family burying-ground.

Urquhart, John; buried near Lynch Station.

Urquhart, Kenneth; buried near Lynch Station.

Ward, Capt. Robert H.; buried in family graveyard.

Webb, John Lewis; buried in Mt. Hebron cemetery.

West, Charles; buried in Mt. Hebron cemetery.

West, Christopher; buried in family graveyard.

Williamson, Calvin; buried in Mt. Hebron cemetery.

Pritchett, James A. (Federal soldier); buried in Mt. Hebron cemetery.

Unknown North Carolina cavalryman, died en route home after surrender; Mt. Hebron cemetery.

Lynch Station

Confederate Soldiers Killed in Action or Died in Service

Brooks, Nathaniel
Brooks, Mosby
Brooks, Whitfield

Brooks, John J.
Andrews, E. Price (son of Rev. Milton Andrews)

Gaines, Richard T., Charles
E. Gaines, William H.
Gaines (brothers of James
Gaines of Rock Wall, Tex.)
Hall Joseph
Hall, Robert
Merritt, Cornelius B. (broth-
er of Marcus T. C. Mer-
ritt)

Snow, Van Buren (son of
Abner Snow)
Stinnett, Whitfield
Stinnett, William
Urquhart, William
West, Loving
West, John
West, Washington

Confederate Veteran State Pensioners in 1926, or Their Widows

Agnew, W. S.
Almond, W. H.
Adams, S. T.
Adams, W. W.
Andrews, W. A.
Armistead, James A.
Armistead, R. S.
Austin, Nannie F.
Barnett, Rodie S.
Bass, Susan F.
Bentley, Martha C.
Black, Mrs. Henry A.
Brown, Ludwell
Burks, Pharoah
Burnett, Samuel H.
Cary, Peter
Callahan, E. W.
Camper, Henry L.
Cardwell, Ann M.
Cardwell, Sallie K.
Cauthorn, J. H.
Clark, Adam
Clark, C. B.
Conley, Sarah

Covington, J. J.
Creasy, Wyatt
Cyrus, Madison
Daniel, William S.
Davis, Victoria
DeJarnette, Julia A.
Dudley, Sallie A.
Duke, Mrs. M. R.
Evans, D. Rees
Evans, Daniel J.
Evans, Nancy M.
Eads, Lethia F.
Elder, R. O.
Elder, Rosa V.
Faris, R. W.
Faris, Emma
Faris, Margaret J.
Farmer, Martha V.
Farmer, Louise
Foster, Mary E.
Foster, I. Y.
Ford, S. A.
Green, Silas (applied for)
(colored)

Guy, Emma E.
Haden, A. Blanche
Haden, J. W.
Hall, W. A.
Harvey, Bob
Harvey, George A.
Hammersley, Minnie
Hicks, Mrs. B. A.
Hicks, Fannie A.
Hill, Sarah L.
Hendrick, W. D.
Hood, Elijah W.
Hunt, Gabe (colored)
Hunter, R. P.
Hunter, Susan T.
Hutter, Charlotte S.
Harvey, John F.
Irby, Sarah E.
Johnson, Wm. H. H.
Johnson, Burroughs W.
Johnson, Malinda S.
Jacobs, Mattie L.
Jenks, G. A.
Jones, Elisha
Jamison, Virgie
Jordan, J. W.
Kabler, Mrs. M. A.
Keesee, Sallie M.
Leftwich, John S.
Lindsay, Maggie J.
Lipscomb, India V.
Lipscomb, Susan A. P.
Lipscomb, Susan P.
Maddox, Robert S.
Martin, Scott
Mason, Susan A.
Maxey, Harman

McBride, James B.
McKenna, Sallie J.
McVeigh, T. Emory
Milstead, Susan A.
Mitchell, James R.
Moore, John (col.)
Moorman, Mollie C.
Morgan, Sallie P.
McMillan, Mattie M.
Organ, James E.
Orr, James P.
Overacre, Susan C.
Owen, Peyton
Perrow, Seth
Phillips, W. M.
Pribble, J. E.
Pritchard, Mary E.
Puckett, Queen E.
Puckett, William M.
Russell, Robert
Reynolds, B. Walker
Robinson, George W.
Reid, Sarah A.
Reynolds, Frances H.
Rosser, George
Rosser, Walter C.
Sandifer, Martha R.
Saunders, Sallie T.
Scott, Maud A.
Snow, Martha A.
Steele, Julia A.
Stevens, James W.
Sublett, George
Swinney, Wilmerth M.
Terry, James (col.)
Thomas, Nannie
Tibbs, Ann

Tucker, Ammon
Tucker, James W.
Tucker, John W.
Tucker, William M.
Tweedy, Sallie A.
Walker, Madora A.
West, William H.
Wheeler, Laura E.

Wilkerson, J. W.
Wood, Laura H.
Wood, W. D.
Woodall, Mary E.
Wooldridge, W. S.
Woodson, Mrs. G. C.
Woodfin, Belle
Ziegler, Henry

Spanish War

Lynchburg furnished three companies of soldiers in the war with Spain.

The Zouaves, Company E, 2nd Regiment Virginia Volunteers

Captain, R. E. Craighill
First Lieutenant, A. B. Percy
Second Lieut., A. S. Burnham
First Sgt., Guy M. Langhorne
Quartermaster-Sgt., M. Allen
Sergeant, W. L. Holt
Sergeant, J. R. Mitcham
Sergeant, H. O. Holt
Wagoner, Spot F. Fulks

Corporal, B. B. Murdock
Corporal, J. M. Tanner
Corporal, Henry L. Johnson
Corporal, L. E. Wingfield
Corporal, George T. Pleasants
Corporal, Harry P. Baker
Musician, L. D. Lewis
Musician, Wm. P. McNeer
Artificer, F. S. Moore

Enrollment of Privates—65.

Home Guard, Company E, Third Regiment, Virginia Volunteers

1st Captain, F. C. Scruggs
2d Lieutenant, W. S. Faulkner
1st Lieut., W. J. Seabury
2d Lieutenant, W. S. Faulkner
1st Sergt., G. R. Lewis
Quartermaster-Sergt., R. L. Stabler
Sergeant, Frank Adams

Sergeant, H. M. Scott
Sergeant, H. C. Snead
Sergeant, J. H. Akers
Corporal, C. S. Adams
Corporal, F. W. Agnor
Corporal, G. W. Gilbert
Corporal, C. D. Hamner
Corporal, R. A. Lacy

Corporal, R. H. Oglesby
Musician, W. H. Tyree
Musician, W. H. Bailey

Artificer, Patrick Kelley
Wagoner, P. M. Jones

Enrollment of Privates—76.

The Fitz Lee Rifles, Company L., 3rd Regiment, Virginia Volunteers

Captain, R. L. Miller
1st Lieut., John D. Clark
2d Lieut., R. H. T. Adams, Jr.
1st Sergt., W. D. Munroe
Quartermaster - Sergt., Alvin B. Scruggs
Sergeant, Ed. Murphy
Sergeant, Daniel A. Broader
Sergeant, John E. Pettus
Sergeant, Wm. P. Gorman

Corporal, William F. Enochs
Corporal, Walter L. Fulks
Corporal, James H. Snider
Corporal, Ernest Hall
Corporal, James C. Peerman
Corporal, James F. Lyle
Musician, Walter Almond
Musician, Joseph L. App
Artificer, Robert L. Adkins
Wagoner, Charles H. Brown

Enrollment of privates—76.

General Thomas Lafayette Rosser (C. S. Veteran), served as brigadier-general, United States Volunteers, from June 10, 1898, to October 31, 1898. He was in command of the 3rd Brigade, 2nd Division, 1st Army Corps, at Chickamauga, Ga., from June 25th, 1898, to August 8th, 1898; on sick leave of absence from August 9 to September 28, 1898; commanding the 3rd Brigade, 2nd Division, 1st Corps, from September 29 to October 14, 1898, at Knoxville, Tennessee, and on sick leave of absence from October, 1898, to date of discharge.

Naval Surgeon

Dr. Henry Tucker Percy, U. S. N., son of Isham and Anne E. Percy, was born in Botetourt county, moved in 1869 to Lynchburg where he attended the school of Prof. C. L. C. Minor: entering the University of Virginia afterwards, he graduated in medicine in one year, then took a post graduate

course at the Jefferson College of Philadelphia and entered the
Navy from Lynchburg in 1873. In October of that year
occurred the incident of the *Virginius,* which came near causing war between the United States and Spain, when five Americans were among the crew shot down at Santiago de Cuba.
The ship on which Dr. Percy sailed at that time was in the harbor of Santiago three days after the occurrence: he was at
Colon when American marines again encountered a Spanish
force. When hostilities opened in the Spanish-American War,
he was surgeon on the *Charleston,* which sailed for Manila; en
route that vessel took possession of the island of Guam, which
the government yet holds as a coaling station. At the close of
the war Dr. Percy returned on the flagship *Olympia* as Admiral
Dewey's surgeon. After two years service in Japan, he returned to Washington, then he was promoted to the rank of
Medical Inspector: filling the duties of that office until March
28, 1909, when he was taken to the Naval Hospital and died
March 31. A Washington paper in reporting the death of Medical Inspector Henry Tucker Percy said "The passing of a
spirit so noble and true has made us see more clearly the
strength and determination of the life purpose of the man;—
the will to perform not only duties of his exacting profession but always to encourage and help. He gave his time and
strength to all who turned to him in need, or who his trained
intellect and sympathetic heart found in trouble:—one whose
life was spent in living for the welfare of his fellowmen."

The Council of National Defence

The Council of National Defense was instituted on April
29th, 1916. April 9th, 1917, state governments were called
upon to organize State Councils of Defense for the purpose
of carrying out the aims of the National Council. Governor
Stuart complied for Virginia by establishing on April 18th
an Agricultural Council of Safety, on April 25th, the Industrial Council of Safety and on April 26th the First Virginia
Council of Defense. In February, 1918 Governor Davis

joined all three of these groups into the Second Virginia Council of Defense. Appointments for Campbell County Council of the Agricultural County of Safety were: W. E. McDonald, county agent, W. L. Garbee, county superintendent of Schools. For the Industrial Council of Safety, Walter E. Addison, Lynchburg *News.*

City and County Councils of the Second Virginia Council of Defense, D. B. Ryland, Chairman:

W. L. Garbee, Lawyers
James H. Steele, Rustburg
R. W. Callahan, Lynchburg
W. E. McDonald, Rustburg
Thomas Tweedy, Rustburg
E. A. Hicks, Evington
E. W. Griffin, Gladys
John T. McKinney, Lynchburg
M. L. Boothe, Brookneal
J. L. East, Alta Vista
E. H. Lane, Alta Vista
B. F. Ginther, Brookneal
J. E. Webbs, Brookneal
Richard Langhorne, Evington

W. T. Oakes, Gladys
A. H. Kirkland, Concord
Miss C. St. John, Rustburg
Miss F. Garbee, Lawyers
Mrs. W. C. Rosser, Jr., Rustburg
Mrs. J. W. Carson, Concord
Miss Rosa Gilliam, Naruna
Mrs. C. Gilliam, Evington
Mrs. Jere White, Brookneal
Mrs. E. H. Lane, Alta Vista
Mrs. Hugh Stephens, Gladys
Walter Fauntleroy, Alta Vista

Local Food Administrator, Howell C. Featherston, appointed May 17th, 1918; resigned June 25th. Local Food Administrator, Lynchburg, N. D. Eller, appointed January 2nd, 1918. Woman's Division, Catherine St. John, R. F. D., November 20th, 1918. Woman's Division, City, Mrs. John H. Lewis, November 20th, 1918. Local Legal Adviser, S. D. Kemp, for Campbell, address, Lynchburg. Federal Fuel Administrator, J. W. Coffey, Lynchburg, volunteer, from November 15, 1917, to February 28, 1919. City and County Fuel Committee, Richard Hancock, chairman; E. E. Menefee, L. H. McWane—volunteer. Mamie J. Rucker, stenographer; A. C. Watts, clerk.

County Registrars, June 5, 1917

The following registrars were appointed for Campbell county precincts for the purpose of registering all males between the ages of 21 and 31 years, regardless of occupation, pursuant to the war registration act:

Rustburg precinct ....Frank Nelson
Concord precinct ....James P. Scruggs
Mount Zion precinct ....Robert E. Mitchell
Brookneal precinct ....J. E. Webb
Mike precinct ....W. F. Wood
Naruna precinct ....Gordon Kent
Hat Creek precinct ....L. C. Asher
Morgan's Mill precinct ....Thomas Whately
Pigeon Run precinct ....W. T. Oakes
Marysville precinct ....G. W. Griffin
Castle Craig precinct ....O. S. Peerman
Lynch's precinct ....C. A. Douglas
Leesville precinct ....John W. Mattox
New London precinct ....W. D. Abbott
Evington precinct ....Eugene Ould
Alta Vista precinct ....Walter Fauntleroy
King's precinct ....John E. Poston
Flynn's precinct ....J. H. Lindsay
West Lynchburg precinct ....David Walker
Blackwater precinct ....W. O. Smith
Rolling Mill precinct ....Seth Perrow

Registration Board

R. L. Perrow, sheriff; S. C. Goggin, clerk; H. P. Brown, M. D.

Local Board members: R. L. Perrow, Rustburg; S. C. Goggin, Rustburg; H. P. Brown, Lynchburg. Chief clerk, B. W. Ballaugh, headquarters, Rustburg. Government Appeal Agents: Frank Nelson, Rustburg, (succeeded by A. H. Light) July, 1917, till March 20, 1918. Medical Advisory Board,

No. 30, Lynchburg: Henry Rawlings, Lynchburg; R. M. Taliaferro, Lynchburg; James M. Morrison, Lynchburg; W. H. Dew, Lynchburg; R. Lemon, Lynchburg; J. A. Rucker, Bedford City; Edward Sandidge, Amberst; F. O. Plunkett, Lynchburg; D. R. Phelps, Lynchburg. Jurisdiction: Campbell, Bedford, Appomattox and Amherst counties and city of Lynchburg. Chairman, A. W. Terrell, headquarters, Lynchburg. Thomas K. Terrell, Lynchburg, served December, 1917, till February 26th, 1918. D. A. Christian, Vera, served December, 1917, till January 16th, 1918. Legal Advisory Board: A. H. Light, chairman; Frank Nelson, Rustburg; W. M. Murrell, Lynchburg.

A call was issued on September 10th, 1917, for 40 per cent of Virginia's quota to be sent to Camp Lee. Then given an extension till October 1st. A display of much patriotism, especially on the part of the Confederate veterans, featured the movement of the contingents of this call to camp Lee. A veteran from Caroline accompanied the men from that county to camp in his gray uniform, reminding them "to remember always you are Virginians." Campbell reported that her examinations had not been completed. The Central Legal Advisory Committee was then appointed and members of the legal boards laid aside their own affairs and without pay gave three months of their time and services to rendering assistance to registrants in completing their questionnaires.

The local board of Lynchburg was the first to report the work of classification and examination complete and Virginia was twenty-sixth of all states in the Union, to render a final report of the classification desired.

Lynchburg organized two companies, one known as the "Home Guards," the other as the "State Guards." Lieutenant L. B. LeGrand, with seventeen years' experience in the National Guard, organized the Lynchburg Home Guards. Applications were signed by sixty men and three officers. Seventy-eight men signed the petition for permission to form the Lynchburg State Guards, and Rozell R. Yoder was selected as leader. The average age of the men of this company was less than twenty-one years. The Lynchburg Home Guards was named for an old Home Guard company of former years. There were three officers and seventy-eight men present at their muster on January 10th, 1918. At the 1919 inspection, inspecting officers reported "this company is dependable for any emergency service which it may be called upon to perform:" every effort was vainly made to induce it to enlist in the National Guard.

The Lynchburg State Guards recruited their company up to the hundred mark, continued an active unit in the Virginia Volunteers, and were mustered in as a National Guard contingent, receiving Federal recognition on July 28th, 1919.

Staff Service

Major Clifford Cabell Early, son of John C. and Mary W. Cabell-Early, grandson of Captain Samuel Early of Lynchburg, graduated from West Point Academy in 1905, was commissioned second lieutenant of the 20th infantry (then in the Philippines); served with that regiment at Monterey, California, in 1906; on duty in San Francisco after the earthquake there, remaining in California until June, 1909; in the Philippines till 1911; promoted 1st lieutenant, March, 1911; with same regiment at Ft. Douglas, Utah; on the Mexican border till December, 1914. Joined the 15th Regiment at Tientsin, China, where he remained from January, 1915, till August, 1917. Promoted captain of infantry, July, 1916; served with the 8th division at Camp Fremont, October, 1917; promoted major in the National Army, November, 1917; served with the 88th Division at Camp Dodge, Iowa, for three months. Detailed on general staff corps in the office of chief of staff at Washington, February, 1918; in Operations Division of General Staff, 1918-19; promoted lieutenant-colonel on General Staff, August, 1918. Demoted to major after the war, with posts, Camp Dix, N. J., Fort Jay, Governor's Island, New York; Camp Benning, Georgia, and Fort Leavenworth, Kansas. At present detailed at North Carolina State College, Raleigh, Professor of Military Science and Tactics.

Second Lieutenant Jubal A. Early, younger brother of Major Early, also of the 20th Infantry (to which he was commissioned in 1908), while a student ot U. S. Naval Academy at Annapolis served on the staff of President Roosevelt in 1905 at his inauguration. He was with the 20th Infantry at Monterey, California, from March, 1908, to June, 1909; in the Philippines from July, 1909, to December, 1911; at Fort Douglass, January, 1912, to December, 1913; represented his regiment in the pistol competition, Western Department, in 1912; on patrol duty at El Paso, Texas, December, 1913 to May, 1914; promoted 1st lieutenant March, 1914; guarded Mexican interned prisoners at Fort Wingate, New Mexico, from May to September, 1914; was drowned in Lake Mariano, near Gallup, N. M., in an effort to save the life of a friend who could not swim and who was in the boat with him when it was upset by a terrific gale. In 1915 the War Department authorized the naming of a battery on the great Fortress of Corregidor, Philippine Islands, "XX Battery Early, in honor of Lieutenant Jubal A. Early, 20th U. S. Infantry, drowned in the line of duty near Ft. Wingate while trying to save the life of a companion."

Naval and Air Service

Lieutenant James Roland Kyle, son of Jas. R. and Alice J. Aunspaugh-Kyle, born at Lynchburg in 1892, was a student at Fishburn Military Academy, at Waynesboro, Va., when he received appointment to the U. S. Naval Academy at Annapolis, which he entered in 1911, graduating from there in 1915. He was then attached to the U. S. S. Brooklyn, which sailed in October of that year for a three-year's cruise in Asiatic waters, and arrived at Manilla in December, 1915. About this time he was attached to the U. S. Torpedo Boat Destroyer Barry, which cruised among the Philippine Islands. In February, 1916, he was detached from the Barry and ordered to S. S. Galveston, then cruising in the Orient. When in April, 1917, the United States declared war with Germany and temporary promotions were made in the Navy, Ensign Kyle was appointed a Lieutenant (Junior grade), from July 1, 1917. On September 3, 1917, Lieutenant Kyle, while at Shanghai, China, was ordered home. Sailing from Manilla on the 18th, on the British liner, Empress of Asia, he reported to the Navy Department at Washington. He was then transferred to the Atlantic fleet, and November 27, 1917, reported at Philadelphia Navy Yard for duty in connection with the fitting out of the Torpedo Boat Destroyer Dent (then under construction, as Engineer Officer thereon, when commissioned, which occurred June 5, 1918, and he became then lieutenant. September 9, 1918, the Dent, fastest ship in the Navy, sailed from New York as ocean escort to the British convoy of American troops for Liverpool, September 17, 1918, and arrived at Buncrana, Ireland, September 28. Proceeding from Buncrana, September 30, arrived in New York, October 9. Again from New York, October 19, arrived at Buncrana, October 29. Back again from Buncrana, October 31, at New York, November 8, three days before the Armistice, Nov. 11, 1918. In January, 1919, the Atlantic fleet went to Cuban waters for winter cruise and target practice, returning to New York in April. May 1, 1919, U. S. S. Dent, in company with six other destroyers, left New York for Trepassy Bay, New Foundland, to take their stations between there and the Azores, to protect the seaplanes NC.1, NC.2, NC.3, NC.4 in their trans-Atlantic flight, the NC.4 being the only successful plane in reaching Portugal; others stopping at the Azores. The fleet was ordered to the Pacific coast, sailed from New York July 12, 1919, touched at Old Point Comfort, Panama, through the Canal, reaching Los Angeles August, 1919. In February, 1920, Lieutenant Kyle, was detached from S. S. Dent and ordered to the Submarine base at New London, Conn., for instruction in submarines. He was transferred to S. S. Minnesota in April, 1920, to navigate the ship to Annapolis in order to take the midshipmen on their summer cruise. On June 4th he was detached from the Minnesota and on the 5th to the Naval Academy for duty under instruction in post graduate course in Engineering. Was commissioned lieutenant, July 1, 1920.

Detached April 1, 1921, from Naval Academy to Naval Air Station at Pensacola, Fla., for elementary and advanced flight training. Reported June 11, and won his wings in September. October 1, 1921, Lieut. Kyle reported to Massachusetts Institute of Technology for post graduate instruction in Engineering, a course he completed in June, 1922. From July 3, to September 1st, he was in the Bureau of Aeronautics, Navy Department, Washington, D. C., then sent to the Aircraft Squads Scouting Fleet (Atlantic), for duty involving flying, and was on the government transport S. S. Wright. Arriving at Pensacola, he was transferred to the Naval Air Station for refreshment courses in actual air-craft flying. Completing instruction, was ordered to the seaplane carrier S. Langley March 12, 1923, and transferred to Naval Air Station, Naval Operating Base, Hampton Roads, Va., Dec. 9, 1923. On January 7, 1924, he reported to the Naval Aircraft Factory, Navy Yard, Philadelphia, for duty involving flying. 1924 and 1925 years were spent in testing new planes built at the factory. Lieut. Kyle was the chief test pilot. In the spring of 1925 the monster seaplane PN-9, an all-metal craft designed for a non-stop flight from San Francisco to Honolulu was completed, ready for its duration flight. Lieut. Kyle and Clarence H. Schildauer were chosen pilots to make the test. The PN-9 took the air about 8 A. M., May 1, 1925, and remained in the air 28 hours, 35 minutes and 27 seconds, thus establishing a new world record in duration flight of seaplanes, a record accepted by the International Aeronautic Federation in Paris. After this flight, Lieut. Kyle and Schildauer entered the parachute school at Lakehurst, N. J., in order to familiarize themselves with the safety devices. On May 22, 1925, the biplane in which they made the ascent being defective, engine trouble developed, the plane refused to rise above 500 feet and was swooping to the ground, when 200 feet up, the instructor signalled the aviators to jump. Lieut. Kyle's parachute failed to open, and he was instantly killed May 22, 1925. His body was brought to Lynchburg and interred in Spring Hill cemetery.

Gordon, brother of Lieut. Roland Kyle, born 1897, graduated from Virginia Military Institute June, 1918. Enlisted in U. S. Marines at that time and did service training recruits in the infantry of the Marine Corps, Paris Island, S. C. Detached from Paris Island October 21, 1918, to Marine Barracks, Navy Yard, Philadelphia. Transferred to Marine Aviation Detachment, Massachusetts Institute of Technology at Cambridge, November 11, 1918. Promoted to Corporal September 27, 1918, to Gunnery Sergeant, October 21, 1918. Honorably discharged from Marine Detachment, Massachusetts Institute of Technology, as a gunnery sergeant, January 18, 1919. On January 27, 1919, received commission as captain of infantry, Virginia Volunteers and Assistant Professor of Mathematics, at Virginia Military Institute, Lexington, Va. Captain Kyle married October 18, 1926, Emma Lawson Adams, daughter of Thomas Tunstall Adams, of Richmond, a descendant of Captain Robert Adams, an early settler in Campbell.

National Guard Service

Robert T. Craighill, attorney-at-law of Lynchburg, and C. S. Veteran, enlisted September 25, 1862, as a private in Company B, 12th Virginia Cavalry, Rosser's Brigade, C. S. Army, and served with that command during the remainder of the war of 1861-65. He was severely wounded near Todd's Tavern at the battle of the Wilderness, May 6th, 1864. His son, Robert E. Craighill, while still a lad, had command of a military company of boys organized by John Clark, who was their first captain. When they attained their majority, they enrolled as state troops, and volunteered for service in the war with Spain. Captain Robert E. Craighill has been promoted through several grades of service beginning with the first period of December 16, 1889, to December 18, 1898. Captain of Virginia Zouaves, Virginia Volunteers, to May 9, 1898. Captain of Company E, 2nd Virginia Infantry, U. S. Volunteers, to December 18,

1898; second period, May 3rd, 1902, to January 14, 1919. Captain and Lieutenant-Colonel, 1st Infantry, Virginia Volunteers to July 24, 1917 (called into Federal service June 18, 1916, for duty on the Mexican border). Returned from Federal to State service January 17, 1917. Lieutenant-Colonel Infantry, U. S. Army, July 25, 1917, to January 14, 1919. Assignments: 1st Virginia Infantry; commanding officer 3rd Officers' Training Camp, Camp McClellan, Ala.; 116th Infantry; 115th Infantry; commanding officer American troops, Calais, France. 3rd Period: May 9, 1821 to January 1, 1927; Captain of Company E, 1st Infantry, Virginia National Guard, to October 2, 1921. Lieutenant-Colonel, 116th Infantry Virginia National Guard, October 3, 1921.

Lynch Station Soldiers in World War

Agnew, Frank Holmes and Russell Agnew, sons of William S. Agnew, courier and Indian Scout, following the surrender of the Confederate army.

Andrews, Clayton, son of Milton and grandson of Rev. Milton Andrews.

Andrews, Hugh A., son of Wyatt A., and grandson of Rev. Milton Andrews.

Anthony, Edwin, grandson of Benjamin H. Anthony.

Arthur, William.

Board, Dr. John Arnold, captain, served in hospital in Scotland; John James Board, sons of Dr. J. J. Board.

Boley, James, naval service.

Bradshaw, Douglas; John Bradshaw, lieutenant in aviation service; grandsons of Rev. Milton Bishop.

Burruss, Wm. H., son of Jas. M. Burruss, lieutenant in field artillery.

Douglass, Chas. Achilles, son of J. L. Douglas, Sr., with Lynchburg Musketeers.

Douglass, Jas. Baxter, son of J. L. Douglass, Sr., railway engineer; now Methodist minister in Colorado.

Douglass, John L. (deceased), in Navy; later editor of Alta Vista *Journal.*

Hall, Thomas, son of William T. Hall, in the Navy.

Hall, William, son of William T. Hall, in the Navy.

Hensley, Albert J.

Hogan, John R.

Oliver, Harry M., son of Richard, grandson of H. M. Oliver.

Reynolds, Robert J.

Smith, Claude M.

Thompson, Capt. J. Victor, (V. M. I. graduate), raised artillery Company, 14th Virginia, in lower end of county; Littlebury Randolph Thompson, bugler 14th Virginia; sons of John C. and Clara S. Thompson.

Tyree, Cuthbert Terrell, son of Joseph Tyree; in Naval service.

Vaughan, Cleveland.

Vaughan, Sidney.

Webb, David Barr, Musketeers; Lewis Snow Webb, R. O. T. C., Virginia University; sons of J. L. and Valeria Snow-Webb.

West, Warren W.

Wilkinson, Dr. Robt. J., son of B. J. Wilkinson; lieutenant; now surgeon for C. & O. Railway. In charge of hospital, Huntington, W. Va.

Twenty-two in the above list were volunteers.

Officers, Lynchburg Home Guards, 1918

Captain, L. B. LeGrand; 1st Lieutenant, L. King; 2nd Lieutenant, J. A. Jones; with the membership of 142 privates.

Officers, Lynchburg State Guards

Captain, Rozell R. Yoder; 1st Lieutenant, John T. Mason; 2nd Lieutenant, James O. Jordan; with the membership of 110 privates.

The classes of 1920-'21-'22 of Lynchburg High School presented a tablet Memorial to the students of the school who were killed while serving in France during the World War, upon which is inscribed their names, and the tablet placed upon the walls of the E. C. Glass High School building in 1922:

Robert Lewis Butler	Allan Lyle Campbell
W. Offutt Cobbs	Jacob Lorenzo Christ
Gabriel B. J. DuVal	Lewis C. Fernald
Saunders Fleming	George Preston Glenn
John Kirkpatrick	Charles John Locker
John J. Murphy	William O. Newbauer
Norman J. Traylor	Clarence Widdifield
Howard Thornton Barger	

A soldier Memorial, designed by Charles Keck of New York and erected in 1926 on November 11th, Armistice Day, at the foot of Monument Terrace, represents a soldier in the trenches with figure in bronze against a background of Indiana limestone, and names of all the dead Lynchburg soldiers engraved upon the stone. The address at the unveiling of the war memorial was delivered by Brig.-General Samuel D. Rockenback, a Lynchburger of the regular army, who at that time was presented with an overseas cross by the United Daughters of the Confederacy, as a lineal descendant of Capt. J. F. Rockenback and grandson of Robert Nicholson, two Confederate soldiers. The list of names includes those of the student soldiers given above also.

Felix Longsdale Banton	Walter J. Mitchell
William Harrison Brooks	Stearns Moon
Harry L. Bryant	Richard W. Pendleton
Herbert A. Butts	Ambrose B. Shenk
Guy C. Finch	Carrington Stevens
Fred George Geophart	W. Austin Thompson
W. W. Hillsman	John H. Wills
Pannill Rucker Jones (col.)	Lennie Joseph Bacon
William G. Ketterer	Charles Minor Blackford
Charles Edward Kruger	Joseph Benjamin Brown
Robert A. Mays	J. Beverly Burks

War Memorial at Lynchburg

Thomas Engene Falwell
Robert Henry Franklin (col.)
John Randolph Harmon
Robert Crusoe Johnson
Robert Lee Kesler
Maynard Kuck
Robert L. Mawyer
Alexander Mier

Marvin A. Moon
Reuben L. Paskiel
George C. Printup, Jr.
Robert Bruce Staples
Charles E. Stone
Harry S. Walker
Abner Odell Witt

*A Roll of Campbell's Soldier Dead in the World War—
White*

Arthur, Private Samuel M., Evington; died of disease, Sept. 14, 1918; buried at Dijon, France.

Brooks, Private William H., Lynchburg; killed in action, Nov. 11, 1918.

Cardwell, Private William A., Rustburg; killed in action, Sept. 28, 1918.

Carey, Private Lacy T., Brookneal; killed in action, Sept. 26, 1918.

Cumbie, Private Volney E., Rustburg: died of disease, Sept. 28, 1918.

Covington, Private John, Gladys; died of disease, October 8, 1918.

Edmonds, Private Chesley, Long Island; died of disease, Nov. 11, 1918.

Falwell, Private Thomas F., Lynchburg; died of disease, Oct. 13, 1918.

Fernald, Sergeant Lewis C., Campbell county; died of disease, Dec. 28, 1918.

Finch, Private Guy V., Rustburg; died of disease, October, October 14, 1918.

*Foster, Corporal Henry L., Brookneal; killed in action, Sept. 28, 1918.

Klein, Private Jacob H., Gladys; died of disease, April 6, 1918.

---

*Corporal Henry L. Foster was interred at Arlington Cemetery, Washington, D. C.

Lash, Private George, Brookneal; died of disease, March 21, 1918.

McDowell, Wagoner Guy, Brookneal; died of disease, March 7, 1919.

Mier, Private Alexander, Evington; killed in action, November 7, 1918.

Moon, Corporal Marvin A., Gladys; killed in action, October 4, 1918.

Perrow, Corporal Robert L., Jr., Rustburg; killed in action, October 15, 1918.

Pugh, Corporal Horace C., Concord; killed in action, October 12, 1918.

Short, Private Flournoy, Alta Vista; kiled in action, October 12, 1918.

Stone, Private Frank H., Rustburg; died of disease, October 16, 1918.

Colored Soldier Dead

Barbie, Private Lafayette, Concord; died of disease, October 16, 1918.

Bowman, Private Samuel A., Rustburg; died of disease, October 22, 1918.

Franklin, Private Robert H., Lynchburg; died of disease, Sept. 17, 1918.

Helm, Private Flem., Evington; died of disease, October 6, 1918.

Jones, Private Pannell R., Lynchburg; died of disease, October 20, 1918.

§Dews, Thomas, Evington; Co. D, 702nd Engineers; killed.

§Gibson, William, Campbell county; Co. C, 511th Engineers; killed.

§Harvey, Robert, Campbell county   .; killed.

The above data is taken from the 1920 report of the Adjutant-General of Virginia, with the exception of the three (§) names, of colored soldiers, given by their relatives.

Parker, Private William, Rustburg; died of disease, October 2, 1918.

Smith, Private Charles, Lynchburg; died of disease, October 7, 1918.

Meggison, Private Charles S., Concord; died of disease, March 19, 1918.

United States Marines—White

Brown, Private Joseph B., Lynchburg; killed in action, June 25, 1918.

United States Navy

Gough, Ernest M., F., 3C, Gladys; December 9, 1917.

Staples, Robert B., E., 1C, U. S. N. R. F., Concord; June 30, 1918.

Stone, Charles E., H. A. 2C., U. S. N. R. F., Lynchburg; Oct., 1918.

(Adjutant-General's 1920 Report).

Names Reported by Relatives and Friends

Dowdy, George W., Campbell county, S. N. R. F. U. S. S., Montana.

Price, Carrington, formerly of Campbell, enlisted in West Virginia; buried at Brookneal.

Snell, J. Bezer, Brookneal, entered service from Illinois; buried at Arlington.

Campbell county furnished 3,700 soldiers, 375 commissioned and 900 non-commissioned officers in the World War; 60 Y. M. C. A. workers, 200 for canteen service with the American Expeditionary Forces in France, participating in the battles of the Meuse and Argonne Forest. In every drive for funds in the prosecution of war measures, the county over-subscribed its quota. The complete list of casualties which occurred among its soldiers has not been obtained, yet at this time there is active movement on foot to secure names and erect a Memorial at the Court House.

Two brothers, Orlie L. Ore, and Thomas Ore, sons of J. P. Ore, of Burton's Creek, and brothers-in-law of Alex. Mier, (listed above), son of William Mier of Evington, were killed.

John H. Johnson, of Forest Depot; Co. G, 318th Infantry; killed in action.

Wounded or Gassed in Service

Almond ———, Campbell county; wounded in action.

Berkley, Thomas G., Campbell county, near Brookneal; wounded in action.

Berkley, Robert; wounded in action.

Bomar, Robert, Gladys, wounded in action.

Cunningham, Wilkes, Brookneal; gassed.

Farmer, William A., Brookneal; wounded in action.

Guthrie, Simmie A., Brookneal; gassed.

Harris, ———, Long Island; wounded in action.

Henderson, W. C., Brookneal; gassed.

Hall, J. T., Gladys; wounded in action.

Lash, Louis, Brookneal; wounded by accident.

McDaniel, Claude, Campbell county; gassed.

Suddith, Roger, Gladys; gassed.

Vassar, Evan S., Gladys; wounded in action.

Wheeler, George A., Gladys; wounded in action.

Williams, ———, shell shot in action.

Yates, John R., Brookneal; wounded in action.

Yates, H. I., Naruna; gassed.

Lynchburg Soldiers Decorated For War Service in the World War, 1918

Lieutenant Edgar A. Jennings, Co. M, 125th Infantry, Congressional Medal of Honor.

Brigadier-General Samuel D. Rockenback, D. S. M., Croix de Guerre, medal of the Legion of Honor, and medal of the English Order of the Bath.

Brigadier-General Meriwether Lewis Walker, D. S. M.

Sergeant Linwood C. Friedhoff, Marines, Croix de Guerre.

Corporal Henry D. Glass, Co. L, 116th Infantry, D. S. C.

First Class Private William Edward Hughes, Co. L, 116th Infantry, D. S. C.

Corporal Dewey B. Lawhorne, Co. G, 120th Infantry, D. S. C.

Sergeant S. Aston Loyd, Co. L, 116th Infantry, D. S. C., and Croix de Guerre.

Major Bernard H. Kyle, 12th Field Artillery, Croix de Guerre.

Captain A. D. Barksdale, Co. M, 116th Infantry, D. S. C., and Croix de Guerre.

Sergeant George Frederick Barksdale, American Ambulance Corps, Virginia Unit, Croix de Guerre.

Lieutenant J. Beverley Burks, Co. G, 114th Infantry, D. S. C., posthumous.

Lieutenant-Colonel John J. Burleigh, 32nd Division, Croix de Guerre.

Major Daniel Warrick Calhoun, Croix de Guerre.

Colonel C. Clark Collins, Hospital Unit 12, D. S. M. and the Companion Order of St. Michael and St. George (British).

Captain Joseph Purnell Cromwell, 11th Infantry, D. S. C.

Sergeant Gilmore G. Tomlin, Co. G, 6th Infantry, D. S. C.

First Class Radio Electrician, Walter Meade Williams, S. S. City of Wilmington, Navy Cross.

Lieutenant Robert Lewis Butler, Co. D, 9th Machine Gun Battery, D. S. C., posthumous.

William White Dillard, son of Dr. John W. Dillard, marine honor medal; supply sergeant in 1917, detailed as gas and dynamite guard at Gievres, France, in 1918, while serving with the Marine Corps.

Colonel Jefferson Randolph Kean (son of R. G. H. Kean, prominent attorney of Lynchburg), who served as a brigadier-general during the World War, entered the army as an assistant surgeon, was awarded a Distinguished Service medal "for exceptionally meretorious and distinguished services as chief of the Department of Military Relief, American Red Cross, a position of great responsibility. By his foresight, marked efficiency and energy, he organized the base hospital which cared for many of our wounded and administered the U. S. Ambulance Service for duty with the French army, greatly assisting our ally. He rendered services of conspicuous worth to the United States."

Other Army and Navy Officers From Lynchburg

Colonel William Owens, Washington, D. C. (deceased).

Colonel Meriwether Lewis Walker, Corps of Engineers, Governor of Panama Canal Zone, Balboa Heights, Panama Zone.

Colonel Thomas T. Kirkpatrick, U. S. Army (Retired), Jonestown, R. I.

Colonel Claude H. Miller, U. S. Infantry, Tank School, Fort Meade, Md.

——— Guy Baker, U. S. Navy.

Lynchburg Post, No. 16, American Legion

Organized in September, 1919. No titles used in the posts of American Legion. Commander, A. D. Barksdale; Adjutant, John T. Owen; 1st officers.

Present Officers:

Commander, A. E. Wood; Vice-Chairman, Dr. Bernard K. Kyle; Adjutant, James H. Tays; Finance Officer, J. R. Franklin; Service Officer, S. R. Tiffany; Chaplain, Dr. T. N. Browne; Medical Officer, Arthur L. Wilson; War Risk Officer, Harry Baumgardner; Sergeant-at-Arms, J. A. Bullock; Executive Committee of the above officers and Fred M. Davis, James E. Canada, A. B. Carter, Dr. J. M. Robeson, and Carter Glass, Jr.

Brookneal Post, No. 153, of the American Legion was organized on May 21st, 1923, with the following officers:

Commander, W. H. Ginther; Vice-Commander, W. J. Lewis; Adjutant, A. T. Canada; Sergeant-at-Arms, W. A. Baker; Chaplain, Hy. T. Younger; with fifteen charter members. W. H. Ginther served as commander two successive years.

The organization has a present membership of 35. The present officers are: Commander, Paul M. Shorter; Vice-Commander, Lacy T. Elder; Adjutant, A. T. Canada; Sergeant-at-Arms, W. C. Henderson; Chaplain, Wm. M. Mason; Executive Committee, H. E. Bates, W. J. Lewis, L. H. Foster; Finance Officer and Historian, W. H. Ginther. The largest percentage of the membership is in Brookneal and Campbell county, but a few residing in Charlotte and Halifax counties. This is the only organization of any World War Veterans in Campbell outside of Lynchburg.

Population and Present Officials

Chapter XIV

Official Enumeration

HE kinds of men forming the population of the nation taken during the century of growth from 1785 till 1900—as enumerated by U. S. Census—were: Beeman, Councilman, Countryman, Iceman, Ploughman, Sickman, Shortman, Smallman, Toughman, Tidyman, Weatherman, Weedingman, Peacemaker, Houselighter, Woolweaver, Landmiser, Pioneer, Pilgrim, Pagan, Pettyfool, Passenger, Grooms, Biters, Fakes, Equals, Drinker, Dancer, Kicker, Cusser, Spitter, Booby, Dunce, Gump, Boor, Crank, Crook, Rascal, Swindler, Knave, Outlaw, Madsavage, Coward, Hero, Double, Goodfellow.

Population in Campbell as taken by Robert Hunter, a citizen, in 1790: county's white population numbered 7,685; slaves, 2,488. That year in the area covered by Campbell and part of Appomattox (then included) of the negro population, 251 were free, 2,488 were slaves.

Sexes in the same area of white population in 1790 were 4,946 males, 2,363 females. Sexes in the same area of white population in 1900 were 25,871 males, 13,106 females. Campbell county population (not including Lynchburg) in 1900, was 23,043. Same area in 1910 was 22,256, as per U. S. census returns. Population in Lynchburg in 1800 were 500 males and females, inclusive. In 1805 Lynchburg was incorporated as a town. Its population in 1870 was 12,020. Its population in 1879-80 was 22,000. In 1899, with 182 manufactories, there were 4,000 operatives. In 1926, after incorporating 8,000 of the county population by annexation of its territory, the city population was increased to 38,473.

In 1816 Lynchburgers petitioned for passage of an act allowing them to send delegates to the General Assembly from the town. Among the early delegates were: William Rives in 1826; John W. Wills in 1836; Thomas Fox in 1839; Richard H. Toler in 1840; John W. Wills, 1850; John M. Speed, 1852; William Daniel, Jr.; Robert J. Davis.

Alexander McDonald, who was State Senator in 1889, later received appointment of minister to Persia.

County Officers in 1926

U. S. Senator, Hon. Carter Glass, Montview, Campbell county.

State Senator, Hon. A. D. Barksdale, Lynchburg.

House of Delegates, Hon. E. A. Hicks, Evington.

Circuit Court Judge, Don P. Halsey, Lynchburg.

County Clerk, C. W. Woodson, Rustburg.

Trial Justice, M. H. Hester, Rustburg.

Commonwealth's Attorney, Wm. M. Murrell.

Sheriff, R. L. Perrow, Rustburg Road.

County Treasurer, R. W. Callaham, Lynchburg.

County Coroner, Dr. J. Wyatt Davis, Lynchburg.

County Superintendent of Schools, J. J. Fray, Gladys.

County Superintendent of Almshouse, C. E. Blankenship, Rustburg.

County School Board: C. C. Scott, Brookneal; Leo A. Arthur, Alta Vista; C. F. Whately, Gladys; G. S. Thomas, Gladys; J. W. Jenks, Evington.

Board of Supervisors: G. W. Griffin, chairman; John Gills; John Rosenberger; Charles Stone; Thomas Whately.

Farm Demonstrator, Bruce Anderson, Rustburg.

Home Demonstration Agent, Mrs. C. L. Ferguson, Rustburg.

Lynchburg Officials in 1926

House of Delegates, Hon. E. Thurman Boyd, Lynchburg.

Corporation Court Judge, Frank P. Christian, Lynchburg.

Corporation Clerk, H. H. Martin, Lynchburg.

Commonwealth's Attorney, Robert D. Yancey, Lynchburg.

City Treasurer, D. L. Taylor, Lynchburg.

State Treasurer, George M. Bell, Lynchburg.

City Coroner, Dr. J. B. Nowlin, Lynchburg.
Superintendent of Schools, E. C. Glass, Lynchburg.
City Manager, R. W. B. Hart, Lynchburg.
City Council: Walker Pettyjohn, Mayor; John L. Caskie,
J. Tanner Kinnier, T. R. Turner, John Victor.
City Collector, H. Minor Davis.
City Auditor, John M. Otey.
City Lawyer, T. G. Hobbs.
Superintendent Water Department, R. F. Wagner.

On March 7th, 1927, the County Board of Supervisors,—
G. W. Griffin, chairman, and C. W. Woodson, clerk,—met
for the purpose of considering and preparing the budget of
the county. An estimate was then made of judiciary expenses,
and compensation from county funds to the supervisors, county clerk, sheriff, commonwealth's attorney, treasurers, and
commissioners, including deputies, and all expenses of administration; as per act of Assembly of 1926, requiring the net
compensation of county officers to be published at the end of
each year and filed for public inspection.

Under this Act the amount received by fee officers from all
sources is limited to a prescribed maximum and two-thirds of
any amount received in excess of this limit is returned to the
localities and one-third paid into the State Treasury.

Family Sketches

Chapter XV

We Live in Deeds

F AMILY life is a unit of community life, and in the characteristics and achievements of its inhabitants, each community provides its quota to the story of county development.

For the first decade or two, Campbell settlers remained satisfied in their occupation of land acquirement and its cultivation, but, as population grew and acreage became absorbed by newcomers, reports of discoveries brought to them, aroused the same spirit of enterprise which had induced younger sons in England to leave their homes and emigrate to America, and many settlers started forth upon new adventures even while Indian hostility made their ventures risky.

Acquirement of bounty land by military warrants, caused veterans of the late wars to move upon the land laid off for them in Kentucky, for that was yet one of Virginia's counties, under the state government; Green river section became their point of destination, then Boonsboro, later Lincoln county. Owners who did not go immediately, gave power of attorney for the locating of their grants and afterwards their heirs went out to take possession: thus we find that the county which became Kentucky state was the *daughter* of Virginia in matter of territory, and largely as to population. Campbell sent Richard Callaway, Christopher and William Irvine, Harry Innes and many others, family names of whom can be found in these pages.

Among the Quaker population, anti-slavery law became established and was strictly enforced. Many neighbors, of other sects, sympathized with and adopted this principle following Quaker example, which embraced the freeing of slaves and emigration to Ohio (part of which territory Virginia had formerly owned) and other non-slave holding states. Miami belt, Ohio, acquired many of Campbell's citizens.

The pioneer spirit—lure of new country—led to the obtainment of *head rights* in the ceded government land in Georgia, which state owes much of its early population to Virginia and North Carolina. Among these, Campbell sent Callaways, Candlers, Earlys and other names still to be found in that home of Virginia expatriates. In 1789 a land company called the Virginia Yazoo Company, composed of Patrick Henry, David Ross, William Cowan, Abraham Venable, John B. Scott, William Cock Ellis, Francis Watkins, and John Watts, was formed and was one of three companies competing for the purchase of territory in Georgia, the disposition of which became known as the *Yazoo fraud*. Virginia company paid no money and secured none of the land.

Following the movement into Georgia, came the exodus to Missouri, afterwards Texas, which seemed justified by the glowing reports of extensive prairie country and fine hunting. The county of Pike, Missouri, drew a number of Virginians, (many of them from Campbell) of the Clark, Anderson, Tyree families.

Excitement over gold discovery in the far west during 1849 induced people from Campbell, joined by their Bedford neighbors, to take their chance of success along with the lucky emigrants, and these went in groups,—as many as ten banded together,—overland to California, others following in smaller bodies; some by way of the isthmus of Darien, but many braving the tedious cross-continent pilgrimage on horseback. Not every one secured a bag of the yellow metal and many of these fortune seekers were drawn back by the tie of mother love to their native county.

Among those who succumbed to the gold fever were Dr. David Ward and Dr. Thomas Dillard, who crossed the continent on pack mules but returned by the isthmus of Darien: Thomas Brown, Charles Clement, Robert Crenshaw, Nathaniel Floyd, Joab Early (who died at Stockton, Calif., in 1853), Dr. Samuel Slaughter, Crow Harris and John R. Maben. Not all names of the roamers have been obtained, but most of those mentioned, returned in the course of years to their Campbell homes where they continued to reside.

Almost every Campbell family chronicles the departure of one or more members from its household, many of whom, through the intervention of time and space gradually lost trace of their original connection.

From the fact that first settlements were made in the eastern country it has become necessary for the east to furnish the west with the background of its past, and restore missing links, incident to removals and misplacement of family papers. Patriotic societies now aid in this restoration, by making it essential that applicants for membership furnish their ancestral lines in order to secure enrollment, thus promote genealogical research : and their requirement has been the means of recovering much valuable information.

It would be a satisfaction to know that every actor who has been instrumental in bringing into use Campbell's natural resources, or who has employed his talents in the promotion of county interests, has been given due credit for service rendered, but this cannot be claimed, because much material known by those most concerned has not been obtained and resort to less sure sources might lead to misinformation. Where continuous record in the following sketches is lacking, it is hoped that sufficient clues are furnished which can enable those in possession of omitted names or dates to make their connection. No attempt is made to join present generations with earlier ones for the reason that this volume, especially designed as a history of the county, would then become too bulky and would defeat its aim, if family extensions tended to displace the more general subject. Enough of family life is embraced to convey information as to the characteristics of the people who chose Campbell for their residence as well as of those who left it and ingrafted their lives into other communities.

The family lists include many who were inconspicuously associated with county affairs in one generation, yet became notable in another, through patriotic service or official preferment; also many of subordinate position in the local social scale, who removed to other sections and acquired prominence and renown in their adopted homes through more auspicious environment. Confusion may appear from the different modes of spelling the same name, which arose from its pronunciation or faulty writing, but enough of similarity is preserved to secure recognition in connecting any branch with its original family stem.

In this summary of community life during a century and a half of a changing population amid shifting scenes of peace and war, facts are given as found in court records, family papers or in print, never tradition unless so stated and obvious.

Adams

Robert Adams, of Welch descent, familiarly known as *old Robin,* was a son of Robert and Mourning Adams of Goochland county, and a grandson of Robert Adams who was a member of the House of Burgesses in 1623-24. Robert (3rd of the name), moved to Albemarle county and married Penelope, the daughter of Charles Lynch, Sr. In 1749 Lynch deeded two tracts of land, containing respectively 400 and 245 acres, to Adams in consideration of his marriage. In 1769 Adams sold 1100 acres in Albemarle and bought land in Bedford; in 1773 he sold 1075 additional acres of Albemarle land, moved from there and settled at *Reed Creek:* his inventory was recorded in 1785 at Campbell C. H.

Children of Robert and Penelope Adams:

—Charles Lynch, b. 1752, m. 1781 Elizabeth, dau. of Thomas Tunstall of Pittsylvania; he was a justice of the peace and member of the Committee of Safety in 1775. His son, Thomas T. Adams, m. Matilda, dau. of Henry Ward and their son, Henry Ward Adams, m. Annie P., the dau. of Dr. N. W. Floyd. Hy. Ward Adams was a colonel in the Confederate army; he died in 1899 at *Old Mansion,* a home built by his ancestor, Major John Ward, which was destroyed by fire and the family moved to *Monteflora,* a residence on an eminence a mile distant, which is now occupied by his son, H. W. Adams,

Jr., and to which is attached a fine landed estate: the old burying ground is near Old Mansion site.

—Robert (4th of the name) is sometimes confused with his father and it appears not entirely settled which one was the

Captain Charles Lynch Adams

Revolutionary captain who served as a member of Lynch's court for the trial of political suspects. It is said that this Robert met with financial losses through his responsibility for a security debt. He married Mary, dau. of Joel and Anna Lewis-Terrell and lived on his estate where Alta Vista now stands. He died in 1790 of typhoid fever contracted while on a visit to his sister, Mrs. Mildred Ward, and was buried at her home in Pittsylvania on Staunton river. Generals Wirt and Daniel Adams of the Confederate army were his descendants.

—James was a captain, 1781, in the Revolutionary army; in 1785-86 he was deputy sheriff of Campbell with John Anthony as his security. He married Mary, dau. of David Irvine of Bedford: moved first to Kentucky, then to Mississippi, and later still to Texas. A grand-daughter, Penelope Lynch, m. Governor Hébert of Louisiana. His son, William, m. Nancy, dau. of Benjamin Chinn, and died in the West Indies in 1821: whose son, Benjamin C., m. in 1840 Caroline Blanks of Mississippi, and their son, Captain Charles Lynch Adams (of the C. S. army), married Lelia, dau. of Samuel C. and Sally Ward-Tardy, thus reuniting two Campbell county families. Capt. C. L. Adams was U. S. Consul to Cadiz, Spain, from 1897-99; he returned to America and engaged, first in the importation of wines and then in tobacco business. He was killed in an elevator accident in 1917 at Lynchburg, Virginia.

—Mildred m. William, son of Major John Ward of Pittsylvania county.

—Elizabeth m. Captain James Dearing of Campbell county.

—Sarah m. Charles, Jr., son of Colonel Charles Lynch, and moved to Kentucky; their son, Charles Lynch, 4th, became governor of Mississippi from 1836-38.

—Penelope married, in 1778, John Shackleford.

—Mourning married John McGee of Bedford county.

—Margaret married, in 1781, John Rice Smith, and lived at *Otterbourne*, Campbell county, a residence which was sold in 1796 *to Staunton* John Lynch: a daughter of this marriage, Mildred Smith, married Matthew Flournoy, and from this last couple was descended the famous beauty, Sallie Ward, of Louisville, Ky. Otterbourne, situated not far from Alta Vista, remains unchanged, having a central building capped by a dormer-windowed roof and extension wings at either end.

Alexander

William Alexander came to Pennsylvania from North Ireland after the siege of Londonderry; he patented 100 acres of land in Lancaster county, Pennsylvania, in 1742, and prior to 1746 had settled in Augusta county, Virginia, in the vicinity of the present Greenville. He was a graduate of Dublin University, and established the classical school which developed into Liberty Hall Academy and later became Washington and Lee University. William Alexander was granted 200 acres of land for serving as a non-commissioned officer in Colonel William Byrd's Virginia Regiment in 1760.

Hand of the Judge

Robert Alexander, also called Robin, a son of William, settled in what was then Bedford, where he held office as deputy to clerk of court James Steptoe, from 1772 to 1782, at which latter date he received the commission of first clerk of Campbell, an office held until his death in 1820. He purchased, in 1783, 400 acres on Molley's creek, beginning at Thomas Haythe's line, along William Brown's land to John Fitzpatrick's, and a year later added 100 acres, on the branches of the same creek, purchased of Shelldrake Brown, lying along Ajonidab Read's line. In 1787 he patented 250 acres on the head branches of Beaver creek and 30 acres on both sides of the main road, southwest end of Long Mountain; in 1803 he patented 150 acres on Molley's creek.

Robert Alexander in 1774 married Ann, the daughter of William Austin (of Elk Island, who had been a captain in the British army), and the grand-daughter of William Callaway. He built a residence on his land near Pigeon Run, which he named *Rock Castle,* because of its massive stone chimneys and foundation: the date, 1819, seen at the present time on a side of the chimney must have been cut into the soft stone about the time Alexander's daughter married Dr. Robert W. Withers, and should not be taken for the date of its construction. The next year Alexander died and Withers came into possession of this home. As Alexander had served with Steptoe in the Bedford clerk's office, when Campbell was formed and its officers were being appointed, he proposed the name of James Steptoe as deputy to himself in the new court.

Rock Castle (side view), Home of Clerk Robert Alexander
Showing One Port Hole

Rock Castle is a well preserved weather-boarded house, built at a time when the country was unsettled, and Indians not infrequently appeared in the community and made attacks upon the white people. The Alexander home was evidently planned with aim of defense against assault and is the only private residence so far discovered which was thus protected. Jefferson noted that houses built in the latter part of the 18th century only lasted fifty years; but there are a number of houses, yet occupied, in the county, which are twice that age and some much older; native stone, or brick, usually was used as base, one or two were built entirely of stone, as were also some outbuildings, such as barns and stables, and this must account for their endurance. The Alexander house is peculiar in having two port hole openings in one end of the stone basement wall, the dungeon-like chamber of which can only be entered from the room above through a trap door opening without stairway. In later times, this secure place was, upon emergent occasions, used as a jail for prisoners. Rock Castle preserves the appearance of substantial construction: its cornice is plain but the roof has three dormer windows, though the center one, for some reason, has been closed. The property is now owned by the Clay family.

The clerk's office occupied by Robert Alexander was in a field outside of his home premises, just above a spring. On court days he would take all the books and records he required during the court term and in company with his deputy (Alexander Austin, half-brother of his wife was his deputy for many years), drive in his coach and four to the court house ten miles distant.

The Alexander family, through father, son and grandson, held the office of clerk nearly 100 years. Robert was county clerk for 35 years, and clerk of circuit court from 1809 to 1819: his son, John, born 1782, died 1838, held the county clerk's office 19 years and succeeded as circuit clerk from 1819 to 1838; John D., better known as "Captain Jack," served as clerk of county from 1838 to 1868 and his son, W. K. Alexander, was appointed clerk for one year. Robert Alexander was noted for his strict integrity and acquired a fine landed estate; he died of apoplexy and was buried in private ground across the road from his old home; a gray stone slab bears his name and dates of his birth and death. His children were William, born 1776, who was deputy clerk to his father, and was murdered in 1800.

—Esther married Micajah Moorman.

—Sallie married Nathaniel Manson of *Pebbleton*, Bedford county.

—John married, 1809, Sarah L. Cobbs.

—Ann married Adam Clement.

—Elizabeth married Dr. John W. Payne.

—Susan D. married, 1819, Dr. Robert W. Withers, and lived at *Rock Castle*.

William Alexander was killed while travelling homewards, when he was supposed to be carrying packages of money (which instigated the crime), but his saddle bags instead contained bundles of nails. After committing the deed the homicide rode to Alexander's home and reported that the latter had been attacked and killed by negroes. Accepting his story the family took him in and he slept that night in Alexander's bed. The dead body was found on the roadside and clinched in one hand was a piece of cloth which exactly fitted into a hole discovered in the assassin's coat, which circumstance betrayed the murderer. Trial of the case was moved to Pittsylvania court by counsel for the defense who claimed that his client could not obtain a fair trial in Campbell on account of prejudicial sympathy of Alexander's large family connection. Children of John and Sarah L. C. Alexander:

—Sarah, m. Dr. Thomas H. Nelson.

—Charlotte, m. Dr. John F. Sale of Bedford.

—Eliza, m. James M. Cobbs of Lynchburg.

—Mary, m. Dr. William Davis.

—Octavia, m. 1st, Robert Camm, m. 2nd Edwin R. Page.

—Susan, m. J. Van Horst.

—Roberta, m. R. A. Hilton.

—John D., m. Mary, dau. of Samuel Pannill of *Green Hill;* John D. Alexander commanded a company from Campbell during the war of 1861-65. His residence at Rustburg adjoined the court house grounds, but was destroyed by fire some years ago.

Esther, the sister of Robert Alexander, married Captain Austin of Bedford, his brother-in-law.

Alexander

Colonel Gerard Alexander, who lived at *The Grove*, near New London, s e r v e d in the war of 1812, and after his return had charge of New London Academy, married

Elizabeth Innes, daughter of Harry and Elizabeth Callaway-Innes. He built *The Grove* (a mile east of New London), at which place he resided. As president of the Academy, in 1830, he petitioned to Legislature for assistance in making repairs there. Alexander lived to be 80 years of age, he and his wife and son, George, were buried in old St. Stephen's churchyard near Forest. His will, executed by his friend, Dr. Harris, was recorded in 1851: gave his personal property to his wife and children, but directed his real estate to be sold and proceeds divided between his sons, Henry and George Douglass, and his daughters, Henrietta, Sally and Nancy; other children mentioned were Edward, Sigismunda Rose, Frances Cole, Lawrence Gibson (eldest son); Henrieta married Ely and Ann married Wallace.

Henry married Sallie Moorman: sons were killed in the Confederate army; dau., Elizabeth, married Pleasant Winston and lived at the Winston home near Lynch's; dau., Sally, married John Nash.

Anderson

George Anderson, a member of Augusta District Militia in 1742, though he moved to Bedford county, was in 1758 still attached to the same military company. He appears to have married twice, the second time to a widow, Mrs. Cofer. His will written in 1778 bequeathed his landed property to his son, Jacob. This son, and his two sons, William and John, were listed with the Bedford county militia, in which Jacob held office of sergeant. His daughter, Sarah Anderson, married Jeremiah Early. Jacob Anderson married Mary, daughter of Colonel William Callaway and his wife, Elizabeth Tilley. Their children were:

—William, m., 1783, his cousin, Sarah, dau. of Colonel Jeremiah and Sarah Anderson-Early. William Anderson was sheriff of Campbell in 1805; died 1806.

—Mary, m., 1806, Richmond C. Tyree, and moved to Tennessee.

—John, m., 1810, Lucy Walton, moved to Lafayette county, Missouri.

—Matilda, m., 1810, Pleasant Tyree, and moved to Tennessee.
—Elizabeth, m., 1816, Samuel Tyree, also moved from Campbell.

—James Callaway, m., 1819, Jane R., dau. of James C. and Janet Robinson-**Moorman**. James C. Anderson served in the war of 1812.

—Lucinda, m., 1811, Rev. Thomas Callaway, son of Col. Jas. and Elizabeth **Early**-Callaway.

—Docia, m., **John** Price.

—Jeremiah Early, m. Elizabeth Brooks. Jerry E. Anderson owned a large tract of land on Goose creek and Staunton river upon which he built a handsome home, *Clover Hill,* on brick foundation, with cornice of dental pattern: the interior finely finished with carved chair boarding in both stories, and stairways, front and back, lead to divided suites for male and female members of the household. Large slabs of light colored native stone are used for exterior steps. This residence rests upon a level plateau overlooking extensive bottoms and heigths across the river. Anderson sold the property in 1836 to Stephen P. Smith of Pittsylvania; a tract of 300 acres, together with 100 acres on Chell's ford adjoining Thomas Leftwich, Mrs. Sally Anderson, and William A. Lee; also 600 acres in Pittsylvania,—on the west side of Callaway's road,—lying upon Staunton river, the sale being by gross and not by acre. Clover Hill is situated near Leesville and is now owned by Walter Smith, of Lynchburg, a grandson of Stephen P. Smith, and son of John T. and Mary King Dunnington-Smith, the property having remained in the Smith family nearly one hundred years.

Jerry E. Anderson moved to Odessa, Missouri; his son, William, Jr., m. a daughter of George P. Venable.

—John, son of Jacob and Mary C. Anderson, m. Sarah, dau. of Capt. Chas. and Judith Early Callaway; children, Judith Early, m. Thomas Franklin; Martha J., m. Capt. John Franklin; Catherine, m. Morton Pannill; Sarah J., m. C. G. Terry; Jacob H., m. Sarah J. Leftwich.

—Docia, dau. of Jacob and Mary C. Anderson, m. Rev. Abner Early (youngest son of Col. Jer'h and Sarah A. Early) who heired his father's old mansion near Evington.

Anthony

Mark Anthony was a trader from Genoa, Italy, who settled in the James river colony and accumulated a fortune: his children married into influential families. A descendant (probably son), Joseph Anthony, was a 2nd lieutenant in the Revolutionary Army in 1778. This Joseph Anthony, Sr., owned land in Hanover, Louisa and Albemarle; moved on Staunton river. In 1782 was living in Henry county, at which time he sold John Clark of Campbell 550 acres on the headwaters of Beaver and Seneca creeks north side of Otter river, along Clement's line, to Lady Mary Read's corner. This property then conveyed to Clark, two years later was sold by him to Robert Alexander.

In 1787 Christopher, the eldest son and heir of Joseph Anthony (dec.) sold John Lynch 150 acres ("formerly owned by Joseph") on both sides of Fishing creek, south side of Fluvanna river, beginning at Daniel and William Candler's ("Achilles Douglass") along by Benjamin Johnson's ("now Wm. Johnson's") Christopher being anxious to complete the contract of his father.

—Joseph Anthony m. Elizabeth, dau. of Christ. and Penelope Clark, sister of Edward, Bowling and Micajah Clark. Children:—Sarah m. Thomas Cooper;

—Christopher, m., 1st, Judith Moorman; m., 2nd, Mary, dau. of Thomas Jordan;—Elizabeth, m., 1st, Wm. Candler; m., 2nd, Cornelius Dysart;—Penelope, m. James Johnson; sons, James, Joseph and Micajah, moved to Georgia;—Mark, m. Nancy Tate, and between 1787-89 went to Georgia;—Agnes, m. Wm. Blakey;—Mary, m. Josiah Carter;—William, m. Miss Carter;—Bowling, m. Nancy Stone;—Rachel, m. James Lane; —Judith, m., 1st, —— Green; m., 2nd, —— Ware.

Children of Christ. and Judith M. Anthony:—Mary, m., 1788, David Terrell;—Joseph, m., 1791, Rhoda Moorman;—Elizabeth, m., 1788, Wm. Ballard.

Children of Christ. and Mary J. Anthony:—Christopher, Jr., m., Anna W. Couch;—Samuel, m., Mary Irvine;—Hannah, m., 1st, ——— Johnson; m., 2nd, John Davis;—Sarah, m. Henry, son of Wm. Davis, Sr.;—Rachel, m. Lot Pugh;—Charlotte, m. Ephriam Morgan.

Joseph and Rhoda Anthony moved first to Henrico, then to Ohio in 1814 with Christopher, Sr., where the latter died in 1815. Samuel Parsons Anthony, son of Joseph and Rhoda Anthony, served in the war of 1812. Afterwards, at Cincinnati, he established the first tobacco factory west of the Alleghany mountains. He studied medicine and settled as a practicing physician in Muncie, Indiana.

February 18, 1769, Christopher Anthony, Sr., was appointed with Micajah Terrell to build a new meeting house at South River, a building completed that year. All of the family were Quakers then. Anthony was appointed elder, and, in 1788, minister, and was very eloquent in the pulpit.

Christopher Anthony, Jr., born 1776, m., 1803, Anna Woolson, dau. of Samuel and Anna Quigg-Couch of Philadelphia, and moved to Lynchburg in 1811. He was a prominent attorney, and a member of Virginia Legislature in 1817.

Christopher and Anna W. Anthony joined the Episcopal church: he died 1835; his wife died 1854. This branch then was no longer represented in the county by the Anthony name. Children,—Mary Anne, m. Geo. W. Cabell of *Inglewood*, Nelson county.

—Samuel, m. Charlotte, dau. of Charles and Ann Rose-Irvine (Charles a native of Ireland), and moved from Campbell.

—Margaret, m. Dr. Clifford Cabell of *Fernley*, Buckingham county.

—Sarah, m. Benjamin H. Randolph of St. Louis, Missouri.

—Caroline, m. Mayo Cabell (2nd wife), of *Union Hill*, Nelson county.

Margaret Anthony-Cabell was the authoress of "Sketches and Recollections of Lynchburg"; her daughter, Mary W. Cabell, m. John Cabell Early of Lynchburg. She was a contributor to various magazines, as her mother had been earlier.

John Anthony, probably brother of Joseph Anthony and therefore uncle of Christopher, Sr., patented several large tracts of land in Bedford county; in 1754 patented 1012 acres on both sides of Otter river, adjoining William Stone. John Anthony was a justice of the peace for Albemarle county in 1745-6. When the proclamation of 1763, allowing bounty lands to soldiers of the late wars was made, John Anthony claimed the pay of captain of a company of rangers raised by particular order of the governor. His 2nd patent was for 674 acres of land at head of Ivy and Blackwater creek in 1759; in 1780 a third patent gave him 1300 acres on the south branch of Otter creek. In 1785-6 he was security on the bond of deputy sheriff Adams, serving under Sheriff John Callaway, who became delinquent to a large amount owing to delay in public business. Adams was reduced to insolvency and Anthony then obliged to pay the amount of his indebtedness. In 1782 John and Micajah Anthony were witnesses to the sale of land from Joseph Anthony to John Clark. In 1785 John Anthony gave Harry Innes and Christopher Irvine power of attorney to settle his real and personal property in Kentucky. In 1793 at the settlement of James Dearing's estate, John Anthony assisted.

The name Mark is peculiar to the John Anthony branch, as Christopher is to the other branch. Christopher's family resided in or near Lynchburg, whereas John Anthony's descendants owned country homes near Evington, Leesville and other county settlements.

The will in 1801 of Elizabeth Anthony lists her children— John Anthony, Jr., Elizabeth Cowan, Abner Anthony, Mary Menges, Elizabeth Robertson, Lucy Jones, grandson Charles Anthony, and grandson, John A. Anthony.

In 1795 Mark Anthony married Sarah Henry Tate; 1794, Mary C. Anthony m. Arthur Goolsby; 1820, James Anthony

m. Patsy Lee; Captain Charles Anthony m. Martha Haden, and lived at Evington. His son, John Anthony, m. Emma, dau. of Col. Reid Arnold. Colonel Abner Anthony married Jane Brown; he was an agent at Lynch's Station.

John Anthony, Jr., lived in an old brick residence at the top of a hill above Anthony's creek, a branch of Goose creek. Members of the John Anthony branch of the family in the county yet bear the Anthony name.

Bailey

In 1754 William Bailey, a soldier in the Virginia militia, was killed at the battle of the Meadows. Henry Bailey served in the French and Indian war. In 1784 Savage Bailey, son and heir of John Bailey, patented 475 acres lying on the west side of Falling river. Marriages, 1788: Kesiah Bailey m. John Evans; 1789, Robert Bailey married Lucy Smith; 1794 Thomas Bailey m. Temperance Bailey; Sarah Bailey m. Adam Driskell. In 1803 Thomas Bailey married Elizabeth Timberlake. He had moved in 1801 from Goose Creek, Bedford county. In 1798 Susan Bailey married Thomas Shepherd.

Josiah Bailey moved from Dinwiddie in 1802; married Susannah Ballard in 1804; was a member of Ivy Creek Meeting the same year, and clerk of South River Meeting in 1809; moved to Miami Meeting, Ohio, with seven children in 1812.

Jonathan Bailey married, in 1808, Sarah Butler; in 1821 Abner Bailey married Charlotte Cocke. In 1817 John and Lucy Bailey sold Thomas Rudd 386 acres lying on Big Falling river, land which Bailey had previously bought of Rudd. The same year John Bailey bought of John and Nancy Rosser 215 acres on Bear Creek, lying on both sides of Lawyer's road and adjoining the lands of Richard Daniel, Micajah, John and William Hubbard, James Shannon and Lindsay Crawley: in the deed of transfer Bailey records himself as then resident in Charlotte county.

Exum and Anna Bailey moved to South River from Dinwiddie during 1817. Philip Bailey was a Revolutionary pensioner, 85 years old, in 1835. In 1771 Richard Bailey patent-

ed 203 acres on both sides of Maple creek a branch of Blackwater. In 1798 Gregory Matthews sold Thomas Bailey 65
acres along Todd's and Driskell's old line ridge path crossing
Ivy creek.

Brown

The family of Brown has been one of the most difficult in
tracing because there are apparently many disconnected families of the name. In 1755 William Brown patented 700 acres
on the south side of Otter river; in 1774 patented 287 acres
on the south side of Staunton river; in 1780 patented 705
acres both sides of Whipping creek, Little Whipping and Lick
creeks including the head waters on the east side of Seneca
and branches of Molleys creek, and 381 acres on both sides of
Cates creek and 70 acres on the south side of Otter. The
first item entered upon Campbell county will book 1, page 1,
in 1782 was the will of William Brown, late of South Carolina, giving the names of his family: wife, Patience Brown,
sons—Elijah . . . —William m. 1788 Elizabeth Dale, m.
2d in 1792 Mary Van North,—Spiers . . . —Samuel m. in
1793, Sarah Roberts—Jeremiah . . ., daughters—Merryan
(Mary Ann?),—Precious Keene. In 1802 Wm. Brown, Jr.'s
will was recorded, mentioning wife, Mary; children, Lucy
Simmons, John, William, Henry, Hubbard, Byrd, Edmond,
Mary Alford and Jenny Butler.

The first deed book records the purchase made in 1784 by
John Brown from James and Ann Martin and Joseph Eads of
196 acres on Catamount branch of the Staunton beginning on
the river at Eads' corner; at this time Brown records his
freeing a slave. The second deed book tells of the purchase by
Brown from Wm. and Martha Alford of 200 acres, known
as Alford's Mountain, near Staunton river, witnesses to the deed
being Micajah Davis, Joseph Childress and John Vest. In 1798
Brown petitioned for a ferry to be established on his land;
his brick dwelling was situated at the top of a hill on a road
leading to Leesville.

In 1783 Shelldrake, Sr., and wife Sarah Brown, Robert and Temperance Brown sold Robt. Alexander 400 acres on Molley's creek beginning at Thomas Haythe's by Wm. Brown's corner along to John Fitzpatrick's; about the same time Robt. and Ann Alexander sold Robt. Brown 120 acres on both sides of Molley's creek at the corner of John Fitzpatrick's line, land lying along the creek and formerly belonging to Shelldrake Brown. In 1785 Shelldrake, Sr., sold Robert Alexander 100 acres on Molley's creek branches along Ajonidab Read's line, and Robert Brown sold Alexander 400 acres in the same locality.

In 1792 Peyton Brown patented 225 acres on both sides of the branches of the south fork of Falling river, including the head of the branch. In 1799 Henry Brown, Jr., patented 784 acres on the north branch of the Staunton, and in 1801 patented 1200 acres near Johnson's mountain.

In 1781 Daniel Brown married Polly, the daughter of Col. James and Sarah Tate-Callaway, and in 1805 allotment was made of Daniel Brown's estate. It seems probable that Daniel was the son of Henry, who was the son of William Brown, 2nd of the name (will recorded 1802).

The last family of Brown became connected by marriage with the Hancock family. Simon or Simeon Hancock was an English emigrant. In 1749 Robert Hancock patented 1400 acres on Straitstone creek. In 1818 John Hancock patented 98 acres on a branch east side of Falling, called Matthews. In 1828 Martin Hancock patented 700 acres in Campbell and Charlotte, principally in Campbell.

Stephen Hancock was a soldier in 1760 in Colonel Byrd's regiment during the Cherokee Expedition. In 1768 he patented 150 acres on Otter river and Sycamore creek. In 1780 Stephen was registered in Kentucky county. Mary, sister of Ammon Hancock married —— Brown. Samuel Hancock, son of Simon, married Mrs. Annie Ammon-Moon, whose daughter, Tolly married Daniel Brown, Jr., parents of James Leftwich Brown, who married Mary V., daughter of Bishop Early.

James Brown, near Leesville, was eccentric in his dress, observed the old fashion of arranging his hair in a cue, and wore a swallow-tailed coat with brass buttons. Thus he would go to mill with his servant behind him. He had a son, Thomas J. Brown; daughter, who married Benjamin R. Turner, and a daughter who married Colonel Reid Arnold; two daughters of the latter married Walter C. and George T. Rosser.

Bolling

Albemarle county, formed in 1745, embraced nine other counties (one of them Campbell), which later were divided from it. The first entry of land on the south side of Fluvanna river was made for Colonel John Bolling, grants covering both sides of the river. Above him was the large grant of Nicolas Davies, also on both sides of the river. This John Bolling, born in 1700, grandson of Robert Bolling, emigrant, was county-lieutenant of Chesterfield, justice of the peace and for 30 years member of the House of Burgesses. He married Elizabeth, the daughter of Dr. Archibald Blair, who was also a member of the House of Burgesses. Between 1740-51 John Bolling entered 20,000 acres of land in the present counties of Amherst, Buckingham, Appomattox and Campbell for himself. and his sons. Bolling's creek in Amherst, south of Lynchburg was named for him. In 1743 he entered for Archibald, his son, 600 acres on Opossum creek, of Fluvanna river. In 1790 Robert and Mary Bolling of Chesterfield sold to Robertson Cheatham of Campbell county, 195 acres on Bolling's road, along Reedy creek, opposite the mouth of Pigeon Run, lying along the dividing line of the old patent, between Thomas and John Bolling. Three sisters, daughters of Archer and Martha Dandridge-Payne married into this Bolling family:

—Dorothea Dandridge, b. 1777, m. Edward Bolling, and had a son, Powhatan Bolling.
—Jane, m. 1st, Robert Bolling.
—Catherine, m. Archibald Bolling. Archibald Bolling had two residences, *Red Oak* and *Retreat,* on the line between

Buckingham and Campbell. He married four times; first, m. Sarah, the dau. of Col. Archibald Cary of *Ampt Hill;* a dau. of this marriage, Sarah, m. in 1792, Joseph Cabell Megginson, a member of the House of Delegates, and son of Captain William and Elizabeth Megginson, (dau. of Col. Joseph Cabell, of *Winton,* Amherst county, near the present town of Clifford). Archibald Bolling m., 2nd, Jane Randolph, cousin of John of Roanoke, a dau., Ann, of this marriage m. 1st, Samuel Shepherd Duval; m., 2nd (1804) Joseph, Jr., son of Col. Jos. Cabell, who moved from *Winton* to *Repton,* in Buckingham county, where he died in 1811 and his widow died 1834 at *The Retreat* while on a visit there. Archibald Bolling m. Catherine, the youngest daughter of Archer Payne. Edward Bolling taught school in Campbell in 1833. Archibald Bolling d. in 1829 leaving to his 4th wife land divided by the Richmond road until it intersected with Joel McKinney's line. Lands adjoining David Robertson, Robert Franklin, ·McKinney, Wm. Ferbush and Henry Christian, he divided between his daughters, Sarah Megginson and Ann E. Cabell and grand-daughters, Pocahontas and Virginia (children of his deceased daughter, Elizabeth M. Robertson), and his sons John R. and Blair Bolling. The last named son, toegther with Wm. S. Diuguid .and Wm. Ferbush, were appointed executors.

Children of Archibald Bolling were:—Dr. Archibald Bolling, m. Ann E. Wigginton and lived on Cheese creek between Clay's Crossing and Boonsboro;—Edward, m. Ann Crallé;—Alexander, m. Susan Gray;—Pocahontas, m. 1st—White, 2nd Hill s. p.

Children of Dr. Archibald and Ann E. W. Bolling:—Wm. Holcombe, m. Sallie White;—Harriet, m. —— Waddell of Mississippi and moved there;—Mary Jefferson, m. a German, Tuesler, a leading medical missionary to Japan.

Children of Judge Wm. H. Bolling:—Rolf E.;—Ann., m. Matthew H. Maury, of Anniston, Ala.;—Gertrude, m. Alexander E. Galt;—Bertha;—John Randolph;—Julian B.;—Richard Wilmer;—Dr. Wm. E.;—Edith, m., 1st, Norman Galt of Washington; m., 2nd, President Woodrow Wilson.

The family of Judge W. H. Bolling moved to Wytheville. Graves with stone markers remain in the cemetery of the old Wiggington-Bolling home in Bedford county.

Bullock

In 1763 James Bullock was an ensign in Captain William Philips' company of volunteers, serving until the company was discharged; at the time he was recorded from Hanover county.

In 1780 James and Josias Bullock were both captains in the Revolutionary army. 1782 Josias and Mary Bullock sold David Herndon of Caroline county 200 acres of land lying upon Lick creek, lines of which were made by Richard Stith, beginning at Brown's road on Little Whipping creek; also sold Achilles Moorman 236 acres on Lick creek between Brown and Bullock property, and in 1783 sold James Johnson 300 acres on the branches of Molleys' creek. 1784 Josias Bullock purchased of John and Elizabeth Traylor 192 acres on the branches of Molley's creek, beginning at the head of Raccoon creek along the old lines of Ormsby North. He acquired the same year 46 acres on a branch of Lick creek, 235 acres on Seneca creek, and in 1786, 335 acres on the Dutchman's branch. A Bullock home stood on the road leading to Brookneal near a rock-walled spring. In 1790 Josias and Mary Bullock sold Anthony Haden 235 acres on Seneca creek. In 1789 Josias Bullock was deputy sheriff to John Hunter and as that officer received notes for hogsheads of tobacco inspected at Manchester and signed by Richard Stith. The same year, Hannah,—widow and administrator of James Bullock, (who died in 1784, leaving five small children to be supported, and a property of ten slaves, five only of whom were workers)—appealed to the Assembly, that as one of those slaves had been convicted of felony, and executed, his valuation be laid out in the hands of trustees for the purchase of a slave, replacing the loss of the deceased Isham, for the benefit of James Bullock's children.

In 1789 Patty Bullock married Bennett Clark, son of Robert and Susan-Henderson Clark: Hon. John B. Clark, of Missouri, was a son of this marriage. Two daughters of Robert Clark,

Mary and Hannah, also married into the Bullock family. Robert Clark had sold his lands in Albemarle county and moved to Campbell in 1765; after 1779 he emigrated to Kentucky.

In 1819 James Bullock, Jr., married Isabella, a daughter of Dr. Humphries, and moved to Lynchburg. In 1823, as trustee for Christopher Clark, Jr., he sold *Sandusky,* near the town, to William Radford, Isaac Otey, Edward Watts and Thomas Moore. Two brothers, James and John Bullock, whose mother was a Miss Henderson, had come to Lynchburg together from Albemarle. John married Lucy, daughter of Wm. Norvell; his eldest dau., Martha, m. John Smith, and died young; William Galt, m. Mary E. Washington, whose only child, Captain John Washington Bullock of the 5th Va. Cav., C. S. army, was killed at Dumfries, and was buried with his family at St. Stephen's church, Bedford county; Mary Elizabeth, m. (2nd wife), Dr. Joseph Virginius Hobson, a practicing physician in Lynchburg from 1840-50. John Bullock was a member of the firm of Galt & Bullock, merchants. He was a Mexican War veteran, held title of Colonel, died at *Clay Hill,* Bedford. Daughters of Dr. Jos. V. and Mary E. Hobson were,—Martha Hobson, m. Dr. E. A. Craighill, who had been a surgeon, raised to the rank of Major, Co. "G" 2nd Va. Inf. of the Stonewall Brigade, C. S. A. Norvell Hobson m. Captain John Holmes Smith, son of John Smith and Susan Leftwich (niece and ward of John Smith who married Martha Bullock): Captain Smith was an original member in 1859 of the Lynchburg Home Guard, which was assigned as Co. "G" to the 11th Va. Inf., and served with that company through the battle at Sailor's creek April 6th, 1865. Commencing as a corporal, he was promoted to captain and as senior captain often commanded the 11th Va. Inf.; and as regimental commander, led this regiment of Kemper's Brigade in the charge at Gettysburg. Captain Smith was severely wounded at the battle of Seven Pines, May, 1862, and again at Gettysburg, July 3, 1863.

James Bullock m. Elizabeth Slaughter and moved South: a dau. married Judge Farrar of New Orleans. Susannah Bullock married Edmund Johns.

Burton-Harrison

Jesse Burton was a justice of the peace for Campbell in 1790. His will recorded in 1795 lent his wife a tract of 300 acres known as Turpin's Lott, which was to descend to his son, John Hudson Burton, at her death. To his son, Alexander, he devised a 300-acre tract which he had purchased from Thomas Jefferson and was known as Ballou's Lott. To son John Hudson, also, 300 acres bought of Thomas Jefferson and known as Jefferson's Lott. The 500 acre lot bought of Joseph Anthony and Thomas Butler was to be sold and money arising from sale to be equally divided between sons, William, Robert and Jesse, Jr.—To dau. Patsy Irvine, he gave 20 shillings; dau. Nancy, slaves and furniture; dau. Sally (m. Samuel J. Harrison of Lynchburg), slaves and furniture. George Cabell, William Irvine and Walter Moseley were witnesses to the will. Burton's lands were situated on Burton's creek, from which circumstance the creek's name was changed from Rock Castle to Burton's, which it has retained. In his will he mentions his brother, Philip Burton. In 1786 when Lynch started the town of Lynchburg on 45 acres of his land, he divided it into half-acre lots, and appointed ten trustees of whom Jesse Burton was one.

His son-in-law, Samuel Jordan Harrison, was an alderman of the town in 1805, and was appointed one of the commissioners to contract for a jail for prisoners and debtors. In 1811 Thomas Jefferson sold Harrison 474 acres on Ivy creek (a tract of land which had been conveyed to Richard Tullos in 1771), and also 100 acres granted Jefferson by patent in 1797. Harrison then moved from Bedford to his Campbell land. Two of his daughters married into the Norvell family, one was the wife of William and the other of Lorenzo Norvell. His son, Jesse Burton Harrison, was an active citizen of Lynchburg. In 1818 he built the *Franklin* hotel, a leading hostelry, the name afterwards changed to the *Norvell House;* still later taken down and replaced by the Guggenheimer Department store. In 1865, when the Lynchburg National Bank was organized, Lorenzo

Norvell was made cashier of it; his daughter, Mary, married John M. Miller, who was cashier of the First National Bank, the position later held by his son, E. P. Miller. His daughter, Lucy Norvell, married Frank T. Lee, of *Westover,* a country place, later divided and incorporated within Lynchburg limits, now covered with residences. Mary Miller, grand-daughter of Lorenzo Norvell married Daniel A. Payne, the president of Lynchburg Trust and Savings Bank.

Callaway, Also Spelt Kellway, Kelleway and Kelloway

The name of the Callaway emigrant seems not to be indisputably settled and is variously given as Joseph, Francis and William, sometimes with the prefix "Sir." In his "Life of Boone," Lyman C. Draper includes a biographical sketch of Colonel Richard Callaway, in which he states that Joseph, the grandfather of Richard, emigrated from England to Virginia, that Richard's father (Joseph, Jr.,) settled in Caroline county, had seven sons and two daughters, Richard being 6th son; that the father, mother and a brother died of fever in a short period while Richard was still a youth, yet the remaining family continued several years to live in the old homestead, then sold out, and about 1740 settled in Brunswick county (the portion which ultimately became Bedford), locating on Big Otter river at the eastern base of the Peaks of Otter. When the war broke out in 1754 the country had become considerably populated and the people collected in forts which Washington occusionally visited. Three of the Callaway brothers held the commission of captain, Thomas at Hickey's Fort, William at Pig River Fort, and Richard at Blackwater Fort. The frontiers were constantly alarmed, marauding parties frequently pursued, and sometimes overtaken and punished. For services in these engagements Richard and William were promoted to rank of Bedford Militia colonels. This account given by Draper is accepted by members of the Callaway family.

The family record, in an old Callaway Bible, gives 2 sisters, Elizabeth and Ann, and 5 brothers;—Thomas, b.

1712, moved from Spotsylvania to Halifax, was appointed in March 1738 constable in the upper precincts of James river mountains; in 1741 an attachment was made on his estate; received pay in September, 1758, for service in the Augusta Militia, as ensign, afterwards as captain of a Halifax company.—William, b. 1714, m. 1st 1735, Elizabeth Tilley, by whom he had 5 children;

James, born 1736, married 3 times, resided in Bedford, died in 1809.

John, b. 1738, m. 1st, Tabitha, dau. of Henry and Sarah Tate; m. 2nd, Agatha, dau. of John Ward.

William, Jr., b. 1740, m. Anne Bowker Smith, resided in Bedford.

Elizabeth, b. 1743, m. Captain Francis Thorp of Campbell.

Mary, b. 1746, m. Jacob Anderson of Campbell.

Of the children of Wm. and Elizabeth Crawford-Callaway (2nd wife), two were daughters:

Charles, the eldest child married in 1768 Mrs. Judith Pate née Early (widow of John Pate), lived in Campbell; he was a captain in the Revolutionary army.

Colonel William Callaway acquired a large quantity of land; he was the first burgess from Bedford, holding the office during the sessions from 1754 to 1765, was also first county-lieutenant of Bedford, with title of colonel; this officer was usually a large landed proprietor, who governed the county, the responsibility of faithful execution of the laws resting upon him; he could call out the militia when demanded and account to the governor and council for his conduct; the militia officers were subject to his orders and he could organize courts-martial. Colonel Callaway gave 100 acres at the county-seat for the establishment of a town there; he and his sons were very active in county affairs; his son William, also bore the title of colonel and records of them, in consequence, may be easily confused.

—Francis, born 1716, moved to Wilkes county, Georgia, and had many descendants there.

—James was a planter in Spotsylvania county, Virginia.

—Richard, b. 1719, patented lands in Brunswick and Lunenburg during 1747-'54; was sergeant, lieutenant and major of
forces active in the French and Indian wars; married Frances,
the daughter of George Walton, who owned land in Bedford;

Capt. Charles Callaway

in 1761, Richard Callaway was appointed one of the trustees
of New London, he patented lands in Bedford during the
period 1762-70; visited North Carolina, with a view to locating there; visited Kentucky several times before settling
there in 1775 when he went with Boone and his road markers
and assisted in the founding of Boonesboro; was a member of

the Transylvania convention which met at that settlement; returned to Virginia and in September, 1775, moved to Boonesboro with his own and other families. In July, 1776, when his two daughters and Jemima Boone were captured by Indians, he led a company which pursued the marauders, rescued the prisoners and the next year aided in the defence of Boonesboro when it was attacked by Indian savages; was elected burgess to the Virginia Assembly from Kentucky county at the first election held, 1777, in Kentucky, was a justice of the peace and colonel of the county, was appointed on the commission for opening a road over Cumberland Mountain to Kentucky in 1779; placed in charge of the first ferry at Boonesboro; a county in the western part of the state was named for him.

On March 8th, 1780, while he and several others were engaged about one mile above the settlement in constructing his ferry boat, they were fired upon by a party of Shawanese Indians and Callaway was killed and scalped; two days later his body was recovered and buried at a spot just back of the fort. Colonel Callaway left a widow (his second wife), and children of both marriages, descendants of whom are in Kentucky, Tennessee, Alabama and Mississippi. Hon. Richard French, for several years a judge in Kentucky, and one time member of Congress, was a grandson.

—Callaway marriages, among early records (Campbell-Bedford):

1758 John Callaway m. Tabitha Tate.
1768 Charles Callaway m. Mrs. Judith E. Pate.
1774 Cona Callaway m. Bourn Price.
1774 Zachariah Callaway m. Susanna Miller.
1775 Elizabeth Callaway m. Harry Innes.
1777 Colonel James Callaway m. Elizabeth Early.
1778 Dudley Callaway m. Patty Trent.
1781 Fances Callaway m. James Steptoe.
1781 Mary Callaway m. Daniel Brown.
     Mary Callaway m. Jacob Anderson.
1784 James Callaway m. Susanna White.
1785 Chester Callaway m. Christiana Galloway.

1787 Elizabeth (ward of Wm. Callaway) m. John Patrick.
1789 Mrs. Susanna W. Callaway m. James Hilton.
1792 Amelia Callaway m. George Dooley.
1793 Sally Callaway m. Daniel Neal.
1793 Joel Callaway m. Lucy Ashton.
　　　Sarah Callaway m. John Anderson.
　　　James Callaway m. Ellen Lewis.
　　　Charles Callaway m. Eliza Green.
　　　Judith Callaway m. William Shands.
1819 John C. Callaway m. Anna Dodson.
　　　Francis Callaway m. Eliza Graham.
　　　Henry Callaway m. Miss Lewis.
　　　William Callaway m. Nannie Crump.
　　　John Callaway m. 1st, Mary Hairston, m. 2nd., America
　　　　　Hairston.
1811 Dr. George Callaway m. Mary E. Cabell.
　　　Abner E. Callaway m. Miss Lewis.
　　　Rev. Thos. Callaway m. Lucinda Anderson.
1813 Henry Callaway m. Pauline DeWitt.
1814 Elizabeth Callaway m. Samuel Read.
1828 John Callaway m. Lucinda Saunders.
1828 William Callaway m. Ann Logwood.
1827 Sarah A., dau. of John Callaway, m., John Hewitt.

At Campbell's formation James Callaway was the most prominent county officer and was transferred from the position of Bedford county-lieutenant to the same office in Campbell. Born in 1736, the son of Col. Wm. and Eliz'h Tilley-Callaway, he had made a fine record to his credit even in a family which had become conspicuous in public affairs; had served in the French and Indian wars; was a member of Bedford county patriotic committee of 1774; held by commission the successive militia offices; built the first iron works, known as "Oxford" (later, Ross'); owned and operated lead mines; in 1780 co-operating with other patriotic citizens he suppressed a conspiracy against the government. Callaway married three times; m. 1st, Sarah Tate; children,—Elizabeth m. Harry

Innes, later of Kentucky;—Frances, m. 1781, James Steptoe, clerk of Bedford, resided at *Federal Hill;*—Polly, m. Daniel Brown, of Bedford; there were other children.

Col. Jas. Callaway, m. 2nd, Elizabeth, dau. of Col. Jerry Early, with whom he was associated in mining properties; ch. of 2nd marriage,—William, a legislater from Franklin county, m. Nannie Crump from Powhatan county;—John, of Franklin, who m. twice, both Hairstons and cousins;—Dr. George, m. 1811, Mary Eliza, dau. of Col. Wm. Cabell of *Union Hill,* Nelson county, and was grandfather of Alex. Brown, Virginia historian;—Abner E., m. Miss Lewis and moved to Missouri;—Rev. Thomas, m. Lucinda, dau. of Wm. Anderson, moved to Missouri;—Catherine, m. Wm. Langhorne, moved to Botetourt, has many descendants.

Dr. Geo. Callaway first made his home in Lynchburg on the estate inherited from his father, which included lands and the mill (afterwards operated by Langhorne and given his name) with property in Madison on the opposite hill; the mill was located at the fork of land between Blackwater creek and the James. Dr. Callaway sold out in 1818 and moved to Nelson county where he built *Glenmore,* still owned by descendants of his name; his son, Paul Carrington and grandson of same name both followed in his profession as practicing physicians.

Col. James Callaway resided near New London and was treasurer for New London Academy; he married a third time but there were no children of this marriage. In 1789 he moved his citizenship back to Bedford where a new county seat had been established on 100 acres of Bramlett's land, donated by Wm. Downey and Joseph Fuqua and given the name of Liberty, first in history to bear it, but the name became changed during the boom of 1890 to Bedford City. At a court meeting held February 23, 1789, an unusual compliment was paid Callaway in the adoption of a resolution that "whereas by his singular services as magistrate in this county before its division and in Campbell county (services from which he has lately removed) merits the attention of the

public, it is the opinion of the court, therefore that he be recommended as presiding member of the county-court of Bedford."

When Andrew Jackson was member of U. S. Congress, it
was his custom to travel by private conveyance to and from
Washington, and he usually made a stop at Echols' Tavern in
New London, which many of the neighboring gentry frequent-

Old Iron Furnace

ed.   Upon the occasion of one of his visits, a young man taking offence at some remark made by Jackson, challenged him
forthwith to combat, asking him to name his choice of weapons.   Jackson humoring his antagonist selected rifles, whereupon the young fellow replied, "That is just my salad," and
left the room to secure the weapons.   Jackson then enquired
of those present, the name of the aggrieved person and upon
learning that he was a son of his friend, Col. James Callaway,
he promptly said he was ready to offer any apology a gentle-

man could require rather than fight the son of a friend; so the affair was amicably settled.

The first lawyer admitted to the bar of Campbell was Harry Innis, the son of Rev. Robert and Catherine Richards-Innis, who married Elizabeth, dau. of Col. Jas. Callaway. Innis was superintendent of the Oxford Iron mines which during the Revolution were operated for supplying the patriot army with materials of war and were owned by his father-in-law. In 1784 Harry and Elizabeth Callaway-Innis sold James Callaway—for £400.—two acres of land bounded by New London on the east, and Colonel Callaway's land on the south and southwest, by the tenement of John Hook on the west, and by Wm. Callaway's land on the north. The Innis family then moved to Kentucky where Harry Innis won distinction in his profession and acquired office as Judge of Court; in the Revolution he had served as an ensign of Bedford militia. Elizabeth, dau. of Harry and Elizabeth-Innis married Colonel Girard Alexander, afterwards a principal of New London Academy.

Candler

Daniel Candler came from Ireland to North Carolina, but settled finally in Campbell; he received a grant of 370 acres embracing Candler's Mountain, on December 1, 1779, which in consequence received his name. He had then been a resident in old Bedford for sometime, as he and his son John were witnesses to marriages at South River Meeting in 1761, and John later was disowned by the Quakers there for using spirituous liquors.

William Candler was perhaps a brother of Daniel. William married in 1746, Elizabeth, the daughter of Joseph and Elizabeth Clark-Anthony, and she was a minister for Goose Creek Meeting, while her husband was a clerk of the Meeting in 1764. William in 1768 sold 170 acres of land (adjoining Edward Bright and Colonel James Callaway), to James Johnson and moved to McDuffie county, Georgia, in 1769; he had nine children, of these,—Mary married Ignatius Few;

—Henry, married Miss Oliver, and was a major in the Revolution army;

—Mark Anthony, married 1st, Miss Young, m. 2nd, Lucy White;

—David, married Sarah Slaughter, of a Campbell family which had moved from Culpeper county.

William Candler became a colonel in the Revolutionary army. Zedekiah Candler, married Anna, the daugher of Zachariah and Betty Terrell-Moorman, and settled near Asheville, North Carolina; his son, Zachariah, married Rachel Thornhill. In 1785, John Candler, married Ann Candler. Eleanor Candler (probably the daughter of Daniel, Sr.), married Byrum Ballard, son of Wm. and Mary Moorman-Ballard, and settled in Campbell about 1763. John Candler, son of Daniel, patented 479 acres on Pocket creek, north branch of Staunton, he inherited the Candler Mountain tract; James, a son of John, married Agatha, the daughter of James Johnson of Amelia county in 1786, and moved from Waynoak, Halifax county, to South River Meeting.

John Candler, Jr., married in 1799, Dorothy Stovall;

Mary, in 1805, married, Benjamin Clement;

Daniel, Jr., in 1810, married, Martha King, in 1812, m. Mildred Candler.

The Candlers became connected by marriage with the Russell family whose property was adjoining, and members of both families still own part of the original tracts.

Among the descendants of Colonel William and Elizabeth Anthony-Candler are Governor Allen Daniel Candler, Asa G. Candler, Honorable M. A. Candler, Bishop Warren A. Candler, Judge John S. Candler of Georgia.

Chiles

The name Chiles, originally Child, became Childs and, after coming to Virginia, was commonly written Chiles. The family was of Irish extraction.

Colonel Walter Chiles was a member of the Council.

John Chiles patented 900 acres of land in Hanover county in 1661; he settled in Caroline county where he entered 300 acres of land. In 1693 he was a Messenger of the Virginia Council, was a member of the Assembly in 1723 and died that year.

He married Margaret . . . .and was the father of Henry Chiles, who bought 400 acres of land on the north side of the Pamunkey river, Hanover county, in 1702; was a justice of the peace in New Kent in 1714; bore the title of captain; was a vestryman in the Episcopal church; died in 1720.

Anna Chiles married Henry Terrell.

Henry Chiles, married Ann Harrelson, and lived in Amelia county where he held the position of commissioner of the peace. He entered large tracts of land in Pittsylvania county and its vicinity; in 1745, patented 104 acres on the south side of Staunton river; in 1746, patented land on Staunton river opposite the mouth of Otter river, four tracts on Falling river, also 250 acres and 300 acres on the north side of the Staunton. Children of Henry and Ann H. Chiles:

—Paul, married Anne . . . . . , in 1748 he patented 400 acres adjoining Henry, Susanna and Elizabeth Chiles.

—Henry, Jr., ...

—John . . . . . .

—Ann, married John Ward, in 1751 she patented 245 acres on Staunton river, including the mouth of Hills creek.

—Susanna, married Micajah Moorman;

—Elizabeth . . . . . ;

The Woodson family-book gives the following Chiles' connections: Captain Chiles, married Lucy Woodson; son, Henry Chiles, married Sarah Cheadle. John Cheadle, m. 1st, Mary Ellen Winston, m. 2nd, Lucy Coleman. Children of Henry and Sarah Cheadle-Chiles: Tarleton W., m. Nancy, dau. of John Chiles,—Fleming, m. Miss Winn,—Judith W., m. Meriwether Smith,—Nancy, m. George Coleman,—Lucy W., m. Wm. McLaughlin,—Elizabeth, m. William Wawes-Blaydes,

—Edna F., m. Dr. Daniel McFall. Children of John Chiles and Mary E. Winston,—Samuel, was a member of Virginia Legislature from Caroline,—Lucy, m. John Coleman of Winchester, Kentucky,—Nancy, m. Tarleton W. Chiles, the son of Henry and Sarah Cheadle-Chiles.

Clark

Christopher and Penelope Clark, the parents of Sarah Clark, wife of Charles Lynch, Sr., settled in Louisa county. In 1722 Christopher Clark and Nicolas Meriwether patented 927 acres of land in Hanover county. Clark cut a road at Green Spring to his land in Albemarle which became known as "Clark's Tract." He was a tobacco planter, captain of a militia company and justice of the peace in Hanover in 1727; entered 5,000 acres in Louisa and Albemarle; joined the Society of Friends late in life, died in 1754. His children were:

—Agnes, married Benjamin Johnson.
—Rachel, m. 1st, Thomas Moorman, m. 2nd, William Ballard.
—Sarah, m. 1st, Charles Lynch, Sr., m. 2nd, Major John Ward.
—Elizabeth, married Joseph Anthony, — Bowling, married Winifred . . . . . ;
—Micajah, married Judith, the daughter of Robert Adams.

Judging from the record of a sale to James Reid of Campbell county in 1784 of 42 acres of land on Blackwater creek (bounded by the lines of John Lynch and Jas. Reid), made by Bowling and Winifred Clark of Surry county, North Carolina, the two latter residents must have previously left the county.

Micajah Clark first settled in Albemarle, and followed the profession of surveying; he laid off land for Thomas Jefferson, who was his friend; moved to Campbell, where he patented 10,000 acres around Lawyers and built *Walnut Hill* about three miles distant from that settlement; there he lived, died and was buried. His children were:—Christopher, Jr., married Millicent Terrell,—Robert, b. 1738, m. Susan, dau. of John Henderson,—Judith, m. Samuel·Moorman,—William, m. Judith Cheadle,—Micajah, Jr., m. Mildred Martin and moved to Kentucky,—John, m. Mary Moore,—Penelope, m. Reuben Rowland,—Bowling, Jr., m. Eliz'h Cheadle,—James, m. Lucy Cheadle.

Robert Clark, Sr., sold out his land in Albemarle to John Grills and others in 1765 and removed to Campbell, and sometime after 1779 emigrated to Kentucky where he died. Children of Robert and Susan H. Clark:

—Christopher, married Elizabeth, dau. of John Hook.
—Robert, Jr., m. Elizabeth M., dau. of Benjamin and Frances McCulloch Shackelford.
—Patterson, m. Frances A., sister of Elizabeth McC. Shackelford.
—Governor James Clark of Kentucky.
—Bennett, m. . . . . . ; Hon. John B. Clark of Missouri was his son.
—James, m. 1st, Susan Forsythe, m. 2nd, Mrs. Mary Buckner-Thornton.
—Micajah, m. Makey Gatewood.
—Frances Henderson, m. Jeremiah Rogers.
—Elizabeth, m. 1st, ... Crawford, m. 2nd, Stephen Trigg.
—Susanna.
—Mary, m. 1st, ... Bullock, m. 2nd, William Winn.
—Hannah, married William Bullock.
—Judith, married John Campbell.

Robert Clark, Jr., born 1793, served in the war of 1812, under General Harrison; was an attorney-at-law but owing to a duel he fought, retired from the bar. He died in 1853 s. p. His brother, Patterson, although but a youth, also enlisted in the 1812 war, was taken prisoner at Dudley's defeat, remained seven years in captivity with the Indians, then escaping through Ohio, he reached his Kentucky home.

John Clark, a brother of Robert, Sr., and son of Micajah and Judith Adams-Clark, was a soldier in the Revolutionary war; in 1784 he sold 550 acres of land on the south side of Otter river road to Robert Alexander, a tract which had been conveyed to him by Joseph Anthony in 1782.

In 1802 Robert and Nancy Clark of Pittsylvania sold Bowling Clark of Campbell, 194 acres lying on Hill's creek, beginning at Charles Smith's corner on James Clark's line. Bowling Clark appointed Austin Easton of Kentucky, his attorney to convey to Robert Goggin, of Campbell, land in the northwest territory, 375 acres on Burley's creek the west branch of Brush creek, part of a tract of 500 acres surveyed for Clark as assignee on three military warrants.

Bowling and Elizabeth Clark settled upon his Hill's creek property where the old home built upon a stone foundation still stands and is now occupied by a grandson, Clark Winston, and his family. Stone is used also as base for the out buildings, and on the stone chimney of the kitchen are found initials and date of its construction. Bowling's children were: —Henry, married Judith Moorman, — Lucy, — Judith, — Charles,—Mary,—Bowling, Jr. and Elizabeth who married in 1820, Pleasant, son of George and Judith Winston.

Lamb's church, built upon the site of old Hill's Creek Meeting House, which stood one mile from Bowling Clark's house, long used for religious services, and well preserved, was accidentally destroyed by fire in 1925.

The will of Christopher Clark, Sr., of Louisa Court, recorded May 28, 1754, bequeathed:

"1st.   To son, Edward, one gun and all my wearing clothes and all things else, that he is possessed of, that was ever mine.

2nd.   To dau., Agnes Johnson, one negro woman and her increase, and whatever else, etc.

3rd.   To dau., Rachel Moorman, 400 acres of land in Hanover county near to Captain Thomas Dancey and one negro woman and her increase and whatever else, etc.

4th.   To dau., Sarah Lynch, one negro boy and all things else that she is possessed, etc.

5th.   To son, Micajah Clark, 500 acres of land in Hanover county the same whereon I now live with all rights and hereditaments thereto belonging, one negro boy, working tools, etc.

6th.   To son, Bowling Clark, 400 acres of land in Hanover county, lying on the northwest side joining the land of Thomas Carr, 2 young negroes, named Nance and Robin, one horse named Spret, one gun, one feather-bed and furniture, 2 cows and calves, my trooping arms, my great Bible and all my law books.

7th.   To dau., Elizabeth Anthony, 400 acres of land in Goochland county on Footer creek, near south forks of James river, 2 young negroes, Moll and Jenny, cows and calves, one feather-bed and furniture.

All the rest of my estate, be it what nature or quality socver, I leave to my loving wife, during her natural life, who I appoint my executor.   Further my will and desire is that my granddaughter, Penelope Lynch, at the death of her grandmother, Penelope Clark, be paid out of my estate, if there be so much remaining, £40. lawful money of Virginia; then if any left, to be equally divided between my children, but not to be appraised.   14th of August 1741."   Christopher Clark.

Witnesses: Thomas and Ann Martin and James Waring.

James Littlepage, Clerk of Court.

Will of Bowling Clark (2nd) 1817

To wife, Elizabeth Clark, plantation and dwelling house including the land purchased of Micajah Davis and a slave purchased of Micajah Clark.

To son, Henry Clark, the plantation on Otter river, Bedford county, 800 acres, known as Bains' old place, and adjoining the lands of Reuben Conrad and Thos. Logwood.

To son, Bowling, Jr., three tracts, land whereon he lived, 830 acres purchased of Micajah Davis (as mentioned in the loan to his wife)—after her death,—the tract purchased of Samuel Moorman, 480 acres, known as Butterworth's tract, and 20-acre tract adjoining which was purchased of John C. Lamb.

To each of his five daughters—Lucy, Judith, Mary, Elizabeth and Sarah,—$500.00 in cash and the following tracts, purchased of William Perkins in Bedford, 490 acres, a tract given him by his father (Micajah Clark) in Amherst county on Stovall's creek, 433 acres, and two tracts in Campbell purchased of Richard Bloxsam and John Organ containing 400 acres and a tract purchased of Robert Clark, 620 acres;—these lands to be divided between them as they came of age or married.   Executors were directed to sell and convey by special warranty, a certain tract in the state of Kentucky of 500 acres to which Clark was entitled by a decree made in the county court of Albemarle of a suit in chancery against the heirs of Bennett Henderson, deceased; also to convey with special warranty two tracts in Kentucky (with all rights) in case they had been sold by Augustine Easten who had been authorized to sell them.

His wife, Elizabeth Clark, friends, William Robinson, John B. Dabney, sons, Henry and Bowling Clark, were appointed executors, with bond of $60,000, secured through signatures of Thomas Moorman, Tucker W. Clark, Edward Lynch, Benjamin Haden, Edward B. Clark, Chiswell Dabney, Alexander Clement and John B. Dabney.

Records of Louisa county contain the will there of Francis Clark; in the bequests of his family he leaves the nominal sum of 5 shillings to Christopher Clark, which appears to indicate, either that he had already given Christopher a portion, or that he considered him sufficiently provided for.   It is presumed that John Clark of Charlotte county was a son of Francis of Louisa, and if Christopher of Louisa was also son of Francis, then the two Clarks, Christopher and John (whose children moved to Campbell), were brothers, but there is no positive proof for this claim. The significant fact that members of a family, locating in a new community generally moved in couples or triplets of brothers, and that in the case of the Clarks they preserved Christian names through generations of Johns and Christophers, would seem to establish the certainty of their common origin; the one at Hat creek, of the Presbyterian sect., and the other on James river of the Quaker Society had little opportunity for intimate association, and in time they drifted further and further apart.

Paulett Clark moved to Campbell in 1798 to teach school at Hat creek, and lived in the home of Major John Irvine, whose daughter, Mary Anne, he married the same year. This couple lived first on Turnip creek, but bought land from Samuel Morris on Entray creek and sold the Turnip creek property to John Hancock. Clark taught again in 1805; he was given the task of collecting funds for re-building Hat Creek Church, of which he was ordained an elder; held the office of justice of the peace for thirty years; he also pursued the profession of surveyor, and in 1842 was appointed sheriff with a salary of $2,700. In 1818 John Clark was sheriff of Campbell county.

After the deaths of Major Irvine and his wife, Paulett Clark bought their home place and sold the Entray creek farm to Parson James Hurt. Clark died in 1855 and was buried at Hat Creek church yard. Children:

—Mary Anne, married Nathan Mason, and moved to Charlotte county.

—Nancy, married Paulett, son of John Clark, Jr.

—Sarah, married K. Conley of Halifax county.

—Catherine, married William B. Smith.

—Orthodox Creed, m. Mrs. Elizabeth D. Payne-Nowlin; their son is Dr. Paulett Clark of Lynchburg, O. C. Clark, b. 1814, d. 1900.

—Susan E. N., married (2nd wife), John S. Payne, she was buried at Hat Creek cemetery.

—John, a successful tobacconist of Lynchburg, died unmarried.

—Christopher, m. Almyra Williams, a descendant of the Morris family, who were among the early settlers in Campbell and for whom Morris Church was named; she was also a descendant of the Armisteads and Olivers. Christ. Clark lived near Lawyers, his family moved afterwards to Lynchburg. Dr. Clark Collins of the U. S. Army, is a son of William J. Collins (a Confederate soldier) and Nannie Clark (dau. of Christopher), of Lynchburg.

—Dr. Abraham Irvine, married Zuleika, dau. of Edward B. Withers of *Ivanhoe*.

Dr. A. I. Clark purchased a home in Lynchburg, where he pursued his profession and spent the last years of his life; there are five of his children living, 3 daus., and 2 sons.

Clay

Sir John Clay is said to have been the ancestor of three Clay brothers who came to America.

Rev. Charles Clay, son of Charles and Martha Green-Clay, was ordained in 1769 by the Bishop of London, as rector of St. Anne's parish in Albemarle county; married, Editha, dau. of Henry Landon and Anne Clayton-Davies of Bedford, to which county he then moved and there died in 1819. He bequeathed to Odin Green, his second son, 1,700 acres of land in Campbell and a lot in Lynchburg. Rev. Chas. Clay was an ardent patriot during the Revolution, and a friend and neighbor of Thos. Jefferson in his Bedford home.

Gen. Odin Green Clay, b. 1800 near the present Forest depot, married in 1822 his cousin, Anne Clayton, dau. of Samuel Boyle and Elizabeth McCulloch-Davies and moved to his estate *Roseland* in Campbell. From 1827, the date when he entered the Virginia House of Delegates from Campbell, his busy, useful and honored life was constantly in the public eye; he remained a delegate for 20 years. He was active in securing the charter for the Virginia and Tennessee (now Norfolk and Western) railroad, and in the construction of this railway, he was the first president of the road continuing in that office for six years, and gave the company right-of-way through his land in consideration of their allowing a station at Clay's Crossing. At Gen. Clay's death his property became divided among his children, the dispersion of whom, finally caused the sale of the land, and the home place, embracing the mill site, is now owned by W. E. Graves of Lynch-

Roseland, Gen. Odin G. Clay's Home

burg, who makes it his summer home, the property having been purchased in former years by Graves' father. In 1835 Gen. Clay was one of the county justices; was appointed in 1854 member of the Board of Public Works and held this position several years. His wife long preceded him to the grave, after her death he spent the winter months at the Norvell House in Lynchburg, and died there in 1882. He had a family of 6 sons and one daughter. His son, Calhoun, married Bettie Lee, granddau. of Nathaniel and Sally A. Manson, and settled at *Leewood* near Lynchburg. Capt. Calhoun Clay was an officer in the Confederate army and was killed in action; four brothers served in the 2nd Va. Cav. A. N. Va.; his son, Odin, moved with his sisters to St. Paul, Minnesota.

The old Clay homestead *Leewood,* still standing, has passed out of the possession of the family, several members of which moved to the northwest section of the country; other descendants of Gen. Clay yet reside in Campbell; his son, Cyrus, married Mary Meriwether, the dau, of Addison and Elizabeth Davies-Meriwether, and left several children.

Clay's Old Mill

General Clay's, brother, Paul, lived near him, but within Bedford lines; had a large family who moved to other sections.

Mrs. Odin Clay was a great lover of trees and flowers, and beautified her lawn with fine specimens brought from other localities; fir, holly, arbor vitæ, cedar, Virginia magnolia, sugar maple, still stand and testify to her good taste and care.

The old brick house is about 100 years old and built on plan of the time, has large square rooms; an old frame house of smaller dimensions, which stands in the yard, was one which Clay first occupied, and the mill he constructed remains as he used it only changed with modern machinery, the old grinding stones, though set aside, are carefully preserved. A tradition of Indians camping in the fields seems justified by the presence of hollowed-out stones upon which it is said they pounded corn to procure meal.

Clemens

Clemens (so spelt) is to be found first in the will of Robert Douglass in 1787, where he gives Polly Clemens as the married name of one of his daughters. Samuel Clemens, married Pamela, dau. of Stephen and Rachel Moorman-Goggin in 1797, and in 1799 Gasper Clemens, m. Polly Caldwell. John Marshall, the son of Samuel and Pamela Goggin-Clemens, was born in 1798, and moved first to Florida then to Hannibal, Mo., married Jane Lampton, and became a justice of the peace; he was the father of Samuel L. Clemens (Mark Twain). In 1841, soon after settling in Hannibal, Clemens was a member of a circuit court jury which found three Illinois men guilty of stealing slaves, the case becoming historic. Slaves working at the mouth of Fabius river were to meet their rescuers, who would escort them to liberty. The negroes told their masters of the plot and actually guarded the three men who came to liberate them, thus preventing their escape.

The family of John Marshall Clemens were buried at Hannibal. Overlooking the Mississippi river and Pike and Ralls' counties, is an old ivy-covered chapel at Mount Olivet cemetery; in the chapel is an old-fashioned flat tombstone inscribed, "Passed on, John M. Clemens, born in Campbell Co. Va., Aug. 11, 1798, died in Hannibal, Mo., Mar. 14, 1847." New markers were placed over the Clemens' family graves by Col. John L. Robards, a close friend of Twain, who authorized replacing of markers for each of his family. An index (near the top of the old slab) points upward; the stone was preserved with the thought that some day Twain would go back to his old home town and see it.

At the completion of the railroad pier at Sewall's Point, there was a gathering of the patrons of the Virginian railway which was made the occasion for much oratory. When President Rogers was called on to address the assemblage he answered that it was his business to make railroads and not speeches, he said he had brought Twain to talk for him. Thus introduced the humorist confided to his audience that the railroad magnate had come to him in great perturbation for advice, saying he wished to learn of some scheme by which he would lose money, that so far every thing he touched had caused him to make money. Twain said he had recommended the construction of the Virginia tidewater railroad, which he was confident would entail loss; then when Rogers reported that he had followed the advice, completed the road and still continued to make money, Twain retorted that he had not carried the road far enough; he should extend it into North Carolina.

Doubtless the nearest point Clemens reached to the old home of his Campbell ancestors was when he passed over the Virginian railway crossing the county's southern section at this stockholder's meeting.

Clement

This name is variously recorded as Clement, Clements and Clemens, and the family is reported as having settled in this country as early as June 10, 1611. Elizabeth Clement came with her three children, Jeremiah, Elizabeth and Nicolas, together with two or three servants on the ship *George*. It is claimed that of all the families which settled at Jamestown and still exist, Clement is the 6th. · Benjamin Clement patented in 1741, 129 acres on the south side of Staunton river both sides of Sycamore creek, and in 1755 patented 529 acres in the same locality. He served in the war between England and France as a private in Capt. Wm. Temple's Company of the 1st Va. Reg., continuing in service till the war ended; his bounty warrant was sent from Charlotte county in 1780. He moved to *Clement Hill,* Pittsylvania county, a property now owned by John Hurt; married Susanna Hill. His son, Adam, married in 1766, Agnes, dau. of Benjamin and Agnes Clark-Johnson, a granddau. of Christopher Clark of Louisa. Adam

Clement commanded a company of Bedford militia in the Southern compaign of the Revolutionary war. In 1780 he patented 102 acres on the head ·branches of Beaver creek; he was sheriff of Campbell in 1784, 1792 and 1804; in 1785 was a member of a committee of 4 justices appointed to contract for building the county court house upon the plan of the old building at New London. He died in 1813; in his will he mentions his wife, Agnes, and his 11 children by name:— William (will written 1843);—Johnson (will 1854), married Miss Scales;—Benjamin (will 1816);—Charles m. Nancy Hamlin;—Adam, Jr., m. Nancy Alexander;—Alexander (will 1866);—Juriah, m. Theophilus Lacy;—George Washington, m. 1st, Stella Smith, m. 2nd, Mrs. Sally Turner Cook;—Susannah, m. Constantine Perkins;—Sallie, m. Mr. Moore;— Agnes.

Adam Clement, Jr., b. 1780, resided on Salem turnpike near Lynchburg and was one of the trustees, of that town, appointed by Lynch. He was a friend of Andrew Jackson, who often visited at Clement's home when passing back and forth from Washington; both were fond of shooting and the cherry tree on Clement's premises to which they fastened a target, was killed by the shots fired into it. Clement in 1806 was appointed captain of a cavalry company and served in the war of 1812. Children of Adam, Jr., and Nancy Alexander-Clement:—Robert Alexander, b. 1812, d. 1872, m. Mary, dau. of General Terry of Bedford county;—Wm. Alexander, b. 1813, d. 1876, m. 1st, Martha, dau. of Thos. Hunter, m. 2nd, Mrs. Mary Perkins, served as clerk of the county;—John N., m. Susan Thompson of Pittsylvania, d. at *Rock Castle;*—Charles B. J., m. Mary Thompson, sister of Susan, went to California in 1849, but d. at *Rock Castle;*—George W., m. Isabella, dau. of Dr. Geo. Washington Clement of Turkey Cock Mountain, Franklin Co., he was a farmer and merchant;—Adam Clement, b. 1826, d. 1916, m. 1st, Martha Cocke, m. 2nd, Ann Cocke, he was Captain of Co. "C" 11th Va. Reg., C. S. Army, later promoted major, was desperately wounded at Boonsboro, Md.; he was twice sheriff of Campbell, and state senator; his dau. Mattie, m. R. Hunter Palmer, member of the Legislature, who lived at *Vineland* on Molley's creek; Nancy A., m. Dr. Geo. W. Clement, Jr., and moved to Patrick county;—Juliette C., m. Charles Slaughter of Danville;—Mary, m. . . . . Jennings of Campbell. Major Adam Clement lived at *Oakdale,* not far from Mt. Zion, a large, brick house, upon stone foundation, which has honey-comb cornice and arched doorway. Robert A. Clement was clerk of circuit court from 1871 till 1886; Wm. A. was clerk of county court from 1838 till 1845. Mrs. Nancy Alex. Clement, Sr., died in 1864.

Children of Wm. A. and Martha H. Clement: Margaret, m. 1st, Samuel Wood, of Fluvanna, who died in Confederate service, m. 2nd, Col. Geo. W. Pettit, of Fluvanna;—Wm. Thomas, b. 1839, d. 1888, m. Mrs. Emma V. Wood, dau. of Jos. H. and Lucy Cobbs-Stone of Campbell, their son, Wm. Joseph, born at *Catalpa Hill,* on Seneca creek, m. Mary E. Frees of Montgomery Co., Pennsylvania; children of the latter: 1. Gretchen, m. O. S. Woodward of Richmond; 2. Wm. Tardy, captain in U. S. Marine Corps, commanding 19th Company, 4th Reg., now enroute to China.

—Robert Alexander, married Louise White of Bedford county, was clerk of circuit court; d. 1887.

—Nancy Alexander, married Captain Benjamin Tardy of Otter river, Campbell county.

—Richard Perkins, married Elizabeth White of Campbell county.

Cobbs

The first of the Cobbs' name, so far ascertained, was John Cobbs of Goochland county. His sons, Colonel Samuel, Edmund and John Cobbs are recorded in Louisa county.

—Samuel, married Mary Lewis, a descendant of Col. Robt. and Jane Meriwether-Lewis.

—Edmund, married Sarah Lewis, and in 1773 patented 500 acres both sides of Ivy creek.

Col. Sam'l Cobbs of Louisa, patented 396 acres on the north fork of Ward's fork in 1743, just one year after John Irvin made his settlement in the county; he acquired a large landed estate; and in his will (recorded 1758) left his brother Edmund and John each 500 acres in the (then Bedford) county. Children of Samuel and Mary Cobbs: Captain Robert, born in Louisa, married Ann Gizaage, dau. of John and Sarah White-Poindexter, he patented 100 acres on Hunting and Hurt's creeks, and 200 acres on Ivy creek; was living in 1795 at a residence called *Plain Dealing,* which is said to have been situated near the present Naruna, where he died; his will was recorded in 1829. Bedford courts of 1778 and 1779 recommended Robert Cobbs for commissions as second and first lieutenants of Virginia Militia, he served as captain, and was in the battles of Camden and Guilford. His widow, Ann G. P. Cobbs, applied in 1841 for a pension, she being then 79 years of age. She died in 1842 at her Campbell county home and her pension was allowed to her surviving children, John P., Robert L., William, Charles L., Sarah W. Weaver, and Elizabeth Ann Motley of Charlotte county. Children of Capt. Robert Cobbs:

—Dr. John P., b. 1785, married Jane Meredith, dau. of Hon. David S. and Jane Meredith Garland.

—Mary Lewis, b. 1787, m. 1st, William Armistead, m. 2nd, Dr. John McClean.

—Robert Lewis, b. 1789, graduated at Pennsylvania Medical College, was brigade surgeon in General Coffee's brigade, served with General Jackson through his campaign; was attorney-general of Tennessee; revised the laws of the state in 1827 and was member of the Constitutional Convention of 1834, died 1856.

—William, b. 1792, m. Mary Ann Stanard, dau. of Major Samuel Scott; bought *Poplar Forest* of Jefferson's grandson; died 1828 and was buried at St. Stephen's churchyard in Bedford; his dau., Emily Williams, married Edward Sixtus Hutter of the U. S. Navy, and lived at Poplar Forest which is now owned and occupied by their son, Christian Sixtus

Hutter and his family, as a summer residence; this historic place has remained in the Cobbs-Hutter family through four generations.

—Samuel Cobbs, U. S. A., b. 1776, appointed (through Hon. David S. Garland, M. C.,) lieutenant in the army; was with Gen. Scott at Lundy's Lane where he was wounded in battle; after war of 1812 was engaged in the Indian wars in Georgia and Florida; died in 1817 of wounds he had received in the war.

—Sarah, b. 1798, m. 1822, William C. McAllister who died in 1841, she m. 2nd, Mr. Weaver.

—Charles Lewis, b. 1800, owned the *Glen Alpine* estate in Bedford, m. Ann M. L. Scott, moved to Indiana in 1848, died at Valparaiso in 1864.

—Elizabeth A., b. 1802, married Joel Motley, moved to Charlotte county.

—Dr. Meriwether Cobbs, b. 1805, educated at Hampden-Sidney College, and Pa. Med. College, d. at the age of 22.

Captain Robert Cobbs in 1824 made a deed of gift to Charles and Thomas Cobbs, Lewis D. Poindexter, John Dixon, John S. Payne, John P. Slaughter, Collins Bradley and Samuel Pannill, self-perpetuating trustees, for sundry causes, particularly to accommodate the neighborhood with a convenient situation for a Meeting House, free for the use of all religious denominations, to be under the control of the trustees and their neighbors, land containing one acre, on the road leading from Cobb's house to a place called *Nickup,* with free use of water from the nearest spring; the Meeting House to be called Grove Spring as long as it was used as such place of worship but should it become disused for two consecutive years at any time, then the land was to revert back to Cobbs' heirs. This deed was witnessed by William L. and Samuel Pannill, Jr., and B. W. Nowlin.

In 1780 Captain Charles Cobbs patented 100 acres of land in which were included the head branches of Falling and Little Falling rivers; four years later he purchased of John Irvine,

Sr., 100 acres on north side of Little Falling to James Gates' lines, the same year he purchased of Gates 18 acres on Sullivan's branch of Little Falling, along his line, for 2,000 lbs. of tobacco.

In 1795 Charles Cobbs was sheriff of Campbell with Charles Hall, Richard Stith, Williston and Charles M. Talbot, Thomas Cocke and Charles Cobbs, Jr., as his securities. When first settled in the county Captain Cobbs affiliated with the Presbyterians and took an active part in Hat Creek Church activities, but later withdrew and joined the Baptists, becoming a minister of that denomination.

In 1784 he was appointed one of the trustees to receive the deed for land given the county by Jeremiah Rust as a site for erection of its court buildings; also for deciding upon the spot where the court house and prison should be erected, and to employ the county surveyor to lay off ten lots of one acre each with proper streets;—i. e.,

—one for the court house and public buildings on the north side of the main street, and in the center facing the sun, and
—two on each side of the court house, the same side of the street, and
—five on the south directly opposite the others, with a street between 60 feet wide: the remainder of the county land to be laid off in such manner as the trustees should think best.

Charles L. Cobbs outlived his wife. His will recorded in 1807 appointed Jesse, John, Samuel and Polly Cobbs as his executors. Children:

—Jesse, who, in 1789, registering himself from Cumberland county, bought of James and Sarah Gates, John and Amy Littlepage of Campbell, 360 acres on Little Falling river, along to Charles Cobbs, Sr.'s still at Thompson's corner. Jesse later sold Charles Cobbs 50 acres of this land lying along the west side of the river.

—John, in 1797, m. Christina Wynn. John Cobbs in 1773 patented 500 acres on Ivy creek. He was a Revolutionary pensioner in 1835, then aged 75 years. He sold John Mason,

Sr., 100 acres on the branches of Falling from Thomas Jones' line along Smith's line to the Ridge road, the deed to which was witnessed by Charles Cobbs, Sr., and Jr. In 1818 his daughter, Nancy, married James Murrell.
—Charles R.
—Caleb in 1791 married Mina Ann Wills.
—William W. as president of Hat Creek Library Society, petitioned to Legislature for its incorporation with all the privilege granted in such cases.
—Samuel D. married Polly. . . . Executors of Sam'l and Polly Cobbs sold land to Samuel Pannill in 1806-7.
—Mary.
—Thomas in 1809 married Susanna Adams; there are many deeds of sale from Thomas Cobbs to members of his family and various other purchasers; his will was recorded in 1825; in settling up his estate, his executors sold a parcel of his land to Robert Smith.
—Frances married —— Rodgers; children, William, Elizabeth Ann, and Ann Walton.

There are indications that Captain Charles Cobbs, the settler of 1780, was nearly related to Captain Robert Cobbs of Plain Dealing, but absence of positive proof of the fact prevents assertion of it.

Edmund Cobbs, Sr., and Sarah Lewis-Cobbs had three sons:
—John Lewis married Susannah, dau. of Nicolas Hamner of Albemarle. Children—Nicolas Hamner married his cousin, Lucy H. Landonia Cobbs, dau. of Edmund and Elizabeth W. Manson-Cobbs.
—Elizabeth married Junius Axle, son of Rev. Charles and Editha Davies Clay;
—Edmund, Jr. (3rd son of Edmund, Sr.), m. Elizabeth Willis Manson, daughter of Nathaniel, Sr., and Lucy Willis Clayton-Manson: children—Lucy Henry Landonia, m. Bishop Nicolas Cobbs; moved to Alabama;—Mary Adeline m. Henry Landon, son of Tamerlane W. W. Davies;—Frederick Augustus settled in the west;—John Cabell, m. Martha B. Carter: lived near Lynchburg.

Nicolas Hamner Cobbs was born in 1796 at *Rose Hill,* Bedford county, within sight of the Peaks of Otter. He received a classical education under a Scotch tutor. His father held the religious views of Thomas Jefferson, while his mother conformed to those of the Church of England. Desirous of giving her son the benefit of church rites, she carried him 60 miles on horseback to have him baptized: the Episcopal church had not been established in her community then.

Bishop Cobbs began his life as an educator; one of his first positions was as principal of New London Academy, his wife being one of his pupils. However, he soon turned to the ministry and was ordained in 1824 by Bishop Moore at Staunton, Virginia. By teaching from house to house he built up two churches in Bedford county—*St. Stephens* near Forest and *Trinity* in the northern part of the county. His efforts were concentrated in the counties of Campbell, Bedford, Amherst and Botetourt; thus he founded the Episcopal church in four counties and at twelve points in Virginia: he held the first prayer book service. Mrs. Cabell, in *"Sketches,"* tells that until the year 1819 Episcopacy was unknown in Lynchburg and neighboring country. About that time a bishop of that church came and his appearance in gown and bands as he walked up the aisle of the church excited the wonder of his congregation, particularly the small boys, who thought the bishop was an elderly woman in a black morning wrapper. Those interested had exerted themselves to procure a few attendants who could respond to the morning service. Female members of three families possessed prayer books and knew how to go through the services, but it was considered necessary to have at least one male voice. Fortunately this was secured in the person of an Englishman who owned a large red prayer book. "He stood in front of the gallery, holding his book conspicuously, responding loudly and surveying the congregation with an air of superiority mingled with compassion for their ignorance." Mrs. Cabell gives Bishop Cobbs credit for the first dawning of an Episcopal church in Lynchburg. Soon after his marriage he made a profession of religion and partly through the influence of Seth Ward he connected himself with the Episcopal church: he assisted in building St. Paul's church. Through Nicolas Cobbs' missionary labors the church was planted in Botetourt parish; in going to officiate in Botetourt he would often travel in a wagon and carry his choir with him. This was on fifth Sundays which he reserved for missionary work. He was installed bishop of Alabama at Philadelphia: died at the age of 65 years in 1861 at Montgomery, Alabama.

Cocke

In 1742-43 Abraham Cocke obtained a grant of 289 acres of land on the north side of Roanoke river. In 1747 Richard Cocke patented 503 acres on north side of Bear's Element creek. In 1748 James Cocke patented 1023 acres on the south side of Staunton river at the mouth of Great Branch, adjoining King's land. In 1784 John Cocke bought 50 acres both sides of Falling river from Ajonidab and Eliza Read. In 1786 John Cocke bought 360 acres lying on Molley's creek (alias Briery), of Benjamin Arnold (the heir of William Arnold, dec.), and his wife, Mary Ann, land which had been conveyed in 1765 to William Arnold by Benjamin and which adjoined the property of George Eagers. Two years later John and Elizabeth Cocke sold this tract of land to William Read. In 1790 John Cocke sold Robertson McKinney 140 acres lying on the South branches of Bull branch at the corner of the patent of Robert Douglass.

In 1788 George Cocke sold Joshua Wynne 82 acres on Falling river, beginning at Hornbeam's, near the mouth of Shoal's branch. The next year George Cocke and Joshua Wynne sold John Minton, hatter, 140 acres on the east side of Falling river, the south side of Shepherd's creek.

The will of George Cocke, recorded in 1892, mentions his sons:

—John in 1796 married Mary Tweedy.
—Thomas in 1789 married Eleanor Hightower.

—William . . . . . .

and daughters:

—Elizabeth married —— Talbot.

—Jemima married —— Gilbert.

—Mary married —— Kent.

—Sarah married —— Kent.

—Nancy married in 1782 Joseph Stith.

—Rebecca married David Marshall.

In 1806 Drury Cocke married Susannah Cox; in 1814 Richard Cocke married Jane Wood; in 1823 Archibald Cocke married Mary Bradley.

Dabney

Cornelius Dabney, ancestor of the family of that name, which lived in Campbell, was a church warden of St. Peter's parish, New Kent county in 1685; his son, George Dabney, lived on the Pamunkey opposite Hanovertown. His son, Col. William of *Aldringham,* Hanover county, died before the Revolution, but William's son, Capt. George Dabney, born 1740, died 1824, was a member of Hanover county committee in 1775 and served in the war of the Revolution.

George Dabney married Elizabeth Price, the grand-daughter of Col. Wm. and Elizabeth Beverly-Randolph; their son, Judge John Dabney, a member of the state senate from 1805-08, was appointed judge in place of Judge Edmund Winston, who resigned office in 1813.

Judge John Dabney married his cousin, Susannah Dabney Morris. Their son, John Blair Dabney, of William and Mary College and of Princeton, a noted lawyer and Episcopal minister, was born in 1795; married 1822 Elizabeth Lewis, daughter of Major Oliver Towles and wife Agatha, the daughter of Col. Wm. Lewis of Sweet Springs. John B. Dabney lived at *Vancluse,* near Campbell C. H. His daughter, Maria Louisa, married in 1844 William Cabell Carrington, born 1821, and moved to Richmond in 1845, where he edited the

"Richmond Times and Compiler." In 1851 Carrington was elected to represent Richmond in the state legislature, but died December, 1851, before he could take his seat.

The *"Southern Literary Messenger"* of September, 1842, pays a tribute to John B. Dabney, in answering a correspondent: "To the question which was some time ago propounded to this journal as to 'What has become of the Cincinnati Oration?' we can reply that it forms part of the exercises of Commencement and that the honor of delivering the last one fell to John Blair Dabney, of Campbell county, who acquitted himself of the charge much to the satisfaction of those who had the good fortune to be present. Washington College, it may be recalled, is the institution to which the surviving members of the Cincinnati Society in Virginia made a few years ago the handsome donation of its funds, one of the conditions of that donation was that an address should be delivered before the college annually forever in defending the society from the aspersions cast upon it by Mirabeau and other French writers. The college is now in condition to fulfill in every respect the wishes of the society."

George William, the son of Chiswell Dabney, was clerk of Campbell from 1845 to 1859 and kept the papers of his office in the most perfect order.

Daniel

Many of the Daniel name appear in the parish register of Christ Church, Middlesex county, which seems to indicate that the family were Eastern Shore emigrants. A William Daniel, of different generations, is found there from 1678 to 1751, a James Daniel from 1704 till 1739. In the U. S. Census of 1785 James Daniel is listed as head of a family in St. Paul's parish, Hanover county; one in Orange, another in Prince Edward; William as head of a family in Shenandoah, one in Orange and a third in Cumberland. Samuel Daniel in 1758 was a soldier in a regiment for defense. In 1742 James Daniel patented 2032 acres of land on the ridge between the head branches of Buffalo and Elk creeks: in 1750 he patented 469 acres on south side of Staunton river.

James Daniel was a Goochland justice in 1742 and sheriff from 1743 to 1744. When Albemarle was divided from Goochland he became a justice there from 1744 to 1745, and then sheriff of Albemarle, Dr. William Cabell becoming his security in both counties. In Albemarle two of Cabell's sons, William and Joseph, were deputy sheriffs under Daniel, and had charge of the business on the north side of the river. Daniel is given the title of captain. He married Elizabeth Woodson; Children:—Chesley, m. Judith Christian;—Abraham;—Josiah;—James, Jr., m. Hannah ———;—Mary;—Susannah. —John Minor in 1772 married Elizabeth Morton; his daughter, Nancy, m. Rev. Wm. Nelson Scott.

James and Hannah Daniel, with four minor children, Rebecca, William, Jaspar and Hannah, moved in 1791 from Goose Creek Meeting to South River in Campbell.

In 1799 Peter Daniel was granted 600 acres on both sides of Bear creek by patent. Peter and Mary Daniel sold Patrick Ratekin 200 acres of land, 100 acres being part of his 600 acre grant and the other 100 part of 282 acres granted William Reid by patent and made over to William Haythe, and from Haythe to William Gibson, and from Gibson to Daniel by deed, land lying on both sides of Bear creek. Peter Daniel died in 1781. Sons: Richard, Peter, William, John; and daughters; Lucy Trent, Sarah Dancy and Jemima Hunter. Marriages of Daniels: 1792, William Daniel m. Edith Sutterfield: 1801, Thomas Daniel m. Polly Jones; 1805, Robert Daniel m. Sarah Douglass; 1811, James Daniel m. Susanna Tanner.

William Daniel, Sr., brother of James, Sr., of Goochland, had a son William, who was an ensign in the Revolutionary army; he married Martha, sister of Archer Allen, member of Cumberland Committee of 1775. His son, William, Judge of Campbell and Cumberland district, married Margaret, daughter of Dr. Cornelius and Mary Briscoe-Baldwin of Winchester. Judge Daniel moved to Lynchburg in 1819 and resided

at first in the town: his children,—Mary C. B., m. Mayo Cabell
of *Union Hill,* Nelson county;—Eliza, m. William J. Lewis
Cabell (son of Dr. Geo. Cabell of *Point of Honor*);—Elvira
A., m. Colonel Charles Ellet, Jr.;—Martha, m. Judge
Wood Bouldin, of Charlotte county;—Judge William, Jr.,
(judge of Virginia Court of Appeals, 1846-65), m., 1st, Sarah
A., dau. of John M. Warwick of Lynchburg; had two children,
John Warwick and Sally (m. Major Don P. Halsey, Sr.);
Judge Daniel, Jr., m., 2nd, Elizabeth H., dau. of Gov. Wm. H.
Cabell of Richmond. He represented Lynchburg in the Vir-
ginia Legislature.

William J. Lewis Cabell and bride died young. They did
not occupy *Point of Honor,* as it was rented at the time of their
marriage. Mrs. Cabell, dying last, inherited this Cabell property, and afterwards her father, Judge Daniel, Sr., heired it
from her and resided there. He married, 2nd, Mrs. Hector
Cabell, neé Pauline Cabell, daughter of Col. John and Paulina
Jordan-Cabell, of Buckingham county. Judge Daniel, Jr., later
built a suburban home, named *Rivermont* from its situation
in view of river and mountain, which afterwards provided the
name for the community that became annexed to Lynchburg.
This occurred when Major E. S. Hutter owned and occupied
the premises. Two grandsons of Judge Daniel, Sr., have represented Lynchburg in the Virginia Legislature: one, Mayo
C. Brown, attorney-at-law, (son of Mrs. Robert L. Brown,
neê Margaret, daughter of Mayo and Mary C. B. Daniel-Cabell,
of Nelson county, and for some years principal of Lynchburg
Female Seminary), a delegate from Lynchburg 1919, 1922-
23. The other, Don. P. Halsey, Jr., (son of Major Don P.
and Sallie Daniel-Halsey), who, when state senator in 1903,
was author of the bill placing statues of George Washington
and Robert E. Lee in Washington Capitol as Virginia's representatives in Statuary Hall. In 1910 he was again a state
senator, and was then appointed by Gov. Mann a member of
the commission to present a replica of the Houdon statue of
Washington from Virginia to France, "The People of the
First Republic": the copy was then made by the Gorham Com-

pany and delivered by Senator Halsey. Appointed in 1925
by Gov. Trinkle to the judgeship of the 6th judicial circuit
of Virginia, he was elected at the Legislative session of 1926
to fill out the unexpired term, made vacant by the death of
Judge William R. Barksdale.

Major Don. P. Halsey, Sr., was mustered into the service
of the Confederate States together with his brothers, Major
Stephen and Edward Halsey, at Forest Depot; became 2nd
lieutenant of Co. "G", 2nd Va. Cav. Reg., commanded by Captain Winston Radford, under Colonel R. C. W. Radford. At
the battle of Manassas he was promoted to 1st lieutenant, later
commissioned aide on the staff of Gen. Samuel Garland; was
wounded at Sharpsburg and taken prisoner, but soon exchanged
and was placed on Gen. Iverson's staff, with title of captain.
Late in 1864 on staff of General G. C. Wharton with title of
major; captured at Waynesboro and imprisoned at Fort Delaware till June, 1865. This Halsey family is descended from
Thomas Halsey, who came to America from England in 1633 and
settled first at Lynn, Massachusetts. Seth Halsey, of Lynchburg, a descendant of Thomas, married Julia D. B. Peters;
was a successful tobacconist. His daughter, Aurelia Halsey,
married Gen. John G. Meem, son of John Gaw Meem, Sr.,
and his wife, Eliza Campbell Russell, (daughter of Andrew
and Anna McDonald Russell). John Meem, Sr., of the Green-
way firm of Abingdon, Va., moved to Lynchburg where he
engaged in the merchandise business and acquired large landed
estates: *Strathmore* and *Mt. Airy* in the Valley of Virginia
being best known. Children:

—William Campbell, m. Miss Matthews; died young.

—Dr. Andrew Russell, m. Ann Jordan.

—Gen. Gilbert Simroe, m., 1st, Gabriella Jordan; m., 2nd,
Nannie Rose Garland.

—Gen. John G., m. 1st, Nancy Esterbrook Cowan; m., 2nd,
Aurelia Halsey.

—J. Lawrence, killed at battle of Seven Pines.

—Fannie Russell, m. Dr. Robert S. Payne, of Lynchburg.

—Eliza C., m. General Samuel Garland, of Lynchburg.

Andrew Russell, father of Mrs. Eliza C. Russell-Meem, was the son of Captain Andrew Russell, Sr., and Margaret, the daughter of Colonel William Christian and Mary Campbell, sister of General William Campbell.

Davis

John Davis of Louisa county married Susannah Smithson; their son, William, born in 1755, married in 1774, Mary, the daughter of Henry and Mary Shelton-Gosney, Mary Shelton being the daughter of Ralph and Mary Pollard-Shelton of King William county. Davis died in 1853; both he and his wife were buried at South River burial ground. Children:
—William, Jr., m. Zalinda, dau. of John Lynch, founder of Lynchburg.
—John, m., 1805, Mrs. Hannah Johnson, neê Anthony, the dau. of Christopher Anthony, and moved to Cincinnati, Ohio, in 1814; died 1830.
—Thomas, born 1777, m. Rachel Davis; children:—Annis Elizabeth, m. Pleasant Preston,—Micajah, m., 1st, Mary E. Phillips, m., 2nd, Sallie W. Selden; died 1884; Zalinda Lynch Davis m. Frazier O. Stratton.
—Henry, born 1779, m., 1801, Sarah, dau. of Christopher Anthony and wife, Mary Jordan. Henry Davis conducted a hardware store in Lynchburg. Children were:
—Mary M., born 1804, married Hobson Johns.
—Sarah A., born 1811, m., 1st, William Ward Smith; son, Wm. W. Smith, Jr. Married, 2nd, Franklin Gillette Smith, rector of St. Paul's church, Lynchburg, 1824-1838, and teacher of a school there; moved to Columbia, Tenn., where he conducted the Female Institute; founded Columbia Athanaeum, which became a factor in Columbia's system of public education; published *"The Guardian."*
—Robert Jordan, born 1815, m. Anne Carrington, dau. of Paul C. and Mary B. Irvine-Cabell (dau. of Wm. Irvine of Bedford). Robert J. Davis was educated at Washington College, where he took his B.A. degree; was a graduate in engin-

eering at the University of Virginia, and graduate of law at Harvard; was for many years a prominent lawyer at Lynchburg and represented the city in the Virginia Legislature. His four daughters, Mary Irvine (dec.), Sallie Anthony, Ann C. and Lucy Lee, have been successful educators; the last named holds the position of Supervisor of Methods in Lynchburg schools and Ann C. Davis conducts an industrial school at Tullulah Falls, Georgia. These two were formerly associated with William and Mary College. Their only surviving brother, Wm. Knickle Davis, for some years engineer in bridge construction, is now located in Roanoke and is engaged in insurance business.

—Lucy Elizabeth, born 1822, m. William Tudor Yancey, a prominent lawyer of Lynchburg; their son, Robert D. Yancey, holds office of Commonwealth's Attorney for Lynchburg.

—Benjamin, born 1785, married Catherine Gilbert, of Pittsylvania county.

—Mary, born 1790, m. Cornelius Pierce; children, Mary, m. Benjamin Brown of Amherst; Susan m. James D. Taylor; Louisa m. Lunsford Lomax Loving; Robinson m. ————.

—Nancy, born, 1792, m., 1814, Peter Dudley; children, John W. married Andusia Fourquerean; Mary E. m. Capt. Thomas W. Johns; Fannie J. m. James F. Payne; Peter L. m. Elizabeth Saunders; Deborah A. m. (2nd wife) Rev. W. H. Kinkle; Maria Rose m. J. Edward Calhoun.

—Mary Annis, born 1805, m. Robinson Stabler of Alexandria in 1828.

Davies

Nicolas Davies, according to the family tradition, early in the 18th century, came from his home in Wales, at the age of 15, to Virginia. The name Davies is to-day not uncommon in Wales. He was a merchant in Henrico about the year 1730 and in 1733 married Mrs. Judith Fleming-Randolph, (the widow of Colonel Thomas Randolph of Tuckahoe), who had two daughters, and a son, William (the heir of Tuckahoe).

Davies was a justice in Goochland in 1741, and at the division of that county to form Cumberland in 1748 he became a justice in the new county. He was living on Muddy creek, on the south side of James river, when he was a member of the grand jury in Williamsburg which presented Rev. John Roane (a Presbyterian minister), Thomas Watkins and Joshua Morris, for reflecting upon the Established Religion. He was a large dealer in lands, locating, entering, patenting, transferring and selling them during his life. Rev. William Stith, the historian, married Judith Randolph, his step-daughter, in 1738, and joined with Davies in entering lands adjoining that of John Bolling and George Braxton: in the division Stith received 1711 acres of *The Forest* tract, and in 1755 he patented 4000 acres on Blackwater, Fluvanna and Otter rivers, ultimately acquiring 6000 acres in the same locality: he died in 1755.

About the time of Bedford's formation, Davies moved to his land in that county, Dr. William Cabell, surveyor, having made an inclusive plot of his lands on both sides of James river between Judith's creek (named for his wife), and the Scotch-Irish Falls. The patent for this land is recorded February 16, 1771, and again July 20, 1784, in the first entry "31,303 acres in Amherst and Bedford counties on both sides of Fluvanna river including the greatest part of Fleming's Mountain, part of No Business Mountain, and part of the main ridge"; almost identical is the second entry, thirteen years later, of 33,797 acres "in Bedford and Amherst on Tobacco Row Mountains both sides of Fluvanna including the greatest part of Fleming's Mountain, part of No Business Mountain and part of the main ridge," making it appear as a duplicate entry of the same tract.

Mary Randolph (Davies' second step-daughter), married Thomas Eston Randolph, a wealthy Englishman who had come to America on a visit to the Tuckahoe Randolphs, yet not known to be related. Randolph met with reverses after his marriage and moved to New London where he resided for a short time, then in 1827 moved to Lynchburg and there his daughters conducted a school for eighteen months. The eldest daughter married Francis Eppes, Jefferson's grandson, and in consequence of her mother's failing health, the whole family moved near Tallahassee, Florida, where Mrs. Eppes died after a few years' residence.

Davies had no children by his first marriage. He married, secondly, Catherine, the daughter of Henry and Anne Bever-

Dr. John J. Cabell

ley-Whiting and had a son, Henry Landon, who married first, Anne, dau. of John and Elizabeth Whiting-Clayton. Children:

—Nicolas, born 1769, m. Elizabeth, dau. of David Crawford.
—Arthur Landon, born 1770, m. Miss Pryor of Gloucester, of which county he was clerk.
—Catherine E., born 1772, m. Francis Thornton Meriwether.
—Samuel Boyle, born 1774, m. 1802 Elizabeth McCulloch.

—Editha Langdon, born 1777, m. Rev. Charles Clay.

—Henrianne, born 1780, m. Dr. John Jordan, son of Colonel John Cabell of Buckingham.

—Tamerlane Whiting, born 1782, m. Jane Smith, dau. of Philip and Elizabeth D. Payne.

Henry L. Davies married, 2nd, Mrs. Lucy W. Clayton-Manson, who had three children:

—Nathaniel Manson m. Sallie Alexander; Mayor N. C. Manson was their grandson.

—Mary Thweat Manson m. Captain Robert Coleman of Orange county.

—Elizabeth Manson m. Edmund Cobbs, their dau. Lucy H. L. m. Bishop Nicolas H. Cobbs.

Children of Henry L. and Lucy W. C. Davies:

—Addison m. Mary, the dau. of Captain Robert Coleman.

—Dr. Howell m., 1st, Harriet Godfrey of Harrisburg, Pa.; m., 2nd, Mrs. Abby Willing Byrd-Jackson. Dr. Davies, graduate of Philadelphia Medical College, was a chemist in Lynchburg. His two daughters of the first marriage were Mrs. Creed Wills and Mrs. Robert Early; two daughters of the second marriage were Mrs. Otwayanna Gilkerson and Mrs. Jas. Bowker Nowlin.

Henry L. Davies heired his father's estate and made his residence at *Pebbleton,* a property which has passed through the hands of several generations, who received their portions, in many instances disposing of the inherited lands to members of other families. Several tracts acquired by Lynchburgers have been built upon for summer homes. The old family burying ground, upon the mountain slope, not far from the site of the stone house first occupied by Nicholas Davies, remains undisturbed except by time and weather.

Davies established an ordinary (inn) at the top of his mountain, where there was a passway leading to the valley on the other side, and there he placed one Ogden as inn-keeper and the place acquired the name of *Ogdens,* also was called *Eagle's Eyrie.* After many years of service the old hostelry fell into disuse. In recent times the land upon which the old L-shaped cabin stood, was purchased by a westerner named Locke, who greatly improved the property and during his several years' ownership attracted many visitors to the place by the charming hospitality of himself and his wife, Margaret Greenleaf (magazine writer), as much as the beautiful panorama observable either side of the mountain. Travel also increased as the pass is on Lexington highway, then under construction but at present almost completed. Thus, by association with its purchaser, former *Ogdens* was christened *Locke's Mountain*, but his cabin home was pulled down to give place to a capacious modern residence, now owned by the Bell family of Lynchburg. The new structure was built by Baron Quarles Von Offert, refugee from Holland during the world war, who lived there but a short while then returned to his native country. He was suspected of being a German sympathizer and was subjected to surveillance by the Department of Justice, but appealed to the Department of State, exhibiting his papers, then was not further molested. Their concrete tennis-court was reported to be the base for long-distance guns to cover Lynchburg and cause its destruction, if war activities reached this country; hence the family became targets for much gossip and annoyance, through exaggerated reports carried to them.

Deering

Edward, the son of Robert Deering of Orange, in 1782 sold Benjamin Johnson 274 acres of his land in that county for six likely negroes about sixteen years of age, and a still containing 53 gallons of liquor, and then moved to Campbell. He died in 1791 while deer hunting with a party of friends who had stopped to rest at a spring near old Shiloh church which stood near Lynch's station; when the others started again they missed Dearing and returning to their halting place found that he had expired. His will, recorded at Rustburg, names his children, Rosamond White, John, James, Anthony, Robert and William Deering, all of whom, except James appear to have died early or left the county.   James married between 1780-85 Elizabeth the daughter of Robert and Penelope Lynch-Adams, and settled at a place on little Otter river between Castle Craig and Evington.   He served in the Revolution from Orange county as a private in Captain Francis Taylor's Company, 2nd Virginia regiment, which was commanded successively by Colonel Alexander Spotswood and Colonel Christian Febiger, his name appearing on the pay rolls of April, 1777 and February, 1778: according to family tradition he rose to rank of captain by which title he was always called.   He died in 1811, and his will gives names of his children:

—Nancy m., 1801, Jonathan White, died before 1811.

—Sally m., 1809, Marston Clay.

—Elizabeth m., 1811, Stephen Clay.

—Mildred m., 1803, John Guy.

—Rosamond, born 1794, died 1836, m. 1814 Howard Y. Bennett.

—General William Lynch S. born 1796, m., 1st, 1817, Mary Terry Harrison; m., 2nd, 1868, Mrs. Nellie McGregor; served in war of 1812, war with Mexico in 1848, and the Confederate war.   Moved to Tennessee.   Mrs. Flora Gillentine, National Officer D. A. R., is a descendant; he died in 1876.

—Margaret m., 1816, John Black; record in Pittsylvania court.

—Colonel James Griffin, born 1800, m. 1834, Mary Anna, dau. of Anselm and Susan Miller-Lynch and grand-dau. of Colonel Charles Lynch.   Col. Jas. G. Dearing was colonel of the county militia, then an important military organization, requiring regular drills of all able-bodied county men when the court was in session.   To gratify his wife, Col. Dearing changed the spelling of his name, and it has since been so used by his branch of the family; he lived for awhile at *Otterburne;* d. 1843, of tuberculosis, leaving three children,—James, m. Roxie Birchett of Petersburg, and their dau. Mary L., married Judge Frank Christian of Lynchburg.   James Dearing entered the Confederate army as 2nd Lieut. of artillery with command of four batteries; became commander of Ashby's Laurel Brigade; was wounded April 6, 1865, while leading a charge on the enemy which was endeavoring to burn High Bridge over the Appomattox near Farmville; was brought to a Lynchburg hospital where he died on the 22nd.

—Mary, m. Thomas, son of Thos. W. Fauntleroy, resided at *Avoca,* which had been the property of her uncle, Charles Henry Lynch, and was named from its supposed resemblance to the Irish valley which Moore memorialized; there her family still continue to live; at its entrance stands the walnut tree used by Revolutionary Vigilants and the old burying ground containing several generations of the family who have passed away, is on the left side of the lawn, guarded by a tall cypress tree.

—Susan, m. Robert H., son of Robert A. and Betsy Terrell-Ward. Robert H. Ward was appointed judge of Campbell county court in 1870 by Governor Underwood.

Thomas Fauntleroy, a lieutenant in the Confederate army, was wounded in service four times, taken prisoner and carried to Johnson's Island, Lake Michigan, where he was detained four months. His eldest son, James Dearing, born in Middlesex county, was a graduate of Va. Mil. Institute in 1888, served in various engineering capacities until 1895, when he entered the Transportation Dept. of the Norfolk and Western R. R. at Norfolk until 1898, then he was enrolled as First Lieut. in the 3rd U. S. Engineers, later commissioned as captain; while serving in Cuba he assisted in mapping out military roads in Pinar Del Rio province. At this time he commanded Co. "B." Returning to the States he was mustered out at Ft. McPherson, Georgia, May 17, 1899. He was commissioned, July, 1899, first lieutenant of the 27th Vol. Infy. and helped organize the regiment at Camp Méade, Pa.; made adjutant of the 1st battalion he went with the regiment to Manila, and as captain of Co. "F" was engaged in suppressing the Philippine insurrection and expeditions against the Insurrectos under Generals Pio Del Pilar and Licerio Geronimo. Afterwards Captain Fauntleroy was appointed city engineer of Manila and had charge of the construction of Junita Market (covering an acre of ground) and of Santa Cruz bridge spanning Passig river about the center of the city. For two years he was a member of the Governing Board of Occidental Negros Province, and as provincial supervisor was in charge of a large program of road and bridge building. It was at his own request in December, 1900, when his regiment was ordered back to the United States, that he was transferred to the Provost Marshall's office (General Franklin Bell) at Manila, where he helped to organize the city's native police force, and became in Jan'y, 1901, assistant city engineer, retaining his military rank until June, when all volunteers were mustered out of service. In 1902 he returned to this country and was married to Frances Hamilton Fox of Evington, Campbell county, afterwards returning to the Philippines where he was made Chief of Provincial Supervisors in the islands with control of all work of 35 supervisors. In this capacity, Dearing inaugurated the road movement there which resulted in one of the most wonderful road systems in the world. In 1904 he was made Sanitary Engineer and had charge of the measure taken to eradicate cholera, bubonic plague and other tropical epidemics. During this period the proper sanitation of Manila with a population of 250,000, was given into his charge, as well as construction of most of the buildings, sewage plant, and water supply system for the Culion Leper Colony, having then 500 lepers. Returning in 1906, Capt. Fauntleroy entered the U. S. Reclamation Service. Until its completion he superintended construction of the Laguna Dam near Yuma, Arizona, practically a mile long and 12 miles from a railroad in the deserts of Arizona. In 1909 he took charge of construction of Bumping Lake Dam, in Washington State, but later was transferred back to Yuma as Resident Engineer of canals and ditches below Laguna Dam. Late in 1910 and beginning of 1911, he was engaged in field work incident to diverting Colorado river back to its old channel, employing 1,000 workmen. He afterwards had the building of power house, cableways, roads, etc., at Elephant Butte Dam, New Mexico. In 1812 Fauntleroy left Reclamation Service and took charge of construction of Lake Hattie Dam near Laramie,

Wyoming, an earth structure one and one-half miles long and 50 feet high; also construction of irrigation ditches covering over 100,000 acres, and of the so-called "Highline" canal, which if completed, would have been 50 feet wide, around the summit of Medicine Bow Mountains at a 9,000 feet elevation. In 1914 he entered the Bureau of Public Roads as Senior Highway Engineer, but shortly afterwards was placed in charge of construction of 32 miles of road in Fairfax Co., Va. In 1915-16 he was in charge of the Bureau of Public Roads' economic investigations until appointed District Engineer when he had charge of all Federal Aid work in Arkansas, Oklahoma, Texas and Louisiana, and was instrumental in organizing the State Highway Department in Texas; was finally appointed State Highway Engineer of Texas, which position he resigned in 1924 and re-entered the Bureau of Public Roads as Highway Engineer in charge of all Federal Aid Highway-work in Virginia. Capt. Fauntleroy is a member of the American Society of Civil Engineers and also of the American Association of Engineers; he now resides at Richmond, Va.

Juliet Fauntleroy, a sister of Captain Fauntleroy, holds position of teacher in Altavista schools, is a student of natural history and a genealogist.

Diuguid

William S. Diuguid, first of the name found in Campbell was a neighbor of Archibald Bolling, and was appointed in 1811, by Bolling, one of his executors together with Blair Bolling, one of Archibald's sons, and another neighbor, William Ferbush. In 1817 Wm. Diuguid of Campbell county bought, of Jesse Thornhill of Buckingham, 236 acres on Buck creek, a branch of Rock Island creek; it appears that Diuguid's land laid partly in a portion of the county which was given in 1845 to Appomattox. George Diuguid was a Revolutionary War Pensioner in 1835, age 72 years.

Sampson Diuguid, brother of William, moved to Lynchburg and in 1817 established what is now known as the Diuguid

Funeral Directing Establishment, second oldest of the kind in the United States. He combined cabinet making with his other occupation, supplying many persons of the community with fine durable furniture. His familiar association with scenes of distress, as undertaker, did not blunt his susceptibilities and, it is told, that at the grave it was often with difficulty that he controlled his feelings. He died in 1856, aged 62 years, and his remains were carried to Appomattox for interment at his former home. Diuguid was succeeded in undertaking business by his son, George A. Diuguid, who lived to the age of 72 years when his son, William D. Diuguid, became head of the establishment.

Perhaps, in its records, no line of business carries so full a history, as this firm, of what transpired contemporaneously at Lynchburg during its century progress,—in its silent reflection of epidemics, wars, crises, depressions, etc., as well as of the march of science in tempering the ills to which flesh is heir. These records give accurate roll call of citizens in their passing, —of the heavy toll in war victims,—of the gradual dismemberment of households.

Embalming was practiced in primitive custom before the War Between the States, and during that crucial period of 1861-65 the method of preservation of bodies for transportation, as found necessary in the case of soldiers sent to their homes,— was by packing the outer casing with charcoal. A later day provided precautions in the use of chemical preservatives, and for this in 1894 Virginia Legislature passed a law requiring the embalming of bodies and licensing of embalmers. This law was sponsored by Virginia Funeral Directors' Association of which Wm. D. Diuguid was president, and Virginia was the first state in the Union to adopt the law.

George A. Diuguid had anticipated the requirement of a doctor's certificate of death, first enforced in 1873, by the use of a peculiar mark of his own selection, to indicate on his books that the certificate had been secured.

The present improved church truck, used for the conveyance of bodies in the building, grew out of the idea suggested to

Wm. D. Diuguid at seeing a picture of the catafalque used for the remains of President Garfield after his assassination. Diuguid conceived the idea of placing wheels on such a car and using it in churches; his suggestion became universally adopted and is now considered an essential accessory.

There are four cemeteries in Lynchburg:—the Methodist, established in 1806,—(an older one on Court House Hill having been abandoned) used later as a reservation for soldier interments; the Presbyterian, established in 1824; the Spring Hill, established in 1855, with violent opposition, causing the first funeral procession to go heavily armed against possible interruption; and Holy Cross Catholic Cemetery, established in 1874. A Jewish cemetery was established on the Amherst Heights; and one for use of colored residents has recently been established near the city. In former years slaves were interred in old Methodist cemetery and plot reservations in the portion divided off from that for soldiers, are still held by their descendants.

Douglas

In 1784 Edward Douglas patented 300 acres of land on Beaverpond creek. 1804 patented 300 additional acres on Beaverpond creek: this Edward may have been a brother or grandson of John: whose children were Charles, Elizabeth, Thomas, Polly, Judith, John, Anne, Achilles and Dorcas.

John Douglas emigrated from Scotland, settled in Orange county where he lived and died. He married Judith, the daughter of Charles and Judith Moorman: their son, Achilles, born 1752, married in 1779 Elizabeth, the daughter of Micajah and Sarah Lynch-Terrell and moved to Campbell county. Achilles Douglas was a member of the Society of Friends at South River and for some years was clerk of the meeting. He manumitted his slaves in 1782. In 1786 he was one of the trustees of Lynchburg. Micajah Terrell, his father-in-law, was a Quaker preacher: the first meeting of the Campbell county justices took place in his home in 1782; he offered a site for the county seat, but though his proposition was taken under consideration and gained many advocates, it was finally rejected in favor of the more central Rust site. Children of Achilles and Elizabeth T. Douglas:

—Sarah, born 1781, married Newby, the son of William Johnson.

—Judith, born 1783, m. Jonathan Johnson, the brother of Newby.

—Mildred Young, born 1785, married Richard Tyree, and was disowned for marrying out.

—Deborah, born 1787, m. Anselm, son of Benjamin and Mary Johnson.

—Elizabeth, born 1790, m. Mahlon Cadwallader.

—John Lynch, born 1797, m. Sally Lynch-Terrell.

—Achilles Moorman, born 1800, m. Anne L. Terrell; their son, Charles Achilles Douglass, born 1830, m. Caroline Matilda, the dau. of Ralph and Susan Lambeth-Smith.

Marriages: 1795, Edward Douglass m. Mary Ann Jude; 1796, Sarah Douglass m. Langhorne Scruggs.

Early

The family of Early moved to Bedford about the time it was established as a county. Jeremiah, Jr., of Culpeper county, first of the name to appear, was followed by his younger brothers, Joshua and Jacob, the latter of whom married into the Robertson family but moved to Georgia during the last quarter of the century. Joshua settled in the locality which remained within Bedford boundary; Jeremiah's property was embraced in the portion which became Campbell, though, as he died in 1779, he did not participate in the division, and his public activities were all in interest of the development and government of the older county, therefore he is not found recorded as resident in the new one.

Jeremiah, born 1730, son of Jeremiah, Sr., and Elizabeth Buford-Early, of Culpeper county, served as a lieutenant from the Augusta Military District during the French and Indian wars. He moved to Bedford with his relatives, James, William and Henry Buford, and in 1755 purchased from John Gibson 200 acres in Russell parish; in 1756 he was a member of a jury formed of the most capable freeholders; in 1756 received an order of court for laying "the court-house floors, sealing the house and making a barr," for which he was allowed 3,743 lbs. of tobacco; in 1758 purchased 200 acres lying upon Elk creek, and obtained a parcel of land, on the north side of the road to Warwick, from the county trustees upon which he agreed to build a house in one year; was appointed overseer of the road and commissioned justice of the peace, an office he held as long as he lived. He had remained in the militia and was promoted captain of his company. In 1759 he was commissioned to procure weights and measures for county use, together with Benjamin Howard he was paid 8,000 lbs. of tobacco for building the prison. This year he bought, from Richard Randolph's executors, 304 acres, part of 1000 acre patent on both sides of Erwin's creek, a fork of Otter; appointed to list tithes in 1760, a year later bought 102 acres on Elk creek of Edward Watts and 241 acres of George Walton; during 1762-63 was appointed to view a new road, lay prison bounds, build stocks and pillory, repair the court house and clerk's office, to have three pairs of handcuffs made for county use and to list tithes from Hairston's precinct up all the waters of James river. At this time he bought 300 acres on Elk's creek and 260 acres around Callaway's and Walton's corner. In 1764 he was appointed to view two new roads from New London; received 5,169 lbs. of tobacco for supplying the county standards; acquired 490 acres on Staunton river and 558 acres on Burton's creek. In 1769 received grants of 275 acres, and 270 acres on Goose creek, erected a mill at the mouth of the creek, and added 100 additional acres there. In 1772 was appointed High Sheriff of the county. He had been promoted major and lieutenant-colonel of militia, and in 1778 was commissioned colonel; was one of the trustees of Russell parish. Died 1779, and his son, Joseph and son-in-law, Colonel James Callaway, were appointed executors of his estate, giving bond in £200,000. His first wife was Sarah, the daughter of George Anderson. Children:

—Jacobus, m. Sarah, dau. of Colonel Charles F. Wall; moved at the close of the century to southwest Virginia, descendants moved to Kentucky.

—Judith, m., 1st, John Pate; m., 2nd, Captain Charles Callaway, of Campbell.

—Jeremiah 3rd, moved to North Carolina, m. Rebecca Freeman.

—Joseph, unmarried, moved to Henry county; died young.

—John, m. Elizabeth, dau. of Dr. Henry Cheatham; was a member of the Convention of 1778.

—Elizabeth, m. (2nd wife), Colonel James Callaway;—Jenny.

—Jeffrey moved, 1784, to Georgia, where he left descendants; sold 937 acres on Staunton river.

—Jubal, m. Mary, dau. of Dr. Henry Cheatham; lived in Franklin county; these were the grandparents of General Jubal A. Early and Captain Sam'l Hy Early of Lynchburg.

—Sarah m. William, son of Jacob Anderson and lived near the present Leesville.

—Abner, m. Docia, sister of William Anderson.

The first wife of Colonel Early died about 1770 and he married, 2nd, Mary, sister of Richard Stith in 1773, died a few years later and was buried within his home grounds. At the division of Bedford, three years afterwards, this property near Evington, cut off into the new county, was inherited by his youngest son, Abner, the only one of seven sons who remained in the county.

The Church of England naturally fell under the bann after the Revolution, and churches of other sects then started. Rev. Abner Early, a follower of Wesley, called "itinerant preacher," travelled around the country in a two-wheeled vehicle like a phaeton but then named "gig." In 1819 he and his wife deeded to his sons and others as trustees, a certain lot on the east side of Flat creek, 1 1-16 acres for the use of the Methodist church. He built at his expense a meeting house which he named *Reheboth*, and with his own hands made the holy table and communion rail. This old church is on Flat creek near Early's mill; when the latter structure was sold the purchaser had to search Lunenburg court to get the record: fire destroyed the mill some years afterwards. Abner Early did not approve of slave-holding and freed 100 of his negroes, who took the name of Freeman. Among early court orders was one appointing surveyors to view a way for alteration of the Richmond road leading through Early's land. In 1804 he was made overseer of the poor. A cousin, Buford Early, his partner in mercantile business, was murdered in 1806, and Abner administered on the estate: Buford was a brother of Bishop John Early. Children of Abner:

—Jacob, m. in 1818, Elizabeth Fitz Patrick, dau. of James Austin; bought 200 acres on Quarry branch known as the Cross Road tract, afterwards called Yellow Branch, moved in 1835, to La Porte, Indiana, where his son, John P., became a prominent politician.

—Henry T., m., in 1821, Peggy D. Haden; their son, Abner, m. Mary A. Kabler; in 1874 Abner and Mary K. Early made a deed of transfer to the Presbyterian church of a tract of land on the west side of the road leading to Leesville in consideration of her interest in the cause of religion, and of his desire to promote the moral welfare of the community.

—Sallie, m., in 1827, Claiborne Porter.

—Elizabeth, m., in 1822, Abner Anthony.

—William, m., in 1833, Mary C. Jennings; moved to Wellington C. H., on the Mississippi.

—John W., m. Miss Lauderdale; family moved to California.

—Matilda, m. A. Pannill.

—Col. Edmund J., m. Ann, dau. of Samuel C. and Jane H. Tardy; inherited his grand-father's old manor place, but grief at the loss there of several children caused him to dispose of that property and build a home, *Oakwood,* a short distance from the old one; Edmund Early was a colonel of militia during War of 1861-65. Children:

—Leverette S. (V. M. I. cadet and Confederate veteran), m. Jean B., dau. of Littlebearry Moon, near Leesville; 2 daughters, and son, Dr. L. S. Early, of Petersburg), moved from the county.

—Dr. Maurice B. moved to New York, where he died.

—Laura J. m. Goggin Moorman, died 1924.

—Peachy H. moved to Washington.

Evans

Two Evans families appear on Campbell records. The first represented by Matthew Evans, who patented 400 acres on both sides of Reedy creek in the section then embraced in Lunenburg. In 1782 William Evans was allotted 204¾ acres, on Wreck Island creek, together with Tarleton Patterson. Evans gave a power of attorney to Charles Lynch, Jr., upon Lynch's payment of £100, he having become the real legatee of Benjamin Clement by purchase of Evans' share of Clement's estate in 1790. Arden and Susanna Evans sold Richard Bloxsam, of Louisa, 384 acres lying on Hills and Cheese creeks.

Rees (written also Rice, Welsh Rhys) Evans, born 1719, died 1813, came from Wales to Chester county, Pennsylvania, in 1752, and two years later to Virginia, settling in Campbell near present Concord station on Norfolk and Western railroad. The receipt for payment of his ocean passage is preserved by descendants and is as follows: "Received of Rice Evans eleven pounds, five shillings (£ English), in full for passage of himself, wife and child from Dublin to Philadelphia, April 7, 1752," signed, Nathan Stokes. The wife was Bridget Evans, and child, his eldest son, Daniel.

In 1776 Rees Evans acquired 340 acres on Naked creek of Falling river, which had been granted to David Rankin of Bedford county in 1771 and which Evans gave to his son Daniel in 1792, at the same time gave him a title to the land upon which he lived, stipulating that Daniel pay his sister, Letty, £20, and, with the further condition that Daniel furnish his father and mother a comfortable maintenance on the plantation during the remainder of their lives. Rees' will, recorded in 1813, made Daniel executor of his estate, gave the widow her dower, provided for the sale of his personal property and for distribution of the proceeds in five lots, respectively, to his heirs, John Davis, John Bryan, Thomas Franklin, Lewis Lewis and Sampson Evans. Children of Rees Evans:

—Daniel, born 1750, married Jane . . . .; had children:— Eleanor, born 1781;—Rees, born, 1783, m. 1835, Martha J., the dau. of James Robertson. He was a militia captain;— Thomas, born 1785, m. Miss Robertson; sons, Dr. Daniel S., of *Cherry Hill* and Dr. Thomas W., of *Mon's View;* he was a militia colonel;—Letitia, born 1789, and Bridget, born 1793.

—Sampson, born 1752, served in the Revolutionary War, was a pensioner of same; aged 81 years in 1835. He bought of his brother, Daniel, 225 acres at the head waters of Falling river in 1783, a tract which had been conveyed to Daniel in 1770. Sampson also owned land around Concord.

—Elizabeth, born 1759;—Nancy A., born 1764;—Catherine, born 1766;—Letitia, born 1769.

Major Daniel J., Jr., son of Captain Rees Evans, resides at *Gypsy Farm,* near Concord, married Lillian, the dau. of Lewis, grand-daughter of Colonel Robert Franklin of the Pilot Mountain estate. He received the title of major of the 117th militia regiment by commission from Governor Henry Wise, entered the Confederate army as orderly sergeant, later made lieutenant of the "Appomattox Invincibles," which was numbered Company "C" of the 20th Battalion of heavy artillery. Afterwards he was detailed to the commissary department with title of captain, and was acting as such in Richmond at its evacuation, under General John C. Breckenridge, escaping over Mayo's bridge after it had been set afire by the Federal forces. His commissary supplies became seized, and his fine horse, which he had loaned to a wounded soldier, was also taken, and he was captured, sent to Washington, and thence to Johnson's Island. Upon returning to Campbell, after release from prison, he followed the profession of teaching. Now retired from business activities, he resides at his home near Concord, advanced in years but mentally well preserved and with keen interest in community affairs. His daughter, Martha, also adopted the profession of teaching and now holds a position in Concord school.

In 1753 Robert Evans patented 400 acres lying on Dry creek adjoining the land of Owen Franklin.

Edward S. Evans, the head of E. S. Evans & Company, of Detroit, Michigan, and the country's foremost loading and shipping engineer, (of Lynchburg parentage), was born in that city in 1880; his father was one time owner and editor of the *Lynchburg Advance,* and his mother a member of the William Murrell family, long resident in the town. Evans mastered the science of automobile loading, turning out loading blocks and crates by millions. Success came to him after many trials and failures, and his early efforts were hampered by ill health and disappointments. It is claimed that he saved the automobile business $60,000,000 and that 90% of all automobiles loaded for shipment are crated, blocked and secured with Evans' material and under Evans' controlled patents. He owns lumber mills and forests in seven states and Canada, from which he draws his timber supplies and is the largest industrial user of pine lumber in America. He heads his own bond and investment house, is vice-president of a national advertising agency and secretary-treasurer of a motor-truck manufacturing company.

Another member of the above Murrell family was Dr. David Murrell, of Paducah, Kentucky, who was at the head of a hospital in that city. He married Cornelia Randolph, of Louisiana, who survives him.

Floyd

Dr. Nathaniel Wilson Floyd, born 1793 near Louisville, Ky., son of Captain Charles and Mary Stewart-Floyd (of Hanover county), who accompanied George Rogers Clark to Kentucky, married in 1819 at *Locust Grove,* Bedford county, Elizabeth West, the daughter of Major John Nelson Anderson (who served in the Revolution under "Light-Horse" Harry Lee), and his wife, Elizabeth West, daughter of Captain John Jones, also a Revolutionary officer, and wife, Frances Barbour, daughter of Lane and grand-daughter of Orlando Jones, noted lawyer of Williamsburg, whose father, Roland Jones, was the first rector of Bruton parish. Mary Stewart was the daughter of Captain John Stewart and Annie Haw, his wife, of Henrico county. Dr. Floyd bought land on Ivy creek, Campbell county, about 1820, and erected a home there, calling it *Brookfield,* a few miles west of Lynchburg. He discontinued the practice of medicine, died 1866, his wife in 1883; children:

—Charles Anderson, m. Mildred, the daughter of Hardin Perkins; enlisted in the Confederate cavalry company under Colonel Radford, and was killed April 6th, 1865 in the battle at Sailor's creek; left a family of nine children.

—Captain Nathaniel Bedford, m. Ellen M. Stith, of Texas; was a member of the 6th Texas Regiment of the Confederate army.

—Captain Nicolas Jackson, m. Mary M. Morrow of Louisiana; served under General Wilcox in the Confederate army.

—Annie Pauline, m. Colonel Henry Ward Adams of "The Mansion," and "Monteflora," near Alta Vista, Campbell county.

—Mary Amelia, m. James Aug. Wiggins, of Alabama.

—Elizabeth West, m. Alexander Spotswood Perkins of Alabama.

—John Buchanon, m. Fannie M. Harris, of Alabama; he served in General Wheeler's cavalry of the Confederate army.

—Letitia Preston, m. Captain John C. Featherston, of Alabama, who had been wounded at the battle of Gettysburg and was brought to Dr. Floyd's home, where he was nursed to health. He was son of Howell Colston Featherston of Alabama, and his wife, Dulaney Odom. Captain Featherston entered the C. S. army as lieutenant of the 9th Alabama Regiment, Wilcox's brigade, and was promoted to the captaincy. He lived at *Evergreen,* near Lynchburg, but during the later years of his life purchased a home in the city to which he moved his family. Elected to Virginia Legislature in 1896, he

served eight years: was a member at the art commission for placing bronze statues of George Washington and Robert E. Lee in Statuary Hall at Washington Capitol. He was appointed business agent for Virginia Farmer's State Grange and United States Agricultural Statistician for Virginia. Children:
—Nathaniel Floyd, held position in Treasury Department, Washington.
—Howell Colston, attorney-at-law, of Lynchburg, represented Campbell county in Virginia Legislature, 1907-08; author of "Origin and History of Lynch Law" an article in "The Green Bag" of Boston.

Franklin

The family of Franklin emigrated from Ecton village, Northamptonshire, England, in 1685; John, founder of the Virginia branch, is supposed to have been a brother of Benjamin Franklin. The name is found among Orange and Culpeper county records about the middle of the 18th century. Owen Franklin in 1773 patented 49 acres on both sides of Morton's creek, a fork of Falling river, and in 1788 bought of Pleasant Branch 182 acres on the south side of Morton's creek, along Thos. Franklin's line, and from Hall's corner to Harris' corner. In 1749 Lewis Franklin patented 850 acres including head branches of Falling river adjoining Edward Nix's line; in 1756 Lewis Franklin patented 118 acres on Callaway's road, between two ridges. In 1793 he patented 215 acres on the south side of Dixon's fork, a head branch of the south fork of Falling river. In 1780 Edmund Franklin patented 252 acres lying upon a branch of Cub creek and Falling river; Edmund and Owen Franklin were ensigns of the Revolutionary army in 1778; Thomas and Thomas P. Franklin were pensioners 75 and 71 in 1835. Owens' will, recorded in 1795, mentions sons, Benjamin and Isaac M. and daughter, Nancy. Robert Franklin administered upon Owens' estate and in 1811 he made complaint that Owen (deceased) who served as deputy sheriff of Campbell had delinquent taxes charged against him for which he was not responsible; he asked that the common-wealth's claims be relinquished.

Colonel Robert Franklin owned an estate near Concord which included Pilot Mountain. He married a Miss Lewis, of Irish birth, who was only eleven years of age. His will recorded in 1831 appointed his sons, Benjamin and Lewis executors, and was witnessed by Robert Franklin, Jr., David Robertson and John Shannon. Children:

—Benjamin . . .
—Margaret, m. John Rosser in 1805.
—Robert, Jr., m. Mary, the dau. of Daniel Perrow.
—Owen . . .
  Mary, m. —— Jennings.
—John M. m. Ann Dinwiddie; had 11 children.
—Lewis, m. Eliza Wood; his daughter, Martha J., m. Daniel Franklin, of Appomattox, and their dau., Lillian, m. Major Daniel J. Evans, near Concord.
—Elizabeth, m. Peter North in 1801.
—Thomas . . .
—Nancy, m. —— Stern.
—Sallie, 1806, m., 1st, Thomas North; m. 2nd, —— Leonard.

Col. Ro. Franklin's will mentioned sons, Owen, John, Lewis, Thomas, Robert and Benjamin, and daughters, Margaret Rosser, Elizabeth North, Sally Leonard, Mary Jennings and Nancy Stern. Lewis Franklin remained in Campbell; other sons seem to have moved away.

Other Franklin marriages: 1794, Elizabeth Franklin m. Alexander Steele;—1794, Milly Franklin m. Arthur Litchford; —1795, Keziah Franklin m. John Thompson;—1805, Elizabeth Franklin m. David Fleming;—1805, Jane Franklin m. John Fleming;—1802, Thomas Franklin, and, 1805, Capt. John Franklin, sons of Edward and Eliza Cook-Franklin, of Appomattox county, married, respectively, Judith E. and Martha J., daughters of William and Sarah C. Anderson of Campbell county. In 1844 Thomas H. Franklin was major of the 117th Va. Mil. Reg.

Garland

The Garlands are allied with the Slaughter family. John Garland, a Welsh emigrant, born 1680, died 1734, had eight children. Of these his son
—James, born 1722, settled in Albemarle county; m. in 1749, Mary, the dau. of David and Mary Howlett-Rice; James Garland, Sr., died in 1812; he had 13 children, his son, James, Jr., born 1753, an officer in the Revolution, was accidentally killed in 1781 at Albemarle Barracks. He married Anne, dau. of John and Mary Hudson-Wingfield, and had 4 children. His three sons were:
—Hudson Martin Garland, attorney-at-law, captain in the war of 1812, and member of the House of Delegates 1805-06 from Amherst; m. Elizabeth Penn Phillips (grand-niece of Wm. Penn).
—James Parker Garland m. Katurah Stone.
—Alexander Spotswood Garland m. Lucinda Rose.
Children of Hudson M. and Elizabeth Phillips-Garland:—Henrietta, m. Rev. Mr. Boyd of the Methodist Episcopal church;—Betsy Ann . . . ;—Maria m ——— Wolfe;—Judge James Garland, of Lynchburg, member of Congress from 1835 to 1841; commonwealth's attorney from 1852 to 1870; corporation judge from 1870 to 1883; blind for many years; died 1883, aged 93 years; his daughters were Mrs. Cole and Mrs. Aurelius Christian of Lynchburg; Hudson Martin, Jr., m. Letitia B. Pendleton;—Gen. John Garland, distinguished in the Mexican War; whose dau. m. Gen. Longstreet.
Children of James Parker and Katurah Stone-Garland:—Bettie . . . ;—Henrietta m. ——— Watts, moved to Alabama;—Addison, U. S. Navy, attempted to land and join the Southern army, but from information given by his wife, was turned back; he died at sea;—Benami Stone;—Alexander;—Catherine Malvina m. 1846, Charles Rice Slaughter, of Lynchburg, son of Dr. Robert Slaughter, of Campbell county;—Al-

thea C. m. ———— Brown, of Alabama, whose daughters returned to Virginia; Kate m. Captain Waite of Petersburg; Lula m. Thomas D. Davis, clerk of Lynchburg court; Bettie m. Charles A. Slaughter, son of Charles R. Slaughter;—Colonel Robert m. Elizabeth Wolfe; he contracted tuberculosis when captured by Federals, and imprisoned; died soon after the war.

Children of Alexander Spottswood and Lucinda Rose-Garland:

—Landon Cabell, Chancellor at Vanderbilt University, Nashville, Tenn; m. Louise Garland. Children—Rose, m. Prof. Lewis of Tuscaloosa Univ.;— Louise, m. Prof. Humphries of University of Virginia;—Maurice, m. Lucy Galt (dau. Mamie, librarian, in Richmond, and son, Herbert, surveyor, in Lynchburg);—Jennie, m. Prof. Smith, of Tuscaloosa Univ.;—Annie m. Prof. Robert Fulton, of Mississippi.

—Hugh m. Ann. Children:—Nannie R. m. Gen. Gilbert Meem*;—Minnie m. Mr. Papan; —Spottswood m. Mary Jenkins;—Maggie m. Robert Hoskins.

—Caroline m. Maurice, Sr., son of Rice and Elizabeth Hamner-Garland, grandson of James, Sr., and Mary Rice-Garland; lived in Lynchburg.

Rice, son of James and Mary Rice Garland, married Elizabeth, dau. of Samuel and Elizabeth Morris Hamner: children: —Samuel, Sr., m. Mary Lightfoot Anderson; he was a member of the legal firm of Garland, Slaughter & Co.; his nephews, Charles R. Slaughter and Samuel Garland, Jr., were included in the partnership.

—Maurice Garland, Sr., m. Caroline, dau. of Alex S. and Elizabeth Hamner-Garland, parents of General Samuel Garland, who m. Eliza, dau. of John Meem of Lynchburg.

—Mary Rice m. Dr. Robert Slaughter of *Oak Hill*, Campbell county.

---

*Four Meem brothers served in the Confederate army: Gen. John Meem, Dr. Russell Meem, Lawrence Meem, adjutant on staff of Gen. Garland, killed at battle of Seven Pines, and General Gilbert Meem.

—Elizabeth Rice m. Henry White of Albemarle; dau., Elizabeth, m. E. C. Hamner;
—Burr;—James;—Hon. Rice;—Austin Garland.

Children of Edward C., Sr., and Elizabeth White-Hamner:
—Samuel Garland Hamner, attorney-at-law, Lynchburg, m. Mary, dau. of Dr. W. R. and Sarah Harrison-Winchester.
—Commander E. C. Hamner, Jr., U. S. Navy, m. Dorothy Lisk, of Beverly, New Jersey.
—Sallie Cole Hamner, assistant librarian at Jones Memorial Library, Lynchburg.
—Bessie, deceased.
—Henry Rawlings Hamner.

Naval Service

Ed. C. Hamner, Jr., son of E. C., Sr., and Elizabeth White-Hamner, of Lynchburg, commander of the Construction Corps, U. S. Navy, was appointed to the United States Naval Academy at Annapolis, as result of competitive examination held by Major Peter J. Otey in 1897.

Entered Naval Academy September 9, 1897, graduated June 1901, and ordered to sea as Watch and Division Officer on the U.S.S. *Lancaster.* In 1902 ordered to the U. S. S. *Brooklyn* as a midshipman, aide to Admiral Coghlan when the *Brooklyn* carried the body of Lord Pauncefort, (British Ambassador to the U. S.), back to England. In 1903 served on the U. S. S. *Indiana* and in June, 1903 was transferred to the U.S.S. *Sylph,* the President's yacht, for duty at Oyster Bay and aide to President Roosevelt. In the fall of 1903 transferred to the U.S.S. *Cleveland* and took part in the Rescue of Predicaris from the bandit Raisuli in Morocco. In 1904 appointed to the Construction Corps and entered the Massachusetts Institute of Technology, Boston, Mass., graduating from there in 1907 with the degree of Master of Science and ordered to duty at the Norfolk Navy Yard. In the fall of 1907 appointed an aide to Admiral Robley D. Evans on his technical staff for the cruise around the world and assigned to the destroyers accompanying the fleet which proceeded from Hampton Roads through the Straits of

Magellan to Mare Island. Stationed at Mare Island one year
and in 1909 transferred to the Phillipine Islands for two and a
half years, holding the positions of Manager of Cavite and
Olongapo Navy Yards. In 1912 ordered to the Navy Yard,
Portsmouth, N. H., as assistant to the Construction Officer;
graduated from the Massachusetts Institute of Technology as
an assistant Naval Constructor and in 1913 promoted to Naval
Constructor, U. S. Navy. In 1916 ordered to New Orleans as
Manager of the Navy Yard, remaining during the war, becoming, in addition to the Manager of the Navy Yard, Manager of
the 8th Naval District, extending from Pensacola, Fla., to the
Mexican border, Head of Inspection Forces for cotton and
lumber in all Southern States and Superintending Constructor
for U. S. Naval vessels building on the Gulf Coast. Detached
from New Orleans late in 1918 and ordered to sea as Fleet Con-
structor to the U. S. Fleet on Admiral Mayo's staff, remaining
in the same position on the staff of Admiral Henry B. Wilson.
Detached in July, 1921, as Fleet Constructor and ordered as
Assistant Naval Attaché to the American Embassy, Court of
St. James, London, England, with additional duties as assistant Naval Attaché at Paris, France, Berlin, Germany, and
Rome, Italy. Detached in September, 1923, and ordered as
Superintending Constructor of the Union Plant, Bethlehem
Ship Building Co., San Francisco, Calif., with additional duties
as Member of the Board of Inspection and Survey for vessels
on the Pacific Coast. In February, 1924, ordered as Manager
of the Navy Yard, Pearl Harbor, Hawaiian Territory, and in
the summer of 1926 detached from this duty and ordered as
Construction Officer of the Navy Yard, New York, N. Y., and
so serving at this time.

Gilliam

First record of Gilliam name in Brunswick county (divided
to form Lunenburg) was in 1745.

John Gilliam in 1756 patented land on the south side of
Roanoke river (Staunton) adjoining property already in his .

possession. In 1780 Zachariah Gilliam patented 562 acres on both sides of Difficult creek, the north branch of Goose creek.

In 1796 Charles Gilliam was one of the administrators of Stephen Perrow's estate. In 1807 Archibald and Sarah Bolling sold Richard Gilliam 100 acres of land.

Gilliams had settled in Buckingham and Prince Edward counties; Richard was the son of Epaphroditus and Elizabeth Gilliam: Epaphroditus died in 1789; his son, Richard, born in 1760, married Elizabeth Glover, born in 1775, whose son, Dr. Glover D. Gilliam was born in 1800. There is a family connection between these Gilliams and Glover Davenport who married Ann P. Slaughter.

In 1827 Dr. Glover Davenport Gilliam of Prince Edward county married Elizabeth Bolling, the daughter of James S. Jones. In 1837 he purchased of William and Lucy F. Robinson several tracts of land lying on Falling river and its branches, one tract including a grist and saw mill, was bounded by the lands of Freeman Moore and John Cobbs. Another tract of 386 acres had been sold to Robinson by Publius Jones and Thomas Rudd, together with 98 adjoining acres; 418 acres lay on both sides of Hickory creek, a tract which had been sold Rudd by John Paul Redd, and 280 acres Rudd had bought of Samuel Morris' heirs, and Thomas and David Jones, formerly belonging to Harfield, on Hickory creek, a branch of Falling river. By various purchases Dr. Gilliam acquired a large landed estate. His place of residence, about 2 miles from Naruna, is called *Landover,* and is situated on Falling river. Several generations of the family were born there. Dr. Gilliam's will, recorded in 1852, mentions daughters:—Eloise G., m. Richard Booker;—Eliza B., m. ——— Price of Texas;—Amanda J., m. Richard Adams;—Olivia F. m. Thos. Woodring;—Martha Virginia m. ——— Epperson; son, Glover E. Epperson, served in the C. S. army. Sons:—James R., m. Annie Davenport, his son, James R., Jr., m. Jessie Johnson, was a successful financier of Lynchburg; whose son, James R., 3rd (Sec. and Treas. Lynchburg Trust and Savings Bank), resides in the Peakland addition of Lynchburg.

—Edward G., m. Emma Gilbert.

—Walter Floyd m. Virginia Hamlet; lived at *Landover,* near Naruna; his dau., Rosa, is the principal of Naruna High School.

—Thomas West m. Fannie Diuguid; he was a successful financier of Lynchburg; his dau., Elsie, served as a missionary.

—Emma m. George Gilbert.

Goggin

The Goggin family was of Anglo-Saxon ancestry. Their original name is said to have been De Cogan, and they were domiciled in South Ireland. Stephen Goggin, Sr., came to Virginia in 1742 from Queen's county, Ireland. He was a member of the Episcopal church. In 1759 he patented 204 acres of land on Flat creek, and in 1773 patented 452 acres lying on both sides of Flat creek. In 1791 Richard Goggin married Nancy Irvine; Richard was probably son of Stephen, Sr. Children of Stephen:

—Stephen, Jr., m. Rachel, dau. of Thomas and Rachel Clark-Moorman; their children were Pamela, m. in 1797, Samuel Clemens;—Polly m. Alexander Gill;—Nancy m. Obadiah Tate; William m. Pamela Tate; Elizabeth m., 1st, Samuel Fulkes; m., 2nd, John B. Witt; Thomas m. Mary Walden; Pleasant M. m. Mary O. Leftwich; Stephen (3rd) m. Janette Robertson.

Mary O., wife of Colonel Pleasant M. Goggin, was the dau. of Rev. Wm. Leftwich (who went by the name of "Black-head Leftwich," and was son of William and grandson of Augustine Leftwich, Sr.) and his wife, Frances, dau. of Col. John Otey. Col. P. M. Goggin was a member of the Virginia Legislature. He died in 1831. Children:

—William L., married twice, Misses Cook, who were cousins of each other. His son, Samuel Cook Goggin, m., 1st, Lizzie D., dau. of Littleberry and Martha P. Moon; m., 2nd, Elsie Lee, dau. of Wm. A. Jones. S. C. Goggin was county clerk of Campbell from 1893 till 1925, when he was succeeded by C.

W. Woodson, his son-in-law.
—Lucian Buonaparte, born 1810, m. Anne J. Curtis.
—Emily, born 1812, m. Edmund Matthews; their dau., Mrs. Cornelia Jordan, was a Lynchburg poetess; a volume of her poems were published by her dau., Mrs. Ambler.
—John O. L., attorney-at-law of Lynchburg, m. Susan S. Holt.
—Elizabeth Frances, born 1818, m. Thomas B. Moorman.
—James Monroe, born 1820, m. Elizabeth Nelson Page.
—Sarah Paulina, born 1828, m. John R. Steptoe.

Hon. Wm. Leftwich Goggin was a member of Virginia Legislature in 1837, and member of Congress 1839-41-43-47; was one of the Visitors to West Point Academy. In 1859 he was an unsuccessful candidate for governor of Virginia; a member of the Richmond Convention of 1861; served in the Confederate army. Colonel Lucien B. Goggin moved to Mason county, Kentucky; served in both houses of Kentucky Legislature.

James M. Goggin, attorney-at-law, was special agent of the Post Office Department to California; established post offices and post-roads in northern California and Southern Oregon. He then moved to Tennessee. He organized a battalion of infantry in the 32nd Virginia Regiment; commanded a brigade at the battle of Cedar Creek; moved to Texas in 1889.
—John Goggin, brother of Stephen, Jr., m., 1777, Lucy Branch. He was a lieutenant in the Continental army.

Hairston

The three Hairston brothers who settled in Bedford were of Scotch origin. Their father, Peter Hairston, the son of Sir Robert, friend and follower of Robert Bruce, left Scotland after the battle of Culloden, having fought on the losing side, sailed for Virginia and landed in Norfolk. First purchased land in North Garden, Albemarle. He had three sons, Samuel, Andrew and Robert, and a daughter, Mrs. Phillips. In 1743 Samuel Hairston purchased of Major William Reed 400 acres on the branches of Rockfish river near the Blue Ridge mountains. In 1746 Andrew had acquired land on branches of Rockfish. In 1747 Samuel and Robert were living in the upper part of St. Anne's parish, Albemarle county. Samuel Hairston was one of the justices of Bedford court in 1754; surveyor of roads and commissioned captain of militia in 1755; appointed surveyor in 1756 from where Callaway's bounds left off to Blackwater Road below Long Mountain; commissioned sheriff in 1757; received 1248 lbs. of tobacco in payment for his services; allowed 500 lbs. of tobacco for going to Williamsburg for commission of the peace and sheriff's commission; was burgess from Bedford 1758 to 1761, with salary of 5522 lbs. of tobacco; major of militia in 1757; the first justice to take oath of office in the new county of Campbell and was appointed with John Callaway to meet the commissioners from Bedford to run the dividing line between the two counties.

In 1781 Samuel Hairston purchased of Charles Caffery, Jr., a large tract of land on the east branches of Beaver creek, both sides of the main road, lying on a spur of Long Mountain for £10,000, and shortly afterwards sold 300 acres of it lying on the creek's branches, beginning at Brown's and Lynch's dividing lines on the west side of Cooper's Mountain, to William Hawkins. Hairston died in 1782 and having no family of his own, devised his manor place and 1060 acres of land to his brother Andrew for his 3 daughters; also 2 tracts of Kentucky land of 2000 and 318 acres respectively, with exception of 400 acres to be deducted and otherwise disposed of. Andrew dying the same year bequeathed his estate to his wife and daughters, having already provided for his two sons, Peter and Hugh. Of the three elder Hairston brothers, Samuel was ensign and lieutenant, Andrew sergeant and Robert ensign and sergeant in the French and Indian War of 1758, with the Bedford county troops. In 1755, Robert Hairston was lieutenant of militia, overseer of roads, and assignee of Jeremiah Rust in 1757; bought of Thomas Cooper 300 acres on both sides of Opossum creek and sold the tract next year to George Stovall, Jr., his brother-in-law. In 1759 he was captain of Bedford militia. He moved to Henry county, where his sons, Peter and George also settled; served as a member of the House of Representatives. Upon leaving Campbell county he sold Andrew Moorman 443 acres in Lunenburg county on both sides of Pheasant creek by Murray's and Williams' lines. Robert Hairston married Ruth, the daughter of George Stovall, Sr., clerk of the House of Burgesses and had three sons and seven daughters. Samuel, son of Robert Hairston, moved to Franklin county; served in the war of 1812, first as lieutenant, later as colonel; his sword and commission are preserved by descendants, who have portraits of him, which were made for each one of his children. He married Judith, the daughter of Peter Hyde and Mary Sparrell Saunders, who was sister of Judge Fleming Saunders of Flat Creek, Campbell.

Hanks

James Hanks of Hat Creek seems to have been the first of his name to purchase land in Campbell county. In 1787 he sold, to Daniel Walker, of Charlotte, 150 acres on the east branches of Hat creek along Mitchell's line to Hank's spring branch. The witnesses to the deed were Thomas, Sarah and Tabitha Hanks. Abraham Hanks bought of James and Thomas Hanks 50 acres of land on Hat creek.

Tabitha Hanks m. Samuel Barnes in 1792; Abraham m. in 1799 Lucy Jennings. Abraham Hanks died in Campbell and was buried in Hat creek churchyard. Among the marriage bonds is found one from Thomas Hanks and James Brooks to Gov. Henry Lee Oct. 23, 1792, of a marriage to be solemnized between Thos. Hanks and Nancy Brooks, both of Campbell county, Wm. Alexander (deputy clerk of court then) the witness, and attached to the bond a note of authority dated 22d, signed by Nancy and Fannie Brooks. To Thomas and Nancy Hanks was born a daughter, who was named Nancy Hanks. Based upon these records a tradition prevails in the county that Abraham Lincoln owed his ancestry to this Campbell family on the maternal side and that he inherited his name from, Abraham Hanks.

But in "A Story of Lincoln's Mother," Caroline Hanks-Hitchcock traced the family from an Englishman, Benjahim Hanks (who first settled in Plymouth county, Mass.), whose son, William, came to Amelia county, Va., a record of which she found in the Hall of Records at Richmond, Va. According to her account, Joseph Hanks of this branch, married Nancy Shipley and moved to Nelson county, Kentucky; their youngest daughter, Nancy, in 1806, married Thomas Lincoln (also of Virginia ancestry), in Beechland, Ky., and three years later their son, Abraham, was born.

Similarity of name and date has caused many genealogical errors and may have in this instance. There is a singular coincidence in the fact that but one member of the Hanks family came to Virginia and settled during the latter part of the 18th century in Amelia, an adjoining county to Lunenburg, a part of which latter county by division became Campbell, where also were the Shipleys (who were Quakers and would naturally affiliate with the nearest Meeting, i. e., South river, Campbell), and that the Hanks' given names were repeated in a Campbell family bearing the same surname about the same period, as the Hitchcock book gives to the Amelia county settlers. Thomas Lincoln moved to Kentucky in 1782, but descendants of the branch of the Lincoln family which remained in Virginia are living in Rockingham county and yet bear that name.

Haythe

1761 William Heath served in a corps raised for defense of state, commanded by Colonel Byrd. The first Heath settled in Northumberland county; the name originally Heath is so spelt in early records. Heathsville is said to have acquired its name from this family. In 1757 William Heath patented 39 acres of land on the north side of Staunton river. In 1771 he patented 333 acres on the south branch of Molley's creek; also 91 acres on the south side of Staunton river. In the last deed his name is spelt Haythe. The same year Thomas Heath patented 250 acres on both sides of the south fork of Bear creek, including its head, and in 1850 Thomas patented 220 acres on the west branches of Molley's creek.

William Haythe first made his home on Long Island, Staunton river; he married Martha . . . His will, written in 1775 mentions sons:—Jesse;—Thomas, m. Martha Gilbert, of Pittsylvania: daughters—Elizabeth Manley;—Eleanor Burgess;—Mary Christian; —and Sarah Cunningham.

In 1794 Haythe sold the Long Island estate and moved to land near Pigeon Run adjoining the property of Robert Alexander. In 1781 Thomas Haythe was a first lieutenant in the Revolutionary army, then promoted to captain. Children—Charles, moved to Chillicothe, Ohio;—Pleasant;—Gilbert, m. Elizabeth Rucker, dau. of an Episcopal minister of Harris creek, Amherst Co.;—John m. . . .; children, Eliza A. and John, Jr.;—William, m. in 1800, Polly Moorman; he sold 264½ acres of land to Alex. S. Henry in 1827;—Benjamin, m., in 1811, Ann E. Ramsay;—Thomas, Jr.;—Jennie Hall.

Thomas Haythe (2nd) devised his mansion house and 300 acres to his wife and appointed her and son, Gilbert, executors of his estate.

Martha G. Haythe, daughter of Wm. and Polly M. Haythe, m., in 1835, William (son of Allan and Jane T. Woodson), and settled in Botetourt county; their son, Blake Lynch Woodson, a student at Lynchburg College, was made lieutenant in the "Lynchburg Beauregards," then promoted in the Confederate army; was a member of Virginia Legislature from Fincastle in 1868-71 ; a partner of R. E. Cowan, until Cowan was elected to the Supreme Bench, married, 1st, Lelia, daughter of Colonel William E. Word, moved to Kansas City, m., 2nd, Nora Delaney of Kansas City. Patsy Haythe m., in 1801, David Layne.

John G. Haythe, son of Gilbert and Elizabeth R. Haythe, married Cornelia F., daughter of Dr. Madison Haden of Evington, Campbell county; he was appointed by Underwood, judge of the county court under the new constitution; in 1866 he moved with his family to Lynchburg. Children:—Massie (dec.) ;—Otway;— John, Jr., and Mrs. Jas. Mason.

Henry

A tract of land purchased by Patrick Henry in Campbell, near Marysville, bearing the name of *The Grove,* because finely wooded, was never built upon, and the fine grove of oaks which so enhanced its value, was cut down some years ago to give place for a crop. In 1796 he patented 200 acres on the east side

Shady Grove, Home of Spottswood Henry

of Falling river and 125 acres on both sides of that stream. Various tracts of land in Campbell were purchased for the benefit of his children. One not far from Pigeon Run (now Gladys), was given to his son, Captain Spotswood Henry and *Shady Grove,* which yet stands in good condition, was built upon it by Dr. George Cabell. This is a large building upon a stone foundation and contains many rooms. The cornice, windows and porch framing are ornamented with beading, honeycomb, and dental work, and it has an arched doorway leading into the front hall, with panelled chair-boarding. An attractive feature of the interior is the beautiful hand-wrought parlor mantel, patterned with a central basket of flowers and pineapple, the symbol of hospitality, at either side, and festooned across the top, a tasselled wreath. Had this old home been situated in a more travelled section, information concerning it and consequent interest would have become more general.

Alexander Spotswood Henry, born 1788, married, in 1814,

Mantel in Home of Spottswood Henry

Paulina (the daughter of Dr. George Cabell of *Point of Honor,* near Lynchburg), lived at *Shady Grove,* and died in 1854. Children:

—George Lafayette, m. Miss Mason, and had 3 sons and 2 daughters.

—Dr. Patrick m. Clara Yancey; had no children.

—John Robert, m. Elizabeth, dau. of W. H. Edwards of Pittsylvania; 4 daughters, 2 sons.

—Sarah W., m. Dr. George Cabell Carrington; 4 sons and 2 daughters.

—Pauline, m. Bartlett Jones, of Danville; son, Cabell Jones.

—Marion F. C., m. Samuel Tyree, tobacconist and realtor of Lynchburg, s. p.

—Antoinette, m. Andrew Hambrick, of Roanoke, s. p.

Captain Spotswood Henry owned a fine library to which he devoted much time and attention, and this caused him to be regarded as a gentleman of leisure, hence there originated, in his community, the saying "clerking to Captain Henry," intended to convey the meaning that the person to whom it was applied was without apparent occupation.

Shady Grove was acquired by Terrell Morgan, who gave it to his son, Richard, and the latter resided there many years, but later sold the place to Captain William C. Perrow, who moved his family there; later still it was acquired by the Suddith family from Brookneal who still occupy it.

Holcombe

At what time the Holcombes, of Scotch descent, came to the Virginia colony, is not now known. Captain Philemon Holcombe, Sr., a veteran of French and Indian wars, is recorded as rendering valuable services in 1756, the year of General Braddock's fatal march. In 1776 he was one of the founders of Hampden-Sidney College and one of its first officials at the time when James Madison and Patrick Henry were among the trustees. Major Philemon Holcombe, Jr., was in the second Regiment of General Lawson's brigade at the battle of Guilford C. H., N. C., in 1781, being attached to the cavalry command of Colonel William Washington; later he served under Baron Steuben, and was with La Fayette at Yorktown and witnessed the surrender of Cornwallis. He lived at *The Oaks,* in Amelia county and was known as "Colonel Holcombe of Virginia." His son, Philemon Holcombe, Jr., married Lucy Maria, born 1756, the daughter of Thomas Anderson of Mecklenburg county, deriving her second name from a great grandmother, Henrietta Maria (for-

merly a maid of honor at the court of Austria and said to be
related to the imperial family), who, with her husband, Baron
Hardeman, emigrated to Virginia and settled in Charles City
county.—Thomas Anderson Holcombe, son of Philemon, Jr.,
and Lucy M. Holcombe, married Mary Royal and lived in
Lynchburg. His daughter, Eliza Holcombe, m. Walter Henderson, and their daughter, Mary Elizabeth, m. George Henry
Caperton, whose daughter, Janie Erskine, m. Massie Warwick
and lives in Charleston, W. Va.—Lucy Holcombe Pickens,
daughter of Beverley Holcombe, youngest brother of Thomas
A., was for many years a regent of Mount Vernon. Thomas
A. Holcombe was one of the elders of the New School Presbyterians, and active in the organization of the Second Presbyterian church of Lynchburg in 1830, when Rev. Daniel L. Russell
served as supply there, and was followed by Rev. J. D. Mitchell.
Mason's Hall was first used for their religious services, then
for two years a store house on Main street, between 6th and 7th
was secured and upon this lot a frame church was built, later
that building was used as a furniture store and was given the
name of "the sacred furniture shop." Their last church, known
as *Westminster*, a brick structure at the corner of Church and
9th streets has recently been sold and a more capacious church
built further out of the city on Floyd and 11th streets. In 1815
Thomas Holcombe conducted a boys' school in Lynchburg, and
in 1824 he was mayor of the city. William J. Holcombe was
on the board of trustees for establishing a Lynchburg Free
School, for the education of poor children, which became incorporated in 1823, as the Lynchburg Charity School. A disturbance arising among the Methodists in the community
caused charges to be preferred against William J. Holcombe
"for endeavoring to sow dissensions in the church by inveigh-
ing against the discipline," which resulted in the disaffected
members uniting in formation of the Methodist Protestant
church in 1828. The corner stone for their place of worship
was laid upon the lot where the present church stands, and Dr.
Thomas Holcombe made the address at the dedicatory service.

Hughes

Benjamin Hughes, born 1763 in Hanover county, was a son of Henry and Margaret Hughes. At the age of sixteen he enlisted as a private in the Virginia troops under Captains Elisha White, Samuel White, Samuel Hubbard, Wm. Tinsley, Thomas Richardson, and Wm. Anderson,—Cols. James Monroe, Mercer, Seawell and Winston. He was in the battles of Brandywine, Malvern Hill, Charles City Court House, and seige of Yorktown; and served altogether about three years. His father's home was burned, but the family records were recorded in the parish register of the Rev. Patrick Henry, who was a neighbor and friend of the family. After the Revolution, Hughes moved to Bedford but in 1805 settled in Campbell. He married a daughter of Littleberry Tucker, of Hanover and was joined in Campbell by his wife's brother, Thomas Tucker. The name Littleberry is preserved in the Hughes family. Children of Benjamin Hughes:

—Littleberry m., 1st, Winifred, daughter of Clement Jordan, who lived at *Far View,* near Gladys. Children,—[1]Emory, enlisted in Confederate army, killed at Gettysburg;—[2]Benjamin, died upon return from the war;—[3] Clement served in the war, moved afterwards to Tennessee;—[4]Patrick;— [5]Susan;—[6]Nancy;—[7]Julia Anne and —[8]Parthenia, m. Jabez Snow. Littleberry m., 2nd, Mrs. Tucker, neê Plunkett, widow of Charles Tucker; children, [9]Thomas;—[10] Sarah Alice; —[11]Margaret; — [12]Charles; — [13]Frank; — [14]Bowling. Mrs. Tucker had five children of her first marriage. Littleberry Hughes m., 3rd, Dionysia Oakes. Children:—[20]Mary;— [21]Virginia;—[22]Tabitha;—[23]Robert, making a household of 23 children.

Daughters of Benjamin Hughes were:—Margaret, m. —— Strong;—Alice, m. —— Roberts;—Katherine, m. —— Roberts;—Tabitha, unmarried.

Benjamin Hughes, while resident in Campbell, made application in 1833 for a pension for his Revolutionary War service, which then was allowed him. He moved to Tennessee, and in 1835 was living in Smith county, sixty miles from Nashville; died 1838, leaving a widow. Littleberry Hughes died 1890, aged 94 years. Patrick, (son of Littleberry), who died young was lively and mischievous. It was the custom of one of the neighborhood preachers, whom Patrick disliked, to spend week-ends at his home. On one occasion, he turned his horse over to young Patrick with the caution, "Feed him high, Patrick, feed him high." The boy disappeared for the day and after dinner, to the chagrin of the preacher, the horse was discovered standing on his hind legs, endeavoring to reach the bundle of oats which was tied to the rafters of the stable. Patrick could not resist the opportunity for his joke, even at expense of the horse. Robert Hughes, youngest son of Littleberry, lives at the old home, *Far View,* two miles west of Gladys. Charles H. Hughes resides at Gladys.

Emory Hughes (killed in battle), had married a sister of James Hughes of a different Campbell family, yet bearing the same name. James Hughes owned property on Ward's Road in the Yellow Branch section, and was the father of Emory and B. E. Hughes of Lynchburg.

Hunter

The founder of the Hunter family was of Scotch ancestry. John Hunter, Sr., came to America from Scotland in colonial times and settled near Fredericksburg, Va., married Henrietta Davidson and had four children, of whom John, Jr., the eldest, married Rachel McFarland and moved south of James river, fourteen or fifteen miles below Lynchburg to a homestead called *Clover Green.* He patented 400 acres on both sides of Russell's creek, 1751, in Lunenburg county. Children:

—John, 3rd, a surveyor by profession, and a Revolutionary War pensioner in 1835, had also served in the Indian War of 1758 as sergeant in a Bedford company, his father being captain of an Albemarle company during the same war. In 1768 John Hunter patented 90 acres on Falling river; his former patent located land on Russell, a branch of Mayo. John Hunter was among the first justices of Campbell. In 1873 he was appointed sheriff with Alexander Hunter, his deputy; again sheriff in 1789 with Josias Bullock as deputy. In 1811 the people of Bedford, Botetourt, Campbell and Greenbrier counties petitioned for the establishment of the Great Western Turnpike from Hunter's, on the main Richmond road through Lynchburg, to Lewisburg, Greenbrier county. John Hunter married Mrs. Mary Stith-Early, sister of Richard Stith and widow (2nd wife) of Colonel Jeremiah Early.

—Robert lived and died at Clover Green, his father's old home, and had a large family, though his will, written in 1827, mentions only his sons, Robert to whom he had lent money, and Ellis, who, with Robert, was appointed executor; and a daughter, Jane S. Rogers, to whom he had also advanced money. A $30,000 bond was required of the executors, for which Washington Hunter furnished security.

1815—Robert Hunter, Jr., patented land, 85½ acres adjoining Jones, Glass, Tanner and Martin, on Reedy creek, and Stonewall road. Colonel Richard Lewis Hunter, youngest son of Robert, Sr., moved to Milledgeville, Ga., and his daughter, Molly, married Judge L. C. Hall of Dardanelles, Arkansas. In 1813 Robert Hunter patented 28 acres on the ridge between Wreck Island and Reedy creeks. Thomas Hunter, in 1795, married Jemmia Fields, and patented land, 14¾ acres, adjoining Jones and Wilson. John Hunter patented 1100 acres on Martin's creek and a branch of Falling river in 1815. Robert Hunter added to his Reedy creek land in 1844.

—Elizabeth married John May of North Carolina.

—James patented land on Wreck Island creek in 1770, moved in 1804 to Russellville, Logan county, Ky.; Rev. Hiram A. Hunter was his son.

—Alexander patented land on the bottom which leads to Mulberry creek, east branch of the north fork of Falling river in 1819. He was an eccentric character, and gave himself the nickname of "Devil" Aleck.

—Major Benjamin Hunter remained in Campbell, had a family of 13 children, and has many descendants in the county.

Descendants of John Hunter, Sr., still reside in Hat Creek neighborhood.

Irvine

The Irvine name of the Scotch settlers who first came to old Bedford is recorded variously as Irvin, Irvine, Irwin and Erwin; and a branch of the latter retains that name to this day. But the Irish Irvin, who located around Hat creek, continued that manner of spelling, only later adding the final letter "e," always in connection with Major John Irvine. The distance in neighborhood prevents confusion of the Irish and Scotch families, though members of both Irvines were active in county affairs. The Scotch emigrants, settling a little later than the Irish.

John Irvin, native of Ireland and Presbyterian in religious belief, married Mary (Molly) Boyd, also born and reared in the Emerald Isle. They happened upon difficult times there, and news of easy living in America induced them to emigrate soon after their marriage. They landed in Pennsylvania, where he acquired land and remained in that state for twenty years; and there all of their children were born. Again reports concerning a land of promise caused him to sell the Pennsylvania land, which had increased in value, and make a preliminary visit to Virginia, in the mountain section, where land could be obtained without great outlay of money. His purpose was to select a place and prepare a home for his family before removing them. Making choice of Hat creek locality, he took up all the land lying in its vicinity for four or five miles; found only one very old white man living within many miles, and his plantation was the first one to be cultivated in a district of thirty-five or forty miles extent. After making necessary arrangements for their reception, he returned for his family, ten white souls and Sam and Moll, two negro servants. Irvin had not long been settled before newcomers began to pour into the neighborhood, and many of these purchased tracts of the land which he had acquired in large acreage. His sales continued over a period of many years, for he sold Charles Cobbs 100 acres on the north side of Falling river extending to James Gates' lines, in 1784, over four decades from the time when he had become a landholder there. In 1805 John Irvine settled up the estate of Samuel Morris. Children of John and Mary Irvin, Sr.—I. Abraham;—William, one time preacher at Hat creek meeting-house;—Robin; —John, a 2nd lieutenant in the Revolutionary army in 1780, acquired title of major of county militia, m. Mary Anne, the dau. of Matthew Tucker (will 1796), and wife, Esther;— Elizabeth;—Mary;—Nancy;—Margaret (Peggy), m., 1793, James Black.

Children of Major John and Mary A. Tucker-Irvine:— Nancy, m., 1791, Richard Goggin;—Peggy, m., 1793, James Black;—Mary Anne, m., 1798, Paulett Clark, born 1771;— James H., m., 1812, Susanna Cobbs;—Mathew T.

Paulett Clark was the son of John Clark of Louisa county, who married Ann Paulett and moved to Charlotte county in 1777. The name Paulett occurs also as Pawlett. Thomas Pawlett, born 1578, came to Virginia in 1618 and was a member of the first House of Burgesses in 1619. In 1641, he was appointed a member of the Council. He acquired the Westover plantation of 2,000·acres, by patent dated January 15, 1637, the estate later owned by Col. William Byrd and well known through its association with Col. Byrd's name. This famous place on James river dates back to 1623 and was built of bricks brought from England. The name of Thomas Pawlett appears with that of another witness in 1626 to the will of Richard Biggs of West and Shirley Hundred. Pawlett's will, dated 1643-4, devised his estate to his brother, Sir John Pawlett.

The name John Clark appears as sergeant in a company of rangers against Indians, in 1764; as a member of the Augusta Militia in 1758; as sergeant of the 1st Va. Regiment, presenting a claim for 200 acres of land in 1774; in Dunmore's war for defending the frontiers in 1774; and on the muster roll of Capt. James Harrod's party, which arrived under Colonel Christian at Point Pleasant after the battle there.

Three Irvine brothers, David, Christopher and William, hailing from near Irvine, Scotland, came to America during the reign of George II, and were among the early settlers in Bedford. They were granted a large boundary of land around New London, Leesville and the present Alta Vista. The grant was preserved in the family at the old Irvine home till burned in a fire which destroyed the house in 1888. In 1786 David Irvine patented 278 acres on Flat creek; in 1787 Christopher Irvine-Clendenning patented 115 acres on the west branch of Flat creek and in 1793 Christopher patented 1140 acres both sides of Flat creek.

William Irvine married Polly Anthony and died in 1767, when his only child, William, Jr., was very small. His widow married Robert Cowan, who was supposed to be related to William Cowan, opposing lawyer to Patrick Henry in the case of Hook against Venable. Wm. Irvine, Sr., built his home, *Otter,* near Otter river about seven miles from New London, and was one of Bedford's justices. Wm. Irvine, Jr., married Martha, the daughter of Jesse Burton, who helped to lay out Lynchburg; their children were:—Edmund, attorney-at-law, moved to Rocky Mount, Va.;—Judge Robert, moved to West Virginia;—James, remained in Campbell county;—Jesse married Clementina, daughter of Col. Wm. and Anne Carrington-Cabell, of *Union Hill,* Nelson county. Children of Jesse and Clementina Irvine were:—Wm. C., m. Mary A., dau. of Meriwether Lewis, of Milton, N. C.;—Ann C., m. David Flournoy;—Edward C., m., 1st, Jane, dau. of Meriwether Lewis; m., 2nd, Mrs. Merrett. Edw. C. Irvine served in the 2nd Va. Cav., C. S. A., was severely wounded in a battle in 1863, and represented Campbell in the House of Delegates, 1873-74;—Sarah C., m. Judge Asa Dickinson of Prince Edward county;—Mary E., m. Philip D. Christian of Lynchburg;—Jesse, m. Margaret, dau. of Dr. Paul C. Venable; he was captain of a cavalry company in Col. Winston

Radford's Regiment, C. S. A., and lost a limb in a charge of his company;—Juliet M., m. Rev. David W. Shanks (his 2nd wife) ; Margaret F., m. Thomas Rosser, relative of Gen. Rosser, of Campbell county.—Alexander, m. Lockie T., dau. of Capt. Henry Brown, a Revolutionary soldier, and their children were:—John B., of Evington, member of 11th Va. Cav. under Gens. J. E. B. Stewart and Jubal A. Early;—Wm. Henry m. Anna, dau. of Col. Jas. Sinkler (of Upper St. Johns, Berkeley Parish, S. C., and his wife, Anna, dau. of Col. John Huger, of Charleston, S. C.,) and had sons, Alexander and Guilford Huger of West Virginia and Dr. James Sinkler Irvine of *Otter,* who married Evie, dau. of Maj. Fleming Saunders and his wife, Mary Gwaphmey of *Flat Creek.*

Christopher Irvine had several sons; Christopher, Jr., was commissioner for Bedford in 1781. He and his wife, Mary Irvine, sold John Hook and David Ross, merchants in partnership, in 1783, 100 acres of land (part of 290 acres patented by him in 1780), lying on both sides of Watery branch, both sides of Irvine's road at Anthony's corner, along John Callaway's line; also sold 190 acres on the South side of Cattail branch along Irvine's road and Watery branch, the West branches of Flat creek, on Hook's line. Irvine in 1784 purchased the old buildings in New London, and the same year made a transfer of land to his sons Charles and Isaiah. Two of this Irvine family, Col. William and Capt. Christopher, moved to Kentucky in 1779, and five years later Christopher was registered in Lincoln county, Ky. He was empowered to locate military land warrants in that state for Campbell county soldiers. Various deeds were made by Christopher in 1790—to Conrad Speece for a tract on Flat creek; to Wm. Harris land on west branch of Flat creek; to James Clark in 1792, land on Quarry branch; to Wm. Watts, land on Flat creek; in the latter deed he signs his name as Christ. Irvine Clendenning. His son, Charles, m. Anne, dau. of Hugh Rose of Amherst, and their dau., Mary, in 1814, m. Samuel Anthony, whose dau., Anne E., m. John Hampden Pleasants, publisher of *"The Virginian,"* in partnership with Richard Toler.

Jennings

In 1800 there was no church building within the town limits of Lynchburg and Mason's Hall was used for religious services as well as court meetings. Here in September, 1800, Bishop Asbury preached when Samuel K. Jennings, then a teacher at New London, was ordained the first preacher in the community to be so consecrated. Jennings afterwards became a prominent physician and preacher in Lynchburg. There are two deeds among county records of his freeing slaves. The first of these states that under authority of an act of the Virginia Assembly, passed in December, 1792, granting to individuals the right of emancipating slaves, Samuel K. Jennings, of New London, "believing that God hath of one blood made all nations of the earth, and—according to our excellent bill of rights—that all are equally entitled to the blessings of liberty," therefore gave up all right and title, which he then had, to the person of his negro man, John Charlsson, at the time 39 years old, late the property of the Rev. Stith Mead, and transferred by deed of sale to Jennings. Therefore, the said John Charlsson was to be considered a free man from the sealing and delivery 'of these presents."

The second deed somewhat differently expressed, yet with similar intent, records that "under the influence of humane feelings, conscious of the rectitude of the thing of itself and authorized by the act of assembly, Samuel K. Jennings did agree to purchase a man named Toby, then about 40 years old, and a woman slave named Sally, 35 years old, with the intention of emancipating them, agreeably to the rules and regulations of the Episcopal church. The purchase was made in 1804 but Toby and Sally were to remain in Jenning's service until January, 1815. The emancipations occurred in 1806, at which time also William Brown, a Scotchman (who started the first dry goods store in Lynchburg, was a banker and agent for nearly the entire county-trading), emancipated a mulatto girl named Judith, "as far as I have a right to her," he stated.

It is found that many of Campbell's citizens were opposed to the perpetuation of slavery. Of efforts to abolish the institution, Jefferson wrote, "There are many virtuous men who would make any sacrifice for its extinguishment, many equally virtuous who persuade themselves that it cannot be remedied. The value of the slave is every day lessening and his burthen on his master increasing, while suffering from the burthen and responsibility entailed, the settlement of this vexed problem baffles the penetration of the wise."

Johnson

Edward and Elizabeth Johnson emigrated to this country in 1701. Their son, Benjamin, married Agnes, the daughter of Christopher and Penelope Clark. Of their children, Sarah m. David Terrell;—Christopher m. Betty Moorman;—Agnes m. Adam Clement;—William m. Susanna Johnson;—Benjamin m. Mary . . . ;—Penelope . . . ;—Collins . . .; —Edward.

In 1763 Benjamin, Jr., and Mary Johnson, settled on Ivy creek. He died in 1769 and his widow married, 2nd, John Miller, and moved to Lynchburg when that town became established.

John Johnson, son of John and Lucretia M. Johnson, m. Elizabeth, dau. of Gerard Ellyson, and settled in Amelia county. Children:

—Ashley m., 1st, Agatha Stanley; m., 2nd, Mary Watkins;— Jesse m. Elizabeth Watkins;—John m. Lydia Watkins;— James m., 1st, Mildred Moorman; m., 2nd, Penelope Anthony; —Gerard m. Judith Watkins;—William m. Agatha Moorman. Ashley and Mary Watkins-Johnson moved from Amelia and settled in Campbell in 1793; John and Lydia W. Johnson settled on Ivy creek in 1780; James Johnson bought 170 acres of land from William Candler adjoining Edward Bright and

James Callaway, in 1768, upon which he settled but moved a year later to McDuffie county, Georgia. Gerard and Judith W. Johnson moved in 1790 to Campbell. He died in 1810; his will, recorded in 1811 provided real and personal property for his wife, gave his 3 daughters, Jean Terrell, Judith Morgan and Elizabeth Johnson, the tract of land upon which Samuel Smithson lived, gave his two eldest daughters property they had in possession, John W. the property in his possession (John moved to Ohio in 1811); Samuel, being incapable of managing an estate, his portion and that of Elizabeth were left in charge of Gerard, Jr., to whom was given the tract upon which his father lived and property lent his mother. Gerard, and friends, John Organ and Henry Brown were appointed executors.

William and Agatha Johnson moved to Campbell in 1789. James, Ashley and Charles Johnson served in the patriot army during the Revolution. Many of the Johnson family intermarried with the Moormans, five daughters of Micajah Moorman marrying Johnsons. A large number of the Johnsons moved from Campbell. In 1806 Christopher and Milly, with 3 children, moved to Miami Meeting, Ohio; Rhoda Johnson and 7 children moved to Ohio in 1809; James Johnson and wife Rachel and 6 children moved to Fairfield, O., in 1810; Samuel and Susanna and 9 children in 1810; Joseph Johnson, Jr., in 1811; Wm. and Susanna in 1812 to Fairfield; Wm., Jr., to Plainfield; Zeptha Johnson moved to Salem, O., and Christopher Anthony Johnson to Miami in 1814; Joseph and his wife, 6 children, and grandson, Alfred Carroll Johnson, moved to Ohio in 1813; James Johnson came to South river in 1775 from New Garden, N. C.; David Johnson in 1780 and James in 1781. Mary in 1782 from Cedar Creek Meeting. Gerard and Judith Johnson and children, Benjamin, Samuel, Gerard, Jr., Watkins, David, Elizabeth and Jane came from Cedar Creek in 1790 and Ashley, Sr., and wife, Mary W., with their minor children, Ashley, Jr., Thomas, Watkins, Drucilla, Anna and Edith in 1793. The Johnson connection was as extensive as the Moormans.

Johnston

Several Campbell residents bearing name of Charles Johnson or Johnston, are among early settlers; and this appearance, disappearance and re-appearance of a certain name in the records raises a question as to whether it is one and the same person first encountered, and becomes confusing in the large connection.

Charles Johnston, "of Goochland county," is found in Campbell deeds, in 1790; eight years later he and his wife, Mary, appear to have exchanged their county property with Caleb Tate for a lot in Lynchburg, and he probably was the Charles Johnson who was the first manufacturer of tobacco in the town.

Charles Johnston, former Indian prisoner on Ohio river, married, 1st, Letitia Pickett, established himself at Richmond, was living there in 1802; had one son and a daughter, Lucy, who, in 1818 married an Ambler. Johnston left Richmond in 1808, purchased 243 acres lying on Blackwater creek of John Timberlake, also purchased 92 acres of Joseph Pratt and widow Timberlake, the latter tract having formerly belonged to William Burton and been deeded by him to Philip Timberlake in 1797. Johnston married, 2nd, Elizabeth, a daughter of James Steptoe and had a large family. About this time Johnston built a home upon his land, naming it *Sandusky,* for the Indian trading post which sheltered him after he was ransomed. He continued to buy Campbell land and in 1810 procured from John Lynch 35 acres near the Quaker Meeting House, adjoining Lynch property; bought land from Thomas Burgess the same year, and, in 1812 bought of James Stanton 83 acres on Rock Castle (later Burton's) creek, running along Timberlake's line to a point opposite the Quaker house. In 1818 Johnston sold Christopher Clark, Jr., 92 acres and the tract of 279 acres where he lived on the south side of Rock Castle creek, moved to Botetourt, where he practiced law and was living in 1827. *Sandusky* changed ownership several times afterwards. In 1823 James Bullock, trustee for Clark, conveyed the property to Wm. Radford, Isaac Otey, Edward Watts and Thomas Moore. In 1826 Isaac Otey in bond of $20,000 with John M. Otey and John O. Leftwich, securities, obtained the property described as lying on the northwest side of the road leading to New London. In 1831 Elizabeth, widow of Isaac Otey made a deed of trust on lands where he had resided to Thomas A. Holcombe, of Lynchburg, and Chiswell Dabney, of Amherst, who sold the property the same year to his son, John M. Otey, for $8,000. Between 1841-2 John M. and Lucy Otey conveyed 512 acres and a small tract of 92 acres (upon which last, widow Timberlake resided for life) to George C. Hutter, a paymaster in the United States army with title of major, and one of the earliest graduates of West Point Academy.

At the declaration of war in 1861 Major Hutter handed in his resignation to the government and retired to private life at *Sandusky* on the plea of age. He was then offered the similar position of general pay-master of the Confederate army by President Davis, which he declined, but his three sons became officers in Confederate service. During his raid on Lynchburg Gen. Hunter made his headquarters in Major Hutter's home, and the family received some little protection from the fact that Hunter and Hutter had been fellow officers in the United States army.

Major Hutter married Harriet, the daughter of Major James B. Risque, a brilliant lawyer of Lynchburg, and his wife, Elizabeth Kennerley. Had three sons:—Ferdinand, m., 1st, Isabel Goggin; m., 2nd, Mary Lyons of Richmond;—Edward, m. Nannie, dau. of Major Jno. S. Langhorne;—J. Risque, m. his cousin. Lottie, dau. of Edward Sextus Hutter, (formerly of U. S. Navy).

The family of Major Risque Hutter yet own and occupy the *Sandusky* home. Ada married Major LeRoy Long.

Ransomed From Indians

Charles Johnston, at 19 years of age, took service as clerk in 1788 in the employment of John May, of Petersburg, then engaged in purchasing and locating large tracts of land in Kentucky. May and Johnston made a trip, by way of what

Sandusky, Built by Charles Johnston

was known as the Wilderness Road to May's lands, returning safely to Virginia. In 1790 a second trip was planned by water travel down the Kanawha and Ohio rivers in a flat, clumsy boat without covering, called an *ark*. This open transport was considered a safe enough conveyance from Indian attack, as long as it was kept in mid-stream of the broad Ohio. They were joined by three fellow-travellers, a man and two women, as was the custom of banding together for protection in unfrequented sections. But, decoyed to the bank by two treach-

erous white men, their boat got caught in overhanging tree
branches, when a party of Indians sprang upon them, killing
May and one of the women, and taking the others prisoners.
These Indians embraced members of four tribes, Shawnees,
Delawares, Wyandots and Cherokees.   In the distribution of
spoil, Johnston was given to Messhawa, of the Shawnees, who
proved a kind master; but as Indians were known to be de-
ceitful and cruel in the treatment of prisoners, they were constantly agonized by fear of the fate awaiting them.

Two Mingoes joined the party, one of whom had killed a
Wyandot husband and father of a family.   The usage pre-
vailed among the savages that if one took the life of another,
he was bound to make reparation either in property value or
by substituting some one to fill the relation of the deceased in
the community, else the murderer for feited his own life. The culprit in this instance represented himself as without the means
to pay the forfeit in property, and begged the gift of a prisoner who might rescue him from his bad plight.   Johnston was
then handed over to him, as substitute for the murdered Wyandot, a situation he viewed not unfavorably, because it suggested a possible means of escape ultimately.   But after two or
three days' separation from his original keepers, they re-ap-
peared and demanded back their prisoner.   Messhawa settled
the dispute, which then arose, by catching two horses, mount-
ing Johnston on one and himself on the other, and, with his
rifle on his shoulder, riding to the Indian town at Upper Sandusky, five miles distant, a town of Wyandot or Huron Indians.

Here Johnston met with a Canadian trader, Duchouquet,
who ultimately succeeded in ransoming him at the price of
$100 worth of goods, paid in 600 silver brooches, on April
28th, 1790, the day Johnston reached his twenty-first birthday.   When Duchouquet was ready to carry his pack of fur
to the trading post at Detroit, he took Johnston with him:
from there the latter was furnished transportation by the
British authorities as far as New York, in which city he was
visited by Washington's secretary, Nelson, and interviewed

by Washington himself.   He had then been absent from Virginia several months, during five weeks of the time a prisoner
in the hands of the Indians, so he returned to Richmond,
where he borrowed a horse and gig and rode to see his brother
who had taken charge of his small estate in Hanover, and
from there rode to Prince Edward on a visit to his mother,
who was living in that county.

Called to Europe on business in 1793, Johnston returned to
America next year on the *Pigeon,* in company with La
Rouchefoucould, author of "Travels in the United States," in
which he included Johnston's experience with the Indians,
but misspelled proper names, and this provoked Johnston to
write his own narrative in 1827, thirty-five years after it had
occurred.   In the meantime Johnston had lived in Campbell
county, built a home he named *Sandusky,* married the second time while there, and finally moved to Botetourt county,
where he died.

Jones

As early as 1742 Thomas Jones patented 323 acres on the
north side of Falling River and the same date Thomas Jones,
Jr., patented 400 acres on the south side.   The next year
Thomas, Jr., patented 3 tracts, 40 acres on both sides of
Crooked Run, 391 acres on the north side of Crooked Run
adjoining his old line and 840 acres on the east side of Little
Roanoke, both sides of Ash Camp creek.   In 1746 he patented
86 acres on both sides of Falling and, together with Charles
Irby, patented 604 acres on Crooked Run.   In 1746-48 John
Jones patented 104 acres and 438 acres on the Staunton river,
and Difficult creek, adjoining Robert Wynn and John Russell,
and an 1736 acre tract in the same locality.   In 1747 Richard
Jones patented 400 acres, and Philip Jones 642 on Little
Roanoke.   In 1787 John Jones registered himself from
Crooked Run, Brunswick county.   In 1781 Thomas Jones was
an ensign and William Jones 1st lieutenant in the Revolution-
ary army.   In 1784 John and Elizabeth Jones sold Thomas
Jones 550 acres in the fork of Great Falling river bounded by

the lands of John Wood, Thomas Jones, Sr., and William
Jones, deceased. Thomas sold Wm. Harris 116 acres both
sides of Simmons' branch, near Dutchman's branch, and Thos.
and Elizabeth sold Robert Alexander 200 acres on the east
branch of Falling river, near Ross and Hook's corner. In
1785 John and Elizabeth Hook sold Thomas Jones 200 acres
lying on both sides of Little Mill creek, a branch of Falling,
which was part of a patent of 565 acres granted Ross and
Hook in 1780: at that time David Ross registered from Prince
George county, and acquired from John Hardwick a tract of
100 acres. Publius Jones patented 320 acres on Entray creek,
eastern branch of Falling; in 1810 Publius rebuilt Hat Creek
church and received £100 as contractor.

It is probable that it was Thomas Jones, Jr., who was en-
sign in the Revolutionary War and later acquired the title of
Major: his son, James S., married Martha, daughter of Major
Thomas West and Elizabeth Blair (dau. of Robert Bolling of
Chilowe, Buckingham county and his 2nd wife Susan Wat-
son), and Eliza Bolling, dau. of James S. and Elizabeth Blair-
Jones m. Dr. Glover Gilliam of *Landover,* near Naruna. The
West family lived above Lynch's Station, towards the Bedford
line, and Charles West drew a pension for war service.

Letter to Major Thomas Jones, from Moses Hoge, president of Hampden-Sidney College, written on the fly leaf of the
1st volume of *Plutarch's Lives,* September 27, 1809:

"Dear Sir: As it is the desire of your sons, James and Buckner, to prosecute their literary studies, it will, I think, be advisable for you to gratify so laudable a desire. They have
conducted themselves well. With the progress of James I am
best acquainted as he recited to me. It has been very considerable. I scarcely ever knew a student to make an equal progress in the same time. It is, however, impossible to obtain
a liberal education in a year. It would be to me particularly
pleasing if he and his brother might be permitted to return
next session.   "I am yours respectfully,

"MOSES HOGE, *President.*"

Below the above is written:

"Major Thomas Jones, C. C. : That Mr. James Jones has completed with much approbation the usual scientific course at Hampden-Sidney College (algebra excepted), and that he has uniformly conducted himself with much propriety is certified by

MOSES HOGE, *President."*

It is not possible to distinguish the various members of the Jones family in Campbell because they bore similar Christian names.   In 1787 John Jones of Crooked Run, Brunswick county, sold Robert Hall 260 acres of land on the south side of Buzzard branch, a fork of Lick creek, head of a branch on the island road to the old line of Ruffin, "now Ruffin's line." In 1804 James Jones patented 50 acres on the south branch of Molley's creek.   James Jones lived at *Locust Level,* on the island road, about a mile from Pannill's *Green Hill* estate, a double stone and gabled building, claimed to be the oldest brick dwelling in the county, still in good condition, and standing near the roadway's present line.   Jones married, in 1791, Catherine, daughter of Richard and Lucy Hall-Stith. Richard Stith, Sr., devised to his son-in-law, James Jones, "the land laid off for him of my daughter Catherine's portion, 73 acres on the north side of the old island road on the south joining his own line, with Buzzard branch on the west side." In 1806 Richard, Jr., and William Stith sold James Jones 977 acres upon which they were living and which had been willed them by their father, land known as *Old Jacob and Nan field,* lying on the north side of Suck creek (formerly Lick creek) along David Jones' and Thomas West's lands.   Agnes Walker, daughter of James and Catherine Stith-Jones, married, in 1811, Richard Gaines Brown, and their daughter, Martha Virginia Brown, married James Lorenzo Morgan, son of Richard Morgan, then living at *Shady Grove,* his father's home, but moved later to Missouri from which state his daughters, Roberta (Mrs. Wm. M. Strother) and Agnes (Mrs. Wm. M. Stokes), returned to make their home in Lynchburg.

In 1780, when collections of provisions in lieu of money tax for army supplies proved difficult, Congress then issued a new species of paper money guaranteed by the states. These bills were to be redeemed within six years in specie, but from the partial compliance of the states, the expedient answered little purpose and a monetary crisis followed in 1781. Jimmy Jones (as known to his familiars), the victim of a hoax, was told that he could sell this continental currency with great profit at some (fictitious) place in North Carolina, and he proceeded to buy what was in the possession of his neighbors. Naturally the fictitious place could not be located and his credulity cost him the amount he had invested in the then worthless paper.

An inventory, taken in 1792, gives an item of 692 dollars paper currency (value 1000 for one) with market value of four shillings and six pence.

Marriages in Jones family, 1782 to 1811:—Joel Jones, m. Agnes Fitz Patrick;—Rhoda Jones m. Thomas Stith;—Elizabeth Jones m. (2nd wife) Col. John Cabell;—John Jones m. Jenny Hightower;—Nancy Jones m. William Stith;—Dorcas Jones m. Achilles Moorman;—Polly Jones m. Thomas Daniel;—Thomas Jones m. Elizabeth Wood;—Judith Jones m. Pleasant Rosser;—Rachel Jones m. William Guthrie;—Polly Jones m. John Smith;—Joel Jones m. Dolly Cobbs. 1823—Sarah Jones m. Henry Brown.

Kabler

In 1807 Frederick Kabler bought of Richard and Judith Chilton 293 acres of land at the junction of Blackwater and Rock Castle creeks from Timberlake's line to Charles Johnston's corner crossing Tomahawk creek on the division line between Alexander and John Burton; again in 1813 Kabler bought of Ambrose and Jane Brown 74 acres at the head of Tomahawk creek along John W. Bradley's and Thompson's lines; in 1823 Kabler added 206 acres to his estate, land purchased from Joseph and Martha Thompson; and in 1846 made a further addition of 140.84 acres which adjoined the property of Dr. Nathaniel W. Floyd and Jas. Addison Meriwether.

Kabler was a surveyor by profession, and accumulated other lands. His widow, Catherine Kabler, received the Robert Burton tract as her dower; other tracts were the Wilkerson tract, the Hobson tract and two tracts lying along Tomahawk and Rock Castle creeks (branches of Blackwater).

Thaddeus Kabler, son of Frederick, in 1821 married Mary, the daughter of Conrad Speece. He sold the land heired from his father's estate and bought tracts on both sides of the road near New London adjoining property his wife had received from the Speece estate. Here he built a residence on the outskirts of the old town, which was burned down some years since. His land was skirted on one side by *Cottontown* road, which in early days had been laid off by Richard Callaway. Thaddeus Kabler lived to be 92 years old. His son, Dr. T. L. Kabler, married Mildred Peyton, the daughter of John Clark and Catherine Leftwich-Moorman; and resided at New London. Children—Dr. Nicolas L., m. Gus Flippen; is resident physician at New London;—Clark Moorman, m. Rosalie Labby of *Federal Hill;*—Ellen Douglass, m. Charles Nelson of Lynchburg.

Langhorne

Maurice Langhorne of Cumberland county was a member of the patriotic committee in 1775, which unanimously passed the resolution "That it be recommended to the inhabitants of this county in particular and the colony in general that all distinction of colonies and counties be laid aside; that there be no other name known among them than that of Americans, and that every man who will heartily join in this common and ever-glorious struggle for liberty be considered and treated as an American born."

Two Langhorne brothers moved to Campbell from Cumberland: Henry married Frances, the daughter of James Steptoe (Bedford clerk), and settled at *Chestnut Hill,* once the home of Charles Lynch, Sr., later of Judge Winston. While Langhorne was residing there, the house caught fire (during his absence) and everything in it was destroyed, his wife, then blind, only saving his valuable papers. A new building was erected upon the old site and the family resided there until 1830, when Mrs. Langhorne's health having failed, they moved to Lynchburg, where she died in 1832. A son of this marriage was Major John S. Langhorne, captain of Wise Troop, C. S. army; he m. Elizabeth, dau. of Chiswell Dabney. Children:

—Nannie m. Major Edward Hutter; resided in late years in *Rivermont*, the home built by Judge Wm. Daniel, Jr., on Daniel's Hill, about a half mile from *Point of Honor*.
—Chiswell D. m. Miss Keen of Danville; he was a successful railroad contractor, moved to Albemarle county. His daughters became noted as the beautiful Langhorne sisters, one of whom is now Lady Astor, Member of Parliament, England.
—Lizzie m. John D. Lewis, a leading lawyer of Lynchburg. Mrs. Lewis is head of the League of Women Voters in Lynchburg, and was an ardent advocate for Woman Suffrage, during the agitation of the question.
—Thomas N. m. Anna K., dau. of Dr. Richard N. Hewitt of Campbell; resided at *Wyndholm,* near Evington; died 1925.
—Mrs. Lucy L. Ficklin, of Danville, died young.

Colonel Maurice Langhorne, brother of Henry, m. Elizabeth Allen. In 1828 he moved to Lynchburg, leased the *Point of Honor* place, then owned by Wm. L. Cabell (son of its builder, Dr. George Cabell). From there Colonel Langhorne moved to the building known as *Bell Tavern,* nearly opposite the Episcopal church in Lynchburg—which he had purchased and remodelled. Colonel Langhorne m., 2nd, Mrs. Samuel J. Cabell, neê Avery of Tennessee parentage. Children of Maurice and Elizabeth A. Langhorne:

—John Archer m. Margaret Kent of Montgomery county.
—James M. m. Ann Norvell.
—William H. m. Mary Epps Buckner.

—Colonel Maurice L. m., 1st, Ann Rodes; 2nd, Elizabeth Morris; 3rd, Nannie Langhorne.
—Dr. Daniel A. m., 1st, Miss Morris; 2nd, Virginia Kent.
—Lizzie Allen m. Anderson Armistead;—Mary m. James Caskie;—Sallie died young.

John Duval Langhorne, of a Kentucky branch of the family, a retired naval officer and successful financier, moved to Lynchburg; purchased *Westover,* a farm belonging to Frank T. Lee (since divided into town lots and incorporated in the city). J. D. Langhorne later purchased property in Washington City to which he moved in 1906, living there till his death. He married, 1st, Mary Potter, of Philadelphia; married, 2nd, Nannie, the daughter of George P. Tayloe of Roanoke county.

Lee

David Lee is the first of the name in county records and appears as early as 1745 when he patented 1800 acres on Ward's Fork.

In 1761 James and Mary Lee came to Bedford county with their son, William.

John and Richard Lee had lived previously in Albemarle, and (according to family report) originally settled in Northumberland and perhaps descended from Richard Lee, the emigrant.

William Lee and his wife, Ava Noel of Bristol, England. Children:—Tabitha m. Thomas Andrews;—Alexander m. Sarah Guthrey, dau. of John Lee;—John, Jr. . . .;—Garnett . . .; Rebecca m. Beverly, son of John Lee, Sr.;—Ava m. William Hicks;—William;—Richard;—Ann.

Richard Lee, Sr., m. Tabitha Andrews s. p., left property to brothers William and John, Sr.

Children of Captain John Lee, Sr.:—Burwell . . .;—Stephen . . .;—Beverly m. Rebecca, dau. of Wm. Lee;—Patty m. John Arnold of Rockbridge county;—Sarah Guthrey m. Samuel Alexander, son of William Lee, Sr.;—Elizabeth m. James Lancaster;—Susannah m. Robert Clark;—

Pamela m. James Crider;—Mary;—Ann m. David Holladay; —John, Jr., . . .;—Richard Henry . . .;—Matilda m. Drury Holland;—Agnes . . .;—Sophia . . .

A very old place, the Lee-Richardson home, burned down about five years ago, which stood near Lynch's Station, with cellar under the front part and at the back a stone room, was built above ground one story, with one door and window. The graveyard adjoining contains many Lee tombstones, the oldest of which was that of John Lee, born 1774, died 1831, aged 57 years, who must have been son of William, Sr., or John, Sr., the last of whom is given the title of captain.

In 1799 John Lee patented 200 acres on the south side of Goose creek. The will of John Lee written in 1818 gives a complete list of his family: his wife was apparently not living then. The document, after making the usual provision for the burial of his body and payment of his debts, takes on a threatening tone as if some one had offended him and would accordingly suffer in the disposal of his property. But further explanation indicates that he had been a careful business man, keeping account of whatever benefits he had given his children, with the view of equalizing the portions in his last testament; and in order to insure having that carried out strictly according to the letter, with the following prelude: "If any of my sons, sons-in-law, daughters or daughters-in-law had done me any favors I have made it my principle and study to compensate, and make that person who did me favors equal amends, otherwise I gave them credit in their accounts on my books for what their service was worth,—which stand as permanent in case they bring in any accounts against my estate: in the latter event they are to forfeit one-half of the legacy allotted them, which is to be divided among legatees who do not contend, and I humbly hope and desire that there be no dispute respecting what I have left behind by the blessing of Almighty God, what He has pleased to bestow upon me, his poor weak and unworthy servant."

To the legatees, then, who observe well and comply with the conditions of his will be began with his son Burwell, to whom he devised the land and plantation whereon he (John Lee), lived, on the north side of Goose creek and Staunton river, being part of a tract purchased of Captain Jacobus Early, with the exception of that part called Darby's Field on the north side of Goose creek at Darby's ford adjoining the lands of Jesse Leftwich and 128 acres taken off to form Leesville at the junction of Goose creek and Staunton river, leaving 246 acres; also to Burwell 246 acres purchased of Robert Owen, adjoining the land "I live on," being 135½ acres.

To sons Stephen and Beverly "I lend during their lives," 140 acres in Bedford county (deeded by Thomas Halley), bought of Thomas Smith, and a mill built upon it, and 500 acres adjoining deeded by William Leftwich and 126 acres deeded by Lucy Pratt; son Beverly equally sharing in the mills. At their deaths and the death of Rebecca, wife of Beverly, the property to be equally divided between their heirs.

To daughter, Patsy Arnold and her husband, John Arnold, slaves and furniture, and to son-in-law, Alexander Lee and wife, Sarah G. Lee, ditto; to son, Samuel Alexander and his wife, Sarah Guthrey-Lee, slaves and furniture; to daughter, Polly Lee, ditto; to son-in-law, James Lancaster and daughter, Elizabeth (his wife) ditto; to son-in-law, Robert Clark, and daughter Susannah (his wife), ditto; to son-in-law, Henry Crider, and daughter, Parmelia (his wife) ditto; to daughter, Mary Lee, ditto; to son-in-law, David Holladay and daughter, Ann (his wife), ditto; to son, John, two tracts of land in Campbell and Bedford, 146 acres granted to Henry Hendrickson, 200 acres adjoining, granted to John Lee, Sr., by patent April 1799; to son, Richard Henry, £500 in cash, slaves and furniture; to daughter, Matilda, and her husband, Drury Holland, slaves and furniture; to daughter, Aggy, slaves and furniture; for daughter, Sophia, $1200 to be raised out of the estate, and put at interest, which was to be paid yearly, and at her death to be equally divided among heirs. There seems to be another daughter, "Shelica," but that may have been a mistake made by the clerk. This enumerates 15 children and the marriages of most c f them. The name of Samuel Alexander Lee repeated produces the appearance of two of the same name; but it appears that a son-in-law bearing that name, was intended.

John Lee's will continues instructions to sell the lots in Leesville, commencing at the mouth of Plumb Tree branch and, together with money from sales already made, equally divided into 9 lots, to be drawn for by his daughters, excepting Sophia, already provided for. The tract bought of John Armistead and that bought of Jacob Cilly (the last deeded to Lee by Henry Brown), both in Bedford county, were to be sold and money therefrom divided between 5 sons, Burwell, Stephen, Beverly, John and Richard Henry Lee.

To Burwell Lee also was given all the lots in Leesville on the west side of 3rd broad street leading from Goose creek, excepting 2 acres adjoining the mill together with the mill seat, which was to be reserved for the estate and allotted for commons for the mill, the 2 acres to extend from the center of the mill house due north. Burwell Lee and 3 sons-in-law, John Arnold, James Lancaster and Robert Clark appointed executors. Witnesses to will, David Quarles, Vincent Snow, John Anderson, Jr., and Charles Noell. Securities in penalty of $60,000, Vincent Snow, John Lee, Jr., Collins Bradley, Benj. Haden, Wiatt Arnold, Jas. M. Haden and William V. Haden.

Captain John Lee was constantly trading in real estate, gave at one time 15 deeds of transfer, which was doubtless in the sale of lots at Leesville.

Leftwich

The family which now bears the name of Leftwich was originally called Vernon. Richard de Vernon accompanied the Conqueror to England and was granted an estate in Cheshire about a mile from Norwich. Two Vernon brothers afterwards lived on a stream called Wich, one on the right and the other on the left bank. The ancestor of the left Wich became known as "Vernon of the left Wich"; in the fourth generation the estate passed to a daughter of the house, whose husband took the name of Leftwich from his wife's estate, about the year 1250.

Records of Kent county show that Ralf Leftwich received grants of land there in 1658, and the Virginia branch of Leftwich is supposed to have descent from that founder. Augustine Leftwich, Sr., moved to Bedford county from Caroline. His sons, Augustine, Jr., William and Thomas, enlisted in the French and Indian War in 1757 from Brunswick county. In 1760 Augustine Leftwich was granted a tract of 212 acres in Bedford, on both sides of David's creek, by Governor Fauquier. Similarity of name makes it difficult to distinguish the property of the two Augustines. William was granted, by George III, 120 acres on both sides of Buffalo fork of Back creek and Thomas 70 acres on the north side of Goose creek.

Two miles southwest of Leesville there is a high ridge bordering on Goose creek, known as *King George's Hill*, on the highest point of which John Perrin killed an Indian chief. Tradition gives to the chief the title and name of King George and tells that the hill was thus named for him, but it seems more probable that it was so called for the English king and the chief was associated with it, because he happened to be killed on that eminence. John Perrin, hero of the episode, was a private soldier in the Lunenburg regiment during the war of 1758 with the Indians, and was later registered from Charlotte county. Situated between King George's Hill and Goose creek is a fine farm of bottom land upon which Leftwich settled. He married twice, the last time he married late in life, Elizabeth, daughter of George Stovall, Jr., and lived to be very old. His will, written in 1795, mentions his wife, Elizabeth, children, and grand-children. Children:

—William, a member of the Bedford Revolutionary Committee of 1775, m. Elizabeth Haynes; he was appointed on the committee to regulate slopes for fish in the mill dams; died in 1820.

—Thomas was captain in General Stephen's Virginia regiment; later was promoted colonel and commanded the rear-guard of Gates' division at the battle of Camden; he married three times; lived at *Mount Airy,* two and a half miles from Leesville; had 21 children. His daughter, Amelia, married Mark Anthony; son Augustine, m., 1st, Mildred Ward; m., 2nd, Elizabeth Williams Clark, of Camden, S. C., and settled in Lynchburg. Alex T., a son of the latter, was Belgian Consul at Baltimore, Md., m. Rosalie V. Lightfoot of Alabama.

—Augustine, Jr., was a lieutenant in Captain Thomas Leftwich's regiment; m. in 1765 Mary Turner; his son, Colonel Peyton Leftwich, was an officer in the war of 1812, lived at *Westerly,* near Lynchburg, a property which was acquired many years afterwards by Major John W. Daniel, who made it his home during the latter portion of his life, and which is now owned by Richard Carrington of Lynchburg.

Col. Peyton Leftwich m., 1st, Mildred Fuqua. Children: —Granville was a captain in the Seminole war and was presented with a silver sword by the state of Florida for his successful bravery in defending a town which was threatened by the Indians, he having, by a hurried march, arrived in time to prevent a massacre: Captain Granville Leftwich died unmarried at Fort Smith, Arkansas;—Beverley, unmarried, Littleton m. Lolly McDaniel;—Lilbourn m. Miss Scott;—Catherine m. John C. Moorman;—Lucinda m. Stephen Terry and moved to Big Lick (now Roanoke).

—John was sergeant in the Continental line for three years: in 1783 m. Susanna, dau. of Guy Smith; in 1784 was given a warrant for 200 acres of land.

—Littleberry m. Fanny Hopkins; was famed as a foot racer, and never beaten.

—Uriah was a captain in the Revolutionary army.

—Joel m. Nancy Turner; served three years as ensign in the Revolution, and in 1783 received a warrant for 200 acres of land; made brigadier-general of the militia force and served in the war of 1812 until after the battle of Tippecanoe, where he gained the title of major-general: was a justice of the peace in Bedford county many years, and member of the Virginia Legislature. He was celebrated in rifle shooting.

—Jabez m. Delilah Stovall: was brigade major of 2nd Virginia Militia Regiment in 1814, promoted brigadier-general: member of Congress from Bedford; member of Virginia Legislature for nine years; in 1825 moved to Huntsville, Ala.; member of Alabama Legislature; died at Huntsville 1855.

—Frances m. . . . Carter.

—Mary m. in 1765 Joshua Early, Sr., and resided near Forest, Bedford county, an estate now owned by Charles Heald of Lynchburg; these were the parents of John Early, bishop in the Methodist Church South.

—Anne m. . . . Peatross.

Lewis

Col. William J. Lewis was the son of Col. Wm. Lewis, of Sweet Springs, and grandson of John Lewis, the first settler in Augusta county. Col. Wm. J. Lewis commanded a corps of riflemen called "Sons of the Mountain," at Yorktown in 1781; he married Elizabeth, daughter of Col. Joseph Cabell and his wife, Mary, the daughter of Dr. Arthur Hopkins of Goochland and Albemarle.

There is a deed from Archibald Bolling dated Oct. 8, 1796, conveying to Wm. J. Lewis a tract of land called the *Buffalo Lick plantation* in Campbell on the Fluvanna river, 800 acres beginning at the mouth of a small gutt called *Slippery,* on the river bank to Horsley's lines and Archie's creek, according to its meanders, and including a mill seat, thence down the Fluvanna river.

Col. Lewis lived upon this land, which he purchased from Bolling, on James river about ten miles from Lynchburg. His residence, called *Mt. Athos,* was destroyed by fire some years ago and valuable heirlooms belonging to the Robertson family, then owners, were lost in it. Lewis was a leading member of Virginia Legislature for many years; and from 1817-19 represented his district in Congress. He died in 1828 and was buried at the summit of the mountain he loved, at a spot selected by himself for a vault which was blasted out of solid rock. Mrs. Lewis moved to Kentucky after the death of her husband and died there in 1855; they left no children. A sister of Mrs. Lewis, Mary H. Cabell, married John Breckenridge and moved near Lexington, Ky.: these were the grandparents of Gen. John C. Breckenridge.

In 1806 Virginia, the daughter of Ann Cabell and Robert C. Harrison, was born in the home of her uncle, Col. Lewis, at *Mt. Athos,* and she was named for the state which her parents were then preparing to leave. She was reared in Kentucky and married David Castleman at *Castleton,* near Lexington, Ky.

Judge John Robertson owned and resided at *Mt. Athos,* and while still held by his family, it was burned and not rebuilt. The property was divided and sold to Messrs. Logan and Herndon.

James Lewis patented land on the south side of Roanoke river adjoining Gilliam.

Lynch

Charles Lynch, founder of the family in Campbell, which became prominently associated with James and Staunton river sections, came to Virginia from Galway, Ireland, between 1715-20, when a lad of 15 years. He was apprenticed by the captain of the vessel, in which he had sailed, for payment of his passage, to Christopher Clark, a wealthy tobacco planter of Louisa county and seems quickly to have won favor for he was received into Clark's household as a member of the family, wooed, won and married his daughter, Sarah, in 1733. He changed his residence several times; in 1741 he was a justice in Goochland; held the same office in Albemarle in 1745; that year he was appointed captain of militia and in August was given leave to keep a ferry from his land across North river (Rivanna) to the opposite side: he represented Albemarle in the House of Burgesses.

There is a tendency in biography to confuse the records of these Lynchs, father and sons, Charles and John, yet in character and career they were distinctly different. Charles, Sr.,

lived only two or three years after settling in Bedford on his
James river property. His sons were still under age, though
Charles, Jr., married not long afterwards, entered official life,
and later was a soldier in the Revolution. John was of a re-
ligious·turn, developed poor health which continued through
life, though he outlived his brother twenty-four years. His
claim to distinction is through his having been the founder
of Lynchburg and promoter of its advancement.

Colonel Charles Lynch, oldest son of the emigrant, married
in 1755, Anna, the daughter of Henry and Anna Chiles-Terrell,
a sister of Micajah Terrell, who later married Sarah Lynch.
Lynch represented Bedford in the House of Burgesses in
1769-74-75; he was one of the signers of the non-importation
agreement and advocated that taxation of the colony be in the
hands of the Burgesses. He was present when Henry delivered his "Liberty" speech. During the Revolution Lynch
served on General Greene's staff in the southern campaign.
He raised a regiment of riflemen and at Guilford C. H. held a
position on Greene's right flank and won laurels for his gallantry there. His young son, Anselm, 16 years old, slipped
away from home and reached Guilford on the eve of battle
and took part there. Lynch's name is perhaps most notably
connected with "Lynch law," as he was constituted judge of
the court which administered it. He was appointed in 1782
colonel of Campbell county militia: made justice of the peace
1784; died Oct. 29, 1796, aged 60 years, and was buried in
the cemetery at his home, *Avoca,* near Alta Vista, his tombstone gives his name and dates of birth and death, and tells
that he was a patriot in the Revolution. His sons,—John, born
1767 and known as "Staunton John," married a Miss Terrell,
emigrated to Tennessee where he died in 1840, aged 73 years;
has descendants at Jackson, Tennessee.—Anselm m. Susan
Miller, of Lynchburg; their dau., Mary Anna, m. James G.
Dearing, whose son was General James Dearing of the
C. S. army; his son, Charles Henry Lynch, never married; was a member of Virginia Legislature; Lynch
(now Clarion) Station, was named for him;—Charles, (3rd of

name) m. Sallie, dau. of Charles Lynch Adams and moved to Kentucky; his son, Charles, became governor of Mississippi.

In 1756 Col. Lynch patented 200 acres on Reedy creek adjoining his own land. In 1759 he patented 81 acres on Otter and 3344 acres on Staunton and Otter; also 4 patents same year of 58, 400, 185 and 121 acres respectively, lying on Bolling's creek, Burnt bridge branch, Blackwater and Beaver creeks; patented with Christopher, John and Edward Lynch 384 acres on Bolling's creek north side of Fluvanna and 343 acres south side of Lynch's creek; in 1793 patented 2300 acres on the west side of Otter river. Anselm patented, in 1806, 200 acres on Pocket creek and, in 1810, 695 acres on Beaver creek.—

McReynolds

Among county records the name McReynolds is found also written McRandle and Reynolds; descendants of the last named continue to discard the prefix "Mc" and thus give suggestion of a different family.

James and Joseph McReynolds came, with their mother, from Ireland to America about 1740. About 1750 James established himself in what was still Lunenburg, four years later became Bedford, in 1782 formed a part of Campbell and about the middle of the 18th century was embraced in the county-slice given to Appomattox. In 1763 James *McRandle* patented 242 acres lying on a branch of Mulberry creek, a fork of Falling river, within Bedford boundary, but twenty years later James *McReynolds* sold this tract along John Ferguson's line to one Dunwoodie(Dinwiddie) : he was probably married before settling in Bedford. His children were:— Thomas, captain in the patriot army in 1779, and given the captaincy of a Campbell militia company at the county formation;—Elizabeth;—Joseph, m. 1803, Catherine McIvor; in 1784 he sold 100 acres on W. branch of Island creek;—James in 1801 patented 184 acres on the east branch of Falling river;—John, m., 1788, Jane Campbell; m., 1796, Olivia Steele; he was a deputy to James Miller, sheriff, in 1832;—Samuel m., 1794, Jennie Campbell;—Robert;—Archibald;—Benjamin m., Elizabeth Wilson in 1798;—Oliver in 1805, purchased of Archibald Robertson, trustee, 172 acres of land formerly belonging to the Archibald Bolling estate; moved with his family to Christian county, Ky., about 1830; a descendant, James C. McReynolds is an Associate Justice of the U. S. Supreme Bench.

James McReynolds, Sr., settled about seven miles south of what is now Spout Spring, an Appomattox station on the Norfolk and Western railroad, and he was buried there. His will, recorded in 1803 (son Oliver, with John Helm and John McAllister, executors), bequeathed to Oliver a 30-acre tract, all other real estate, excepting four poles square (including his stone-walled graveyard) was to be sold and the proceeds equally divided between his children and grand-children, only Oliver, James, Archibald and Benjamin being mentioned by name. A bequest of £10 (English) was devised for support of the Gospel at Concord church, if service should be continued there by the Presbyterian denomination, otherwise the money was to revert to his children.

The settlement of William McReynold's estate occurred in 1800 when allotments were made to Martha Thomas (neê McReynolds) and to Joseph McReynolds of Washington county, Va. Some descendants of the latter moved to East Tennessee and Logan county, Ky. Judge James C. McReynolds (a descendant of John and Oliver McReynolds through the marriage of cousins), upon a visit to the early home of his ancestors was shown the well-kept minutes of the Concord Presbyterian church, which he since had rebound in new leather. This secures the covering, but does not conceal the original mottled boards. In recent years a history of the church has been prepared by the minister, Rev. R. L. McNair, in charge at New Concord church. The oldest inscribed gravestones in the churchyard are of Captain Isaac Rucker, 1808-1889, and Dr. Daniel S. Evans, 1824-1895.

Marriages in the Reynolds family: 1791, Rachel Reynolds to John Haden; 1792, William Reynolds to Martha Wilson;

1797, Nancy Reynolds to Henry Trent; 1805, Sarah Reynolds to Robert Daniel.

Miller

A sister of Samuel Pannill of Green Hill, Sarah Bailey Morton Pannill, married David Fitz Patrick and their daughter, Francis E. Fitz Patrick married Samuel T. Miller; the latter were the parents of William A. Miller, Lynchburg's fine old citizen who lived within three months of his century mark,— useful and honored to the last,—his death caused by a fall followed by pneumonia.

Samuel Thomas Miller opened a female school at New London in 1811, but the next year he enlisted under Captain Adam Clement in a cavalry company to serve during the war of 1812 which was sent to Mount Holly, N. J., but remained idle. He returned to New London and re-opened his school. He married in 1817 Frances Elizabeth Fitz Patrick of Pittsylvania; bought property in New London and taught there ten years. He bought 600 acres on Staunton river. In 1821 he took charge of New London Academy, where he remained two years: he then opened a boys' school in New London, but sold his property there and moved to his plantation on Staunton river; built *Woodburne* in Pittsylvania and conducted there a classical school which was patronized by families who lived in the surrounding country. He had a household of fourteen children, eight sons and six daughters; died in 1870, aged 80 years. Many of his children lived to old age. His son, Thomas, a Confederate veteran, was for many years a prominent teacher in Lynchburg schools; a son, Hartshorn Miller, was on the staff of the *Lynchburg News* and contributed to other papers. William A. Miller married Margaret Henry, a granddaughter of Patrick Henry.

Moorman

The family of Moorman is of English extraction and the name is derived from moor, the prairies or commons of England, i. e., "man of the moor." They were Quakers and long before the Revolution, in order to avoid persecution in their own country, they emigrated to America. Zachariah, his sons, Thomas and Charles, and daughter, Sally A., settled in Nansemond sounty. Thomas Moorman's eldest son, Charles, Jr., married Elizabeth Reynolds and located in Louisa county, where he patented three tracts of land: also patented 400 acres in Albemarle county at the junction of Mechum and Moorman rivers, from which circumstance the latter stream received its name. Later he secured a second tract in the same locality; he died in 1757.

Micajah, son of Thomas, Sr., born 1735, owned land near Lynch's ferry in 1757, entered 394 acres on the north side and 250 acres on the south side of James river and purchased two tracts of 200 and 770 acres respectively on Ivy creek; also purchased land on Molley's creek.

In 1762 Thomas, Jr., son of Charles, Jr., bought 200 acres on Tomahawk creek and moved there in 1767 from Golansville, Caroline county, having previously married Rachel Clark; they carried to South River Meeting the following certificate: "Thomas and Rachel Moorman having removed from under our care and within the verge of your Meeting, requested a recommendation to you. After due care we do not find but that he has settled his worldly affairs to satisfaction and they have always been esteemed as orderly persons and held in good unity among us"—signed in behalf of the Meeting by Samuel Hargrave, clerk.

In 1763 Zachariah, born 1732, son of Thomas and Rachel Moorman, settled five miles south of Lynch's ferry; in 1784 he sold to Achilles Douglass 766 acres on Seneca creek, that being part of Blair's Order, on the dividing line between Christopher Anthony and his land. Samuel, a son of this Zachariah Moorman, lived at *Walnut Hill,* near Lawyer's Station, where there yet remains the family burying ground, and old residence. In 1782, John Murray, executor of James Murray, sold to Achilles and Charles Moorman, 3030 acres of land on both sides of Seneca creek, (which had been granted to James Murray, late of Prince Edward county),—excepting 200 acres which he conveyed to Andrew Moorman,—the lines being run by Nicolas Meade. In 1791 Andrew Moorman devised his land—beginning on both sides of the creek and extending to Venable's line till it intersected with Jesse Moorman's line—to his wife, Judith Moorman; to son, Achilles, a tract of land on Rough creek; and provided for the sale of land called "Carver's," and an entry called "Poe's." The Moorman's, by intermarriage with other Campbell county families, seem to have a more extensive connection than any other family in the county: many from the different branches removed to northwest and southwest sections, descendants of whom may be found still bearing the name.

1. Zachariah Moorman, emigrant; his sons Charles and
2. Thomas, Sr., his son.
3. Charles, Jr., m. Elizabeth Reynolds; children:—
    Thomas, Jr., m. Rachel, the dau. of Christopher Clark.
    Judith m. John Douglass.
    Charles m. Mary Adams.
    Achilles m. Elizabeth Adams.
    Ann m. Thomas Martin from Galway, Ireland.
4. Thomas and Rachel C. Moorman; children:—
    Mary m., 1st, Benjamin Johnson, m., 2nd, John Miller.
    Zachariah m., 1st, Elizabeth Terrell; m., 2nd, Elizabeth Johnson.
    Micajah m. Susannah Chiles.
    Mildred m. James Johnson.
    Agatha m. William Johnson.
    Achilles m. Frances Herndon.
    Andrew m., 1st, Mary Gill; m., 2nd, Mrs. Prudence Anderson.
    Charles m., 1st, Rebecca Leftwich; m., 2nd, Nancy Hancock.
    Clark T. m. Rachel Harris.
    Rachel m. Stephen Goggin.
4. Charles and Mary Adams-Moorman; children:—
    Elizabeth m. Christopher Johnson.
    Lucy m. Benjamin Johnson.

Charles m. Judith Moon.

Mary m. James Taylor

Thomas m. Elizabeth Leftwich.

Agnes m. John Venable.

Robert m. Sarah Moon.

Judith m. Christopher Anthony, Sr.

4. Achilles and Elizabeth Adams-Moorman; children:—
Charles m. Mary Venable.
Silas m. Mary Moon.
Andrew m. Sallie Moon.
William m., 1st, Jane Haden; m., 2nd, Judith Venable; m., 3rd, Eliza M. Haden.
Jesse m. Elizabeth Buckner Stith.
Judith m. William M. Haden.

5. Zachariah, son of Thomas and Rachel C. Moorman; their son;

6. Samuel m. Judith, the dau. of Micajah and Judith Adams-Clark in 1796; children:
John Clark m. Catherine, the dau. of Colonel Peyton Leftwich.
Zachariah m. Martha Brown of Cumberland county.
Dr. Granville m. Mary Crawford, settled in Augusta county; was member of Va. Legislature.
Frances m. Colonel Joel Breckenridge Leftwich.
Sallie m. (2nd wife) Henry Alexander; lived between Lawyers and Lynchburg; their dau., Mary E., m. Charles J. Winston and lived at the Winston home near Lynch's (now Clarion) station on the Southern R. R.; their dau., Sallie m. John Nash.
Elizabeth Moorman m. Mr. Hoffman, whose sons joined the Confederate army and were killed in service.
Rev. Samuel Moorman, was educated at Hampden-Sidney College; his son, Thomas, m. Rose Winston, whose dau. m. Charles Roller, the founder of Augusta Military Academy.

7. John Clark and Catherine L. Moorman; children:—
Granville L. m. Mary Moorman.

Pauline J. m. Dr. Hobson Clark.
Littleton L. m. Marian S. Gordon of Forest, Bedford county.
Mildred Peyton m. Dr. T. L. Kabler, of Evington.
Ellen G. m. Major Marcellus Moorman, a member of a Kentucky branch of the family, and settled at a Moorman home situated then on the outskirts of Lynchburg, but now incorporated within the city limits. Major Moorman commanded a regiment in the C. S. army; later engaged in tobacco trade.
Lucinda m. E. Steptoe Moorman of Rustburg.
Mary J. m. Dr. Robert Withers Morgan of Gladys.
The family of Jno. C. Moorman lived at the old *Walnut Hill* home, near Lawyers, which is now owned by descendants of Joel Breckenridge Leftwich.
5. Micajah and Susanna C. Moorman; children:—
Thomas m. Apharacia Hope.
Elizabeth m. Moorman Johnson.
Rachel m. James Johnson.
Millie m. Christopher Johnson.
Rhoda m. John Johnson.
Susannah m. Samuel Johnson.
Docia m. Joseph Stratton.
Nancy m. John Paxson.
Sarah m. Mahlon Stratton.
Molly m., 1st, Pleasant Moorman; m., 2nd, John C. Moorman.

Other Moorman marriages among Campbell's earliest records:

1791.	Nancy Moorman to Robert Clark
1792.	William Moorman to Eliza Martin.
1795.	John Moorman to Rachel Haden.
1787.	Wm. Moorman to Elizabeth Rosser.
1798.	Achilles Moorman to Dorcas Jones.
1799.	Jas. C. Moorman to Jane Robinson.
1800.	Polly Moorman to Wm. Haythe.
1803.	Elizabeth Moorman to Jas. C. Clarkson.

Ludwick A. Moorman, born 1809, m. Elizabeth Mc-
Culloch, dau. of Samuel Boyle Davies; their dau.,
Elizabeth A. McC. Moorman, m., 1st, James B. Anthony; m., 2nd, Morton Pannill, both of whom rendered service in the C. S. army.

Morgan

Members of the Morgan family seem to have settled first in
Bedford, before moving into Campbell. Thomas Morgan, a
Bedford county soldier, will recorded in 1774. In 1745 Philip
Morgan patented 120 acres on both sides of Stith's creek.

Reuben Morgan patented in 1755 four hundred acres on the
lower side of Miles' creek, adjoining Stith's property. Haynes
Morgan, sergeant major in 1758, served seven years in the
80th British Regiment; in 1771 was an attorney in Bedford.

In 1802 Hugh Morgan came from Deer creek, Harford
county, Md.; married Judith, the daughter of Gerard and Judith Johnson; purchased land from Terrell Morgan in 1803.

Among Campbell deeds is one from John Morgan in 1806
and Andrew Morgan in 1810. In 1814 Terrell Morgan purchased 735 acres lying on Whipping creek of Joseph and Elizabeth Poindexter, along the lines of John Poindexter, John Bullock, Dr. John Slaughter, south of the creek; in 1817 purchased 140 acres from John Morgan. About the year 1830
he acquired *Shady Grove,* the Spotswood Henry home, which
he deeded in 1837 to his son, Richard Morgan, who resided
there many years, but in 1862 disposed of it to Captain C. Perrow, and moved to property at Pigeon Run (now Gladys), belonging to the Haythe family. The will of Terrell Morgan in
1840, provided for his wife, Dolly (Dorothea), 4 daughters,
Sally, Mary, Jane H., Mrs. Nancy Dillard and her daughter,
Henrietta, of Winfall and sons Richard, David C. and Mc-
Gilcrey.

Richard Morgan, born 1801, married Sophia Weston Jones;
Richard Morgan appears to have engaged in tobacco business.
In 1825 he was an inspector of tobacco at Spring Warehouse

in Lynchburg. He sold Bowling Haythe and Elliott each 200 acres of his land, sold Shady Grove and spent the last years of his life at Pigeon Run (Gladys). Of his children—William H., attorney-at-law at Floyd C. H., m. Ann, dau. of Capt. Wm. Cox of Rustburg;—James Lorenzo m. Mary V., dau. of Richard G. and Agnes W. Brown, moved to Missouri; George moved to Asheville, N. C.; engaged in tobacco business;— Dr. Robert Withers m. Mary J., dau. of John C. Moorman; moved to Lynchburg;—Sophie Jones;—Taylor m. Sallie Moorman; resided near Pigeon Run. Four of these brothers served in the Confederate army; two of them, William H. and Robert Withers, were captured at Milford on May 21st, 1864; the first named was imprisoned at Fort Delaware for one year. In 1911 he wrote and published reminiscences of the war, giving account of each member of his company.

Murrell

The earliest appearance of the Murrell name in Virginia records was when William Murrell was appointed on a committee of three to view the tobacco crop in a Charles City county parish, as per an act passed in 1639 by *Grand Assembly,* that "Tobacco, by reason of excessive quantities made, being so low that the planters could not subsist by it or be enabled to raise more staple commodities to pay their debts, enacted that the tobacco of that year be viewed by sworn viewers and the rotten and unmerchantable and half the good, be burned."

About a century later Thomas Murrell, a descendant of William, of Charles City county, was living on his large landed estate in Goochland county, married and had a number of sons, one of whom was William of Lunenburg, who married Miss Estes and whose will was probated in that county in 1780. His will mentioned that he had previously conveyed his land to his sons, James and Drury, and appointed sons Jeffrey and Drury his executors. His son James was fatally injured in November, 1781 while building his house, and his will was probated in 1782; an only child, born soon after his father's death, was given the name James after his parent. This James

Murrell moved to Campbell, settling 6 miles south of Rustburg on east ferry road at *Seneca Hill* on the creek of that name. He married first in 1805 Obedience Rudd, m., 2nd, in 1818, Nancy Cobbs, dau. of John and grand-daughter of Rev. Chas. Cobbs. Among the children of his first marriage were Thomas Rudd and Rufus Albert, both prominent educators. Thomas R. Murrell educated at the Univ. of Virginia in 1835, taught in his father's family several years but was living at Champagnolle, Ark., at his death in 1846, then in his 35th year. Rufus A. Murrell taught until his father's death in 1859 when he made his home with his sisters, Louisa, Evelyn (Mrs. G. A. Dinwiddie) and Julia. He represented Campbell in Virginia Legislature of 1870 and was there when the gallery of the Supreme Court room crashed onto the floor of the room and then into the Hall of Delegates, killing and wounding many persons, but he had just slipped out of the crowded room and escaped unhurt. He died at *Seneca Hill* in 1880, aged 66 years.

John Cobbs Murrell, a child of James Murrell, Jr.'s second marriage, born 1820 in Charlotte county, was a prominent lawyer in Campbell and from 1865 till his death in 1879 was commonwealth's attorney for the county. He married Frances Cornelia Smithson. Children:—Edgar, m. Charlotte, dau. of Henry L. Davies; at his death his widow married Dr. Newell of Baltimore.

—John Cobbs, Jr., moved away.
—William M. m. Flora Scott, dau. of Ro. W. and Blanche T. Payne-Withers.
—Walter m. Miss Lee.

William M. Murrell attended the classical school of Prof. C. L. C. Minor at Lynchburg, at Roanoke College, from which he graduated in 1874 with degree of A.B.; entered the Law Department of Virginia University same year, and started the practice of his profession at Rustburg with his father in 1877; was elected in 1879 to the office of Commonwealth's Attorney for the county, holding the position until January

1st, 1912. In November, 1922, he was appointed by Judge Wm. R. Barksdale, Judge of the Circuit Court of Campbell, to fill the unexpired term as commonwealth's attorney of his predecessor, who resigned. In 1923 he was elected to the office for the term beginning January, 1924, which position he yet holds. He is a member of the Virginia Bar Association, as well as the American Bar Association. Some years ago he moved with his family to Lynchburg, where he yet resides.

A second family bearing the name of Murrell, coming from Mount Holly, N. J., settled in Lynchburg during the second quarter of the 18th century, and have descendants of the name still residing there. Two sons, John and Hardin, were postmasters in the town. John also was a merchant and accumulated a large fortune, which he liberally shared with his family. His sister married Samuel Claytor, a Lynchburg tobacconist. Senator Daniel married Julia, daughter of Dr. Edward Murrell of Lynchburg, a member of this Murrell family.

Norvell

Captain William Norvell, Sr., born 1770, son of William and Martha Norvell of Hanover county, Va., was among the Campbell residents, who moved there from Amherst county. In 1797 Captain Norvell made fifteen purchases of land in Campbell county. He also purchased from Alexander Stuart and John Dabney a half acre lot in Lynchburg. He was the first corporation court clerk in Lynchburg; in 1811 was elected a member of the town council. The manner of elections at this time was peculiar. The council appointed commissioners, and the city sergeant, according to order, gave notice, by sending the bell around, to inform all freeholders and householders entitled to vote, that the election of 12 common councilmen would be held at Mason's Hall, then used as the court house.

William Norvell was appointed in 1813 a member of a committee of three to build a new market house in the south western side of Second and Water streets (now Main and 9th streets). Norvell was one of the directors of the Exchange bank, organized in 1814. The first effort towards public education in Lynchburg was started by private subscription, with a board of managers, the first of whom was Wm. Norvell, who applied to Legislature for articles of incorporation, which resulted in the incorporation in 1823, of Lynchburg Charity School.

The old Franklin Hotel, corner of Main and 11th streets, (opened by Charles Hoyle), built in 1818 by Samuel J. Harrison, became changed to the Norvell House after the family of that name. This site is now occupied by the merchandise store of C. M. Guggenheimer Co. Captain Norvell resided at a country home called *Radcliff,* near Candler's mountain. He married Anne, second daughter of Col. John and Wilhelmina Jordan-Wyatt, the latter a daughter of Col. Samuel Jordan and sister of Mrs. Wm. Cabell of Union Hill, Nelson county, and Mrs. John Cabell of Green Hill, Buckingham county, and of whom there were nine sisters. Martha, a sister of William Norvell, married Seth Ward of New London.

In 1828 Captain J. E. Norvell commanded the Lynchburg Artillery Company; in 1823 he had been promoted major of militia. Children of William and Ann Wyatt-Norvell:

—Wm. Wyatt Norvell, born 1795, m. Ann M., dau. of Samuel J. and Sally Harrison in 1818

—Martha Ann, born 1797, m., (1st wife), Chiswell Dabney of Hanover county in 1814, died 1815.

—Lucy Wilhelmina, born 1801, m. John M., son of Isaac and Elizabeth Otey, in 1817.

—Elizabeth Emmeline, born 1799, m. Edward Trent of Cumberland in 1815; she died in 1819. Edward Trent died in 1818, and their daughter, Martha Ann, died in 1818.

—Susannah Carolina, born 1803, m. John M. Warwick, son of William and Leanna Dawson-Warwick, grandson of Abraham and Amy Warwick; Mr. and Mrs. John M. Warwick were grand-parents of Major John W. Daniel and Mrs. Sallie Daniel-Halsey; their daughter, Sarah Ann, who married Judge

Wm. Daniel, Jr., died in 1845, aged 24 years; the inscription on the tombstone reads:

"This day without a cloud is passed,
  And thou wert lovely to the last.
  Extinguished, not decayed, as stars that shoot along the sky,
  Shine brighter as they fall from high."

—John Edmondson, born in 1805, called, because of his polished elegance, a D'Orsay.
—Samuel Gustavas, born in 1807; m. Champe Carter Bradfute, moved to Cincinnati, Ohio.
—Fayette Henry, born in 1809, moved to Shelbyville, Ky.
—George Edward, born 1811, died 1839, aged 27 years.
—Martha Maria Louisa, born 1814, m. ——— Waller.
—Flora Ann Emmeline, born 1817, m. Daniel Warwick, of Baltimore, later Lynchburg.

Letter to William Norvell from James Callaway, Sr.:

Amherst, 30th October, 1792.

Dr. Sir: Mr. Nichols was with me on Sunday last about the execution I sent over which you were kind enough to have levied on him for me. He has a letter from Mr. Austin to me to give credit for seven pounds, which I requested Mr. Clarke to do. He also informed me he had about 7 or 8 pounds in money and knew not how to raise the balance, unless I would take some Merchants' Assurances. If he will pay 8 or 10 pounds and you, Mr. Brown or Mr. Irvine, get him to work for you and give your assurance to pay the balance by the 1st of December next the Sheriff may be directed to return the execution postponed by order of Plaintiff. I am Sir,

Your mo. obt.

JAMES CALLAWAY.

The family of Norvell were allied by marriage with the Warwick family, then resident in Amherst county, the name appearing as Warrick, Warick and Worrick. Abraham Warwick is recorded in 1781 in Amherst; in 1785 he is listed among census returns as head of a family of 8 white souls in that county and William Warwick as head there of a family of 3 whites; William held title of major and had a brother, Capt. James Warwick; both of the latter spent much time in Lynchburg. The family were long lived, the mother of William and James living to be 102 years old. Major William Warwick was a prominent bank officer; m. 3 times; children:

—Mrs. Stuart.

—John M. m. Susanna Caroline Norvell, their dau. Sarah A. m. Judge Wm. Daniel, Jr.

—Corbin;—Abram;—moved to Richmond, Va.

—Daniel m. F. Ann E. Norvell, moved to Baltimore.

—Mrs. Saunders.

—Mrs. Thomas Leftwich, of Bedford county.

Otey

(A Bedford family, many of whom lived in Campbell).

Family of John and Mary Hopkins-Otey (born 1739).

—Isaac, m. 1789 Elizabeth Matthews of Rockbridge.

—John Hopkins, m., 1st, Elizabeth Buford, 1790; m., 2nd, Mrs. Mary C. Wainwright.

—Frazier, died 1825; m., 1st, Mildred Leftwich, 1793; m., 2nd, Mrs. Mary Latham, 1814.

—Frances, born 1772; m. Rev. Wm. Leftwich 1788; she died 1825.

—Walter (died 1823); m. Mary Walton of Botetourt in 1800, moved to Huntsville, Ala.

—James Otey, born 1774; died unmarried.

—Armistead, born, 1777, died 1866; m., 1st, Sarah Gill in 1806; m., 2nd, Nancy Lumpkin, 1834.

Major Isaac Otey, born 1765; died 1835 at *Sandusky;* m. Elizabeth Matthews of Rockbridge county, born 1767, died 1855. Children:

—Sarah Maxwell, b. 1789, m. Major William Cook; died 1832.

—William Otey, born 1791, died 1845, unmarried.

—John Matthews, born 1792, m. Lucy Wilhelmnia Norvell, died 1859.

—Mary J. A., born 1794, m. Colonel Edward Gwatkin.

—Isaac Newton, born 1796, m. Prudence Buford Otey, died 1875.

—Frances Ann, b. 1798, died 1822, m. Captain Paschal Buford, b. 1791, died 1875.

—James Hervey, b. 1800, m. Eliza Davis Pannill, d. 1863.

—Armistead Otey, b. 1801, m. 1st, Susan J. Terry of Tennessee; m., 2nd, Martha Ann Nolley of Mississippi; died 1863.

—Mildred Leftwich, born 1804, m. John Hopkins Otey, Jr.

—Walter Luke, born 1806, died 1876, m. Ellen Kyle of Raleigh, N. C.

—Littleton Waller Tazewell, born 1808, died unmarried.

—Robert Taylor Otey, born 1811, died in 1877, unmarried.

Owen

Owen and Jane Owen of Augusta county were among the early settlers of Lynchburg, where they established a school, which nearly every child in the city attended. This institution is said to have been one of the first in Virginia to adopt the use of Webster's Spelling Book at a time when his pronunciation and manner of dividing words was ridiculed.

Mr. and Mrs. Owen brought to the town influences which greatly advanced its prosperity and refinement, in their love of flowers, drawing and painting, which latter arts were taught together with plain and fancy needle-work in the school. The Owens also established a circulating library which fostered a taste for the best writings as the *Owens Circulating Library* afforded facilities for making many readers acquainted with the standard authors and stimulated them to pursue their reading still further. Mrs. Owen survived her husband many years and continued the school after his death. Of their children:

—Sarah married —— Hughes, died in 1820, leaving children.

—Benjamin Franklin, and —Septimus D. died young.

—Dr. William married Jane Latham of Culpeper county;—a sister married Dr. Henry Latham who established himself in Lynchburg where he pursued the practice of medicine. Many of the Owen connection devoted themselves to that choice of profession; Dr. Gray Latham, son of Dr. Henry, was one of this group. Dr. William Otway, son of Dr. William Owen, Sr. achieved much distinction in his practice. Colonel Robert Owen, another son of William, Sr., was for many years president of the Norfolk and Western Railway Company; his son, William (dec.) was in the Medical Department U. S. Army with the title of colonel; a second son, Robert, Jr., has long been a United States Senator and resident in Washington City many years.

Pannill

The name Pannill is first seen among Campbell records in a deed of sale to Pierce Butler Pannill from Williston Talbot of 177 acres of land extending from Talbot's corner to Drinkwater's line.

Samuel Pannill, from Orange county, in 1797 purchased of William and Moses Fuqua 600 acres on the north side of Staunton river from Wade's and Hick's corner, on Fuqua's road, along Henry's line and Hill's creek. William Fuqua was a resident of Lunenburg county; his son, Moses, in 1759, married Judith Woodson and settled in Campbell. His children: —Obediah m., 1785, Mary Morton of Prince Edward;—William m. Sarah . . .;—Nancy m., 1790, Josiah Morton, a soldier who had fought at Guilford C. H. and Yorktown;— Samuel m. Polly Armistead;—Lavinia m. John McCoy;— Elizabeth m. William Dupuy;—Polly m., 1803, Jeremiah Ward, Jr. After the sale of their land the Fuqua family moved to Kentucky, where Moses died in 1814.

Samuel Pannill was descended from William Pannill, of Richmond county, who married Frances Prows, and their son, William, m., in 1735, Sarah Bailey, and son, William (third in line), born 1738, married Ann Morton. This last William served in the Orange county Committee of Safety, of which James Madison was a member, in 1774; he had been sheriff of Orange and as that officer, made the proclamation from the court-house steps of the accession of George III to the throne of England. Wm. Pannill died in 1790; his son, Samuel, born 1770, moved to Pittsylvania, married Judith Boughton in 1795, and two years later bought the Fuqua land upon which he loccated his home. In 1800, through Richard Stith, trustee, he acquired 100 additional acres of the same tract. A ferry had been operated from Joseph Echols' land in Halifax across the Staunton to Fuqua's opposite bank, but it had fallen into disuse because managers of Echols' estate had let the boat drift away, and though appeal had been made for ferry re-establishment in 1793, there was still no provision made for it in 1797 when Pannill settled there; therefore petitions for it again were sent from Campbell, Halifax and Pittsylvania, urging the necessity. The ferry then established was later replaced by Pannill with a toll-bridge.

In 1807 Pannill bought of Jesse and John Cobbs (sons and executors of Charles Cobbs, dec.), 358 acres on Little Falling river, that being the upper part of Cobbs' estate at the west end of James Hurt's mill dam, along Wynn's creek to Boughton's land and adjoining his own. He acquired large land acreage and many slaves; was a member of Virginia Legislature from Campbell, on the Board of Public Works and president of the Roanoke Navigation Company. *Green Hill,* his home, constructed of brick and native stone, is the most complete private residence in the county. Situated at the top of a hill, there are various buildings surrounding it, such as loom-house, kitchen, double laundry with water and waste connections, stone stables, partitioned tobacco barn and other out-buildings, connected by rock walks and roadways, enclosed everywhere within stone walls. The original main entrance to the residence was through an avenue of cedar trees, across a wide lawn to a long side porch having round brick columns and flagged flooring upon which the front hall opened, with parlor and dining room either side and stairway leading to the dormer-windowed upper rooms. The present approach is by roadway, at the back of the premises, into a wide, walled avenue, separated from the rear yard by a stone wall through which there are square openings, large and small, for the egress and ingress of dogs, and a gateway with stone columns, leading into a box hedged walkway. The abundance of native rock caused free use of it in construction, and brown stone was obtained across the river in Pittsylvania. The group of buildings on the hill was designated *Upper Town*. Though simpler in ornamentation than many county residences, the interior of the dwelling-house has hand-carved wood work on its elaborate parlor mantel (reaching to the ceiling), high chair-boarding and stairway rail, with built-in cabinets for the dining room. Three flights of stairs lead to the various suites for male and female members and for guests, as these apartments were disconnected, each from the other, after the custom of the day.

The merchant store, chapel and mill called *Pannill's,* near which were the slave-quarters, were also known as *Lower Town*. Flour made at his large mill was shipped by batteaux manned by his slaves, to market at Weldon and Gaston, N. C. Gabriel Hunt, a former slave at Green Hill, now janitor at Campbell court house, takes much pride in recalling operations which were conducted at the old plantation. In 1801 Pannill patented 900 acres on the branches of Whipping creek and Watkins' road, including the head of Little Whipping creek, six islands in Staunton river opposite Big Island and including smaller islands and 141 acres embracing islands, rocks and shoals in Staunton river. He died aged 94 years, and in the distribution of his estate Green Hill fell to his son, John Pannill. Children of Samuel and Judith Pannill:

—John ⎫
—David ⎬ died unmarried.
—Samuel, Jr. ⎭
—Catherine m. Robert Wilson of Danville.
—Elizabeth m., 1841, Robert Rives, Jr., a member of the House of Delegates from Nelson county, 1823 to 1826 and again from 1827 to 1829.

—Mary m. Captain John D. Alexander, clerk of court at Rustburg.

—Ann m. ——— Graham.

—Judith m. Colonel John Wimbush. Their sons, Captain Abram, Samuel and James, served in the army of the Confederacy. Colonel Wimbush acquired the Green Hill property, upon which he lived for some years, then negotiated the sale of it to a purchaser named Randolph, said to have been of foreign birth, who paid for it with fraudulent bonds, and this so incensed the sons of Wimbush that one of them, coming upon Randolph when he was examining the deed of transfer, shot him dead. The homicide was tried by court but was acquitted.

Afterwards Green Hill was purchased at public sale by James Franklin, Sr., of Lynchburg, who, at his death, bequeathed it to his nephew, Samuel Hale of Bedford, and the property yet remains in the ownership of Hale's family.

Long Island is not far from Green Hill and the village nearby furnishes a station on the Virginian railroad, thus connecting it with Brookneal. At the time that Samuel Pannill lived at Green Hill, Long Island was owned by William Clark. Conrow Falls is opposite Long Island.

Payne

George Payne, ancestor of the Paynes of Campbell county, came from Bedfordshire, England. He and his brother Robert came to America together, Robert settling in Fauquier county. George held a grant from King George, embracing land in Goochland, Buckingham, Bedford and Campbell counties and land lying on Dan river in southern Virginia and northern North Carolina. He married Mary, the daughter of John Woodson; was a justice of the peace from 1728-29, and sheriff of Goochland from 1734-37; died in 1744. His son, Colonel John Payne, born 1713, inherited a large fortune and the family seat *White Hall,* in Goochland. He was a member of the House of Burgesses from 1752 to 1768 inclusive, lieutenant-colonel of militia and member of the Revolutionary

Committee of Safety of Goochland; married, 1st, Miss Archer. Children:—John m. Mary, dau. of John Chichester;—Archer m., 1st, Martha, dau. of Captain Nath. West Dandridge of the English army; m., 2nd, Betsy Brooks and lived at *New Market,* Goochland county, an estate given him by his father in 1775;—Robert died unmarried in 1776.

Children of Archer and Martha D. Payne:—Anne Spotswood m. —— Bryce;—Martha . . .;—Archer, Jr. . . .; —Dorothea D., born 1777, m. Edward Bolling, a nephew of Thomas Jefferson, and their son, Powhatan, patented 138 acres upon the head branches of Joshua's creek, Fluvanna river;— Elizabeth . . .;—America . . .;—Alexander Spotswood m. Charlotte, dau. of Archibald Bryce of Scotland, who bought 700 acres on Ivy creek, Campbell county, upon which he built a residence called *The Cottage,* and to which he moved in 1840 from *New Market,* the old Payne home;—Jane m., 1st, Robert Bolling; 2nd, James Ferguson;—John Robert Dandridge m. Susan Bryce, and lived for many years in Lynchburg; three sisters, Mrs. Nancy Bryce, Mrs. Susan Payne, and Mrs. Lilias James also lived there;—Lillias m. Dr. Richard Potts James; —Catherine m. Archibald Bolling (was 3rd or 4th wife);

Children of Alex S. and Charlotte B. Payne:—Dr. Robert Spotswood m. Frances Russell, dau. of John G. and Eliza R. Meem of Lynchburg;—David Bryce m. Helen James;—James Ferguson m. Frances, the dau. of Peter Dudley of Lynchburg; —William M. m. Frances A. Mitchell;—Charlotte E. born 1829, married John H. Winston;—Harriet, born 1831, m. Captain William Steptoe.

The old family burying-ground at *The Cottage* contains nine graves which are marked by tombstones: Jefferson Bolling, 1845; Mrs. Catherine Bolling, sister of Alexander S. Payne; Susan Payne, the wife of John R. D. Payne and sister of Mrs. Alex S. Payne; Alexander Spotswood Payne, 1858; Josephine Mitchell, the dau. of Rev. J. D. Mitchell; Charlotte Payne, wife of Alexander S. Payne; Harriet Steptoe, wife of Captain William Steptoe; Ida, the wife of Major William Payne; Kate, the sister of Captain William Steptoe.

Colonel John Payne, m., 2nd, Mrs. Jean Smith-Chichester, widow of John Chichester and dau. of Philip Smith of Northumberland, and his wife, Mary, daughter of Baldwin Matthews. Children:

—Anna, born 1758, m. Colonel James Gordon of Lancaster county.
—Philip, born 1760, m. 1783, Elizabeth, dau. of Capt. Nath. W. Dandridge, and sister of Mrs. Archer Payne.
—Jean, born 1762, m. William Lee of Northumberland.
—Smith, born 1764.
—George Woodson, born 1767.
—Robert, born 1770.

Colonel Philip Payne, a militia officer, resided at *Airy Mont,* on Seneca creek, near Marysville, a house yet standing, and near its entrance is a rock stable. Children:

—Jane Smith, born 1784, m. Tamerlain W., son of Henry Landon Davies of Bedford; her children:

Henry Landon m. Adeline, dau. of Edmund and Elizabeth Cobbs.
Elizabeth Wortley m. J. Addison Meriwether.
Catherine A. m. Benjamin Hunt and moved to Georgia.
George Washington m. Mary Landon.
Hennanne m. Charles Wall.
Martha Whiting m. —— Miller, of Iowa.
Edith m. —— Plamonda, of Oregon.

—John Smith, born 1786, m., 1st, Susanna Scott; m., 2nd, Susan E. N., dau. of Paulett Clark.

John S. Payne inherited Flat Creek Quarter; he built a residence called *White Hall,* after his grandfather's place in Goochland. Children:

Amanda m. George Yuille of Lawyers.
Clementine m. Frank Scott.
Elizabeth D. m., 1st, Robt. W. Nowlin; m. 2nd, O. Creed Clark; son, Dr. Paulett Clark.
Susan m. Jesse Hargreaves.

Philip W. m. Julia Ogden, grand-daughter of John M. Gordon.

Walter Tazewell m. Elizabeth R. Ligon.

Ann m. Jack Elliott of Naruna.

Martha m. Marco B. Carter.

Blanche T. m. Colonel Robert Withers, clerk of Campbell county.

—Elizabeth S., born 1788, m. Wm. Syme Cabell and moved to Mississippi in 1831,

—Dr. Nathaniel W., b. 1790, m. 1812, Catherine W., dau. of Robert Alexander.

—Philip Matthews, born 1794, m., 1st, Eliza Cobbs; m., 2nd, Mary E. Mitchell; lived at *Oak Grove,* Staunton river.

—Baldwin Matthews, born 1796, m., in 1827, Catherine Coles; lived at *Airy Mont,* on Seneca creek.

—Ann T., born 1799, m. Jeremiah Pannill.

—Eveline Washington, born 1801, m. Edward Ball Withers, of *Ivanhoe.*

—Camilla West, born 1803, m. Samuel Scott, Jr.

—Louisa Woodson, born 1807, m. John Coles.

—Clarissa Aylett, born 1809, m. Robert Wyatt.

Philip M. and Eliza Cobbs-Payne. Children:—John Alexander m. Isabella Perrow;—Missouri m. Dr. Horace Lemmon. Philip M. and Mary E. Mitchell-Payne;—Catherine M., born 1836, m. Dr. F. A. Perrow.

—Lucretia V., born 1837, m. Capt. Wm. E. Johns; children, Elizabeth, m. Davis; Lucretia; Sallie m. Harvey; Wm. E. Johns and W. Perrow Johns.

—Sarah, born 1845, m. F. C. Perrow.

—Samuel Garland, born 1847, m. Isabella Jones.

—Mosby Hale, born 1848, m. Mary Morriss of Lynchburg.

—Helen, born 1853, m. A. C. Berryman.

—Charles R., born 1842, died in the war of 1861-65.

Perrow

The family of *Perault* were Huguenots, who escaped from France after the Edict of Nantes in 1685, to England and from there, with the assistance of William of Orange, emigrated to America. A colony of them settled at Manakin town about the year 1700, on the south side of James river, 20 miles above Richmond in Prince William county, (now Powhatan). In a list of heads of these families, Charles Perault's name appears fourth from the top. In the registry of baptisms occurs in 1728 "Charle Pero, son of Daniel and Marie Pero," and in 1735 "Estiene Pero, son of Daniel and Marie Pero." From Daniel are descended the Perrows of Virginia; a name variously spelled Pero, Perro, Peros, Pierro and Perreau. From Manakin-town, members of the family migrated to Buckingham county, and settled on Slate river, where they owned slate and gold mines. In the latter part of the 18th century Stephen Perrow and his nephew, Daniel B., sold their lands in Buckingham and moved to Campbell county, where they settled upon adjoining farms along Beaver creek, near the court house road. The name had then become Anglicized Perrow. In 1783 Daniel B. Perrow was listed in the U. S. census as head of a family of five and located in Amherst. Daniel married Elizabeth, the daughter of David Fleming. He had previously purchased lot No. 6 at Campbell court house, which he and his wife sold in 1787. Daniel B. Perrow was a man of large property, and sporting proclivities; he maintained a stable of thorough-bred horses and built a track in a field near his house which is still called *race track field*. He was an ensign in the American Navy during the Revolutionary war, but bore the title of colonel, was later probably a militia officer. He represented the county in the Legislature for 11 terms, twenty-two years altogether. In 1815-16 he was sheriff of the county, with Nicolas Harrison as his security. His daughter, Mary, married Colonel Thomas Franklin of Pilot Mountain estate; no males bearing his name are now living, but he has female descendants; he died in 1821. Stephen's inventory made by Adam Clement, John Depriest and Charles Gilliam listed 265 acres on both sides of Beaver creek, near the property of David Ross and John Lynch. It was from Stephen Perrow that those bearing the name now, have descent. Stephen lived at *Apple Grove,* where much of the building now stands. His children were:

—Mary Ann m. ——— Bailey.

—Elizabeth m. Neilly Powell of Amherst.

—Stephen m., 1804, 1st, Dollie, dau. of Benjamin Cox; m., 2nd, Amy Green; children of 1st marriage:

Polina m. ——— Stewart.

Capt. William C. m., 1836, Uramia V. Cowling of Richmond.

Stephen W.

John F. m. Martha Cowling; in 1810 sold his brother, Stephen, his land and left the county.

Andrew J. m. Miss McGehee.

James S. m. Miss Ogden.

Caroline m. ——— Stephens.

Dolly m. ——— Rucker.

Betsy m. ——— Walthall.

Children of Stephen and Amy Green-Perrow:

Dr. Ferdinand A. m., in 1856, Catherine M., dau. of Philip M. Payne.

Isabella m. John A. Payne.

Thomas B. removed to Missouri.

Ann m. ——— Murrell.

Dr. Ferdinand A. Payne—graduate of University of Virginia, University of Pennsylvania, and College of Physicians and Surgeons,—of Marysville, Campbell county, was a prominent physician. His son, Dr. Ferdinand M. Perrow, follows the same profession in Lynchburg, where he is located.

William C. Perrow, born 1810, died 1887, was captain of militia during the war between the states. He purchased from Richard Morgan, in 1862, *Shady Grove,* where he afterwards resided. Four of his sons served in the Confederate army;— Alexander, born 1837, died 1915, m., 1st, Fannie Brooks; m., 2nd, Nettie Spriggs; he was a member of the first company organized in Campbell, Co. B, 11th Va. Reg., commanded by Capt. Robert C. Saunders: was captured at the battle of Seven

Pines, imprisoned for four months, exchanged and re-entered Company G, 2nd Va. Cavalry, commanded by Captain Jesse Irvine.

—Stephen C., born 1840, died 1907, left college at the outbreak of the war and joined an infantry company in Lynchburg, commanded by Captain Samuel Preston, of which he was elected lieutenant. In 1864 he resigned his commission to join Mosby's command. After the war he graduated in law at the University of Virginia, and practiced at Halifax C. H. with success and distinction.—Fletcher C., born 1842, died 1915, m. Sallie A., dau. of Philip M. Payne. Mrs. Perrow died at *Sunnyside,* and was buried at the Payne graveyard at *Oak Grove.* F. C. Perrow joined Company G, 2nd Va. Cav., under Capt. Jesse Irvine, participating in Manassas, Fredericksburg, Gettysburg, The Wilderness and Petersburg battles. —Willis L., born 1845, died 1895, m. Nellie Brooks; was a courier to Gen. R. E. Lee at the age of 16 years.

Dr. Mosby G. Perrow, son of Fletcher and Sallie A. Perrow, is Director of Public Health in Lynchburg.

R. L. Perrow, son of John F. and Martha Cowling Perrow of Route 18, between Rustburg and Lynchburg, is sheriff of the county.

Preston

Thomas Preston in 1773 patented 454 acres of land on the north side of Staunton river.

John and Rebecca Preston, with their eight minor children, moved from Goose creek in Loudoun county to South River Meeting in 1792; these children were:

—Zenas m. Elizabeth . . .; children, Albert, Vickers and Urban.

—John, Jr., in 1798, was disowned by the Society of Friends for laying wagers.

—Amos moved in 1810 to New Garden Meeting in Ohio.

—Moses was among the witnesses, in 1798, to marriages at South River Meeting.

—Sarah.

—Peter.

—Ann.

—William.

John and Rebecca Preston were witnesses to the marriage of William Davis (son of Samuel and Annis Davis), to Zelinda, the dau. of John and Mary Lynch, in 1793. Rebecca Preston was clerk of South River Meeting in 1803.

Motto on Preston coat-of-arms, "Leaving the towers of earth, we soar, D. V. to heaven."—

Marriages—Margaret Preston m. John T., son of Samuel and Anne Lipscombe-Davis, formerly of Louisa county, moved to Bedford; they were buried at South River Meeting burial ground;—Pleasant Preston m. Annie Elizabeth, the dau. of Thomas and Rachel Davis of Lynchburg, Capt. Samuel Preston, an officer in the Confederate army and attorney-at-law, was a son;—Moses Hurt Preston, son of Isaac and Sallie Hurt-Preston, m. Elizabeth D., dau. of Richard Tyree.

John Preston, born 1791, m. Martha B., the dau. of Captain Joshua and Martha Strange-Early, and moved in 1834 from Campbell to a residence twenty-seven miles from Nashville, Tenn. Children of this marriage were:

—Martha E. m. Abner E. Christian, Jr., son of Abner, Sr., and Frances E. Christian.

—Stephen Smith, a captain in the Confederate army, m. Ann M. Keyes, of Aberdeen, Miss. Capt. Preston represented his county in Tennessee several years previous to his removal to Memphis, where he was living in 1900.

—Captain William B. was killed in the Confederate army; left two sons and two daughters.

—Margaret E. m. James Coskey, and had three daughters.

—Docia K. m. Daniel Du Bose, who was killed in the Confederate army.

—Capt. Thos. Pleasant, killed 1864 in the Confederate army, left 3 daughters.

—Amorilla . . .;—John Clement m. ——— a farmer in Grimes county, Tenn.

—Joshua E., born 1841, held office in the Confederate army; later was an attorney-at-law, Navasota, Texas.

—James Steptoe, unmarried, killed in the Confederate army.

—Frances Early.

Pleasants

John Pleasants emigrated from Norwich, England, in 1665, to Virginia, settled on James river in 1668; his son, Joseph, m. Martha Cocke, whose son, John m. Susanna Woodson; they were Quakers. Thomas Pleasants was a preacher in 1739 at Cedar Creek Meeting, Hanover county, m. Margaret Jordan; Joseph m. Elizabeth Jordan; James in 1775 was a member of a select committee to procure ammunition for county use.

The recurrence in many Campbell county families of Pleasant as a given name, seems to indicate extensive connection of that family with others, yet this supposition is not confirmed by the marriage bonds on record, and popular use of the name may have merely testified the regard felt for Preacher Thomas Pleasants.

John Hampden Pleasants, son of James Pleasants of Goochland, moved to Lynchburg, where he established *The Press* at the time when the press of Lynchburg was at a low ebb, and he produced a revolution in the printing establishment. He married Ann Eliza Irvine.

Prewitt

The name Prewitt is variously given among county records, Prewitt, Prewett, Pruitt. In 1750 Richard Prewitt, together with Timothy Murrell, patented 465 acres both sides of Hall's creek, adjoining Hall's line. In 1755 Thomas Pruitt patented 437 acres on Catawba creek. The will of Daniel Pruitt was recorded at Halifax court in 1750 and his two sons, William and John, were executors, their mother, Sarah Pruitt, executrix. Michael Prewitt settled in Campbell and appears to have married two sisters, first, Sarah, dau. of Moza and Phoebe Hurt, and secondly, her sister, Bettie Hurt. The father of Michael Prewitt emigrated from Ireland many years before the Revolution. He patented 1770 acres on Falling river between 1773 and 1780. Children of Michael Prewitt:

—Robert, m. Patsy Candler, and moved to Lexington, Ky.; he possessed a Bible in which he wrote "My father was Michael Prewitt of Campbell county, Virginia," and on the fly-leaf was the name of his son "William S. Prewitt, given to him by his father, Robert Prewitt, as the testimony of the esteem of his father, March 8, 1815." Robert had a second son, Nelson Pruitt-Prewitt; descendants in Missouri and California.
—Rachel m. Robert Shipley.
—Jane . . .;—Elisha . . .;—Judith . . .
—Michael m. Elizabeth Simpkins; had a son Joseph (who m. Leah, the dau. of Frederick and Sarah Tomlinson-Moss), and dau., Martha Tomlinson, who died in 1870.
—Byrd, m., 1782, Sarah Hurt;—Joseph . . .;—Joshua . . . .;—Elizabeth . . .

A petition was sent on June 8, 1782, to the Assembly requesting that a passage be kept open in the dam, in order to conserve supplies of fish in Falling river. The petition contained complaint against Michael Prewitt for having built a grist mill across the river within two miles of its mouth. This bill was rejected, yet five years later a similar one stating that before the passage up the river was obstructed by Michael Prewitt's erection of his mill near the junction of Staunton river, the river was well supplied with fish for the support of their families, but had been wholly deprived since, along a boundary of twelve or fifteen miles; they therefore requested that Prewitt be compelled to remove his mill. Assembly refused to interfere between Prewitt and his neighbors in the charge of river obstruction and he was left free to reap the benefit of his milling operations. In 1784 Prewitt sold to David Hutcheson 450 acres lying on the south side of Falling river, beginning at Mitchell's corner and crossing a branch several times till another branch was reached along Dougherty's line. Again in 1805 Michael and his wife, Sarah Preitt, sold Thomas Scott 496 acres adjoining Staunton and Falling rivers. In 1778 a Michael Prewitt m. M. Thurston of Halifax county. The marriage of Frances Prewitt to Thomas Murrell in 1811 is among the marriage bonds in Campbell. Anthony Prewitt m., in 1785, Susannah Ghoulson of Halifax county.

Robertson

In 1783 John Robertson patented 1604 acres of land lying on both sides of Cub creek. In 1756 Robertson patented 200 acres on both sides of Avents branch in Lunenburg county, adjoining Manning's line.

James Robertson (born 1744, died 1819), married Rachel, the daughter of Edward Phair, and his wife, Elizabeth, dau. of John Beard (will 1780), of Campbell county. Children:

—Nancy m., 1818, 1st, Captain Samuel Doak; m., 2nd, Colonel Bell, of Missouri; she died 1844.

—John, born 1763 (died 1814, aged 45 years), m. Miss McDearman; son, Dr. John Robertson.

—Joseph, born 1769.

—Isabel, born 1774, m. ———— Gibson.

—Mary, born 1777, m. in 1812 ———— Galbreath; dau. Rachel, m. ———— Woodson.

—James, Jr., born 1779, died 1845.

—Abraham, born 1782.

—Captain David, born 1785, m. Eliza Steele (b. 1799), dau. of John and Margaret D. Thompson; he was a soldier in the war of 1812, died in 1856; dau. Margaret, born 1820; m. George T. Reveley, had 3 sons, Wm. Wirt, Geo. Francis, and David, cadets at V. M. I., when the war of 1861-65 started; sent to drill recruits; the two eldest died from exposure. David

R. Reveley m. Alice Gibson of Rockbridge county: a dau., Bettie Croton.—Major James Ewen Robertson, born 1832 (died 1907) married Mary Jane, dau. of Major John W. and Maria F. West. Children, William Walter, born 1856; James Ewen, born 1872, died 1923.—William Walter Robertson represents the Charles E. Merrill Company, of New York, in Oklahoma City, Okla.—Elizabeth Bruce Robertson m., 1st, Colonel John T. A. Martin; m., 2d, Jesse Thornhill Davidson: children of 1st marriage, John R., Willis V. and Chassie B. Martin.

Captain David Robertson died in 1856. All of the older members of the family are buried in the family burying-ground at the old Robertson home, which was formerly in Campbell, but when a strip of the county was given Appomattox in 1845 and another in 1848, the Robertson lands became registered in Appomattox. Their home was about two miles from what was Appomattox Depot on the Norfolk and Western R. R., now the Court House. Old Appomattox C. H., situated near the scene of Lee's surrender, was burned down in 1892 and all records in it were then destroyed. Only a few tax receipts remain: among these are found listed 2167½ acres, embraced in eight tracts on Falling river, belonging to David Robertson as certified by William A. Clement, clerk of Campbell, and Allan L. Wyllie, commissioner of revenue: the lands of James Robertson, Sr., and Jr., William Robertson, of Richmond, Abram and Archibald Robertson. Edward Robertson (living on Richmond Road in 1847) was taxed on five parcels of land aggregating 326 acres lying in Appomattox county. The descendants of Dr. John Robertson live around Spout Spring on the N. & W. R. R., and are Dr. D. Mott Robertson and John Robertson; and a brother, Robert G. Robertson, in Lynchburg.

Elizabeth S., wife of David Robertson and only child of John and Marg. Davidson Thompson, lived in a brick house a mile or so from the present Court House, which has recently been renovated and become occupied, about three miles from the Robertson burying-ground. Six graves are marked with engraved stones: James Robertson, Sr., aged 75 years, died 1819; Rachel Phair Robertson, aged 73 years, died 1822; John Robertson, aged 45 years, died 1814; David Robertson, born 1785, died 1856; Mrs. Nancy Robertson, aged 59 years, died 1844; James Robertson, Jr., aged 45 years, died 1849.

Rosser

John Rosser, entitled to 200 acres of land by the proclamation of 1763, patented land in 1765. In 1779 Jonathan Rosser patented 230 acres on the east side of Martin's fork of Falling river; in 1782 Jonathan Rosser (formerly of Bedford county), sold David Rosser of Campbell 470 acres of land lying on the north fork of Falling river, being the plantation upon which David Rosser lived and which extended from Jonathan Rosser's to Henry Terrell's line on towards McMurtry's mill, by Joseph Tweedy's and Thomas Helm's lands, and joining Richard Elams. In 1786 Jonathan Rosser was an inspector of tobacco at Lynch's ferry.

In 1790, David Rosser's will was recorded in court, with his wife, Ann Rosser, and John Forbes executors; devised a tract on Falling river and his grist mill to be divided between his sons, Andrew and Samuel; mentioned daughters, Elizabeth, Susanna, Sarah and Ann; also dau., Winny, wife of Andrew Torrence and her son; Joseph Tweedy and Robert Richardson, witnesses.

In 1817 John and Nancy Rosser sold John Bailey of Charlotte county 215 acres on Bear Creek, both sides of Lawyer's road, adjoining the lands of Richard Daniel, Micajah Hubbard, John Hubbard, Wm. M. Hubbard, James Shannon and Lindsey Crawley. In 1823 John Rosser petitioned to have his marriage to his deceased wife's sister legalized. General Thomas Rosser of the War Between the States and the Spanish-American War was of this family. When after the surrender in 1865 he was retreating, with the aim of joining General Johnston in North Carolina, his horses gave out and he was forced to leave his cannon and buried them on Ward's road, the route he was pursuing; they have never been recovered. He burned the bridge over Staunton river and it was not replaced for many years. There are a number of marriages in this family recorded in the court marriage lists:

1786. William Rosser to Elizabeth Wood.
1792. Thomas Rosser to Nancy Tweedy.
1795. Sarah Rosser to Samuel Moore.
1794. Patty Rosser to John Arrington.
1796. Lavinia Rosser to William Glass.
1797. Betsy Rosser to William Moorman.
1799. Ambrose Rosser to Sally Finch.
1803. Pleasant Rosser to Judith Jones.
1805. John Rosser to Mary Franklin.
1809. John Rosser to Nancy Wood.
1810. Sally Rosser to Charles Arrington.
1812. John Rosser to Vicey Tweedy.
1814. Joel Rosser to Nancy Glass.
1818. Jesse Rosser to Elizabeth Finch.

Russell

Records of many members of the Russell family are to be found, but no indication of the relation they bore to one another. Thomas Russell married Sarah Asher in 1796. In 1738 John Russell patented two tracts respectively of 281 and 137 acres of land on the south side of Staunton river. In 1749 he had acquired land on Difficult creek. In 1740 William Russell patented 300 acres on the south side of the Staunton: in 1758 he was serving as a private under Major William Caldwell in Lunenburg county and in 1760 one of the same name was a sergeant in Captain James Gunn's company, of Col. Bryd's regiment, in the expedition against the Indians, and was registered in 1780 from Pittsylvania county. In 1742 Andrew Russell was a private in Company No. 4; in 1758 Samuel Russell was a member of a company from Brunswick county: the same year Henry Russell was listed among those officers of the Virginia Regiment, who made an humble address upon Washington's retirement as commander of Virginia troops December 27th, 1758, which was directed "To George Washington, Esq., colonel of the Virginia Regiment, and commander of all Virginia forces." David Russell is mentioned under date 1784 and his property is recorded in early court archives. Philemon and Jeffrey Russell jointly patented 400 acres on Miles creek.

Robert Russell, who patented 350 acres on both sides of Flat creek, seems to have been the ancestor of those of the name who remained in Campbell, and his original patent has been handed down to his descendants. He patented two other tracts in the same section, but the patents for those were lost in their transmission to a branch of the family living near Franklin, Tennessee. This Robert Russell married in England Ann Bard; his will (1791) mentions his wife, Ann, sons James and Robert, daughter Elizabeth, who married Jerrard Dougherty, and had a son, John; daughter, Catherine, unmarried; daughter Millie married a Fleming, daughter Eleanor m. John Robinson; daughter Mary m. James R. Rowland and moved to Kentucky, carrying with her the family Bible; daughter Ann m. James Boaz and lived on the headwaters of Flat creek; had two children, Robert and Tabitha, and a grandson, Pleasant Russell.

—James Russell m. Rosanna Rutherford; had a large family of children, some of whom moved to Tennessee, others to Mississippi; his dau. Polly m. Barnard Rucker, and resided in Bedford county; dau. Patsy, m. Willis D. Elliott and lived near Winfall; dau. Nancy m. John Hay, and lived on Seneca creek and their son, James Russell Hay, was a captain in the Confederate army, and for 40 years county surveyor of Campbell. Captain James, Jr., youngest son of James and Rosanna Russell, born 1800, married in 1836 Mary W. Fitz Patrick; owned 1800 acres on Flat creek and its branches; was captain of a cavalry company in the Virginia Militia in 1828, and a justice of the peace from 1846 to 1851. His children were:

—Edmund, of the Confederate army, who was killed at the battle of Seven Pines.

—Rosanna m. Burnley P. Johnson, died in 1911; children, Bessie P. (of Lawyers), and Mary B. who married Samuel B. Rosser.

—Martha A.

—James, 1st lieutenant of artillery in the Confederate army, died at Gordon, Texas, leaving daughters, and son, Richard C.

—Robert, of Flat creek.

—William H. m. Miss Candler; son, Robert A. state senator from 1920 to 1922, appointed on Board of Visitors of V. P. I. College by Governor Byrd.

—Richard H., daughters, Mollie R. Duke, near Lawyers, Mrs. Charles Boaz Fitz Patrick of Gordonsville, and Mildred G. Crews, of Aspen, Va.

A part of the original Russell tract lying on Flat creek was purchased by Lynchburg for the City Farm and lies just east of Candler's mountain.

Scott

Members of the Scott family settled in Caroline, Prince Edward, Bedford and Amherst. Mrs. Anna M. Scott, wife of Roy Scott, possesses a family Bible of 1715 (printed at Oxford, England), which contains much of the Scott history. James Scott (born 1690), an emigrant from the Highlands of Scotland, belonged to the Clan McGregor. He and his son, Thomas, bought tracts of land from the royal governor of Virginia Colony. Thomas was born in 1718 in St. Mary's parish, Caroline county; m., in 1742, Martha (born 1721, died 1777), daughter of Rice and Frances Williams; children:

—Rice, born 1743.

—Frances S., born 1745, m. 1766 James, son of Dudley and Sarah Gatewood.

—John, born 1747.

—Thomas H., born 1749, was a captain in the army; m., in 1767, Isabel ———; she died 1770.

—James, born 1752.

—Samuel Beverley, born 1754, m. 1784, Ann, dau. of John B. Roy, of Spotsylvania.

—William, born 1756, m. 1781, Ann, dau. of Gabriel and Martha Waller-Jones of Spotsylvania.

—Robert, born 1758, died ————.

Thomas Scott's will, recorded 1773, devised 1000 acres to his son, Rice, in Prince Edward, where Rice was living; to his son, John, £70 to pay the balance due on land where John lived in Amherst; to his son, Thomas, slaves and furniture; to James 400 acres in Prince Edward, purchased of John Bagby, where he lived; to Samuel and William and Robert, slaves; to daughter, Frances Gatewood, for her sole and separate use, and not her husband's, slaves and furniture (itemized); to grand-daughter, Martha Gatewood, a slave. The land upon which he lived and other in his possession to be sold and the money equally divided between 3 sons, Samuel, William and Robert. His wife to have the liberty to live on his home place with whichever of his sons should live there till she thought proper to move. Capt. Hawes, John B. Roy, George Gates, and sons, Rice and James, were appointed executors. A codicil was added to the will as follows:

"As James Gatewood has brought suit against me since I had this will wrote it is my desire if he should recover more than herein bequeathed to my daughter, Frances, which he married, that all I have bequeathed to her and her daughter, and my account of sundry articles delivered to my daughter and her husband, shall be recovered out of the sum he recovers by law suit, if it amounts to more than I have given him."

Signed, THOMAS SCOTT.

Two sons of Thomas Scott, Major Samuel and Colonel William Scott, at the close of the Revolutionary War, settled in Campbell. Samuel Scott enlisted as lieutenant of Virginia Cavalry. In 1777 was captain of Georgia cavalry; retired from this service January 18, 1779; afterwards was a major in the Virginia troops and so served until close of the Revolu-

tion. He was in the battles of Savannah and Guilford C. H.
and others; was wounded in the foot in an engagement with
Jones. His widow, Ann Scott, was allowed a pension upon
her application Sept., 1838, when she was 76 years old and
then living in Lynchburg. Major Samuel Scott in 1786
bought of Chiles Terrell of Albemarle 400 acres lying on
both sides of Turkey branch at Henry Tate's corner, land lying between Benjamin Rucker and Chiles Terrell. In 1790
Samuel Scott went on William Henderson's sheriff's bond to
Gov. Randolph. Scott's home was on the Forest road, a property now owned by the Barksdale family, and there Major
Scott and his son Beverley are buried. The inscription on the
tomb of the latter reads "Beverly Roy Scott, b. Jany. 11, 1796,
son of Major Samuel and Ann Roy Scott, d. June 3, 1837."
He was an officer on board the Caroline when it was blown up
near New Orleans during war with Great Britain and escaped
by jumping overboard and swimming to shore. He afterwards
fought under Gen. Jackson in the memorable battle of New
Orleans on Jany. 8, 1815; and lost a leg in that battle. In
applying for a pension Ann Scott gave the record of both her
husband and her son, Beverly R.

Major Samuel Scott's home on Forest road was called
Locust Thicket. In 1804 he was one of the justices of the
peace in Campbell. That year he patented 114 acres and 54¾
acres on Ivy creek and the south branch of Ivy. Court ordered
the way viewed for a road from the Quaker Meeting House,
running by Scott's Mill to the public road leading from Bedford to Lynchburg. In 1807 Edmund Tate petitioned for authority to erect a toll bridge across Blackwater creek on the
road from the county line by Samuel Scott's property to
Lynchburg. Children of Samuel and Ann Roy-Scott:

—Belinda Roy m. James Moseley.

—Agnes Walker m. John M. Gordon, children, Ann B. and
Louisa P. Gordon.

—Aphire Beverly married William Rose in 1805.

—Emily Williams m. Patrick P. Burton, and had a son, Philip
Burton.

—Marian Stanard m. Wm. Cobbs; their dau. Emily m. Edward Sextus Hutter.

—Beverly Roy m. Almira Anderson.

—Samuel McGregor m. Camilla West, dau. of Philip Payne.

Major Scott died in 1822 and his will then recorded, reserved for a burying-ground forever one acre of land back of his garden, gave his wife one half of his estate except the tract lying in Bedford, called the Ivy creek tract, which he devised to his son, Samuel, and his mansion house and plantation at *Locust Thicket,* where he lived; Samuel and son-in-law Gordon, were appointed trustees of the property devised to his daughter, Belinda Roy; he had conveyed 250 acres of land in Bedford on Cheese creek (bounded by the lands of Benj. Wigginton, George Cabell and others), in trust as permanent provision for his daughter, Aphire Beverly; to Mary Ann Stanard he gave a lot in Lynchburg adjoining John Lynch and Wm. Radford. To Beverly was devised land lying in Bedford and Campbell, called *Blankenship's* tract, conveyed to him by deed November, 1818. Samuel M. to receive two tracts, *Locust Thicket* and *Ivy creek* upon condition that he conveyed to executors in trust the tract called *Blackwater,* hereafter conveyed to him. Executors, J. M. Gordon, Beverly R. and Samuel M. Scott.

Colonel William Scott, first a lieutenant in the Revolutionary army, raised a company of his own and became its captain. In 1776 he went with his brother, Thomas Scott, to Savannah, Georgia, and was assigned to Captain Letty Mosby, Jr.'s, Company in Colonel Crittendon's Georgia Regiment. It is said that upon one occasion when five of his wife's brothers were killed in battle, he conveyed their bodies from Norfolk to his home for interment; he was engaged in the battle of Great Bridge, Va.; was taken prisoner at Briar creek, carried to Savannah and confined during the siege. In 1784 James Gatewood of Bedford county sold William Scott, for £2000, 1150 acres of land lying on both sides of James river in Bedford, Campbell and Amherst counties.

Children of Colonel William and Ann Jones-Scott:
—Gabriel died unmarried.
—Robert m. Miss Price of Charlottesville.
—William Waller, born 1795, lived in Amherst, m. Eliza, dau. of Reuben Pendleton and his wife, Eliza Garland.
—Thomas Hazelwood, lived in Campbell and m., 1st, Margaret Parks Burks of Amherst county; m., 2nd, Malinda Grigsby.
—Hugh Roy, lived at the *Grove* in Bedford; m. Elizabeth J. Burks of Amherst; had 3 children, Dr. Samuel Burks, m. Sallie Patterson of Buckingham county.

Frank Goode m. Maggie Scott, dau. of Rice Scott.

Elizabeth Roy m. Captain John Cabell Ward of Lynchburg.
—Martha m. Thomas Goode of Richmond.
—Nannie m. William Harrison of Lynchburg.
—Susanna m. (1st wife), John S. Payne of Campbell county.
—Harriet m. Benjamin Wigginton of Culpeper county.
—Anne M. L. m. Charles Cobbs of Bedford county.

Thomas Scott lived at *Homestead,* Campbell county. Children: Rice, Margaret, Roy Beverly and Nannie.

Children of William Waller and Eliza Scott of Amherst county:
—William Preston m. Miss F. Tinsley of Amherst; son Dr. Edward Waller Scott of Amherst.
—Rev. Hugh Roy, m. Miss J. C. Harrison of Richmond; m., 2nd, Miss A. M. Scott, of Washington, D. C.. Children: Roy Waller; Florence Gadsden, m. in 1883, Herbert B. Henry, of New York; issue, 2 sons.
—James Pendleton m. Miss J. Kirkpatrick of Richmond. Children: John K., Bessie P., Jellis, Walter, George, Chester, Fortune, Nannie, and Mary Deane.
—Robert Garland m., 1st, Miss L. Shelton of Amherst. Children: Lizzie, Florence, Fannie, Robert, William, James, Roy, Waller and Edward; Robert G. Scott m., 2nd, Miss Ida Bailey of Lynchburg.

—Frances m. George Dameron of Amherst. Children: Charles, Emma Roy, Anna, George, Robert, Fannie;—Eliza Adelaide m. William Steen and moved to Wheeling.
—Mary Camden m. C. C. Wingfield of Lynchburg. Children: Charles, Walker, Ossie.

Scott

A Scott family of Scotch ancestry settled near Brookneal, where descendants are still living and are prominently associated with the business of the town. Joseph Scott, Sr., married Sarah, dau. of William Mayo, of Powhatan county, who helped Colonel Byrd run the dividing line between Virginia and North Carolina. Mayo had married Frances, the dau. of Enoch Gould, a leading merchant of the Barbadoes, where he had been banished for participating in the Monmouth Rebellion in 1685.

Joseph Scott served in the Revolution, beginning as a 2nd lieutenant in 1775 and passing through the intermediate grades to major under General Muhlenburg; was wounded at Germantown in 1777, and transferred to the 5th Virginia Regiment in 1781. His son, Joseph, Jr., was also an officer in the war waged for independence, having received the commission of second lieutenant under Captain Thomas Nelson in 1777, later made first lieutenant and 1780 became captain. The younger Scott left Hampden-Sidney College to enter the army and equipped a company at his own expense.

Major Scott was living in Amelia, before moving to Campbell and there his son, Captain Joseph Scott, born in 1752, married in 1778 Elizabeth, the daughter of Edward and Henrica Booker: children of this marriage were, daughters, Elizabeth, Judith, Sarah and Nancy; and sons, Edward Booker, Joseph, 3rd, and Jack; the latter married Sarah Munroe, and moved to Halifax near Brookneal: his children were:—
—Charles m. Sallie A., dau. of James and Nancy Clark-Adams;
—Alex married Margaret, dau. of Nathan Hancock;—Elizabeth m. John E. Fore, Sr.;—Tom, John and Polly unmarried;

—Kitty m. Richard E. Adams, Sr., brother of Mrs. Charles Scott.

Charles Scott was a railroad contractor; owned 1000 acres on Cottontown road; iron works in Southwest Virginia; a flour mill in Lynchburg (where he settled); and acquired a nitrate plant at Saltville. He furnished the Confederate government with flour and nitrate from his mills. The wife of Charles Scott was descended from John Adams, whose people came from Massachusetts, and he had moved from Fairfax county, settling about 4 miles from Brookneal, where he built a home still standing and occupied by his descendants. Children of Charles and Sally Adams-Scott:—James m. Lucy Mullens;— August W. m. Maggie Seay;—Charles, Jr., m. Kate duVal;— Susan m. Richard H. T. Adams;—Robert C. m. Mary C. Terrell;—Ella m. Cleland K. Nelson;—Henry m. Lizzie O. Hatcher.

Children of Alex. and Margaret Hancock-Scott:—Ida m. W. J. Poindexter;—Ora B. m. John T. Jennings;—Charles m. Nannie Tanner;—Annie m. Rev. W. L. Fisher;—Hallie m. Philip Withers, of Danville;—Wm. W. m. Eloise ———, of Detroit.

Children of Elizabeth Scott and John Fore:—Wm. m. Maria Johnson;—John E.—Sallie m. John Hines and moved to Bowling Green, Ky.

Children of Richard, Sr., and Kitty Scott-Adams:—John J. m. Nannie Callaway;—Mary E. m. Capt. Wm. P. Graham, of Del Rey, Calif.;—Nannie m. James Clark.—Richard E. m. Mattie Cook, of Brookneal;—Emma W. m. G. B. J. duVal, she died and duVal married, 2ndly, her sister, Jennie;—Jesse, T. m. Lou. E., dau. of Rev. Rd. E. Booker, and lives at the old home built by John Adams, the first of his name to settle there.

Slaughter

Robert Slaughter married Frances Ann, daughter of Cadwallader Jones (will 1725), his son, Robert, m., in 1723, Mary, daughter of Augustus Smith, vestryman of St. Mark's Parish, Culpeper county. Robert Slaughter, 3rd in name and line, (born 1724, died 1790), married in 1750, Susannah Harrison. In 1785, when members of the Slaughter family emigrated to Kentucky (among them Gabriel Slaughter), Charles, a brother of the latter, remained in Virginia; married Elizabeth, (born 1757, died 1780), daughter of John and Sarah White Poindexter of Louisa county. A deed between Charles Slaughter, Daniel and Elizabeth Marshall, John and Patience Marshall and Robert Cobbs (who married the sister of Slaughter's wife), was recorded in Campbell, involving the transfer of 282 acres of land lying on Whipping creek in 1804, showing that Slaughter had then moved to Campbell.

In 1823 there was a settlement of Charles Slaughter's estate, when the widow received one-fourth and the balance was divided between his four children,—John P. Slaughter (named for his grand-father Poindexter)—Ann P. Davenport (neê Slaughter)—Robert Harrison Slaughter, and Eliza F. Bullock (neê Slaughter).

Charles Slaughter ran away from boarding school to join the Revolutionary army, as a private in Capt. Alex Spotswood Dandridge's troop of light dragoons, commanded by Col. Theodore Bland from July, 1776 to Dec., 1778. His eldest son—Dr. John Poindexter, seems to have married three times; 1st m. in 1805, Patsy Armistead of Charlotte county; children:

—Charles Darwin m. Judith E. Clemens, had 2 sons, Dr. John and Henry Clay.

—Sarah m. Josiah Hunter; 3 children, Dr. Joseph E., Robert and Jane.

—Pauline m. Robert Hunter; children, Mrs. Selina Dinwiddie and Rev. Joshua Hunter.

Dr. John P. Slaughter, m., 2nd, Agnes Cobbs of Bedford; children, 1 daughter, Susan Agnes. Married, 3rd, in 1816, Vera Kirkpatrick. His will, recorded in 1837, mentions daughters, Mrs. Sarah A. Hunter, Mrs. Paulina A. Hunter, Mrs. Susan Arabella Nicolas and son, Charles Darwin Slaughter. Daughters of Charles and Elizabeth P. Slaughter were:

—Ann Poindexter, born 1782, m. in 1801, Glover Davenport.

—Elizabeth F., born 1796, m. in 1810, James P. Bullock.

—Dr. Robert Harrison, 2nd son of Charles Slaughter, Sr., born 1786, m. 1st, Miss Harrison, s. p.; m., 2nd, Mary Rice, daughter of Rice and Elizabeth Hamner-Garland of Albemarle county. Children:—Charles Rice, born 1819, m., in 1846, Catherine M., dau. of James Parker and Katurah Stone-Garland;—Dr. Samuel Rice, m. Elizabeth Henderson: went to California in 1849;—John Flavel, born 1828, died 1893, m. Mary Harker of Mount Holly, N. J;—Celeste Pauline m. (2nd wife), in 1881, Jas. Madison Cobbs, s. p.;—Austina W. m. Ro. Withers Broadnax, whose dau., Mary Roberta m. George Cameron of Petersburg, Va.

Children of Charles Rice and Catherine M. Slaughter were:

—Mary E. m. Judge J. Singleton Diggs, son of Rev. Thomas and Elizabeth Ford-Diggs of Matthews county, Va.; children, Catherine, member of Lynchburg Public School faculty and Dudley of the Int. Gen. Elec Co., with office at Schenectady, N. Y.—Charles Alex, m. Bettie Garland Brown, daughter C. Althea m. J. M. Vest of Huntingdon, W. Va.;—Catherine Lightfoot Slaughter.

Mary Roberta, only child of Dr. Saml. Slaughter, m. Chas. Matson Harker, Jr., of Mount Holly, N. J.

Children of John F. and Mary H. Slaughter were:—Dr. Charles, m. 1st, Mary Duke; m., 2nd, Hattie Gray.

—John Flavel, unmarried;—Robert m. Augusta Bannister of Alabama, sons Robert and Munroe;—Dr. Samuel G. m. Mayme Richardson; children Rosalie, Willis and Samuel;— Edith Ridgway m. Judge R. T. W. Duke, Jr., of Charlottesville; 5 children, Mary, R. T. W., John S., Eskridge and Helen;—Dr. B. Rosalie m. Baxter Morton; she was engaged during the World War on special relief work in Servia; was instrumental in securing scholarships in the United States for Servian students; decorated for service rendered Servia.

—Judge William Austin Slaughter, of Mt. Holly, N. J., m. Florence, dau. of Rev. John K. Lewis.

Charles R. Slaughter was an M.A. of the University of Virginia; member of Virginia Convention of 1861, and drew up the articles of the secession of Virginia; died in 1862. John F. Slaughter, alumnus of Virginia University, was a member of the "Committee of Nine," who interviewed Gen. Grant in Washington at close of war, and helped to secure an early re-admission of Virginia into the Union; was president of the First National Bank of Lynchburg from 1876 till 1892; his sons, Charles, Samuel G. and William, are alumni of Virginia University and daughter, Rosalie, is an alumna of the Philadelphia Woman's Medical College.

The Slaughter-Garland home place, *Oakley*, Campbell county, stood not far beyond the present Westover section of Lynchburg, but the house was destroyed by fire, in recent years.

Electric Service

Dudley Diggs, graduate of Virginia Military Institute, entered service with the General Electric Company at their Lynn plant on a graduate testing course of one and a half years; was then transferred to the commercial section of the company in the street lighting department with charge of Headlights, Intensified Arc Lamps and other arc lamps. While located at Gloversville, N. Y., he received the shock of an electric flash which prevented the use of his eyes for nearly a year. At the time the Ornamental Luminous Arc lamp appeared he was put in charge of the sales of the new lamp and was called upon to deliver talks before technical and commercial associations at Indianapolis, Atlanta, Detroit and other places most important of which was at Michigan State Section of the National Electric Lamp Association, which chartered a steamer and held meetings for a week, while they cruised through Lake Huron, Georgian Bay and other places. This was the first large delegation before which the new lamp was presented. Diggs was sent to other conventions to make similar addresses. He conceived the idea of co-operative selling by a group of

pole manufacturers in conjunction with the General Electric
Company and received an appropriation for this purpose, and
held a joint meeting at Lynn. From this meeting grew one
of the permanent policies of this section of the company, far-
reaching in effect, as to the manner of selling the type of lighting to the public. Since then co-operative selling of an idea
by a group of manufacturers of an association has become
an every-day incident.

In New York district Diggs was detailed as street lighting
and general lighting specialist, covering New York city, part
of Pennsylvania, New Jersey and Connecticut from 1913 to
1920. During the World War his service was protective lighting of Ellis Island,—which was used as a place of detention
for German spies,—protective and utilitarian lighting of shell
loading plants, ship building plants, protection of New York
bridges, New York water supply and points of embarkation.
In 1920 he was engaged with the International General Electric Company, which handles export business of the General
Electric pendants and other manufactures, negotiating agree-
ments for exclusive representation abroad. In 1924 was sent
to South America to study merchandising methods in order
to assist the companies operating there and especially to assist
in a large lighting proposition in Santiago, the capital of Chile.
He also assisted local engineers in laying out a complete new
lighting scheme.

Later the Chilean government sent its foremost engineer to
the United States in company with the Construction Engineer
of the Electric Properties of the large public utilities in Chile,
and the financial managers of the Whitehall Securities Corporation of London, to study methods in the United States and
to place order for complete equipment for this project. Diggs
had charge of the delegation; after an examination, they decided to adopt Electric Company material and placed order for
all the material. This was the first city in the world with over
a half million population to change its entire lighting for the
whole city at one time. Its lighting cost millions and will make
of it the best lighted city. A separate electrical merchandis-

ing company was formed and at Diggs' recommendation an agent was sent from the United States to start it. The store inaugurated by this company is the most up-to-date in Chile, and is a joint enterprise of the International General Electric Company and the International Machinery Company, which is a Chilean representative of the General Electric Company.

Under auspices of the local technical societies and universities Diggs lectured at Buenos Aires and Rosaria, Argentine, San Paula and Rio de Janeiro, Brazil; with a special moving picture and lantern slide lecture at the Universities in Santiago, Chile, and before officials at Valparaiso, Chile; he was sent in 1926 to England to investigate conditions in a subsidiary company and map out a course of observation for the manager, who came to America in conjunction with one of their directors. Dudley Diggs is located at Schenectady, N. Y., at the present time.

Snow

Four Campbell families connected by marriage, were those of Hughes, Snow, Thompson and Walden. In 1765 Henry Snow received a grant from George III of 410 acres lying on the north side of Staunton river and Plum Tree branch, including what was later known as the Moon place. In 1783, Henry Snow married Martha Cheek.

Thomas, Jr., and Mark Snow, sons of Thomas, Sr., and Winifred Snow, served at the battle of Guilford C. H., with Richard Walden; Thomas Snow, under Capt. James Rice and Mark under Capt. Jacobus Early, in Col. Charles Lynch's regiment. Mark Snow later married Elizabeth Torrence. Sold 115 acres of land (beginning at a line patented by Henry Snow to Watery branch) to Capt. Jacobus Early and moved to Georgia a power of attorney being sent from Wilkes county, Ga., in accordance with an act "enabling persons living in other countries to dispose of their estates in this commonwealth with more ease and convenience." Mark Snow settled in Gwinnett county, Ga.

Richard Snow, born 1754, was a Revolutionary pensioner, aged 81 years, in 1835.

James Snow patented 167 acres on both sides of Crab Apple Tree branch in 1780; and John Snow patented 300 acres along Ward's Ferry road on the heads of east branches of Troublesome creek. Children of Thomas and Winifred Snow were: —William, Thomas, John Henry, and Mark; daughters Sally Adams and Mary Bennett.

Thomas Snow, Jr., married Rachel, daughter of Peter and Frances Bennett in 1781; a letter filed with their marriage bond, dated Oct. 27, 1781, is as follows:

"To the Clerk of Bedford Court, Sir: Please to grant the Lysence of Marriage between Thomas Snow and Rachel Bennett, and this our note shall prevent *dammidges* occurring. In witness whereof we have set our hands and seals," signed Rachel Bennett, Sr., Elizabeth Perry, Frances F. Bennett: Thomas Adams, security for Thos. Snow's marriage bond.

Vincent Snow of *Mt. Airy,* (a son of this marriage), m. Mary Walden in 1803. He is said to have been in the war of 1812. His son, Thomas, emigrated to Kentucky in 1835, carrying a son, Joseph, aged 3 years. Joseph H. Snow, born 1836 at Leesville, Campbell county, moved with his parents to Greenup county, Ky.; moved in 1857 to Missouri, by steamboat to St. Louis and on horseback across the state to Davis county, where he engaged in teaching in 1860; America J. located in 1867 at Stewartsville: son, William David Snow, a banker of Stewartsville, Mo. In 1908, after seventy years had elapsed, Joseph returned to Virginia in search of relatives and by chance inquiry at Lynchburg, discovered that Mrs. John Thompson, neé Clara Snow, of Lynch Station, was a first cousin. Descendants of Joseph Snow yet remain at Stewartsville, Missouri. The will of Sarah K. Snow of record November, 1844, mentions brothers Jabez and Jehu, and sisters Clarissa, Winifred and Frances B. Snow. Jabez Snow married Parthenia, daughter of Littleberry Hughes. Children were:

—Jabez, Jr., m. Susan P. Pannill of Albemarle;—Valeria m. John L. Webb of Orange;—Clara V. m. John C. Thompson.

Three sons of Abner Snow were Van, Robert and John; the two former served in the Confederate army.

Early records of the Snow family give the connection with Dr. Thomas Gerard, who was for a long period Chancellor in Maryland but was banished from Maryland for taking part in the insurrection of Josias Fendall in 1659. Provided a refuge in Virginia in 1650, obtained a patent of land there. He married Susanne, daughter of Justinian Snow, one of the founders of Maryland and Lord Baltimore's factor in Indian trade. Two of his brothers in England were Abel Snow, clerk in Chancery office, London; and Marmaduke Snow.

Children of Dr. Thomas and Susanna Snow-Gerard were Susanna, Temperance, Frances, Justinian and John.

1778—Family of Peter and Frances Bennett:—William (in the Revolutionary war) Reuben, Micajah, Abner, Richard, Mary Lawson, Elizabeth Perry; Rachel m. Thomas Snow.

David, a brother of Joseph H. Snow, moved first to Washington county, Va., later to Arkansas: son, David Victor Snow, a banker of Camden, Ark.

Stith

In appointment of officials for newly established Campbell, the selection of Richard Stith was appropriate as he had been assistant surveyor to his brother, Buckner in Bedford, having received his commission for that office from the president and professors of William and Mary College, "if he truly and faithfully to the best of his knowledge and power discharged and executed his trust, office and employment according to law and his commission."

Colonel John Stith, first of the name in Virginia, took up grants of land in Charles City county; was sheriff in 1691, and burgess from 1685-92 and 93; he married Jane ———, and their son, Drury, the first clerk of Brunswick, married Susanna Bathhurst, whose son, Colonel Drury Stith, was a Burgess from Brunswick in 1748, married Elizabeth Buckner and their son, Richard, who had settled in Bedford, as surveyor of Campbell in 1782, was appointed to run the dividing line between the old and new counties. Richard was born in 1727, married in 1753 Lucy, the daughter of John and Ann Cocke-Hall, a grand-daughter of Robert and Anne Cocke-Bolling, Robert Bolling having been son of Colonel Robert of *Kippax,* Prince George county, and his second wife Anne, the daughter of Colonel John Stith of Charles City.

The county surveys made by Richard Stith are preserved in the clerk's office at the court house. Stith acquired a large estate in land. He began writing his will, disposing of it, when he was 54 years old, twenty years before his death, and as time passed added four codicils to the original instrument, covering several pages in the records. It is considered the best prepared will at the clerk's office. His whole estate was left to his wife, to revert to his children, the portion for each one being specified. In the 3rd codicil he says "I have left them in comfortable circumstances," in the 4th he devised his still and its appurtenances to his widow and son Richard; he first appointed Edmund Winston, John Fitz Patrick and Charles Cobbs his executors; ten years later he added his wife's name to this list, as executrix. His land embraced 1150 acres including Mt. Hermon on Jumping run, 1150 acres on Stony fork of Goose creek including Buck mountain, 1460 acres both sides of Molley's creek; 1200 acres on the branches of Falling river; 400 acres near the head of Little Falling river on Mulberry creek, including the Narrow Passage branch; the land on Buzzard branch along the island road leading toward the old mill; land south side of Goose creek opposite Flat Top mountain, including Harpeth and Shalum; land at the mouth of Lick creek and 1054 acres on Lick creek, including the seat *Old Jacob and Nan;* land on branches of Enoch's creek (according to a patent of 1787); part of Stony Fork tract. If Richard, Jr., was not satisfied with his portion he was to take land beginning at the mouth of Pompey's branch, up the same, passing by the mouth of Saucer towards Mr. West's mill. To his son-in-law, Drury Hardaway, was devised 1050 acres on Lawson's creek, which was not altogether a gift, as he had made compensation. To Luke Morris Valentine was given 80 acres, (which Charles Talbot, Sr., "acknowledged,") in Campbell on Falling river, including the little old plantation on Lick creek, with mouth of the creek.

Children of Richard Stith:—Joseph m., 1782, Nancy Cocke; —Benjamin . . .;Thomas m., 1792, Rhoda Jones;—John m. Lucy Ann Hardaway;—Richard, Jr.;—Anne m. Drury Hardaway;—Elizabeth m. Jesse Moorman;—Lucy m. William Jordan of Bedford county;—Patsy m. David J. Saunders of Buckingham;—Catherine m., 1792, James Jones;—William m., 1796, Nancy Jones; two brothers and a sister marrying three members of the Jones family.

Strange

Many emigrants, bearing the name Strange, came to America in early times. In 1619 one of these in the employment of the British government under the command of Yeardley, —took passage in the ship *George;* returned to Great Britain and came again, with a brother, on the *Pauline,* and settled near Jamestown, Va., where he became a large land holder. A grant was given him, (with others) of 1290 acres near Jamestown, "extending into the woods," in recognition of meritorious service to the government, and was signed by Governor West (as recorded 1635 in Charles City county).

Alexander Strange was a private in the Lunenburg county regiment under Major William Caldwell in September, 1758.

The first of the name found in Campbell was John M. Strange, who was born in 1719, came to Virginia in 1747 and married that same year, Fannie Smith; in 1782 he patented 346 acres of land on the south fork of Falling river; purchased of Williston Talbot 332 acres on the north side of Morton's creek, a north fork of the south fork of Falling river, on both

sides of Naked creek, extending from Burnley's to McReynold's line. His will, probated in 1815 mentions the children
of his deceased son, James;—

—children of his deceased son, John, who married Evelina
B. Watson, and had two daughters, Evelina, and Elizabeth
(who married James Reynolds, attorney-at-law, and moved to
Seattle, Washington) ;—

—Robert, who m. Elizabeth, the dau. of Joshua Early, Sr.,
of Bedford county, and had three sons, Nathaniel, Robert and
Thomas and Sophia, who m., in 1815, William Day.   Robert
Strange, Sr., was major of the 1st battalion, 117th Va. Reg.,
in the war of 1812;

—children of son, Nathaniel, Sr., to whom was given the
homestead.   Nathaniel's will (1811) names wife, Martha;—
daughter, Elizabeth, who m., 1814, John R. Jennings; son,
Robert, who m. Eliza R. Watson; daughters Edith, who m.
———— Andrews; Fannie, who m. Robert Woods; and Martha,
who m., 1790, Captain Joshua Early, Jr.   Captain Early of
Dickinson's 3rd Va. Reg., was killed on Nov. 3rd, 1814, in
the engagement at Ellicott City, Md., aged 46 years, and his
inventory was recorded in 1815 at Bedford C. H., with Alexander Austin, John Thompson and William Irvine, administrators upon the estate.   In 1798 Nathaniel Strange, Sr., patented 150 acres on the south fork of Falling river.   Children
of Capt. Joshua and Martha Strange-Early:

Frances m. Abner W. Christian—family moved north;
descendants in Pennsylvania.

Martha m. John Preston—family moved West and South.

Amorilla m. Charles Little, moved to West Virginia.

Lucy m. Robert Leftwich, moved to Kentucky.

Eliza m. Thomas Key; son died in the Confederate army.

Charlotte A. m. Wilson Matthews, moved to Texas.

Silas killed in the Confederate army.

Clement moved first to Louisiana, m. Lou, dau. of Colonel Thomas Holladay; moved to Kentucky, and left an
orphan daughter, Lottie, who came to reside in the home
of her great uncle, Bishop Early, where she died.

Talbot

From Charles Talbot, of Maryland, descends the family of that name which settled in Virginia. Matthew Talbot, born 1699, son of Charles, moved to the state and married in 1722, Mary Williston, who died in 1736; had sons, Charles, Matthew, Jr., James and John. Matthew, Sr., married, 2nd, in 1737, Jane Clayton, and children of this marriage were Isham and Martha. Charles Talbot, Jr., married Drucilla, daughter of David Guin of Lunenburg county.

In 1742 Matthew Talbot patented 241 acres on the south side of Licking Hole, in Brunswick county; 1746 patented 600 acres, embracing an island in Staunton river below the mouth of Seneca creek; 1747 patented 143 acres on the south side of Staunton river; 1749 patented 400 acres both sides of Twitty's creek adjoining Charles Talbot; the same year Charles Talbot patented 315 acres on both sides of a branch of Ward's fork adjoining David Lee, and 380 acres on Licking; 1786 John Talbot patented 1265 acres west side of Otter on branches of Callaway's and Irvine's creeks. Members of this Talbot family were living in Lunenburg at the time of its division to form Bedford, and Matthew and Charles were appointed to define the boundary between the two counties. Matthew made a proposition to donate a site on his land for the court house but it was not considered sufficiently central; he furnished a meeting place for the justices at the first meetings in 1754, the last of which was November 25, when a writ of adjournment was read and two days later court adjourned from Talbots' to the building on Callaway's land. Matthew and Charles were among the first justices of Bedford. In the following year Charles received the commission of sheriff and both brothers became vestrymen of Russell parish; Matthew was made colonel and James lieutenant of Bedford militia; in 1757 Charles was appointed captain of militia and Matthew sheriff of the county; 1758 Matthew, Jr., was commissioned captain of militia; that year Colonel Matthew Talbot died and his estate was divided between his widow, Mrs. Jane Talbot, 5 sons and daughter Martha Arthur; Charles was bequeathed the

great family Bible and a godson, Abraham Chandler, was bequeathed 400 acres on the lower side of Flat creek, joining
property of William Arthur. In 1773 Charles, John and Isham
were Bedford justices; John a captain of militia in 1776, was
a Burgess from 1761 to 1765, and member of 4 conventions
held during 1775-6. Williston Talbot, son of Charles, was
lieutenant of militia in 1778, and in 1780 a commissary of provision for collecting Revolutionary supplies. Charles Talbot
died in 1779; his will provided for his wife during her widow-
hood, gave the family Bible to his son Williston, his land on
Whipping creek, adjoining Robert and Pierce Pannill and on
Dry creek—as far as David G. Talbot's—to sons Charles Moile,
David Guin, Providence, George, and Ezekiel and daughters
Mary Thurston and Christiana Talbot.

John Talbot was one of the first justices of Campbell county.
In 1784 he bought of Matthew Talbot, Jr., 450 acres on both
sides of Callaway's branch, part of a tract granted to Isham
Talbot in 1771 by patent and containing 1254 acres, which was
conveyed to Matthew, Jr., in 1772.

At one time John Talbot was the presiding magistrate in
court and he and his large family connection had control of
the bench. During the war with Great Britain in 1812 there
was great financial trouble, when many suits were brought to
enforce the collection of claims; whenever a judgment of execution was likely to be ordered against any of the special sup-
porters of the presiding magistrate, he would order the sheriff
to adjourn court and his order would be sustained by the controlling faction, seriously impairing the income of the clerk,
Robert Alexander, then in office.

Williston Talbot was sheriff of Campbell in 1793 with John
Irvine, Daniel B. Perrow and Sackville King as his securities.
He married, 1st, in 1769 Elizabeth Cock; at her death m., 2nd,
Nancy Keesee in 1827 and willed his land on Whipping creek
to sons, Charles, Pleasant, John and Hilary,—to the last two,
bequeathed his land above Sulphur Springs branch, together with
heirs of his son, Williston; to son Allen 10,000 weight of inspected tobacco; to sons Elbert Gale, Melville and Henry, and

daughters, Mildred Ann, Paulina M., Addeline, and children of daughter, Louisa Galleon, daughters Sally McReynolds and Betsy Buckler, the undivided half of his estate; sons Elbert, Gale and Melville to have all of his books. In 1820 Williston Talbot, Jr., married Ann Arnold. Colonel William A. Talbot organized a company to serve in the Mexican War.

Tate

Joseph Tate patented 270 acres lying both sides of Russell's creek, a branch of Mayo river, adjoining the lands of John Hunter, in 1751. Ten years later Henry Tate patented 300 acres on Cheese creek, and 14 acres on Blackwater creek. His will, written 1784 mentions his wife, to whom he willed the plantation upon which he lived, and home;

—dau. Mary m. Chesley Davis.

—son, Jesse, ensign in the Revolutionary army.

—Charles.

—Nathaniel in 1794 patented 1000 acres on the east branch of Troublesome creek.

—Edmund in 1807 petitioned for permission to erect a toll bridge across Blackwater creek on the road leading from the county line by Major Samuel Scott's plantation to Lynchburg; in 1809 he patented 16 acres on the west side of Blackwater.

—Caleb, in 1803, patented 290 acres on Green Spring creek; in 1782 the brothers, Caleb and Edmund, purchased of Benjamin and Tabitha Clark, 236 acres on Blackwater.

—Tabitha m. (1st wife) Captain John Callaway; children, James and Elizabeth.

—Eliza m. ——— Harris; Anne m. ——— Anthony.

—Euphenia m. ——— Rucker;—Sarah Henry m., in 1795, Mark Anthony.

Other marriages in the Tate family: Obediah Tate married Nancy, daughter of Stephen and Rachel M. Goggin; Pamela Tate married William Goggin, a brother of Mrs. Nancy Goggin-Tate; in 1818 Alice Tate married David G. Murrell.

Tate Spring, situated on the property of Colonel Edmund Tate, near Lynchburg, became much frequented for its chalybeate and sulphur mineral water. Col. Tate planned splendid improvements at the spring, but he died before his scheme could be carried out. In 1828 a ballroom and cottages were erected and balls were held there occasionally, but the last one was broken up by a terrible storm and they were not repeated. Through intermarriage with the Murrell family the property came into the possession of the latter and is still held by them.

Terrell

William Terrell, of English birth, a persecuted Quaker, went to Ireland, and after a temporary residence there, emigrated to America and settled in Virginia between 1665 and 1700. He had three sons, David, Henry and James. David Terrell in 1787 patented 178 acres east side of Seneca creek on both sides of Phelps' road. David, born in Virginia, married there and had 7 sons and 3 daughters; of these Henry, a Quaker, was a wealthy lawyer and lived in Hanover (then Caroline), m. Anna Chiles and had 4 sons and 5 daughters. Children:

—George was a Revolutionary soldier, at Camden, S. C., under General Gates.

—Thomas m. Rebecca Peters and descendants moved to Ohio;

—Ursula m. Mr. Raglan.

—Abigail m. Col. Durrett, of Albemarle.

—Henry, born 1735, lived in Spottsylvania; m. Mary, dau. of Capt. Wm. Tyler; emancipated his slaves, and moved in 1787 to Montgomery county, Ky. David Terrell's son, Micajah, came to Campbell (then Bedford), from Caroline; married, in 1754, Sarah, daughter of Charles and Sarah Clark-Lynch, who died in 1773. The Terrells were among the first worshippers at South River Meeting, having received the following certificate of recommendation:

"Monthly meeting of Friends held at South river: Our friend, Micajah Terrell, having removed from our monthly meeting within the verge of yours, without our certificate, these are to certify you that we have made enquiry into his life and conversation whilst amongst us and find that he was a member in unity (in most respects) and we recommend him to your Christian care and oversight. Signed by order and on behalf of our meeting held at Golansville, Caroline county, 7-9-1762." A similar certificate was granted Sarah Lynch-Terrell from Cedar creek, Hanover county, 8-14-1762. Children of Micajah and Sarah L. Terrell: Robert, Elizabeth (m. Achilles Douglass), Agatha, Charles Lynch, Ann and Mary. In 1799 Micajah Terrell, Anna and Achilles moved to New Garden, N. C. In 1798 James Terrell married Penelope Adams.

In 1795 Samuel Terrell was disowned for allowing himself to be so transported with passion as to utter some very unbecoming speeches and threats to the dishonor of Quaker profession.

In 1793 David Terrell married Patty, daughter of Ashley and Martha Johnson of Louisa county, at Cedar Creek Meeting house in Hanover. In 1806 David Terrell and wife, Mary, and children, Pleasant, Christopher, David, Judith, Sarah, Joseph and Mary, moved to Miami Meeting, Ohio.

In 1805 David Terrell, Jr., the brother of Micajah Terrell, died, aged 76 years. Edward and Mary Terrell moved from Cedar Creek, Hanover County, Va.: their son, Edward, Jr., m., in 1794, Jane Johnson, who died in 1815.

Edward and Jane J. Terrell, with their children, Elizabeth, Mary, Johnson, Judith, Christopher and Gerard, moved from Goose Creek, Bedford county, to South River Meeting in 1801; —Christopher, Jr., born 1798, m. Susan Kennerly, of the Valley of Virginia, and moved to Missouri; died at Boonsville in 1833. Children:

—Judge Alexander Watkins Terrell, of Austin, Texas, minister to Turkey.
—Dr. John Jay Terrell, born 1829 at Penn's store, Patrick county, m. Sue Wade.
—Capt. Joseph Christopher Terrell of Fort Worth, Texas.

Dr. John J. Terrell, who was 14 years old at the time of his father's death, then returned to Virginia to make his home with his aunt Judith Terrell. This home was *Rock Castle,* supposed to have received its name from Rock Castle creek, now called Burton's creek after a landholder whose property lies adjacent. Dreaming creek also flows through the Terrell farm, and in a grant dated 1762 to John Anthony, the first owner, it is defined as lying on Dreaming creek, and tradition gives the reason for its name. Settlers clearing land along the stream, growing tired, rested and fell asleep. One of them had a vivid dream that Indians were coming, which so impressed him with the thought that Indians were near, he rushed off to warn the neighbors, and none too soon, for the red men did appear and his dream saved their lives and furnished an appropriate name for the stream.

Dr. Terrell was conversant with the history of Campbell and its founders. His grand-parents and aunt were Quakers and he attended services with them. He was at the last meeting when but two or three gathered in sad recognition of their passing from this section. The Meeting was "laid down" in 1858 after 100 years activity and in 1902 the stone walls then standing were sold to the Presbyterians, some of whom owed descent to the Quakers who had worshipped there. When the church began falling to decay, Dr. Terrell preserved the corner stone, having the date 1791, which had been used for the original building, and was again used in the restoration into Quaker Memorial church by the Presbyterians who purchased it.

During the War of 1861-65 Dr. Terrell was assigned assistant surgeon to Dr. Wm. Otway Owen, Chief of Staff, and placed in charge of Burton's Hospital in Lynchburg. He represented Campbell county in Virginia Legislature from 1885-89, was on the Board of Health almost from its formation, was an intimate friend of Samuel Miller, philanthropist, and appointed by him on the board of directors of Lynchburg Female Orphanage.

Mrs. Terrell died 1919, and Dr. Terrell survived her 3 years, dying at age of 93. During the course of his long life he won the esteem and affection of those who came in intimate contact with him.   Members of his family reside in Lynchburg and in the county home on Dreaming creek.

Thompson

In 1761 William Thompson patented 170 acres on Flat creek adjoining Wylie's lines.

Campbell August Court, 1783, recorded the inventoried estate of Wm. Thompson, dec.; John Thompson, administrator; appraisers being Wm. Creasy, James Robertson and John Caldwell.

In 1760 John Thompson patented 244 acres on Quarry branch and 199 acres on Dreaming creek; in 1761, 360 acres on Tomahawk and Dreaming creeks, this last tract he received by grant from George III through Gov. Francis Fauquier for 40 shillings lawful money paid to the Receiver General of Revenues for the Colony and Dominion of Virginia.   The land touched Bramlitt's line and Callaway's corner and adjoined the land acquired later by Thomas Jefferson.

John Thompson's will, 1791, devised to his wife, Margaret, £10 yearly during her life (the amount to be paid her by his sons, John and Andrew), and certain personal property; lent John and Andrew the land on Tomahawk and Dreaming creeks, supposed to be about 1450 acres, at their death to be divided between their children equally; lent to his son, Matthew, use of his land in Prince Edward and Buckingham counties, lying upon the Appomattox river, at death of Matthew to revert to his children.   104 acres adjoining Edmund Franklin and Simon Woolridge to be sold and divided between the children of John and Andrew; 400 acres bought of John Beard upon which son William had lived were left in trust for support of William's children, mentioning by name among the latter, Margaret, when she came of age; this 400 acre tract was to be sold and equally divided between William's children.   £1500 and upwards due on a bond given by John Callaway to be divided between John, Andrew, William's children, Elizabeth Gill, Jane Mitchell and

Esther Phair. To John Thompson, son of Andrew, the tract upon which he (John 1st) lived, containing 300 acres, he paying to David Thompson, son of William, £30 two years after he came of the age of 21 years;—that being land bought of John Cundiff; for the better support of his daughter, Elizabeth, wife of William Gill, certain slaves, to be held in trust by John and Andrew Thompson, and hired out for the benefit of Elizabeth. The remainder of his home tract,—about 700 acres,— to be equally divided between the sons of John and Andrew, who were requested to assist Matthew with what they thought necessary for him and his family's support. The still was given Andrew, who had it in his possession. Slaves were given John and Andrew—others for better support of Matthew, also for better support of daughter, Esther Phair. Witnesses to will: Charles Patterson, William Campbell and Jacob Watkins. In 1794 Sarah Thompson m. James St. John. In 1796 John Thompson, Jr., married Keziah Franklin; in 1809 he patented 81 acres of land lying on Little Beaver creek. Jane Thompson, dau. of John and Margaret Thompson m. William Mitchell; son William Mitchell.

Thorpe

In 1742 Thomas Thorpe purchased 200 acres from Richard and Frances Shackleford of King and Queen county, Va.

In 1769-70 Francis Thorp patented land on Goose and Buffalo creeks.

William Thorp was a sergeant during the years 1755-62 in the French war. John Thorp was a soldier under General Forbes in 1758, and regularly discharged, in 1779; William, his heir-at-law, applied for his claim. Thomas Thorp, of Caroline county, a corporal in the war 1759-62, served in Colonel William Byrd's regiment in 1860, till properly discharged. William Thorp's claim to service was signed by Brigadier-General Charles Scott.

In 1780 Francis Thorp patented 1264 acres on Goose creek and north fork of Buffalo; 794 acres on both sides of Buffalo; 346 acres were patented, together with Jones and Read, 620 acres both sides of Buffalo; and together with George Callaway patented land on Elliott's branch.

Captain Francis Thorp married Elizabeth (born 1743), the daughter of Colonel William and Elizabeth Tilley-Callaway.

In 1782 Francis Thorp was appointed by the governor, first sheriff of Campbell county.

In 1787 Pamela Thorp married Thomas Crump; 1790 Elizabeth Thorp married Wm. Jones.

In 1792 Francis Thorp patented 140 acres of land on the west branches of Buffalo creek; this apparently was a son of Francis Thorp, Sr., who died without having made a will and his inventory was taken in 1790 by John Campbell, Jacobus Early and William Scott, justices of the peace, with William Harris, administrator.

Thurman
(In all early records this name is written Thurmon.)

The Thurman family were settled in Bedford before its division, two members, William and Richard, being on record among Campbell's early entries. Richard Thurman married Anne . . .

In 1779 Rd. Thurman patented 415 acres on Seneca creek; in 1785 James Gatewood of Bedford county sold John Thurman for £1000 specie, 314 acres on the north fork of Pigeon branch, William Thurman a witness to the deed.

In 1782 Richard Thurman purchased of George Vest 130 acres of land at the corner of a locust thicket adjoining Benjamin Gilbert's, John Traylor's and Micajah Terrell's lines; this was the property upon which he resided, and it was situated upon a branch of Seneca creek; he and his wife, Anne, sold this place in 1784 to Shelldrake Brown, and also sold Brown 415 acres lying on both sides of Phelps' old road along the east side of Seneca creek, beginning at Benjamin Gilbert's. Following the disposal of his land he moved to Lynchburg, and for some years (until 1822) he was tobacco inspector at Spring Warehouse with Edward Lynch and Thomas Franklin securities on his bond to the governor. It was perhaps his son (or brother), John Thurman, also located in Lynchburg, who was affectionately known in the town as "Uncle Thurman." When very young he had held, during the Revolutionary War, a position in the army, and had the privilege of residing for some time with Washington and La Fayette in the stone building in Richmond now so valued on account of its distinguished inmates at that time. When General Lafayette visited Richmond in 1825 John Thurman went to call on him there,—dressed in the same clothes he had worn while living in the stone house with the two generals—and was received affectionately by Lafayette with open arms.

Thurman lived to extreme old age. His son, John, married a daughter of Mrs. Essex, also of Lynchburg, and lived not far from the old town reservoir.

John Thurman, Jr., was a saddler by trade. He was of a very religious disposition, and established the first Sunday school that was started in Virginia. This was in 1817 and the school was then held in the old Methodist church.

John Thurman, Jr., died in 1855, leaving a large family of children. Richard Thurman married Sallie Lewellen, a woman of large charities, who supplied many poor persons with food from her bakery. Placed at one period of her life in great poverty and difficulties, by patient industry, energy and economy, she not only retrieved the fortunes of her husband but reaped a fortune for herself. Mrs. Thurman died in 1840, leaving two children, one of whom was Samuel Thurman of Lynchburg. A sketch of Mrs. Thurman, portraying her fine traits of character and her magnanimity, was written at the time of her death by Richard K. Crallê of Lynchburg. In 1785 John Thurman, Sr., was one of a committee of four appointed to view the nearest and best way for a road from the county line near Richard Timberlake's, leading past Samuel Scott's plantation and Tate's mill to Lynch's ferry. In 1920 John Thurman, Jr., was mayor of Lynchburg.

William Thurman, son of John, lived at a place called Thurman's Spring (named for him, though he was not its first occupant). The ground upon which it stood (near Lynchburg), was purchased by a man named Williams, who built there a very expensive house, one room of which was designed for a mercantile store, and extended over the spring. He also built a large brick warehouse, which caused the place to be called Williamsburg; but Williams only remained a short time, and the warehouse was destroyed. The dwelling was rented at various times; Rev. Samuel Tompkins kept a boys' school there. Henry Thurman married Quintilla Adams, had seven sons; this family moved to Franklin county.

Senator Allan G. Thurman, whose family moved to Ohio, the state he represented in the United States senate so notably, was of this Campbell county connection. A Lynchburg member of the branch which remained in the county, E. Thurman Bond, is at the present time the delegate in Virginia Legislature from Lynchburg. He married Lucy Lillian, daughter of Edwin Wills, and descendant of John W. Wills, one time delegate to Virginia Assembly, from Lynchburg.

Tyree

Richard Tyree, of New Kent county, moved to Campbell in 1800. Three half brothers, Richmond, Pleasant and Samuel, came with him, married three Anderson sisters in Campbell and moved west. Richard Tyree in 1806 m. Mildred Y. Douglass. Bought lot 104, Sixth alley and Third street at Lynchburg in 1808 from John Lynch and built a home there. Richard Tyree was inspector of tobacco at Liberty Warehouse, 1811-12-13. Children:—John Henley, born 1806, m. Ann Phoebe, dau. of Samuel and Phoebe Walton-Bransford. He purchased land about three miles below Lynchburg upon which he built the house still standing at Tyreeanna, named for himself and his wife. Children:—Cora V., m. Thomas L. Johnson of Lynchburg;— Elizabeth B., m. Samuel W. Younger of Lynchburg;—Charles Hudson, m. Bettie M. Sclater; served in the Confederate army, wounded at Drury's Bluff, and died at his father's home in 1864;—Samuel Bransford, C. S. soldier, killed at bat-

tle of Seven Pines;—Rosa Kent, m. William S. (C. S. veteran) son of James D. and Ann E. Wms. Gregory;—Walter Preston, m. Martha, dau. of Colonel Logan Anderson;—Ann Ammonette, m. Charles Sinton of Richmond.
—Achilles D., m. Martha Tisdale McKinney.

Tyreeanna. Home Built by John H. Tyree

—Elizabeth D., m. Moses Hurt, son of Isaac and Sallie Hurt-Preston.
—Sallie Johnson, m. Andrew C. Elliott.
—Judith Ellen married Charles Simpson.
—Anna Lynch married Moses Lacy.
—Samuel, m. Marion Fontaine Cabell, dau. of Captain Spotswood Henry.
—Mildred D., m. George G. Williams.

John H. and Samuel Tyree were successful tobacconists in Lynchburg; later Samuel Tyree engaged in real estate business which still bears the name Tyree and Wilkins.

Venable

The Venable name was first spelled with a final s. Abraham Venables emigrated from England to Virginia in 1685 and married in 1699 Elizabeth, the daughter of Hugh Lewis, of James City county. Their son, Abraham, Jr., who married Martha, daughter of Nathaniel and Elizabeth Hughes-Davis, of Amherst, was friend, client and political supporter of Patrick Henry; was also, for a time, county-lieutenant of Louisa and for 20 years member of the House of Burgesses from Louisa. His son, William Venable, nominated Henry in the county meeting as a candidates for the House of Burgesses in 1765. From this Venable are descended the Virginia members of the family. His son, John (7th child), married Agnes, daughter of Charles Moorman of Louisa. He belonged to the Society of Friends and was among the first to set his slaves free. Abram Venable in 1759 patented 2065 acres on Falling creek; in 1754 patented 340 and 740 acres on Little Falling creek.

John Venable was assistant commissioner of provision to Christopher Irvine at the time he impressed John Hook's steers. This occurred during the time of distress in the patriot army consequent upon the joint invasion of the enemy's forces under Cornwallis and Phillips in 1781 when levies were made upon the citizens for contributions of supplies. John Hook, a Scotchman, was a prosperous merchant and farmer who was suspected of being unfriendly to the American cause. The taking of his steers for use of the troops had not been strictly legal and by advice of William Cowen, an attorney of some distinction, in 1783 Hook brought suit against Venable personally in the district court of New London, where Patrick Henry appeared for the defendant. The legal record shows the verdict to have been for the plaintiff "one penny damages," but an appeal resulted in a command to take John Venable into safe keeping to answer Hook's plea of trespass, with damage of £40 at the court house in Richmond, April 5, 1783. The case was continued in general court till September, 1789 with issue to the plaintiff of one penny damages. Costs in court were 500 lbs. of tobacco. Hook became the victim in this suit.

In 1784 the estate of Thomas Faland sold to John Venable 300 acres of land which had been conveyed to Faland by Lady Mary Read, on both sides of Seneca creek. Abraham Venable was a member of the Virginia Yazoo Company. John Venable in 1786, with William Martin, Jonathan Rosser, and Griffin Lewis, was appointed inspector of tobacco at Lynch's Ferry.

Venable moved, with his family, to Georgia, in 1791, but that there were Venables left in the county is proven by the marriage of Nathaniel Venable to Nancy Kelly in 1816 as recorded among the bonds in the clerk's office at Campbell court house.

Wade

As early as 1536 Armigil Wade of a Yorkshire family, was called "the British Columbus," because he was the first British explorer of the American Indies. In 1589 Thomas Wade was one of the Company of London merchants to whom Sir Walter Raleigh transferred the colony of Virginia.

In 1656 Daniel Wade of Surry county petitioned Lieut.-Governor Nicholson to remit a fine of 10,000 lbs. of tobacco imposed upon him for re-planting tobacco after the first of July, a restriction made to prevent over-production that would lower the price of the product upon which the farmer depended for his revenue.

The first meeting of justices appointed for Halifax county occurred in April, 1752, at the house of Hampton Wade; and in this county are found the wills of Andrew Wade in 1766 and of Edward Wade in 1776.

Henry Wade, Jr., of Hanover county, born 1740—son of Henry, Sr., (died 1760), and Judith Wade,—married, in 1761, Lucy Turner, born 1740. Children:

—Luke, born 1763, m., 1785, Martha Stanley, of Halifax county.
—Oneida, born 1765, m., 1801, Richard Jones of Halifax;

—Andrew, born 1770, m., 1790, 1st, Sarah Petty, of Halifax; m., 2nd, 1795, Elizabeth Kimball of Anson county, N. C.
—Zachfield m., in 1799, Mary Johnson of Campbell.
—Polly m., 1797, Thos. Stokes of Lunenburg.
—Henry, born 1778, m. in 1806, 1st, Polly Stone of Halifax; m., 2nd, in 1810, Mary Waene of Halifax.
—Sarah, born 1786, m., in 1811, 1st, Matthew Hobson; m., 2nd, ——— Sweeney of Lynchburg.
—John, born 1782, m., 1812, Elizabeth Hobson of Halifax.

Children of Zackfield and Mary Johnson-Wade, as mentioned in his will, May 6, 1849:
—Richard Jones m., 1855, Lucie Martin Hancock of Charlotte county; he died 1898; she died 1866.
—Luke m. ———; children Bettie and Brack; moved to Texas.
—John H. m. Sarah W.; children, Ben, Luke and John.
—Mrs. Elizabeth Martin;—Lucy . . . ;—Sally . . . ;
—Henry m.; died early; left children;—William . . . ;
—Zackfield, Jr., m. Mary Boone of Franklin county; both died early; left 2 daughters:

> Susan, born 1840, m., 1857, Dr. John J. Terrell at Mrs. John Boone's in Franklin county.
> Catherine married a cousin, Benjamin Wade.

Children of Richard J. and Lucie M. Hancock-Wade:—Edward R. of Knoxville, Tenn., and Mary Elizabeth, m. ——— Betterton, of Chattanooga, Tenn.

Zackfield Wade gave bond to the governor 28 times, starting from 1811, as inspector of tobacco at Friend's Warehouse in Lynchburg; in 1843 he deeded a piece of property to his son, Zackfield, Jr., provided in his will for his children, and the children of his deceased sons, Henry and Zackfield, Jr. His son, Luke, was appointed executor. His property was on Pigeon creek, which runs through the Presbyterian Orphanage farm into James river at the old iron mines near Reusen's, near which his home stood, and at the back of the house was the family burying-ground; he requested that this reservation be enclosed and preserved.

The name *Zackfield* may have resulted from the mis-spelling of *Sackville,* as occurred in the records of Sackville King, witness to a Wade deed.

Walden

The history of the Walden family is traced from John Walden, son of Lord John Walden of Ravensworth Castle, England, who settled in Leyton, Essex county, Va., in 1715, moved later to his home *Walden Towers* in Caroline, site of which is about nine miles from Bowling Green; the house was destroyed by fire about the middle of the 19th century.

Richard, son of John, Sr., married Candace Hubbard. He received several grants of land in Pittsylvania county in 1761 and the same year was granted a tract of 565 acres lying across Staunton river in Campbell county; was commissioned captain of militia in 1767. It is not known that he served in the Revolutionary army, but he furnished supplies of beef and teams for use of that army.

His will, dated 1790, mentions sons John, Charles, Richard; daughters Lucy Hudson, Mary Whitworth, Millie Mourning, Sarah, Fanny Bobbitt and Elizabeth Ballard. John married Sally ———— and settled in Caroline; was given a tract in Pittsylvania. Charles, who was after his mother's death to receive the home tract in Pittsylvania, married Elizabeth, daughter of Col. Charles F. Wall. His daughter, Tabitha H., married John Ward, 3rd of the name and son of William and Mildred Adams-Ward of *Edge Hill,* Pittsylvania county. Charles Walden served in a number of battles during the Revolution. Richard, Jr., third son of Richard, Sr., received from his father his 565 acre tract of land in Campbell, on the north side of Staunton river, which had been granted by patent from George III. Richard, Jr., was commissioned an ensign at Bedford court, served under Captain Jacobus Early at the battle of Guilford court house and afterwards acquired the title of captain.

Milly, daughter of Richard Waldren, married Thomas Ward, the youngest son of Major John Ward in 1791 and moved to Ohio.

Polly Walden married Thomas Goggin, son of Stephen and Rachel Moorman-Goggin.

Martha, daughter of Charles Walden, married John L. Adams.

Richard T. Walden m. . . . .;

Mary Walden married Vincent Snow; they were grandparents of Major David Richard Snow of Campbell county.

Steuart and Steuart, a legal firm of Baltimore, Md., were employed by the descendants of Lord Walden in Virginia to endeavor to recover a portion of the English estate but it was found that it had reverted to the crown and the castle is used as a museum for antiquities.

Charles Walden's will (1829) leaves to wife Elizabeth Walden, land at mouth of Jasper's creek on Staunton river along Thomas Adams' line (formerly Henry Ward's line), to the old pocket road, on to Austin's (formerly James Smith's line), to a mountain called Tinker's and onwards to a branch called Harry Hatcher's. To Joel L. Adams and Richard T. Walden, the lower plantation on Staunton river, formerly belonging to Richard Walden, Sr., and Callaway, along to Anderson's corner, thence along Austin's line on Tinker's creek to James Anderson's (formerly James Callaway's), thence running with May's line. For benefit of daughter, Martha Adams, the tract of land on small branch above canoe landing along to Polly Snow's (formerly Vincent Snow's), to the corner on Sophie Dobyns, crossing Terrell's Mountain and McDonald's road, thence with Leftwich's lines; daughter Tabitha H. Ward and Polly Walden, after death of his wife, to have the tract upon which he lived. To grand-children, James, John, Ravenscroft, Louisa, Sarah, and Mildred Anderson, $100 each in money. 133 acres on Back creek in Campbell and Bedford, adjoining Anderson, Parsell and Quarles, to his three daughters.

Ward

Joseph Ward patented 731 acres on the north fork of Little Roanoke in Brunswick county in 1739. The next year John Ward patented 400 acres on the south side of Rose's creek; in 1742 Richard Ward patented 1700 acres on Staunton river; in 1750 John Ward patented 425 acres on Hunter's branch on the north side of Hunter's creek and a year later patented 550 acres at the head of Jenita creek. Two or more families bearing the Ward name were recorded in Campbell, and the names John and Richard are found among Major John Ward's descendants, but nothing has been found concerning these early patentees. In 1753 the two brothers, John and Jeremiah Ward, of Albemarle, patented 3200 acres of land on the north side of Dan river in Pittsylvania county, which were located (as designated) "in the mountains." John then settled at *Reed creek;* and some years later Jerry moved to Cabell county on the Guyandotte river. John Ward married the beautiful Anne, daughter of Henry and Anne Harrelson-Chiles of Pittsylvania. He built a second home, *The Mansion,* east of the mouth of Otter river near its entrance into the Staunton and only a few miles from where Alta Vista now stands; here he lived, and, dying (over 100 years old), in 1816, was buried in the family grave-yard nearby. Major Ward married, secondly, 1766, Mrs. Sarah Clark - Lynch, daughter of Christ. Clark and widow of Charles Lynch, Sr., for which she was disowned by the Quakers, Ward not being of the sect. He received his title in 1778 as Major of Bedford county militia, an office he resigned in 1781 on account of his great age.

In 1778 Major Ward established a ferry across the Staunton, having previously kept there a boat free to passengers, and in 1810 he obtained permission to erect a toll bridge near his ferry. As early as 1769 he built mills at Sinkler's and Chile's creeks; raised large yield of hemp upon his land. Included in his estate was a tract called *Indian Camps,* which received the name from its use by Indians. He surveyed the road leading to Lynchburg which still bears his name and which, though recently improved by shortening of curves, filling of depressions and sand-clay resurfacing, is not materially changed from its early lines; in providing cross-country passage for his neighbors, Ward builded better than he reckoned, for his road now forms part of a highway which runs through the state, and connects with routes leading north and south.

Children of John and Anne H. Ward:

I.—John, Jr., never married, was ensign of Bedford militia in 1781, and lieutenant in 1782; he owned a large estate in land, of which he willed (1826) the larger part to his nephew, John, the son of his brother, William. *Indian Camps,* was part of his inheritance.

II.—William, born 1745, married Mildred, eldest daughter of Robert and Penelope Lynch - Adams, owned land above Leesville; was a justice in Pittsylvania in 1777, member of the Committee of Safety in 1775, captain of militia, in 1780 was allowed £53.14 for provisions furnished Mrs. Atkinson, the wife of a soldier.   Children:

> Robert Adams m. Betsy, dau. of Charles L. and Sally Lynch-Terrell in 1807; their son, Robert H., was appointed by Underwood in 1870 judge of Campbell county court; a son, Charles, m. Martha K., dau. of Nathaniel and Virginia Woodson-Henry.
> John (3rd of the name), m., in 1805, Tabitha Hubbard, dau. of Chas. and Elizh. M. Wall-Walden, gr.-dau. of Col. Chas. F. Wall, and gr.-dau. of Rd. and Candace Hubbard-Walden. John Ward was killed in 1838 by a tree falling on him, when he was having ground cleared; his home was *Edge Hill,* Pittsylvania, near Leesville. He had 12 children of whom—Mildred, the eldest, m. (1st wife), Augustine Leftwich and died young;— Henry Chiles m. Sally Winston, dau. of Dr. John J. Cabell; their son, Capt. John C. Ward of the C. S. army, was imprisoned at Johnson's Island, where he contracted consumption, and died two years later: m: Elizabeth, dau. of Hugh Roy Scott;—William Walden m., 1836,

Elizabeth M. Adams; owned 1302 acres on Staunton river and Cheese creek, along Lynchburg and Pittsylvania turnpike: will recorded 1845;—Charles m. Martha A. Dillard, 1835; soldier in Mexican War, remained and died in Texas;—Three next sons died unmarried; —Dr. David C. went with the gold hunters in 1849; returned to Virginia; died, unmarried, 1906;—Addison Whitfield, m., 1st, Wilmouth W. Adams; m., 2nd, Mary C. Anthony; m., 3rd, Fanny S. Terry;—Sally Wilmouth m. Samuel Clark Tardy, Jr., son of Saml. C. and Jane Haden-Tardy, and moved first to Richmond, then to Lynchburg, where he conducted a wholesale grocery. Their daughter, Eva, youngest of a large family of sons and daughters, married Wm. McAdoo, secretary of the Navy under Cleveland;—Lucy E. m. James M. Spindle of Wytheville;—Alex Tazewell m. Ann, dau. of Wm. Lee. Major Ward devised his lands, above the mouth of Old Woman's creek, adjoining Staunton river, to his son, William.

III.—Agatha m. (2nd wife) Col. John Callaway, and lived near Evington, died in 1812. To her Major Ward gave his lands on Smith river in Patrick, Franklin and Montgomery counties, jointly with his son Henry.

IV.—Ann m., 1st, Christopher, son of Charles Lynch; m., 2nd, Benjamin Dillard, to whose 3 children their grand-father bequeathed 850 acres on Sycamore creek above Early's mill.

V.—Major Henry, a commissary during the Revolution, was active in providing for the American troops and was also issuing commissary to the Catawba Indians from February 21st till April 20, 1780. It is probable that these were the Indians who occupied the Camps and whose friendship Henry Ward gained by acts of kindness to them. After his death they came back to make him a call and were distressed to learn that their friend had passed away. In remembrance of his service to them they performed certain religious ceremonies to obtain by favorable sign the assurance that Ward had passed to the happy hunting grounds; this was effected by knocking heads together till the blood flowed from their nostrils and was caught in straws which they then held to the sun to discover if light showed through, thus indicating that he had reached the desired goal,—the perception of a favorable sign gave them much satisfaction.

Henry Ward received from his father, the land adjoining the ferry on the south side of Staunton river, land and the home place on the north side of Staunton and Otter rivers and Cheese creek, the mill and tract on Old Woman's creek, the tract on the south side of the Staunton purchased of Henry Chiles and known as *Jack's Place*. Children of Henry Ward: Matilda Callaway, born 1800, m. Thomas Tunstall Adams of Pittsylvania;—Lucinda Dillard, born 1801, m. 1823 Dr. John Biddle Rutledge of Maryland, their daughter, Martha Henry m. James Carter, whose daughter, Maud, married Nathaniel E. Clement, a member of the House of Delegates from Pittsylvania, who has served two terms, also as state senator. Dr. Rutledge built *Monteflora* and resided there; after his death Major Henry Adams bought the place and lived there until it was burned, when he moved to the old *Mansion* home which was also burned down seven or eight years ago. *Monteflora* was rebuilt by H. W. Adams, a son of Major Henry W. Adams, but the *Mansion* has not been rebuilt.—Juliana, born 1808, m. John Wheeler Rutledge and moved to Maryland;—Henrietta, born 1810, m. 1828, Dr. William J. McIlheiny of Baltimore; moved to St. Louis;—William, born 1814, moved to Missouri;—Robert A. born 1817;—Edwin Jeremiah, born 1821 moved to Arkansas.

VI.—Jeremiah Ward, Jr., moved to Texas.

VII.—Thomas Ward m. Milly, daughter of Richard Walden, and moved to Ohio.

Three families of Wards located in Campbell county at different periods. The second to come was Seth Ward, 5th or 6th in family line bearing that full name. Seth Ward of Henrico county, in 1632 was granted 60 acres of land in Varina;

he died in 1677. His son, Richard Ward, had four sons, the eldest of whom was Seth, who lived at Sheffield and who died in 1732. The third of these brothers was Joseph (who died in 1743) and he had six sons, the second of whom was named Seth.

In 1823 David J. Thompson sold Seth Ward the "Buffalo Mills," and distillery on Buffalo creek (reserving the carding machine) near the town of New London on the east side of Turner's branch.

Seth, son of Seth and Mary Goode-Ward, born between 1720 and 1730 in Powhatan county, married Martha, the sister of Captain William Norvell of Lynchburg and settled in New London. Episcopalian in faith, he built Chax creek church near Trinity, and was instrumental in building St. Stephen's church, a brick church still standing and not far from Forest depot. His son, Seth Ward, married Ann Hardwick in 1818. The family of Seth and Martha Norvell-Ward moved to Tennessee. Rev. William Norvell Ward, an Episcopal clergyman, was a son of this Seth Ward; the daughters were Mrs. Williams, Mrs. Kerr and Miss Ward.

Giles Ward, who made his home in Lynchburg, was the third of the name to settle in Campbell, coming to Virginia from Connecticut. He possessed considerable dramatic talent and started in Lynchburg the Thespian Society, of which he was made the president.

Giles Ward married Adeline, the daughter of Major James Risque, and his wife, Elizabeth Kennerly, and their son, James Beverley Ward married Harriet Emmaline, daughter of John Buford and Angeline Brown-Otey; they resided on a farm near Forest but moved to Lynchburg. Of this family only two daughters, Mrs. Emory McVeigh and Mrs. Will Johns, remained in the locality; other sisters and brothers moving south; daughters—Ella, Addie (m. McVeigh), Annie, Julia (married Johns); sons: John, Otey, Charles (m. Helen Cartmell of Lynchburg). Ferdinand Ward went West.

Harriet, eldest daughter of Major Risque and sister of Mrs. Giles Ward, married Major George Hutter, of *Sandusky*.

Watts-Saunders

William Watts, who settled in Campbell, was a soldie. Captain John Smith's company of a regiment, raised in 17 by Colonel William Byrd for the immediate defence of th state, and commanded by Byrd.

Watts married Mary, the daughter of Francis Scott of Prince Edward county. In 1796 Conrad Speece sold a tract of land on both sides of Flat creek to William Watts, the property which had been purchased of Christopher Irvine in 1790 by Speece. The same year Christopher Irvine (who had then added Clendenning to his name), sold Watts another tract on Flat creek and the residence built upon it was given the name of *Flat Creek,* which it still retains; dying in 1803, this manor place was willed to his widow, his brother, John Watts and brother-in-law, Thomas T. Scott, being appointed executors of his estate.

Alice, daughter of William and Mary S. Watts, married Judge Fleming Saunders, in 1814, and they acquired the Flat creek property, lying near Evington, and it has since been the home of this Saunders family and their descendants.

Judge Fleming Saunders, born in Franklin county 1778, was descended from Jesse Saunders, of English ancestry, who settled in Powhatan county and married Phyllis Dudley (said to have been of the same family as Lord Guilford Dudley who married Lady Jane Gray), who was heiress to a fortune in England, which was never recovered by her descendants, it is said, because of the burning of a marriage record. It was also said that Saunders was related to Edward Hyde, Lord Chancellor of England in 1658; he gave the name Hyde to each of his five sons, one of whom received the full name of Chancellor Hyde.

Peter Hyde Saunders, eldest son of Jesse, born 1748, married in 1767 Mary Sparrell, who had been brought to this country by her father, but he died on his return trip, leaving her an heiress, and she became the ward of Governor Giles, to whom she was related. Saunders moved to Franklin country after

his marriage, settling at *Runnet Bay,* where the men would have to go very far to the mill and leave Mrs. Saunders with only her maid servant. The two females, for self-protection, were forced to shut themselves in the cabin and fight wolves and bears off with shovels of hot coals thrown from an open window, for that country was then but sparsely settled, and wild animals roamed about. In 1775 Saunders was a member of Pittsylvania County Committee and in 1780 he was a collector of specific taxes in Henry county. Children:

—Judith, born 1769, m. Colonel Samuel Hairston, an officer in the war of 1812.

—Elizabeth, born 1772, m. John Ingles.

—Fleming, born 1778, m. Alice, dau. of William Watts of Campbell county.

—Samuel, born 1783, m. Mary Ingles.

—Mary (Polly), born 1788, m. Captain Wiley Woods of Franklin county.

—Docia m. John Hale; a grandson, Wiley Hale, died while scaling the walls of Chapultepec, during the war with Mexico in 1848.

Judge Fleming and Alice W. Saunders. Children:

—Mary Elizabeth, m. ———— Davis.

—Peter m. Bettie Dabney, moved to Franklin county.

—Ann M. m. Prof. Thomas Preston, of the University of Virginia.

—Major Robert C. m. Carietta Davis, lived at *Caryswood* near Evington; was an officer in C. S. army.

—Captain Fleming m. Mary Gwaphmey of Norfolk, lived at *Flat Creek;* was an officer in C. S. army.

—Louisa Morris m. Richard T. Davis.

Winston

Isaac Winston, of this family which settled in Virginia, married Mary Dabney and was the grandfather of Judge Edmund Winston, whose father, William, married Sarah, the daughter of George Dabney, was a hunter, Indian fighter and orator, and bore the nickname of "Langaloo Billy." There are many anecdotes extant of this William Winston.

Judge Edmund Winston was a native of Henrico county, had practiced law prior to locating in Campbell and was a judge in his district for many years after the Revolution. He resigned his judgship in 1813. He married, first, his cousin, Alice, the daughter of Anthony Winston and wife, Alice Tay-

Point of Honor, Home of Dr. George Cabell

lor; secondly, married the widow of Patrick Henry, the orator. From his farm, *Chestnut Hill,* (former home of Charles Lynch), in Campbell, Judge Winston moved to *Hunting Tower,* in Buckingham county. His eldest daughter, Sarah, married Dr. George Cabell (son of Colonel John Cabell, county lieutenant of Buckingham), who lived on his farm in the forks of Blackwater creek and James river, near Lynchburg, a place which received the name of *Point of Honor,* from a duel which was fought there, a point of land long since incorporated within the boundaries of Lynchburg. Dr. Cabell, who was educated in Hampden-Sidney College and the Medical University of Pennsylvania, became a noted surgeon.

—Alice, 2nd daughter of Judge Winston, married Frederick Cabell, brother of Dr. George Cabell, in 1801, and resided at *Strumon,* Nelson county, Va.

—Caroline Winston married Mr. Moseley of Bedford county.

—Mary married Colonel John Johns, died and was buried at *Chestnut Hill.*

—George Winston married Dorothea, daughter of Patrick Henry; moved to Alabama.

—Edmund, Jr., married Eliza, daughter of Colonel John Wyatt; resided in Amherst.

Paulina, eldest daughter of Dr. George Cabell, married Alexander Spotswood Henry, son of Patrick Henry; a daughter of this marriage, Marion F. C. Henry, married Samuel Tyree, a tobacconist and later real estate man of Lynchburg, and brother of John Tyree of Tyreeanna. John Breckenridge Cabell, son of Dr. George Cabell, married Martha, daughter of Judge Thomas T. Bouldin, M. C., who, in 1834, rose in Congressional Hall to announce the death of his constituent, John Randolph of Roanoke, and fell dead. John B. Cabell lived on Opossum Island, James river, at the mouth of the creek of that name, but moved from this Campbell home to Greenbrier county, now in West Virginia; George Kuhn Cabell, son of Dr. George, m. Eliza, daughter of Hon. David S. Garland, of Amherst; Alice, 2nd daughter of Dr. George Cabell, married Walter C. Carrington of Halifax county.

Alice Winston, the daughter of Jno. B. Cabell, m. William A. Withers (who bore the nickname of "Rip"), son of Dr. Robert W. Withers, of Campbell, lived at *Hollywood,* on Little Seneca creek and had a family of nine children.

George Winston, born 1759, died 1826, youngest son of Nathaniel and Jeremiah Winston of Caroline county, m. in 1790, Judith ———; children:

—James, born 1791, m. 1813 Ann R. Ricks.

—Pleasant, born 1792, m. 1820 Elizabeth, dau. of Bowling and Elizabeth Clark of Hills creek.

—Nathaniel, born 1797, m. 1819 Zelinda Lynch; he died in 1845.

—Elizabeth H., born 1799, m. 1818 William Clark.

—Lucy Ann, born 1801, m. 1820 Hazlett Kyle.

—Amelia H., born 1806, m. 1832 George Simpson.

—Virginia born 1815, m. ———— Butler; died in 1871.

Children of Pleasant and Elizabeth C. Winston:

—Bowling H., born 1822, m. Julia W., the dau. of Alfred and Mary Ann Ricks.

—George Clark, born 1825.

—Pleasant, Jr., born 1827, died 1899.

—Liberia Indiana, born 1829, m. George W. Winston.

—Elizabeth Virginia, born 1834.

—Ambrose Whitlock, born 1835, served in the Confederate army, died 1897.

—Charles Jones, born 1837, m. 1867 Mary E. Alexander, served in the Confederate army; died 1889.

—William H. H., born 1840, m. 1866, Nancy Powell Moorman; served in the Confederate army.

Pleasant Winston, Sr., was opposed to the institution of slavery; moved his family to Indiana; his wife died in 1852, and his sons returned to Virginia; the three youngest joined the Confederate army. He gave a tract of several hundred acres lying upon Hill's creek to his former slaves.

Bowling H. Winston lived near Castle Craig.

Mary E. Alexander, wife of Charles J. Winston, was the daughter of Henry Alston Alexander, and his 2nd wife, Sarah Ann Moorman; their son, J. Clark Winston, m. Sallie Stuart, the daughter of Wm. Withers and his wife, Pauline (dau. of J. Breckenridge Cabell of Opossum Island, James river), who lived at Hollywood, Seneca creek; J. C. Winston lives at old Bowling Clark home, on Hills creek, built on secure foundation of native stone, still well preserved.

Lindley M. Winston, son of Bowling H. and Julia W. Winston, moved to California, and is president of the Highland Fruit Exchange at Redlands; m. twice; 2nd wife, Gladys D.

youngest daughter of Thomas and Mary D. Fauntleroy of *Avoca,* Charles Lynch home.

Henry Alston Alexander m. 1st, Elizabeth Cole Irvine and had sons, Jack Cole and Henry J. Alexander.

Withers

John Withers, of Lancaster, England, emigrated to America in the middle of the 17th century and settled in Stafford county, Virginia. He owned a large property in land, one tract of which called *Chotank,* by a train of casualties in the family, fell finally into the possession of Augustine Washington.

Thomas Withers, a descendant of John, married and had a large family.

Enoch Keane Withers, born 1760, his fourth son, married Jennet Chinn in 1786, and died of apoplexy at his home, *Green Meadows,* Fauquier county in 1813. The mother of his wife was Janet Scott. Of Enoch's children, Robert Walter, born 1795, married Susan Dabney, daughter of Robert Alexander, the clerk of Campbell, studied medicine and first settled in Lovingston, Nelson county, then moved in 1820 to Campbell and began the practice of his profession there. His father-in-law, dying soon afterwards, he settled at the old Alexander residence, *Rock Castle.* In 1836 Dr. Robert W. Withers, was a member of Virginia Legislature. He had several physician neighbors, of these Dr. Nathaniel W. Payne was a brother-in-law, who lived 1½ miles distant and Dr. John Slaughter, four miles from him, thus it will be seen that the community had all facility for medical attention. Children of Dr. Robt. W. and Susan D. A. Withers were:

—Jennet Ann, m. Dr. Robert Thornton Lemmon, and lived 12 miles from *Rock Castle;*—Dr. Robert Enoch m. 1846 Mary Virginia, dau. of Joseph and Elizh. Royall, of Lynchburg;— Mary Elizh. m. George D. Sanders;—Flora V. m. Philip T. Withers;—William A. m. Alice, dau. of J. Breckenridge Cabell;—Dr. John T. m. Henrietta Alexander; he was Assistant Surgeon in Col. Thomas P. August's 3rd Va. Inf. Reg., died

1861 in a Richmond hospital and was buried at St. John's churchyard, near Pigeon Run, in Campbell;—Edward Horatio died aged 16 years;—Susan C., m. Patrick C. Massie of Nelson county;—Henry Howard m., 1st, Mary T. Anderson, of Nelson; m., 2nd, Miss Adams of Campbell; he was a member of Company "C," C. S. A., from Campbell;—Walter L. m. Bettie Hamilton of Nelson;—Austin C. m. Missouri T. Riddick, of Suffolk: all of the brothers served in the Confederate army.

Captain Edward Ball Withers, a brother of Dr. Robt. W. Withers, also settled in Campbell, at *Ivanhoe,* situated not far from old Oxford Iron furnace, *Chestnut Hill,* and Six Mile bridge. He married Evelina W., dau. of Philip and Dorothea Dandridge Payne of *White Hall.* Children of Edward Ball and Evelina W. Withers:—Philip T., m. his cousin, Flora V., dau. of Dr. Ro. W. Withers; lived first in Rustburg, but sold his residence there to Judge Frank Nelson and moved to Lynchburg;—Dr. Edward Withers moved to Danville;—Janet m., 1st, Horace Lemmon; m., 2nd, Samuel Holt;—Walter m. Mollie, dau. of Christopher Clark;—Robert Woodson m. Blanche T. Payne;—Zuleika m. Dr. A. Irvine Clark and moved to Lynchburg. *Ivanhoe* was sold to the Rode family, who have been living there many years: it is reached by the river road from Lynchburg or by soil road back of Long Mountain from Rustburg.

Wyatt

The Wyatt family is of English extraction. Among early records the name is found spelt Wiat, Wiatt and Wyatt, differently even with members of the same households. Colonel John Wyatt, first of his name in Campbell, was an officer in the Revolutionary army and was present at the battle of Guilford court-House. He married Wilhelmina, the daughter of Colonel Samuel Jordan, who was a sister of Mrs. William Cabell of *Union Hill,* Nelson county, and of Mrs. John Cabell of *Green Hill,* Buckingham county. Colonel Wyatt settled first in Amherst county, but moved to Lynchburg, and had a large family

of children.   He was mayor of the city in 1806, died in 1827.
His daughter, Caroline, married Edmund Winston of Am-
herst: Anne, his second daughter, married Captain William
Norvell.

Captain Samuel Wyatt, a tobacconist of Lynchburg, married,
first, Mary, daughter of Benjamin Brown, of Amherst, who
died in 1825; married, 2nd, Sarah, daughter of Matthew
Brown of Lynchburg, who died in 1842.   Captain Wyatt commanded the Lynchburg Rifles in the war of 1812.   He fought
a duel with Henry Langhorne at *Point of Honor,* Dr. George
Cabell's former residence, which was given the name from that
incident by Lewis Cabell (son of Dr. George), who was then
owner of the property.

Thomas Wyatt, a younger brother of Colonel John, moved
in 1787 from King and Queen county to Lynchburg, where he
became an active citizen.   He married Sarah Miller.   In 1793
John Miller deeded to Thomas Wyatt lot No. 15 in Lynchburg.
In 1795 Caleb Tate sold Thomas Wyatt and William Norvell,
merchants in partnership under the name of Wyatt and Norvell, one-half acre lot in the town.   In 1804 Jesse Tate sold
Wyatt one-half acre lot; the same year John and Mary Lynch
sold him a half-acre lot below Lynchburg, and a half-acre upon
which stood Miller's Tavern opposite the lot purchased by
Colonel John Wyatt.

At the first meeting of Hustings court in Lynchburg, 1805,
Thomas Wyatt, Sr., was appointed recorder, and John Wyatt
was security with William Warwick on the bond of William
Norvell, then appointed clerk of court.

Mary, a daughter of Thomas Wyatt, married D. Hoffman;
another daughter, Martha, married (2nd wife), William Massie of *Pharsalia,* Nelson county, whose daughter, Ellen, married ———— Warwick.   Thomas Wyatt was a trustee and treasurer for the Methodist church of Lynchburg; and a director in
1814, of Exchange Bank of Lynchburg.   Thomas Wyatt, Jr.,
was one of the teachers in the public schools in Lynchburg, established in 1871—one of which buildings later was named for
him.

Robert Wyatt married Clarissa Aylett, daughter of Baldwin and Catherine Coles-Payne of *Mt. Airy,* Campbell county, Seneca creek neighborhood, whose old home still stands and has near its entrance a large native stone stable. Robert Wyatt lived in Hills creek section near the old Bowling Clark residence. His daughter, Sallie Elizabeth, married Hays Otey, of Lynchburg, and resided in that town; daughter, Nannie, married Philip Yuille, of Lawyers; and son, Thomas, married Mary Bell.

Yuille

Charles Yuille (or Ewell, as a branch of this family is now called) came to Virginia from England in 1690 under contract to build the capital at Williamsburg, accompanied by two brothers. They were said to be sons of John Yuille, of the clan Buchanan. A stone in Bruton church-yard is inscribed to the memory of John, son of Thomas Yuille of Darleith, Scotland, Dumbarton county. John died in 1746 aged 27 years. Thomas, a descendant of Thomas Yuille of Darleith, married Lucy Fletcher, of England, settled at a place now called Clarkton, in Halifax county. Children:

—Frances, born 1806.

—George, built a home, *Prospect Cottage,* at Lawyers in 1840; m. Amanda V. (dau. of John Payne, of *White Hall*).

—Jane, m. Winston Henry, lived in Charlotte county, near Brookneal, Campbell county.

—Mary m. ——— Hairston.

—Antoinette m. Colonel John McCraw.

—Melvina m. Colonel Daniel Easley.

—Alexander unmarried.

In 1770 Thomas Yuille patented 473 acres on the south side of Troublesome creek and in 1780 patented 1180 acres on the north side of Otter, both sides of Troublesome creek.

—Capt. Thomas Yuille served in the Revolution from 1777 to 1781.

Children of George and Amanda V. Payne-Yuille:

—William Murdock m. Lillian Winfree, lived in Lynchburg.

—Thomas m. Miss Hunter and moved to Kansas; lived for some years in Campbell county.

—Sue m. Colonel Richard Burks of Rockbridge county.

—Andrew unmarried.

—John Matteau (named for Dr. Matteau, friend of the family, of Prince Edward county), m., 1st, Susan Burks, of Rockbridge county; m., 2nd, Nancy Coleman Hundley (his first cousin) and lived in Halifax county; a son of the first marriage, Thomas Burks Yuille, of New York City, was vice-president of the American Tobacco Company, until its dissolution, President of the Universal Tobacco Company, now owner of *Prospect Cottage,* his great-grandfather's old home.

—Philip Payne m. Nannie Wyatt; lived near Lynch's station.

—Alexander Campbell m., 1st, Sally Moon of Halifax county; m., 2nd, Sue Massie of Nelson.

—Helen m. S. Flynn, of Culpeper county; lived in Danville and Washington, where she died;—Horace, died.

—Fletcher Campbell, m., 1st, Sally Butler Scott; m., 2nd, Addie Armistead, gr.-grand-dau. of Patrick Henry. John Matteau and Fletcher Campbell resided at *Prospect Cottage.*

John Matteau, Philip Payne and Alexander Campbell Yuille served in the Confederate army, and in the engagements around Lynchburg; J. Matteau with General McCausland's command.

Five generations of Yuilles have lived in Campbell county. An old diary written by Thomas Yuille 1785-87 is preserved by the family. George owned a great deal of land and many negroes; he died in 1861 aged 51 years. His wife lived to be 90 years old and died in 1905, both died at Lawyers where they were buried in the family graveyard.

Emigrants to Ohio in the Early Part of the 19th Century

Thomas Clark Moorman, born 1755, son of Micajah and Susannah Chiles-Moorman, gr.-son of Thos. and Rachel Clark-Moorman, married, in 1775, Apharacia Hope of Caroline county.

He was known as "Big Tommy," his diminutive wife lived to be nearly a hundred. Their children were:—Chiles, Thomas, James, Charles, Reuben, Micajah, John Hope and Nancy. Thomas, Sr., purchased of Col. John Watts of Lynchburg 1000 acres of land in the *Miami Belt* of Ohio, afterwards in Silver Creek township, Green Co., Ohio. They started with all their family excepting John Hope and Reuben for the Wilderness in Ohio. A few years after they had gone, Zachariah Moorman in 1732, who married Bettie Terrell (dau. of Henry Terrell, who was a captain in the 5th Va. Revolutionary army), also moved to Ohio. Zach. Moorman was father of Henry Moorman, one of the principal contractors on the James river and Kanawha Canal. Zach. Moorman; m., 2nd, Elizabeth Johnson, children of whom were Zach., Jr., m. Catherine Ellis, and Lucy, who m. Benj. Baugham.

In 1810 another emigration to Ohio from Campbell was made by Anthonys, Terrells, Johnsons and Thurman. Among these was Christopher Anthony, Sr., whose eloquence as a pulpit orator had attracted wide attention for a quarter of a century. son of Joseph, his grand-father was Mark Anthony. Dr. Charles Anthony, a distinguished surgeon for 30 years in the U. S. Navy, and Lynch Anthony, who died in the Canadian Topographical Engineering Corps at Halifax, N. S., in 1860, were descendants: George Ellis Pugh, attorney-at-law, was a descendant of Christopher Anthony, also Mrs. Emma Anthony Cartmel of Springfield, Ohio.

The Terrell descendants are scattered over Ohio, Iowa, and California. Anthony Clark Terrell was a jurist of considerable fame in Minnesota. His nephew, David Terrell, forged himself to the front as an Engineer in the U. S. Coast Surveys on the Pacific coast. David Anthony settled with his brother, Samuel, in Highland county, Ohio, and many of their descendants are still in the region of New Lexington, Ohio.

Hon. A. D. Candler became Governor of Georgia; E. D. Candler, member of Congress from Mississippi; Warren A. Candler, of Atlanta, Bishop of the Methodist Episcopal Church South, were all of Campbell ancestry. Terrells in the South are represented by Judge A. W. Terrell, of Austin, later minister to Turkey, under the Cleveland administration; and Judge Jos. Terrell of Fort Worth; these were brothers of Dr. John J. Terrell of Lynchburg.

Benjamin Butterworth, who married Rachel, daughter of Zachariah and Bettie Terrell-Moorman, moved to Ohio in 1812; his son Henry Thomas (married his cousin, Nancy Irvin Wailes), was a prominent railroad contractor and general internal improvement commissioner. He settled on Little Miami river; his widow lived to be nearly 100 years old. A daughter was Mrs. Jane B. Foster of Athens, McMinn county, Tenn. Moorman Butterworth, a brother of Henry T. (married Fanny Smith), left a son, Clark Butterworth of Waynesville, Ohio, who was an encyclopedia of family history. Another brother, Benj. Butterworth, Jr., (born 1794, m. Judith Welch, a cousin), attorney-at-law, was a state senator and for several years represented the Cincinnati district in Congress. Upon the election of Benjamin Harrison to the Presidency, Butterworth was made a cabinet officer and was Commissioner of Patents at the time of his death in 1869.

Descendants of Micajah and Sarah Lynch-Terrell settled on the Ohio river belt and on the Great Lakes. Johnson descendants scattered from Ohio to California; several members were managers of manufacturing establishments and railroad enterprises in Wisconsin, Iowa, Michigan and Ohio.

Clark Moorman Terrell and Robert Moorman went to Texas in 1861, joined a Confederate battery, remaining in the army during the war, and returned to their Texas homes after the termination of hostilities.

These Western and Southern settlers were all of the Quaker sect from Campbell county.

Index to Chronicles

Allied County Families

Adams—Lynch.
Alexander—Austin.
Anderson—Callaway.
Anthony—Clark.
Anthony—Moorman.
Bailey—Timberlake.
Bolling—Cary.
Bullock—Clark.
Burton—Irvine.
Brown—Hancock.
Cabell—Davies.
Cabell—Winston.
Callaway—Crawford.
Callaway—Tilley.
Candler—Anthony.
Chiles—Harrelson.
Clark—Adams.
Clark—Irvine.
Clay—Davies.
Clemens—Goggin.
Clement—Hill.
Cobbs—Lewis.
Cobbs—Poindexter.
Cobbs—Scott.
Cocke—Stith.
Cocke—Talbot.
Dabney—Price.
Dabney—Morris.
Daniel—Allen.
Daniel—Woodson.
Davis—Gosney.
Davis—Lynch.
Davis—Smithson.
Davies—Clayton.
Davies—Godfrey.
Davies—Manson.
Davies—Nowlin.
Dearing—Adams
Dearing—Lynch.
Douglass—Moorman.
Douglass—Tyree.
Early—Anderson.
Early—Wall.
Early—Callaway.
Evans—Robertson.
Evans—Murrell.
Fauntleroy—Dearing.
Floyd—Anderson.
Featherston—Floyd.
Franklin—Lewis.

Franklin—Callaway.
Fuqua—Woodson.
Garland—Rice.
Garland—Wingfield.
Gilliam—Glover.
Gilliam—Jones.
Goggin—Irvine.
Goggin—Moorman.
Hairston—Saunders.
Hairston—Stovall.
Hanks—Brooks.
Harrison—Burton.
Haythe—Arthur.
Haythe—Moorman.
Haden—Reynolds.
Henry—Cabell.
Holcombe—Royall.
Hughes—Tucker.
Hunter—Davidson.
Irvine—Boyd.
Irvine—Clark.
Irvine—Anthony.
Jennings—Davis.
Johnson—Clark.
Johnson—Moorman.
Johnson—Terrell.
Johnston—Pickett.
Johnston—Steptoe.
Jones—Bolling.
Jones—Stith.
Kabler—Speece.
Langhorne—Allen.
Langhorne—Steptoe.
Lee—Noel.
Leftwich—Turner.
Leftwich—Fuqua.
Lewis—Cabell.
Lynch—Bowles.
Lynch—Clark.
Lynch—Terrell.
McReynolds—Campbell.
Miller—Fitz Patrick.
Moorman—Reynolds.
Moorman—Johnson.
Morgan—Jones.
Murrell—Cobbs.
Murrell—Estes.
Murrell—Rudd.
Norvell—Wyatt.
Otey—Hopkins.

Otey—Matthews.
Owen—Lathan.
Pannill—Boughton.
Payne—Archer.
Payne—Smith.
Perrow—Fleming.
Perrow—Cox.
Preston—Davis.
Preston—Early.
Prewitt—Hurt.
Robertson—Phair.
Rosser—Wood.
Russell—Bard.
Russell—Fitz Patrick.
Russell—Rutherford.
Scott—Adams.
Scott—Jones.
Scott—Roy.
Scott—Williams.
Slaughter—Jones.
Slaughter—Poindexter.
Slaughter—Smith.
Snow—Bennett.
Snow—Cheek.
Stith—Hall.
Stith—Buckner.
Strange—Smith.
Talbot—Guin.
Talbot—Williston.
Tate—Callaway.

Tate—Goggin.
Tate—Murrell.
Terrell—Chiles.
Terrell—Johnson.
Terrell—Kennerly.
Terrell—Lynch.
Thompson—Franklin.
Thurman—Lewellen.
Venable—Moorman.
Wade—Turner.
Walden—Hubbard.
Walden—Ward.
Ward—Adams.
Ward—Chiles.
Ward—Risque.
Ward—Norvell.
Ward—Warwick.
Watts—Scott.
Watts—Saunders.
Winston—Taylor.
Winston—Cabell.
Winston—Clark.
Withers—Chinn.
Withers—Alexander.
Withers—Payne.
Wyatt—Jordan.
Wyatt—Miller.
Yuille—Fletcher.
Yuille—Payne.